Teaching E
to Children

From Practice to Principle

Edited by
Christopher Brumfit
Jayne Moon *and*
Ray Tongue

Longman Group Limited
Longman House, Burnt Mill, Harlow,
Essex CM20 2JE, England
and Associated Companies throughout the world.

© John Millington Ward 1984

First published by Collins ELT 1991

This impression Longman Group Ltd. 1995

ISBN 0-17-556889-8

Printed in China
LREX/02

Contents

Christopher Brumfit, Centre for Language in Education, University of Southampton, England

Introduction: Teaching English to children

THE LAST FEW YEARS have seen a revival of interest in the teaching of English to young learners. After much interest in the 1960s, the period of communicative language teaching saw a concentration on adults or secondary level work, with relatively little concern for primary level activity. Now this is changing.

In part this was because the emphasis on needs analysis was particularly unhelpful for learners who were by definition too young to have clearly identifiable needs. Yet it was strange in many ways to observe this neglect of young learners, for many of the approaches that came in the 1970s and 1980s benefited from our experience of working with young learners in general education. 'Humanistic' approaches to language teaching share concerns with good primary school teaching practice, and the emphasis on language use and language context simply draws upon the commonplace expectations of good primary school teachers.

In the 1950s and 1960s, educational innovation at primary level led a process of liberalisation that changed classroom practice. Jean Brewster's first paper discusses the current practices deriving from this approach, which received its synthesis in Britain in the official Plowden Report (HMSO 1967). Throughout the world during this period classes were increasingly working in small groups on projects which integrated work from a number of previously diverse subject areas. For many traditions, changes of this kind were very radical, and it has taken several generations of teachers to assimilate them into normal practice. At the same time, we have to recognise that language teaching innovation at this level emerged more from practitioners than from theorists. Non-native-speaking teachers working in normal classrooms without extraordinary resourcing were the people who had to accept new ideas if they were to be of any value in the long term.

This book attempts to provide a basis for work by primary level teachers of all kinds, whether native speaker or non-native speaker. The contributors have experience in many countries, and include both native speakers of English and non-native speakers. The first part of the book is concerned with the practice of teaching, and contains a wealth of ideas of various kinds. The papers in this section move from the practical towards the theoretical as the section progresses. The second part contains the basic background which is necessary to make sense of the practical principles which have already been demonstrated. Thus Section Two is more theoretical and more academic than Section One. Between them, the two parts provide a thorough overview of the theory and practice of teaching English to young learners.

What I hope to offer in this introductory paper is a general framework for more detailed examination of specific problems – but the value of such a framework needs to be constantly tested against the experience of particular learners in particular education systems, with particular groups of teachers.

Variation at primary level

Let me start by asking a fundamental question. Is there any such thing as 'primary English Language Teaching' in a general sense? Clearly in many countries there is English Language Teaching in schools for young age groups. But the key elements in the concept of primary ELT vary considerably from culture to culture.

For example, what we mean by 'childhood' itself varies considerably from country to country. In many parts of the world 'children' take on 'adult' responsibilities at ages when in other countries they are still protected within their schools. These differences will lead to differences in the purposes of language learning. Similarly, attitudes to authority, to teaching and to learning in general vary from culture to culture. Nonetheless, perhaps we can list some of the characteristics which young learners share:

a) Young learners are only just beginning their schooling, so that teachers have a major opportunity to mould their expectations of life in school.

b) As a group they are potentially more differentiated than secondary or adult learners, for they are closer to their varied home cultures, and new to the conformity increasingly imposed across cultural groupings by the school.

c) They tend to be keen and enthusiastic learners, without the inhibitions which older children sometimes bring to their schooling.

d) Their learning can be closely linked with their development of ideas and concepts, because it is so close to their initial experience of formal schooling.

e) They need physical movement and activity as much as stimulation for their thinking, and the closer together these can be, the better.

Most primary level learners will share these characteristics – though the age range of primary schooling will vary considerably from country to country. For the purposes of our discussion, we shall assume that we are talking about children in the early stages of their schooling, up to the age of 13 or 14.

Why teach English at primary level?

There is a considerable debate about whether young learners learn language better or more efficiently than older children or adults. In general the evidence is unclear. What is certainly clear, though, is that effective teachers can help learners to progress rapidly at any level of schooling. Much of the discussion in Section One of this book is an attempt to pass on some of the successful practices of effective teachers.

However, there are a number of reasons for teaching English at primary level that do not rely simply on the claim that that is the best time to learn languages well:

• the need to expose children from an early age to an understanding of foreign cultures so that they grow up tolerant and sympathetic to others.

• the need to link communication to the understanding of new concepts.

• the need for maximum learning time for important languages – the earlier you start the more time you get.

• the advantage of starting with early second language instruction so that later the language can be used as a medium of teaching. (These issues are surveyed by Singleton 1989 pp. 242–5.)

If you think about your own situation in relation to these reasons, you will quickly realise that different countries have different needs, and no one country will wish to teach foreign languages to young learners for all of these reasons. How much money is available, how good the teachers' knowledge of English is, whether English is a second language (used for social purposes outside school) or a foreign language (only normally used while it is being learnt in school), and other factors will determine which of these needs are relevant.

Many of the broader issues raised by Singleton are not within the control of individual teachers, however, and some of them will reflect general social views which education cannot directly change at all. Nonetheless, it is useful to recognise the claims that may be made about the role of education – even if we conclude that we cannot do much about them!

Second language learning at a young age

I said earlier that it is unclear whether children learn languages better at a young age. Many people believe that they do, however, and a number of different explanations have been offered.

It may simply be, of course, that young children have more opportunities than adults. They are learning all the time without having the worries and responsibilities of adults; their parents, friends and teachers all help them in learning. Furthermore, they have a strong personal need to learn if they are surrounded by people speaking the second language, and there are strong social pressures to do what their elders expect!

The main explanations for better learning that have been suggested are these:

a) That the brain is more adaptable before puberty than after, and that acquisition of languages is possible without self-consciousness at an early age.

b) That children have fewer negative attitudes to foreign languages and cultures than adults, and that consequently they are better motivated than adults.

c) That children's language learning is more closely integrated with real communication because it depends more on the immediate physical environment than does adult language.

d) That children devote vast quantities of time to language learning, compared with adults, and they are better because they do more of it.

Nonetheless, there are problems with most of these explanations. If the child's brain is really more adaptable, why do so many adults learn so well? Children do perhaps learn accent better than adults (though even this claim has been disputed), but it is unclear that they learn anything else more efficiently. Many adults are very successful and economical language learners. Further, some of these advantages do not apply when the child is not immersed in the foreign language culture, so their relevance to many foreign language situations is not obvious. Altogether we need to be a little cautious about over-strong claims. At the same time, there is no evidence to suggest that teaching foreign languages to young children actually produces bad results, unless the teachers are untrained or there is no satisfactory resourcing. The two most recent book-length surveys of the age factor in language acquisition conclude that while an early start does give advantages, and certainly need not do any harm, there is no theoretical agreement over exactly what the advantages are (Harley 1986, Singleton 1989).

What do teachers need?

I hope it is clear from my discussion so far that there are no strong reasons to do with children themselves or the ways in which children learn for refusing to teach them second languages. There may, however, be strong reasons which relate to teachers and materials – there is little justification for exposing learners to teachers who themselves lack confidence in their ability to teach and use the target language. What kind of support do teachers need?

First, teachers need the language. Basic competence is essential. However, we should note that this may pose problems in some educational traditions, especially where foreign rather than second languages are being learnt. Opportunities for foreign language access will vary considerably from country to country. It may therefore be necessary to train foreign language competence closely co-ordinated with teaching methodology for this level.

Secondly, of course, teachers need competence in primary teaching methodology. The skills necessary for teaching at this level are very different from those needed elsewhere in the education system. We need to emphasise the role of story (Garvie 1989), dance, roleplay and puppet activity, model-making and so on, and we shall need to centre much of our teaching on topical rather than formal organisation. Experienced primary teachers will already be familiar with these procedures, but EFL teachers who wish to move from other levels to work with young children will have to reorientate their teaching expectations – at least as great a change as for an experienced primary teacher learning a new language. The first section of this book gives a substantial overview of major ideas drawn from good primary practice.

Bibliography

Central Advisory Committee for Education (CACE). 1967. *Children and their Primary Schools (the Plowden Report)*. London: HMSO.

Garvie, E. 1989. *Story as Vehicle*. Clevedon: Multilingual Matters.

Harley, B. 1986. *Age in Second Language Acquisition*. Clevedon: Multilingual Matters.

Singleton, D. 1989. *Language Acquisition: the Age Factor*. Clevedon: Multilingual Matters.

Section One

Things to do and why

This section contains 14 papers.
The first one introduces principles of good primary practice.
The remainder move steadily from practice to principle.

Jean Brewster, Ealing College, England

1 What is good primary practice?

Jean Brewster outlines in this opening paper the basic principles of good primary practice, and thus provides a framework for all the papers in Section One of this book. The first part of her paper summarises many of the themes which we shall return to in Section Two, and shows the links between general psychological theory and the practice of primary teaching.

A T A RECENT CONFERENCE on 'Theory and Practice in Primary ELT' interesting questions were raised by Professor Christopher Brumfit regarding the teaching of English to young learners. They serve as a salutary reminder that there is a need for constant reflection on what we are trying to achieve in teaching English to young learners and how we might best approach its implementation:

a) Is there a best way to teach primary EFL?

b) Is the model underlying British primary teaching exportable or does it conflict with the cultural settings in which primary EFL operates?

It may be worth first delving into some of the background which leads us to pose these problematic yet fundamental questions and perhaps to find the beginnings of some answers.

What is good primary practice?

In addressing this question we can first pinpoint certain key issues which arise from the theoretical perspectives offered by the fields of education, psychology and applied linguistics. Nunan (1988) writes of the benefits to be derived from applying general educational theory and research to language teaching:

> while theoretical linguistics will continue to be an important base discipline, it is important that it not be seen as the only discipline which has anything of value to contribute to decision-making on what, how and when to teach. While the learning of a second language has unique aspects, it is not so unique as to have nothing to gain from general educational theory, practice and research. (p.180)

It is clear that greater knowledge and understanding of theories of child development and learning, the ways in which children learn a foreign language and studies of the kinds of classroom conditions which promote foreign language learning will all contribute to our understanding of good educational practice in the teaching of English to young children.

How do children think and learn?

Children at primary level are learning how to cope with school life, learning to become literate and continuing to develop concepts. How might children's cognitive development influence classroom methodology?

Primary education has generally been influenced by attempts to discover the ways in which people think and learn, most notably in Britain by Piaget (1967), Vygotsky (1962) and Bruner (1966).

The most well-known aspect of Piaget's theory holds that all children pass through a series of stages before they construct the ability to perceive, reason and understand in mature, rational terms. Teaching, whether through demonstration, asking questions or explanation, can only influence the course of intellectual development if the child is able to assimilate what is said and done. This view has led to the concept of 'learning readiness' which has influenced, for example, the teaching of reading.

The three stages — 'sensori-motor' (birth to 18 months approximately), 'concrete operational' (18 months to 11 years approximately) and 'formal operation' period (11 years onwards) — are ascertained by means of cognitive tasks. The concrete operational period is sub-divided into two further periods — the 'pre-operational' which lasts until around the age of seven during which the 'concrete operations' are being prepared for, and the 'operational' proper during which they are established and consolidated.

Piaget's work has more recently been criticised, notably by educationalists such as Donaldson (1978). The argument motivating many studies which call Piaget's views into question is that children do not pass through stages of development in which they are unable to learn or be taught how to reason 'logically'. Rather it was the unfamiliarity of the tasks which the children were given to assess their information processing skills that led to failure. Donaldson writes, for example, about a task where children had to press buttons to obtain a toy: 'the difficulty lies not in the inferential processes which the task demands, but in certain perplexing features of the apparatus and procedure.' (p.54)

Piaget's views strongly influenced the work of the Plowden Committee (1967) which advocated a child-centred approach to teaching. This in turn led to the encouragement of individualised learning in primary classrooms, where children's individual needs were catered for by tasks pitched at different cognitive levels.

The work of Bruner and particularly of Vygotsky has become influential more recently. Piaget was primarily interested in the structure of mature thinking, while Bruner sought to describe the different processes that are implicated in problem-solving. Both emphasise the importance of action and problem-solving in learning and believe that abstract thinking should grow out of and be abstracted from material actions. From both perspectives, teaching that teaches children only how to manipulate abstract procedures without first establishing the deep connections between such procedures and the activities involved in the solution of concrete problems is bound to fail.

Piaget and Vygotsky differed in their views on the nature of language and its effect on intellectual development. Piaget argued that language exerts no formative effects on the structure of thinking; mental actions and operations are derived from action, not talk. Vygotsky argued that in the beginning speech serves a regulative, communicative function; later it serves other functions and transforms the way in which children think, learn and understand. It becomes an instrument or tool of thought, not only providing a system for representing the world but also the means by which planning and self-regulation to achieve goals takes place. Thus speech comes to form what Vygotsky referred to as the higher mental processes, including the ability to plan, evaluate, memorise and reason. These processes are, in Vygotsky's view, culturally formed in social interaction. Seen in this light, language gives structure to and directs the processes of thinking and concept formation themselves.

Both Bruner and Vygotsky place a greater emphasis than Piaget on the role of language, communication and instruction in the development of knowledge and understanding. Indeed, Vygotsky placed instruction at the heart of human development, defining intelligence itself as the capacity to learn through instruction. A central tenet of his theory is the zone of proximal development (ZPD), which was introduced to account for the discrepancy between product and process in IQ tests. Vygotsky (1978) defined the ZPD as 'the distance between the actual developmental level as determined by independent problem-solving and the level of potential development as determined through problem-solving under adult guidance or in collaboration with more capable peers.' (p.84) This theoretical construct emphasises the social nature of knowledge acquisition, since through collaboration the child is able to solve more complex tasks. In this way, the child internalises the processes required for working out a particular task. Bruner, strongly influenced by Vygotsky, is one of the most notable contemporary exponents of the view that children's language and learning development takes place through the processes of social interaction. Bruner introduced the concept of LASS, an acronym for Language Acquisition Support System. Bruner proposed that for language development there needs to be a child component, incorporating an innate propensity for active social interaction and language learning, together with an adult support and help component. The interactional partner provides a structure or framework which Bruner referred to as 'scaffolding'. (For a more detailed analysis of the theories of Piaget, Vygotsky and Bruner see Wood (1988) and Garton and Pratt (1989).)

How have these theories influenced primary classrooms?

The main features of primary practice in Britain between the 1960s and

1980s, which derive to some extent from these theories, can be listed as follows:

a) Teacher autonomy, i.e. no nationally agreed 'scheme of work' to be followed by all schools.

b) A child-centred curriculum and methodology, i.e. where the child's needs and interests were paramount. This led to a concern for the education of the whole child, including his/her moral, physical, emotional and intellectual growth.

c) Individualised learning, where children were free to work at their own level and pace. This often led to the 'integrated day', where there was no set timetable and it was hoped that children would develop autonomy and self-discipline in planning their own timetable from a selection of activities.

d) A topic-based approach, developed out of child-centredness and emphasising the integration of different aspects of the curriculum, such as mathematics and science.

e) A methodology whose emphasis was 'learning by doing' and problem-solving, involving frequent use of work in small groups.

Today primary practice in Britain is undergoing enormous change following the introduction of the National Curriculum. In the recent past Britain has been proud of its tradition of 'child-centred' primary education based on a flexible curriculum which was not assessment-driven. Research into UK primary schools has shown, however, that there was frequently a grave mis-match between the rhetoric of government reports, such as that produced by the Piaget-influenced Plowden Committee (op. cit.), and the survey of actual practice in primary schools by Galton *et al.* (the 'Oracle Report' 1980). There are now real fears that child-centred education may become a thing of the past as teaching falls under the grip of national testing.

To reassure teachers, the National Curriculum Council is at pains to state that it does not wish to interfere with what has been regarded as good practice, but rather wishes to ensure that examples of good practice are made more explicit for all teachers to draw upon. It is interesting to note the way in which the Department of Education and Science (DES) document (1989) lists the features which, in the teaching of English, are held to represent good primary practice, a term which is frequently used but rarely defined.

1 Using language to make, receive and communicate meaning, in purposeful contexts.

2 An 'apprenticeship' approach to acquiring written and oral language, in which the adult represents the 'success' the child seeks and yet offers endless help.

3 Maximum encouragement and support whilst errors are mastered; the appreciation that mistakes are necessary to learning.

4 Working on tasks which the children have chosen and which they direct for themselves.

5 Employing a variety of forms with a clear awareness of audience.

6 Working with teachers who are themselves involved in the processes – albeit with special expertise – as talkers, listeners, readers and writers.

7 Reading literature for enjoyment, responding to it critically and using that reading for learning.

Although intended for teaching English in the UK, many EFL teachers would probably agree with most of these points. Points 1 and 5 are very much in line with the communicative approach to ELT and views on process writing. The implications of Points 2 and 3 for pupils and teachers are that risk-taking is important in children's learning and that the making of mistakes can reveal evidence of learning rather than being detrimental to learning. Many errors made by young learners of English resemble those of the developmental stages of first language learning, such as simplification of syntax and overgeneralisation of rules. As Mayor (1985) writes, 'the important thing is that a child should be given the space to experiment and take risks with the language, on the principle that fluency is more likely to lead to accuracy than vice versa.' (p.118)

Point 4 is more controversial and probably represents the kind of classroom activity which is viewed as typically British – children walking around the classroom freely, selecting their own activities, sometimes purposefully, but not always! Point 6 has emerged mostly from the teaching of literacy: educationalists argue that, if children see teachers reading with enjoyment, experiencing difficulties in their own writing and sharing their own writing processes in the classroom, the pupils are more motivated to develop their own literacy. Point 7 fits in with most people's intuition about the importance of stories and rhymes in children's learning and their frequent use in primary EFL classrooms.

The earlier DES report (1988) had included a note on classroom organisation: 'Effective English teaching may occur where a whole class listens attentively or engages in a lively question and answer session; in small group teaching in which a high degree of interaction is possible; and in a one-to-one setting where a child may receive individual help and support.' (2.6, p.7)

The inclusion of a variety of teaching styles is a realistic reflection of what actually goes on in primary schools; it is not all collaborative group work, as an influential report on English teaching, the 'Bullock Report' (1975), had advocated, nor Plowden-style 'individualised' learning. Indeed, in many schools abroad class sizes of 40 to 100 would seem to militate against the use of many of the central tenets of British primary practice outlined earlier. It takes ingenuity and skill to introduce group work in such large classes, although one could argue that there is even more need for such classroom organisation to ensure that every child has a chance of actually speaking English.

How do children learn a foreign language?

Investigations of the relationship between interaction and second language development (SLD) have tended to follow in the footsteps of first language development (FLD). Research on SLD by Ellis (1984) derived in some part from work on FLD directed by Gordon Wells at Bristol University. Ellis suggests that there are eight features of classroom discourse which may be important in SLD. These features can be grouped thus:

The teacher's use of language

1 Quantity of intake
2 An input rich in directives
3 An input rich in 'extending' utterances

Types of activity used and support provided

4 A need to communicate
5 Adherence to the 'here and now' principle

The learner's use of language

6 Independent control of the propositional content
7 The performance of a range of speech acts
8 Uninhibited practice

The first three features concern the nature of the language input. Qualitative and quantitative aspects of the speech addressed to a child are important in both FLD and SLD. In SLD, however, a crucial factor is the quantity of 'intake', that is, not simply the amount that is comprehensible, attended to and subsequently converted into 'intake'. We have already seen how theories of children's learning require that young learners be supported by moving from the concrete to the abstract and through being involved in activity. The structured activities used in mathematics, where children weigh, measure and sort real objects, are a good example of providing 'comprehensible input' which, along with the 'scaffolding' provided by adult support and help, allows for more intake of the mathematical concepts involved. It would be surprising if there were not parallels between the processes by which children develop concepts, recognise patterns and make hypotheses in mathematics on the one hand and learn a language on the other.

An input rich in directives (Point 2) is seen by Ellis as particularly useful in SLD since it frequently requires a non-verbal response and refers to concrete features of the environment which makes decoding of the propositional content easier. Many primary EFL classrooms use the approach to ELT called 'total physical response' (TPR), which is one means of providing an input rich in directives. Using this approach children follow instructions in a game-like atmosphere which usually involves them in some kind of activity or involves manipulating objects in the classroom.

The use of extending utterances (Point 3) is a feature which is paralleled in FLD – more rapid development takes place when adults behave as though the child's language is meaningful even when it is not. They react to its content by elaborating and expanding on what the child has said. Many teachers provide a model for children by expanding their utterances; these expansions will not necessarily be copied immediately but provide input for the child's hypothesis formation about learning English.

The second group of features deals with the types of language activity in which the learner is engaged. Point 4 refers to the need for language teaching to be based on purposeful communication. This is one of the chief characteristics of children's FLD as control over language is a means of controlling other people and hence, to a certain extent, their environment. We have already seen the ways in which both Vygotsky and Bruner stressed the importance of social interaction and genuine communication in FLD, paralleling recent developments in the communicative approach to language teaching. Point 5 fits in with theories of children's cognitive growth and refers to the need to move from the concrete to the abstract in order to support children's understanding of the propositional content of a message. Story-telling, for example, will make more sense to the child if visual aids are used to contextualise the language. If these visual aids are also available afterwards to encourage children to rehearse the language of the story in retelling or rewriting, the teacher creates a learning environment where intake is more likely.

The third group of features concerns the types of language used by the learner. If the classroom is the only venue for foreign language learning, this is entirely dependent on the kind of language the teacher uses and the kinds of activity in which he/she is engaged. Children learning their first language are generally free to express their own meanings and initiate social interaction. Ellis suggests that SLD is likely to be more successful if children are also free in the foreign language learning context to initiate interaction as well as respond to others' use of language. They can thus deploy their developing language resources in a flexible manner and are more likely to use a range of speech acts, another important characteristic of successful SLD.

To ensure that children have the opportunity to use a wide range of language, teachers must include a variety of task types based on games, stories, collaborative problem-solving or information-gap activities which will provide wherever possible a context and audience for the production of spoken and written language. For example, children can produce written or tape-recorded work which is read or listened to by other children who in turn respond by answering questions, making a drawing, filling in a chart, labelling a diagram and so on.

How can children be helped to learn a foreign language?

It is not surprising to note that a child's concentration span increases as he/she grows older. Holden (1980), for example, writes that 'children cannot concentrate on one thing for a long period' and that lessons should therefore be divided into a series of activities lasting no longer than five or ten minutes. This, she explains, is because children are bombarded with new experiences and information. Teachers should keep the number of new language items introduced to a reasonable level and present and practise new language items in a number of different ways.

Wood (1988) explains the ways in which younger children are more 'distractable' than older ones, writing that the ability to keep on task and to ignore distractions is a symptom of the child's intellect, and changes in concentration span are related to intellectual development. He adds that 'we have to recognise that when we ask children to pay attention and concentrate on tasks that we have set and which provide little by way of concrete, perceptual support, they may find it impossible to comply with our demands.' (p.70)

Vygotsky argued that mature mental activity involves adaptive 'self-regulation' which develops through social interaction. In this view, instruction and schooling play a central role in helping children to discover how to pay attention, concentrate and learn effectively. Wood (op. cit.) writes

> Attending, concentrating and memorising are activities. Simply asking a child aged five or six to pay attention, concentrate, study, learn or remember is unlikely to bear fruit. Unless we embody the material to be learned and remembered in a task that makes sense to the child, one that involves objectives [he/she] can realise and that draws [his/her] attention 'naturally' to the elements we wish [him/her] to take in, our imperatives to concentrate, memorise or learn are almost bound to fail.

Wood argues that activities or interactions are more likely to enable a child to memorise items since they are more meaningful to the child. Rehearsal is a powerful aid to deliberate memorisation which, when linked to the imposition of some structure or meaning on what is being memorised, is more likely to lead to success. Young children can be helped to learn that rehearsal, especially saying things out loud, is an effective strategy and they need to be shown how to do it. Although children of five or six can learn these strategies they will not use them spontaneously. With prompting they will learn gradually to use them autonomously. An example is given by Wood of children being asked to memorise the names of toy animals. If they are asked to point to and verbally label each animal, they are more likely to be able to remember the names than when simply asked to remember the names without accompanying actions. Such a task provides a concrete external cue for the child and involves practical demands in his/her performance, and he/she is assisted in learning how to remember.

Is there a best way to teach primary EFL?

Given our present state of knowledge about teaching and learning processes, it would be naive to imagine that there is a straightforward answer to this key question. It may be useful, however, to consider two models of classroom practice which are held to exert the greatest influence on the development of a pedagogy for young learners: the classical EFL practice model on the one hand and the mainstream primary practice model on the other.

A stereotyped version of classical EFL is characterised by a presentation and practice model, developed largely with adults and focusing on questions of language and communication. Mainstream primary practice embodies a less structured conception of language, more appropriate to the educational needs of children, which focuses on questions of curriculum content and cognitive development. Figure 1 outlines these two approaches by reference to the models of language, syllabus design, language acquisition and classroom practice which are often their distinguishing features.

What is required to develop a pedagogy for primary ELT is an exploration of the possibilities of drawing upon both of these approaches. In my own teacher-training experience on the RSA Diploma in 'Teaching English across the curriculum', I have frequently witnessed a synthesis of the two approaches in the classroom practice and materials development of primary teachers working with developing bilinguals. In EFL contexts where constraints of time, resources and training militate against teacher-made materials, explorations of this kind can be found in some course materials, such as *Jigsaw* (1980) and more recently, *Stepping Stones* (1990). A departure from the more traditional use of course materials is demonstrated by publications such as Ellis and Brewster (1991). This work uses stories produced originally for English-speaking children as a starting point for the teaching of EFL and links language learning to the primary curriculum and children's conceptual development. Materials such as these demonstrate that the cross-fertilisation of ideas derived from the two models outlined in Figure 1 can create a fruitful and rich language learning environment.

Indeed, certain aspects of good primary practice which have been developed over the last 30 years have already influenced certain aspects of teaching English to adults. It is interesting to note some of the parallels between the central tenets of mainstream primary practice and relatively recent developments in teaching English as a foreign language – see Figure 2. These parallels stem from a recognition that the best of primary practice, with its emphasis on leaner-centredness and the creation of a supportive learning environment, serves the needs of language learners of all ages equally well.

Implications for the training of primary ELT teachers

There is a pressing and growing need to train teachers in this newly developing field. Training courses will find themselves attempting to address at least two major issues: the development of language awareness and awareness of children's learning. In terms of language awareness it seems that the specialist skills of primary teachers of English should equip them to do the following (adapted from Clegg 1990):

• choose an appropriate topic (curricular or otherwise) and derive from it a

Figure 1 A comparison of two methodological models for teaching English to young learners (adapted from Clegg 1990).

		Classical EFL	Mainstream primary practice
Model of language and syllabus design	1	Syllabus tends to be mainly linguistic and mainly structural/functional.	Syllabus is orientated to topic and concept rather than language.
	2	The model of language relies mainly on the categories of structure, function and skill, listening, speaking, reading and writing.	Skills categories are applied within topics. Language categories which might be used to set objectives within tasks are discourse, function, structure and lexis.
	3	Teaching objectives are usually framed and tasks set in terms of one or more of these categories.	Topics are selected for their potential for exploring aspects of the curriculum, e.g. maths, environmental studies. Tasks will often foster the development of study skills such as survey skills or collecting and recording data in investigations.
Model of language acquisition	4	Teacher control of the input is important. The input is often dominated by an ordered sequence of language items. Spoken language is acquired by a combination of form-orientated practice (repetition) and meaning-orientated practice (communication).	The teacher creates a learning environment which facilitates language acquisition and communication. This is achieved through enquiry which generates opportunities for small group work, and teacher-pupil communication.
	5	Tasks are often shaped in order to generate discourse in which specific items determined by a syllabus are used. Listening, reading and writing skills are also acquired via a combination of form-orientated and process/communication-orientated activities.	The teacher provides contextual support (e.g. pictures, matrices) and support at different levels of language for skills development. This support aims to provide access to tasks for learners with varying levels of cognitive and linguistic ability.
Model of classroom practice	6	The work of the classroom is orientated towards language/communication practice. Oral work often takes the form of specified stages: presentation of new language, controlled practice and communicative practice, often but not necessarily in that order. Reading, writing and listening activities are often subordinated in their purpose to the linguistic/communicative orientation of the oral work.	Learners explore topics through a sequence of problem-solving and research tasks. Final products and the audience for those products are important both for motivation and the learners' attention to language use. The teacher intervenes in the selection and sequencing of tasks, task design and group composition. He/She may model language, shape and correct pupils' discourse and offer support at an individual's level of language ability.

Figure 2 A comparison of the central tenets of mainstream primary practice and recent developments in TEFL.

Good primary practice	Recent EFL developments
SYLLABUS	
Syllabus derived from topics and concepts.	Use of projects and theme-based language work.
METHODOLOGY	
Topics used to promote activity-based learning, including surveys, investigations and problem-solving often involving small group work.	Development of task-based methodologies. Use of pair- and groupwork for surveys and problem-solving.
LANGUAGE AND LEARNING PRODUCTS	
Pupils' spoken and written products, e.g. taped stories or written instructions, provide the input for other pupils to work with.	Production of materials by learners with an audience other than the teacher, e.g. fellow pupils, pupils in other classes.
Display of children's work considered important for motivation.	Increasing use of e.g. poster presentations, class magazines.
VIEW OF THE LEARNER	
Child-centred approach led to a holistic view of the child's education, including a concern for creativity and self-expression through music, drama and art.	Interest in the learner-centred curriculum and humanistic approaches. Use of roleplay, jazz chants etc.
Children treated as agents of their own learning, leading to promotion of independent learning, use of self-access work and pupils setting their own agenda.	Development of learner-training; development of procedural syllabus.
VIEW OF THE TEACHER	
Experiments in classroom practice led to diversification of teacher's roles to include monitor, facilitator, consultant etc.	Growing interest in a range of teacher's roles and teaching styles.
CULTURAL CONTEXT	
Child-centred approaches led to a concern with cultural appropriacy and development of 'multi-cultural' education in its best sense, e.g. avoidance of tokenism or stereotyping.	Developing recognition of importance of cultural issues in planning context-sensitive materials, training courses etc.

set of learning tasks which pursue subject matter and cognitive objectives appropriate to a given age group.

- plan these activities in sequence, taking into account both whole class and small group forms of organisation and a variety of both language and study skills.

- analyse the language demands of these activities in terms of discourse, skills, functions, structures, lexis, pronunciation.

- analyse the language needs of the pupils using the same kinds of category.

- match these demands and needs in such a way as to pinpoint what the main language problems of the lesson are going to be.

- modify activities which may be linguistically too exacting; provide language support where necessary, for example 'scaffolding' in the form of rehearsal of useful language and strategies through judicious use of conventional controlled practice involving visuals, games, dialogues and so on.

- develop an understanding of language processes in talk, listening, reading and writing.

- develop a wide repertoire of activity types for skills work and match these to specific text types, for example recognise different text types such as narrative, description or instructions, and know which kinds of comprehension activity (sequencing, filling in a chart, labelling a picture) 'fit' the text.

An extension of the teacher's repertoire of activities should facilitate the provision of suitable work for children operating at different linguistic and cognitive levels. Alongside the analysis and rehearsal of language pertaining to a particular activity, a wide range of activity types should also provide opportunities for developing freer practice where children work independently of the teacher.

In terms of curriculum content and learning at primary level, teachers should know more about the following:

- the role of different determinants of curriculum design such as curricular content, cognitive development, learning skills, language development.

- the range of learning activities which might be described as conventional in the young learners' classroom, for example different types of 'product' which demonstrate language learning and which provide a purposeful context and audience for the learner. These might include taped stories, labelled drawings, pupil-made comic books, graphs, a model, a dramatised story.

- the relation of ELT to the rest of the curriculum and to local educational philosophy.

All of these skills taken together will enable teachers to provide a rich language learning environment and should allow for the tailoring of tasks to the children's needs and interests.

Figures 3 and 4 provide a framework for ways in which a topic can provide a starting point for language learning and show how one topic can be analysed to derive a set of specific language activities. After suitable modelling, trainees on a course might be encouraged to develop a set of lesson plans using a similar framework, possibly in conjunction with topics used in published course materials.

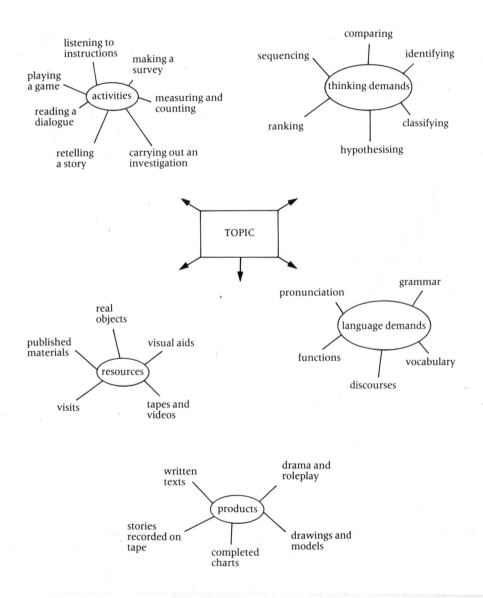

Figure 3 A framework for planning topics.

13

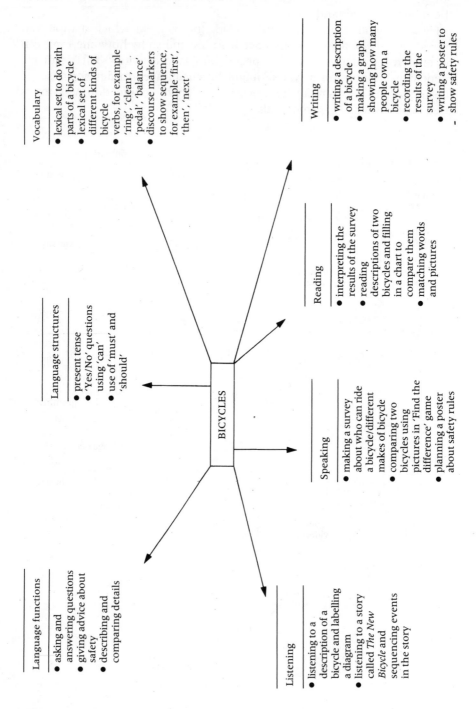

Figure 4 A framework for planning a specific topic.

Is British primary practice exportable?

The British model has to a certain extent been exported to various English-speaking countries with large populations of developing bilingual children, such as Canada, Australia and New Zealand. Good primary practice in these countries has flourished and has in turn been a source of inspiration to the UK. In terms of EFL, aspects of primary practice are currently exported to some degree to countries such as Singapore and certain parts of Africa.

One example of ELT at primary level which has been influenced by the mainstream primary practice model is the Molteno Project developed for black primary schools in South Africa. This course places emphasis on a child-centred approach with extensive use of small group work to promote independent learning. 'Discovery learning' via surveys and investigations is an important component of the course, as well as more structured activities to promote communication and literacy. The use of stories is emphasised and each class is provided with a box of graded book stories at different language levels; a set of puppets accompanies the stories for retelling and the creation of new stories.

One of the most important factors to consider in exporting aspects of primary pedagogy to other countries is the role English plays in the wider community. The EFL/ESL continuum can be said to contain at least four different contexts determined by the answers to the questions in Figure 5.

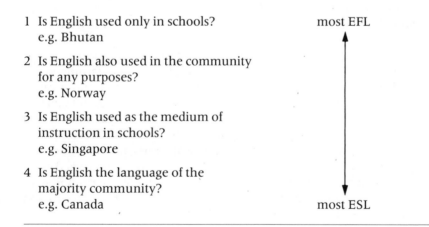

1 Is English used only in schools?
    e.g. Bhutan

most EFL

2 Is English also used in the community
    for any purposes?
    e.g. Norway

3 Is English used as the medium of
    instruction in schools?
    e.g. Singapore

4 Is English the language of the
    majority community?
    e.g. Canada

most ESL

Figure 5 The role of English in the wider community placed on an EFL/ESL continuum.

The features of the contexts which emerge in answering these questions will have a strong influence on the development of a pedagogy for primary ELT. Further questions which need to be posed concern language acquisition, the syllabus, methodology and view of learning.

LANGUAGE ACQUISITION

How far does the context affect pupils' motivation?
How much exposure to English do pupils receive?
What is the potential for natural acquisition?

SYLLABUS

Which particular skills are emphasised?
How credible is the functional syllabus?
What is the role of grammar?
Is there potential for linking ELT with the primary curriculum?

METHODOLOGY

Is there potential for groupwork?
What is the role of controlled practice?
What is the role of the teacher?

VIEW OF LEARNING

Are children encouraged to engage actively in learning?
What importance is attached to independent learning?
How far is rote learning considered important?
What part does testing play in learning?

The answers to these questions will determine the extent to which aspects of mainstream primary practice outlined in this paper could be considered methodologically or culturally appropriate. While involved in teacher training abroad I have been struck by comments from non-native speakers working in primary ELT who expressed the wish that innovation in ELT at primary level might trigger off a change in attitude to other learning in the primary school. This raises concerns about the need to avoid the so-called 'colonialisation' of ELT by native speakers. Where pains are taken to ensure the 'ownership' of innovation by non-native teachers and trainers and where aspects of the learning context have been taken into account, such moves may be appropriate, albeit ambitious. British practitioners of course have a part to play in offering their view of what is good primary pedagogy in ELT, particularly in the fields of materials design and teacher training. In all cases, however, the development of a sensitivity to learners' needs and teaching constraints in differing contexts is vital.

Conclusion

Professor Brumfit stated clearly that the questions he posed and the search for answers to them were problematic. The challenge to create a new pedagogy suited to the needs of children is one which the profession urgently needs to address. It will be interesting to see whether consensus can be reached on what constitutes the best practice for primary children learning English in different contexts. In meeting this major challenge, reflection and the sharing of ideas ought to provide interesting possibilities for a variety of educationally attractive solutions.

Bibliography

Bruner, J.S. 1966. *Towards a Theory of Instruction.* Massachusetts: Harvard University Press.

Central Advisory Council for Education. 1967. *Children and their Primary Schools.* London: HMSO.

Clegg, J. 1990. Report on a course leading to the RSA Certificate in TEFL to Young Learners. (Unpublished).

Department of Education and Science. 1975. *A Language for Life.* London: HMSO.

Department of Education and Science. 1988. *English for Ages 5 to 11.* London: HMSO.

Department of Education and Science. 1989. *English for Ages 5 to 16.* 3.1;3.4. London: HMSO.

Donaldson M. 1978. *Children's Minds.* London: Fontana.

Ellis, G. and J. Brewster. 1991. *The Story Telling Handbook.* London: Penguin.

Ellis, R. 1984. *Classroom Second Language Development.* Oxford: Pergamon Press.

Galton, M., B. Simon and P. Croll. 1980. *Inside the Primary Classroom.* London: Routledge & Kegan Paul.

Garton, A. and C. Pratt. 1989. *Learning to be Literate: the Development of Spoken and Written Language.* Oxford: Basil Blackwell.

Holden, S. (ed). 1980. *Teaching Children.* London: Modern English Publications.

Krashen, S. 1981. *Second Language Acquisition and Second Language Learning.* Oxford: Pergamon Press.

Mayor, B. 1985. 'What does it mean to be bilingual?' *Language and Literacy* Vol I, p.118. Milton Keynes: Open University Press.

Mercer, N. (ed). 1985. *Language and Literacy* Vol I. Milton Keynes: Open University Press.

Nunan, D. 1988. *The Learner-Centred Curriculum.* Cambridge: Cambridge University Press.

Piaget, J. 1967. *Six Psychological Studies.* London: London University Press.

Vygotsky, L.S. 1962. *Thought and Language.* Sussex: Wiley.

Vygotsky, L.S. 1978. *Mind in Society: the Development of Higher Psychological Processes.* Massachusetts: Harvard University Press.

Wood, D. 1988. *How Children Think and Learn.* Oxford: Basil Blackwell.

Jackie Holderness, Oxford Polytechnic, England

2 Activity-based teaching: approaches to topic-centred work

An exploration in practical detail of the role of topic-centred work. It can be linked with Edie Garvie's overview later in this section, while activity-based learning is taken up again in papers on fun and play activities (especially Shelagh Rixon and Julia Khan) and on drama (Anne and Gordon Slaven).

THIS PAPER PROPOSES to give a brief introduction to the merits and practicalities of topic-centred, activity-based language teaching, moving from consideration of the general (the ways in which children learn) to the specific (how these ways may be integrated into the EFL classroom). While the specific needs of the young EFL learner must of course be addressed, the basic principles by which all young learners operate provide the framework for topic-centred work. These create, in turn, a need for us as teachers to look again at coursebooks and methodologies which we may have inherited from traditional models of primary education or even the adult EFL situation. Making adult teaching methods simpler is definitely not the solution. Ignoring the implications of research into children's learning (Vygotsky, Donaldson, Wells and so on) is unfair to the children we teach.

Children deserve to have teaching that is child-centred and teachers of children deserve to have their specific requirements and skills recognised within the adult-based EFL world and marketplace. Topic-centred, activity-based learning has evolved precisely because it fulfils the needs of the young learner.

Topic-centred learning

Topic-centred learning is a concept familiar to most primary teachers in the UK. It means teachers not teaching to a timetable strictly divided into lessons or periods for different subjects. History, maths, English and so on are not always taught separately.

Instead the day is regarded as 'integrated'. The children explore a topic, for example transport, materials or opposites. The teacher structures the children's learning so that in their topic work they are involved in a wide range of activities. These activities may be scientific, creative or investigative.

The children will therefore approach almost all their curriculum from the perspective of the topic. One may ask why this should be a good thing. There are several answers to this question.

First, there is the question of *context*. It is important that the children appreciate where their learning fits into their experience. In language learning this is vital. A word without a sentence is rarely meaningful. A sentence without a context is hard to understand. The incoherence of traditional language exercises must have created all kinds of confusion in pupils' heads. Sentences unrelated to each other or to anything else, in certain language exercises, have forced children to jump conceptually in a meaningless acrobatic display of linguistic competence.

From context comes the second important issue, *meaning*. If the topic chosen is directly relevant to children's experiences or interests, topic-centred learning can be more meaningful to them. Children will want to search for meaning if the content of the topic is interesting. Focusing together on the content of the topic, the children will be able to explore it in greater depth, leading to more stimulating challenges than those provided by superficial language exercises.

Through the topic, then, the children are guaranteed interesting content, a shared context and an emphasis on meaning. These provide the children with a genuine *purpose* both for their language learning and for their learning in general. They are no longer learning language for its own sake, but in order to extend their learning horizons in a cross-curricular, holistic way. Language becomes their passport to finding out, to increasing their knowledge.

This approach has been accepted for some time in mainstream primary education. In language teaching, however, teaching the target structure or function has often taken precedence over consideration of the quality of the children's learning. Activities have tended to isolate features, which are then taught, produced and practised for their own sake. This has involved children in an artificial approach to language.

For most children language is not intrinsically interesting: it is the currency of action. They see little purpose in studying sentences that do not make sense in their world, yet they do understand the purposes of language to communicate, identify, persuade or find solutions. They use language to find out more, share information or to achieve something.

To summarise, the advantages of topic-centred learning are that it provides a clear context which makes learning more meaningful and creates a genuine purpose for learning and for using language in the classroom.

Activity-based learning

When children are allowed to be themselves, they will be active. They are irrepressible doers, because it is by doing that they learn.

Various forces stimulate children into activity, most evident among them play, creativity and curiosity. In play, children are active symbol-makers, imitators or actors. Within the relative safety of the play situation, children will take greater risks than in real life and try things out in their fantasy and imagination. This is closely related to their creativity. Children want to make and invent things for themselves. They need to create and recreate representations of their experiences. They are also curious – curious both about the world within their experience and the world beyond it. Full of hypotheses, they want to experiment, to find out and to see if . . .

In the language classroom, the teacher can exploit what children do naturally. Activity-based learning is lively and enjoyable. Yet it can focus on the language skill to be learned. It is concerned with making the *how* of learning more effective, rather than changing the *what*.

The children will, of course, learn a lot more than the target language item, and more than the teacher might have expected. This is especially true in the topic-centred classroom where the cross-curricular approach encompasses wider fields of experience than traditional subject-based teaching. At the primary level this is very important because the children are still developing as learners and as people. The activities within their language curriculum should enhance their cognitive and manual skills as well as develop their target language skills.

Practical guidelines

It is difficult to be practical without being specific. Each reader's/teacher's situation will be unique. Teachers may have class sizes anywhere between seven and 70. Pupils may receive anything from one to five hours of English per week. They may be following an immersion-style course or studying in an English school in a second language (ESL) context. There may be adequate supplies of paper, scissors and glue or none at all. Whenever an alternative teaching situation is described, it is with the knowledge that it remains an impossible dream for many teachers. While being realistic, however, it is valuable to keep in mind something to aspire to. Each teacher will at best be able to adapt some of the ideas presented in this section of the paper.

Planning the topic

The teacher first needs to choose a topic that is appropriate for his/her particular group of pupils. The topic needs to be wide enough to appeal to varying interests and levels of ability and perhaps both boys and girls. The school environment or locality will to a certain extent dictate the topic choice. For example, studying boats in an area where they are never seen would be difficult. The following list features topics which should be widely suitable: School, Jobs, People, Buildings, Shops, Toys, Clothes, Families, Accidents and Safety, Books and Stories, Friends, Animals, Pets, Transport, Music, Materials, Hobbies, Plants, Weather and Communications.

Having chosen a topic, a quick brainstorm is a good idea. It may produce a topic web like Figure 1.

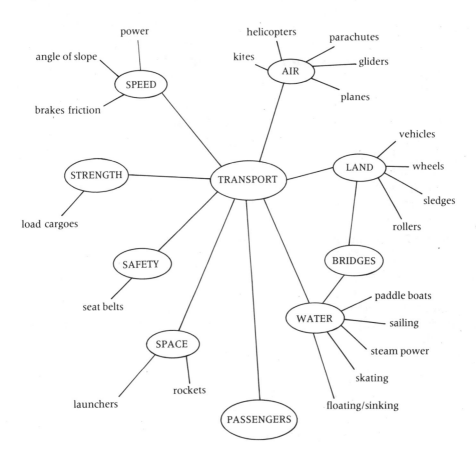

Figure 1 A topic web (*topic:* transport).

A topic web is a free exploration of ideas – you would be unlikely to attempt to cover all the ideas first noted. By laying out ideas in this way, however, you can check for balance and identify the structures, activities and resources required.

At this point it is valuable to glean from the children (in the mother tongue if necessary) what they would like to find out about the topic. Their questions will reveal much about what they already know and where their interests lie, for example 'How do aeroplanes stay in the air?' or 'Who wrote the first book?' Indeed their questions can provide a framework for the topic and generate ideas for activities.

Identifying language skills

Having decided upon a topic and produced a topic web, more specific planning is essential. A table as in Figure 2, which is both a planning aid and a record of pupils' experiences and the teacher's achievements, is useful.

Activity	Language focus	Lexis	Functions	Comments
Match jobs & tools cards	need + noun	jobs tools	expressing need	
Miming + guessing game. What do I do? which job does this?	verbs	jobs tools	describing action	

Figure 2 A planning aid and record (*topic:* occupations).

There can be no hard and fast rules about creating a lesson. Sometimes an activity will generate the language focus. Usually the teacher will identify a language requirement (for example, the ability to express the future) and devise an activity where the language will genuinely be needed and can be taught purposefully (see Figure 3).

Language focus	Activity	Lexis	Functions	Comments
'going to' 'travel by' + noun	Guessing game using photos of different forms of transport	Forms of transport	Expressing future action Describing modes of transport	

Figure 3 An activity/language table (*topic:* transport).

The pupils' coursebook will identify the language skills deemed appropriate for the age group or ability level, but the teacher may find that they need a particular structure or skill earlier. The teacher can then devise a topic-centred activity to introduce and practise the target language.

Devising activities

There are several different kinds of activity. If children are to understand the nature of a task, the teacher him/herself will first need to be clear what the activity is demanding of the pupil. Activities can include one or several of these cognitive skills:

describing	comparing
identifying and recognising	sequencing
matching	remembering
sorting and classifying	solving problems
making connections	testing theories

The type of activity chosen will depend upon the language available, the language targeted, the resources required, the size of the class and groups and the material in the pupils' coursebook.

Let us suppose that the coursebook is dealing with comparatives ('bigger than, smaller than'). The class has been looking at colours as a topic. The teacher could devise several activities that would use the new language while recycling the old.

Example 1. The children make/have made a series of shapes – triangles, circles, squares of different colours and thicknesses (a set of these may already form part of their maths equipment). In pairs each pupil tells his/her neighbour about the relationships between their shapes. Each pair makes a poster showing three examples.

Example 2. A simple game can be made, using mathematical shapes or lexis items familiar to the children. Let us say shapes are being used. A large games board is made, with numbered spaces leading to question boxes. In the question boxes, a shape is drawn and a question asked, for example 'Is your triangle bigger than this? Yes/No?' Each child has one example of each shape. He/She compares his/hers with the shape on the board and then picks up a Yes card or a No card. This says how many steps forwards or backwards he/she must go. This could be played with animals, household items or anything which can be described with the comparative or superlative.

Example 3. In pairs children sequence simply made pictures that tell a story, for example blobs of colour getting bigger and bigger.

Example 4. The teacher sets up an experiment. He/She provides squares of different types of material and asks pupils to find out, for example, which is stronger or more waterproof. Alternatively coloured threads could be used with questions such as, 'Which is longer than 30 cm?' 'Which is shorter?'

Example 5. A pair of children have two similar but not identical pictures of coloured geometric shapes and lines. Each child hides his/her picture from his/her partner. They ask questions to find out what the differences are.

The factors to take into account when devising activities include language, skills, resources but finally and most importantly cognitive challenge. Young language learners are too frequently presented with simplified tasks where all they really need is simplified language or 'scaffolding' (Bruner). They find tasks which are cognitively challenging more interesting than those with obvious solutions. A ten-year-old beginner in English is not a beginner in conceptual cognitive functions. Activities need to be matched carefully to the child's developmental level if motivation is to be sustained.

Providing challenges

Among the most challenging learning activities we can provide for children are open-ended activities, where the outcome or answers are not known. This leads us into the realm of problem-solving and investigations. The children become real learners, where they actually have to think rather than simply remember. They quickly realise that this kind of activity is less threatening because there is no established right or wrong. They are encouraged therefore to be more confident and creative.

Figure 4 shows examples of both closed and open-ended activities. The examples demonstrate that both closed and open-ended activities can be challenging, but the open-ended tend to allow for greater creativity and responsibility. The open-ended activities may involve the teacher in a lengthier briefing session before the children can proceed. Once they have understood the task, however, they should not need to keep checking for accuracy and the teacher is much freer to provide language input, focusing on structures and lexis as and when necessary. With closed activities, where

Open-ended activities	Closed activities
A *Experiment:* Roll a toy car along different surfaces. Which surface is best?	1 Match the pictures and words (transport).
B *Problem-solving:* Mr X must travel to 15 countries, always going east. He can only stop in countries beginning with 'A'. Can he do it?	2 Draw a route on a map following taped instructions.
C *Game:* Can you form pairs by making connections between these pictures/objects with wheels?	3 Put the pictures from this story about a train into the correct sequence.
D *Group task:* Make a life-size skeleton out of newspaper.	4 *Pairwork:* Each pair uses a tall book or equivalent to make a screen between them. A chooses and describes a picture featuring movement from a selection of pictures. B tries to draw what A describes, then hunts through the pictures to find the original and compare it with his/her drawing.

Figure 4 Examples of open-ended/closed activities (*topic:* movement).

the solutions are known, the teacher can of course free him/herself as well by encouraging pupils to check their own work.

A varied approach combining open-ended and closed activities is probably the best. The ultimate factor, as in many teaching decisions, may be the resources available.

Organising resources

In the primary EFL classroom, the most obvious single resource is the pupils' coursebook. In more affluent settings this may be enhanced by a write-in activity book and, ideally, by other resources such as reading books, dictionaries, cassettes, games and videos. Let us assume that the coursebook is the only book. Even if it is monochromatic and unappealing, it is the teacher's central resource. As the teacher prepares the next term's work he/she can analyse and plan how best to exploit the coursebook as a resource: he/she can build a wide variety of challenging activities on it, weave stories, topics and investigations into it, and extend it to involve the interests of the children, the local environment and the children's lives outside school.

When planning a topic, the teacher needs to refer constantly to the coursebook. Bearing in mind the practicalities of the timetable, he/she can identify places in the book where topic work naturally arises. Some exercises might be replaced by more meaningful and enjoyable activities. Structure, balance, challenge and variety are the key words here.

The next task in planning the coming term is to identify and list the materials and resources that will be required. Most primary teachers collect odds and ends that may come in useful some day, and these will be a good starting point for collecting the items on the list. Building up a bank of pictures, objects with particular qualities and different examples of text is an ongoing process. A more specific collection, however, is required for exploring a topic. If the topic is transport, a collection of pictures of forms of transport is the first step. Library books in the mother tongue can be used for reference and can form part of a display. Once under way, the display area itself becomes a valuable resource.

A transport display, thanks to the children themselves, should soon feature model/toy cars, buses and horses, train tickets and so on. The class can then label the display so that it becomes a tangible word bank. Supplemented by a class dictionary of topic words and wall posters made by the pupils (on related subjects such as road safety, local transport, advertisements) the classroom itself becomes a lively language resource.

All these resources will need organising. Pictures can be stored alphabetically by subject or topic in wall pockets or in boxes where they are accessible to the children. Items like old corks, containers, string and paper scraps also need to be available to pupils and well labelled.

A book making area, with paper, old card, glue and thread, is a common feature in many primary classrooms in Britain, but would not be feasible in most EFL situations. However, the EFL teacher might be able to make a large, simply bound book at home, using card covers and large sheets of paper folded and sewn in place. The children could write something individually for the book, for example a collection of stories, poems or opinions. They could also collaborate on a class story, with the teacher writing down the ideas in large clear letters. The children could provide the illustrations to go with the text. A combination of photographs of the children, say in class, together with their descriptions of the photos works well too.

All these ideas mean that the EFL classroom is gaining valuable reading material, created by the children themselves. Before long, the idea will take root and children will start bringing in books they have made themselves at home.

A collection of target language/English books, especially picture and story books, is of course an ideal language resource. If a full reading box or corner is an undreamed-of luxury, a start can be made with old comics and magazines. If there is an English community in the area, a request in the community newsletter for children's books might prove very rewarding. Building up a large collection of resources may produce its own problems. The teacher may be unable to leave the materials in the classroom in between lessons. The collection could be stored in a large box and kept safe in a cupboard in the classroom or staff room and the pupils themselves could be made responsible for packing and unpacking it at each lesson – a good opportunity to revise vocabulary.

The teacher's role

The topic-centred, activity-based approach does not call so much for a change in the teacher's role but for an extension of it. The teacher will still have to introduce new language and provide practice with repetition in order to consolidate what is learned. With thoughtful planning, however, this practice can be invested with greater relevance for the pupils and can offer them learning experiences within the language programme that increase their involvement and motivation.

As well as content and activities, the teacher needs to consider the following issues when planning classwork: preparing the children, language support, strategies for managing the classroom and a system for feedback and assessment.

Preparing the children

First, the children need to be prepared linguistically to give them the confidence to use English – the target language. This will involve initial input and ongoing support and feedback.

Second, they will need to be prepared for the topic in general and the activity in particular. Some time may have to be spent in discussing pairwork and groupwork if these are unfamiliar ways of operating. A clear understanding of the nature of the task is essential. Does it involve matching or sequencing? Is it open-ended or can the answers be checked somewhere? What materials will be needed to perform the task?

Third, the teacher will have to spend some time preparing the children for working in an 'English-speaking' environment. Certain classroom language is essential in order to locate resources, ask for help and maintain discipline. Codes of behaviour and noise level all form part of this area of preparation.

Providing language support

Experiences in mainstream primary education have revealed that without careful planning, topic-based teaching can imply a move away from structure towards a curriculum based on chance. This is of course unsatisfactory and the teacher must be clear as to what language he/she will teach, together with its context (topic) and activities.

The kind of language support the teacher gives will vary from situation to situation. The long-term objective is that children develop their own strategies for support, for example dictionary and reference skills.

Meanwhile the teacher, working in the role of facilitator, creates learning situations where children must use the target language structure but are also challenged.

Activity-centred learning frequently involves groupwork. The teacher may need to interrupt an activity from time to time and call the groups together to teach or reinforce a language point. A highly developed sense of timing is required, along with considerable sensitivity to pupils' needs.

The use of structures to highlight intonation, word order and tense formation may continue as before, but pupils are helped to understand the reason for knowing something. They can see the need for the structure in their activities and recognise that they are learning more than just the language.

Managing the classroom

Mobility is the key here. If neither desks nor children can move freely, the teacher will find it difficult to set up groupwork. Conditions may allow some

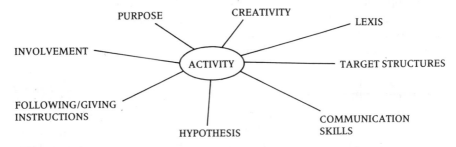

Figure 5 The target structure is just one of the learning outcomes for the child.

activities to be pursued in the open air but this will need careful supervision. In a classroom where mobility is limited and the teaching style is restricted to chalk and talk, read and discuss, the topic can still be central. At least paired activities can take place, possibly using this formula:

whole class → pairs → whole class → make different pairs → whole class. In this situation, tasks need to be desk-top, such as information-gap, sorting and investigative activities. The topic can be approached via cognitively challenging puzzles using paper and pencil, and children can play and make desk-top games, make books, lists and so on. In a more freely arranged classroom, the teacher can form groupings as required. One day the children might work in fours, on another in sixes. The smaller the group, the greater the children's involvement. The groups do not necessarily need to be doing the same kind of activity simultaneously. For example, imagine a group of 40. They have been divided up into ten groups of four. Each group is given a different task. Look at Figure 6.

Figure 6 Ideas for group activities (*topic:* people).

1 Making a dictionary of people who help us.
2 Sorting pictures of people to find famous people. Labelling and displaying.
3 Same as 2, but looking for occupations. Labelling and displaying.
4 Making a class book or a poster about young and old.
5 Same as 4, but about people in the class/school.
6 Looking from window to record how many men, women and children pass the school . . . then drawing graph.
7 Same as 6, but looking for people in uniform, with animals, etc.
8 Same as 6, but people using wheels or walking.
9 Looking at a well-known story (well-known to the children) and making a poster to show the people in it, their jobs/characters, etc.
10 Matching sets of words, e.g. adjectives describing physique or mood, to pictures of people.

Having each group produce something different from the rest creates a genuine reason for sharing activities.

The topic of people may have been inspired by the coursebook. Imagine the chain of events. The current unit highlights occupations or family relationships. The teacher encourages the children to collect pictures of people and to think about and collect words relating to facial expressions, clothes, actions and so on. The words go into the class dictionary. The class works together on lexis and a few structures. They complete worksheets individually. The teacher reads them stories which feature a lot of people, for example *The Great Big Enormous Turnip*, *The Emperor's Clothes* or *Cinderella*. The classroom walls feature posters about people, families and film stars. The children add photographs of the people in their own lives. There are population graphs as well (older age range).

Managing such a diversity of experience and activity needs firmness. It is worth establishing ground rules in the first few lessons about the use and sharing of resources, levels of noise and standards expected. The teacher may wish to use the mother tongue if necessary to ensure understanding.

Children do need to know if they are allowed to use the mother tongue, for what purposes and for how long. If the teacher doesn't want it used at all, this must be made clear. Some teachers feel that a flexible approach works best – as the children become absorbed in the task and focus on meaning, they may lapse into the mother tongue to make themselves understood. They are not penalised for this, but the teacher can exploit the opportunity to model the structure that they have been unable to produce in the target language/English. Other teachers insist that English only can be spoken. Where several teachers work together, it is vital that they agree on a common policy to avoid confusing the children.

Once ground rules are established, the teacher can explain to each group what they have to do. Where tasks are similar, groups can be given instructions together. Other groups who are waiting for their instructions can do a straightforward exercise, perhaps revising words, reading, practising spelling or dictionary skills.

As the groups understand their tasks, they can be sent off quietly to collect resources, plan and get started.

As the children become involved in their activities, the teacher is gradually left free to go round to each group and provide language support until he/she senses the need to call everybody back together for specific language teaching or to share something that one particular group has discovered or achieved.

Providing feedback and assessment

In order to develop confidence in the children, teacher-to-child feedback should always be supportive and positive.

By creating the opportunity for groups to share their tasks and the end-results, the teacher enables the children to provide feedback for each other.

In closed activities, the children can assess their own achievements by matching their results with the predicted outcome, while the teacher keeps an overview of pupils' competence and progress. The language focus of the lesson can be tested orally or in writing, depending on the age and ability of the pupils. Testing, however, is only encouraging to those who do best. For some children poor test scores can signal the beginning of the end of their motivation.

The teacher needs therefore to balance testing with assessment based on classroom observations. Levels of confidence and fluency can best be measured by listening in to the pupils' interchanges. Levels of motivation, attitudes to problem-solving and overall development can also be noted.

Children can be directly involved in the assessment process by filling in a questionnaire (see Figure 7) or simply commenting on their own learning orally in response to questions in discussion.

Look at these questions. Think about them carefully. Draw a circle around the number you want. 1 means 'Not at all'. 6 means 'Very much or very good'. Numbers 2, 3, 4 and 5 are in between.

How interesting do you find this topic?	1 ② 3 4 5 6
Do you like learning English songs?	① 2 3 4 5 6
the coursebook?	1 2 ③ 4 5 6
stories in English?	1 2 3 4 5 6
working together?	1 2 3 4 5 6
How good are you at speaking English?	1 2 3 4 5 6
reading English?	1 2 3 4 5 6
writing English?	1 2 3 4 5 6
understanding English?	1 2 3 4 5 6

Figure 7 A self-assessment questionnaire.

The answers will give the teacher a valuable insight into the pupils' perceptions of their own learning.

A quick note in the teacher's record book of which children were successful and which had difficulty for each activity will identify the range of ability within the group and help the teacher to steer a sensible course in the future, refining the match between language needs and the pupils' conceptual levels (see Figure 9).

Such records are invaluable for report writing and as a basis for discussion with parents. They enable the teacher to remember, for example, that Miguel, who scores low in lexical terms is the acknowledged group leader in problem-solving. A much rounder picture of the pupil is made available and strengths upon which the teacher can build are identified. More effective planning and more successful task/child matches should follow.

A briefer record sheet might be preferred. Each child in the group is named and a short comment or an indication of the child's degree of success added. These abbreviated reflections would serve as a reminder to the teacher of specific responses and as a planning aid.

Activity	Date	Successes	Difficulty	Language needs	Comments
Make a group story		Miguel— good sense of story structure	José— verb confusion	Revise past simple with all	Nina needs more extension— get activity ready for her.

Figure 8 A teacher's record sheet (A).

	Activity A	Activity B	Activity C	
Giulia	+	+ +	too noisy	
Miguel	+	– past continuous		

Figure 9 A teacher's record sheet (B).

Conclusion

A consideration of the topic and activity-centred approach may involve the teacher in a review of both the content and the methodology of his/her English teaching. The rewards in terms of learning and motivation may be great, but such a review may daunt many teachers for several reasons.

First, parents may be unsympathetic to what seems to them a deviation from traditional learning patterns. They may expect their children to learn languages as they did. This can be a serious problem because negative parents can undermine the children's confidence and rob them of motivation. The teacher needs the support of parents at all times, even if this involves a note home explaining the topic, and the value and purpose of the activities offered at school. Alternatively, the teacher might invite the parents into the school to see the results of this approach and to discuss together the benefits of working in this way. Enlisting the parents' support and then encouraging them to read to their children in the target language (if books are available) and join in the resource bank collection would be ideal.

Second, teachers themselves may not see the need to alter their ways of working. Certainly, change for change's sake is absurd and time-wasting. However, if teachers could at least experiment, tentatively to begin with, I think they would find the results encouraging and beneficial. Convincing one's colleagues can be harder even than convincing parents, but teachers are not immune to example. Once other teachers begin to see the fruits of the topic approach in one classroom, they may be inspired to try it in their own.

Third, the teacher might fear that the children will exploit the more flexible classroom situation and create too much noise, disturbing other classes. One could argue that a good language classroom should be the scene of a lot of talk, but with a large class the borderline between communication and mere noise is very thin. If time is spent establishing acceptable and unacceptable ways of working, and if classroom management is carefully considered, this need not become a real difficulty. Indeed, pupils' increased motivation, stemming from their recognition of the learning purpose, usually leads to more sensible behaviour.

It is best to move cautiously to begin with, building up confidence in the topic-based approach. There may be time, perhaps, to adopt this approach for some of the lessons initially, or for part of longer lessons. The aim is to achieve as much coherence and meaning in the children's learning as possible. If the teacher begins to search for connections which will make learning relevant, the pupils will soon respond. They will soon start searching for connections themselves.

The place of topic and activity-centred learning is as central to teaching English to young learners as it is to teaching them any other subject. The decisive factor is our involvement, as EFL teachers, with the overall development of our pupils as learners. The way we teach them English can enhance the way they view all learning and help them to grow in confidence and competence.

It is vital to retain as the focus of our teaching a clear view of how younger children learn best.

This checklist of questions can be internalised and used by teachers to ensure that their language teaching is concerned with the overall quality of the child's learning:

a) Which concepts are involved here?
b) Which language structures do I want to focus on?
c) Are the activities cognitively challenging? How? Are they open/closed?
d) Are they relevant to the children's experiences and interests?
e) Which strategies for feedback and assessment are needed?
f) Classroom management – how will I organise the lesson?

If teachers plan their lessons with these questions in mind, the language classroom should become a place where children enjoy using English as a passport to activities that interest and challenge them. By focusing on the way young learners learn – by doing, by testing ideas, by solving problems and by using their creative imaginations in play – the topic-based approach gives children a more active role in their learning of English and a greater sense of relevance and enjoyment. If an activity is worth doing, it's worth thinking about and talking about – and that is exactly what the children will do!

Bibliography

References

Donaldson, M. 1978. *Children's Minds.* London: Fontana.

Tann, S. 1988. *Developing Topic Work in the Primary School.* London: Falmer Press.

Vygotsky, L.S. 1962. *Thought and Language.* Massachusetts: MIT Press.

Wells, G. 1968. *Language and Learning and Education.* Slough: Nelson/NFER.

Further ideas

Bright Ideas series. Various authors. Titles include *Environmental Studies* and *Language Games.* Leamington Spa: Scholastic Publications.

Fisher, R. 1987. *Problem-Solving in Primary Schools.* Oxford: Basil Blackwell.

Fisher, R. 1990. *Teaching Children to Think.* Oxford: Basil Blackwell.

Kincaid, D. and P. Cole. 1979. *Science in a Topic* series. Amersham: Hulton Educational.

Shelagh Rixon, The British Council, London

3 The role of fun and games activities in teaching young learners

Shelagh Rixon offers many principles and many practical ideas for using play in the primary classroom. This theme will be taken up later in Julia Khan's paper, which links these ideas with the theories that underlie primary teaching.

B Y 'FUN AND GAMES' I mean all those activities that we loosely think of as involving play and enjoyment. Singing, clapping hands, chanting rhymes, solving puzzles, drawing, colouring, model-making, games. I hope that will be the only loose thing about this paper – it is too easy to be unanalytic about such a seductive subject as fun.

It is a commonplace that young children learn better through play or at least can be induced to go along with teaching that is tempered by 'fun' activities. I would not want to take issue with that basic proposition, but it can be a dangerous one if acted upon by teachers or course designers with insufficient thought and rigour. We are all apt to be so delighted by the fact that children do get absorbed in play or fun in a language classroom that we tend to assume something worthwhile must be going on. We might all take more care about exactly what the children are absorbed in. Fun should have a role in, rather than just be a feature of, children's education. Here are some of the pitfalls:

a) That we provide an activity which is absorbing in itself but is of negligible pay-off in terms of language acquisition or else takes too long for too little return. Fun, but a waste of the limited time usually available for language learning. An example of this would be a board game whose rules are so complicated that the children are more absorbed in its mechanics than in the language comprehension or production work that it was originally designed to stimulate. Little English and a lot of native language will be heard in this case. 'Colour the picture' without any linguistic challenge is a good activity for calming children down, but if it goes on too long, time is being wasted.

b) That our best endeavours to provide a game or fun activity that is good for English are being distorted by the ingenuity of the children themselves. Very often they can create a 'better' game in their own terms. Where it is better both for them and for the main objective of their being in that class – getting to grips with a bit more English – this is clearly a case where we should steal the idea and use it. However, I have seen many cases where the 'new' activity was not quite so useful.

I well remember a game played in a native language classroom by six-year-olds. It was a form of Pelmanism (a game in which players try to remember the whereabouts of pairs of cards which are turned face down on a table. If a player can remember and make a pair, he/she can keep the cards. The player with the most pairs when the cards are used up is the winner). This version of the game had word and picture cards which went together, to train word and image matching. Excellent in itself (for EFL learners too) except that the teacher was not monitoring what was going on. This particular group had changed the rules, and was taking bets (in sweets) about remembering the locations of the picture cards alone. The word cards were ignored. The group was having great fun, but the objective of the original game had gone out of the window.

c) That adults are too snooty about humble-seeming activities and deny them a place in language lessons. I hope to make a case for some too easily despised activities which I have seen to work well. Many everyday puzzle activities can play their part in language development, if they are used at the right moment and contain the right clues or challenges.

In all three cases there are two messages to the teacher. First, we need to monitor what is actually, rather than seemingly, going on in class. Second, we need to develop a clear understanding of the mechanics and effects of different activity types.

To this end, the main section of this article attempts a categorisation of types of fun activity, and gives suggestions within each category of the types of pay-off we might expect for the children.

My main claim to be writing this paper at all is the five-year period in which I worked in Italy during the long run-in to the introduction of foreign languages into primary school, and my thinking has been very much influenced by discussions I have had with Italian colleagues on the language objectives and general educational aspirations this move reflects. My view is certainly not an official Italian one, but I think at least that I have arrived at it through my own and colleagues' serious thinking about a very concrete situation.

Four main objectives for foreign language learning at the primary stage stand out:

1 Language learning should assist the general educational objective of encouraging the conceptual development of the child.

2 Language learning should form part of the skills/conceptual and cultural/ social development of the child – literacy, numeracy, general language

awareness, some curiosity about the world around him/her and outside the borders of his/her own country.

3 Primary school language learning should promote the formation of a positive attitude to language learning in general. It should form a good basis for secondary school studies, but not ape the style of learning that may later be imposed. Rigorous grammatical analysis does not seem to be appropriate to this age group, though discovery of rules may be a useful pay-off of pleasant informal activities.

4 Last – primary language learning should result in the acquisition of some appropriate elements of the actual language studied.

I always put Point 4 last because of the danger that this rather obvious objective might swamp and distort the other three. In fact, I think the approach to learning English or French or German at primary level should be shaped and determined by the first three.

A crude summary of the type of course implied is as follows. One that includes scope for children to apply intelligence and intuition as well as or above rote learning. One that has interesting content matter. One that does not put the child off for ever from learning a language, and is not a mere rehearsal for the formal study of languages that he/she will inevitably meet in secondary school.

Fun activities can play their part at all points in this list. The Appendix summarises how some of the activities discussed in this article might meet one or more of the above objectives.

Language pay-off

Language pay-off is one of the most obvious parameters to consider. What can a child be expected to absorb or learn in language terms from particular types of activity?

Language learned by heart as part of an activity

Activities which help the child gain command of 'pre-fabricated' chunks of language involve the most humble level of endeavour at which fun activities can operate. Many games in this category are drill-like but have an added fun and competition element.

■ 'What's the time, Mr Wolf?', a native-speaker game in which children chant the title phrase while cautiously circling a 'wolf', certainly helps fix the 'What's the time?' structure. The wolf in his/her turn has to repeat innocuous times such as three o'clock or ten o'clock, but every now and then bursts forth with 'It's tea-time/dinner time' which is the signal to chase the 'sheep'. If a sheep is caught, he/she becomes the wolf. This game needs space but it serves a good purpose and may be played in break-time once children are familiar with it.

■ A quieter more language-orientated game is 'I went to market and I bought . . .'. The first student says one item (for example 'some apples'), the next student lists the apples and adds an item of his/her own. The third student repeats the sentence, lists the items already mentioned, then adds one, and so on round the class. There can be a penalty for forgetting items on the list or getting them in the wrong order. A player may be declared 'out' or lose a 'life', but often it works just as well if the class co-operates, prompting the speaker who forgets, to see how many items can be remembered corporately. Yes, it does practise 'went', 'bought' and 'some/a/an' but the students' attention is on the feats of memory they can perform. Concentration, close listening and memory strategies are amongst the general educational benefits this game may promote.

■ Songs learned by heart have less controlled language but may give the child access to language chunks which he/she can incorporate into general language use. In the best of possible cases songs and rhymes learned by heart may form part of a child's linguistic data base from which generalisations may be made. Suitable songs include 'If you're happy and you know it, clap your hands' – an action song, often sung by native speakers, in which the children do the actions suggested in each verse. Once the basic verse has been learned, children can suggest other actions to fit into the verse.

> If you're happy and you know it, clap your hands,
> If you're happy and you know it, clap your hands,
> If you're happy and you know it, and you really want to show it,
> If you're happy and you know it, clap your hands.

Other actions could be 'stamp your feet', 'turn around', 'nod your head'.

'The ABC song' is another 'real' song. The rhyme and the rhythm of this song help to fix the names of the letters in English. It is inconvenient for learners of British English that 'zed' must come out as American-style 'zee' for the sake of the rhyme, but otherwise it is a simple and enjoyable mnemonic.

A B C D E F G, H I J K
L M N O P, Q R S T U and V
W X Y and Z.
Now I know my A B C, why don't you sing with me?

Language picked up as a result of an enjoyable activity

Telling stories to students can result in natural language acquisition on their part, but one needs to be careful about the type of story used. My Italian colleagues had the right instincts – that well-known universal fairy stories might be a good starting point. The children would probably know the story in their own language and would be able to follow it better as a result. They would appreciate knowing that many of their own stories existed in other cultures. The stories were guaranteed 'good' since they had stood the test of time. However, some teachers reported disappointing results. Stories like *Cinderella* fell rather flat. The children did not seem to follow very well, they were passive and seemed bored. We analysed the problem together. Two obvious defects of the Great Romantic Stories were the frequent changes of scene and the wide range of vocabulary involved. Also there was nothing for the children to do while the story was being told. So we started looking at another category of universal stories, the ones where part of the fun is for the children to predict the next step and join in. Here are two examples.

The Great Big Enormous Turnip is a Russian folk tale which can be found in many versions. Basically, it concerns a poor farmer who planted one seed, a turnip seed. The seed did very well. In fact, 'It grew and it grew and it grew.' The farmer, being hungry, decided to pull it up and cook it for supper for his family, so 'He pulled and he pulled and he pulled – but he could not pull it up!' One by one he called members of his family. 'He called his wife. And they pulled and they pulled and they pulled – but they could not pull it up! He called his son. And they pulled and they pulled and they pulled – but they could not pull it up!' And so on, through his daughter, the dog, the cat and finally a tiny mouse who tips the balance and up comes the turnip, which is promptly eaten by all. In a story like this, the children quickly recognise the repeated bits, and with encouragement from the teacher they will begin to join in. This story bears retelling and acting out (great fun). The lengthening line of 'pullers' can also be drawn. I found to my pleasure that a class of eight- to nine-year-olds in Liguria that I told it to 'cold' had already done the story in their Italian lessons, only in their version it was a great big enormous carrot. They showed me their exercise books where they had done drawings and captions to fit. A story like this can also provide a framework for other stories, perhaps made up by the teacher or even by the pupils themselves. A modern version which I have used is about a lengthening line of people pushing a car which will not start.

Another traditional story like this is *Chicken Licken* in which a panicky chicken who thinks the sky is falling meets more and more friends on his way to 'tell the King'. The list of friends grows, until they all meet the final 'friend', Foxy Loxy, who takes advantage of the situation, leads them all into his hole and eats the lot of them. Phrases such as 'Good Morning, Chicken Licken. Where are you going?' recur every time a new friend is met. Then 'They all went down the road to find the King.' Or any other phrases that you can work into the story.

I have always used these stories primarily as 'listen and join in' activities. I would not expect a young child to learn the whole story off and retell it, though many can repeat much of it. These pre-fab phrases, learned from an enjoyable and active experience, often stick, and can be reused spontaneously by a child either in a situation which calls for them, or as a source of language data from which the brightest and most creative may make generalisations and come out with phrases of their own, for example, 'I looked and I looked, but I could not find it.' A fuller list of such stories is given in the Bibliography.

Creative use of language in an activity

Some activities allow more creative use of the language, where 'new' utterances can be produced by the child. We have already seen a limited form of creativity where the verses of the song, 'If you're happy and you know it', can be extended by the children to include new actions. Games which allow children to use known language at their discretion and in response to what another speaker has said include the whole gamut of communication games, usually played in pairs or small groups.

■ 'Find the difference' is well known. Two players have two similar but not identical pictures and (without looking at the other person's picture) have to ask each other or tell each other about their own picture to discover four or five differences. This is an example of a 'game framework' which needs planning by the teacher to be sufficiently targeted to what students can say and to a particular area of language. Differences can be made in several ways. The two pictures could simply contain different sets of objects. In this case the expected language might be, 'Have you got a . . . ?', 'I can see a . . .'. If the focus of the lesson is prepositions or location, the pictures might contain the same objects but in different spatial relations, for example, 'On the right of the house . . . On the left . . .'. The same objects with different colours could be used to practise colour words. Making the pictures for such games may seem a lot of work, but the children can do it themselves. Once they are familiar with the game framework, you can put up on the board a list of objects for them to choose from and ask each student to draw his/her own secret picture in his/her exercise book and then use it to play the game with a partner. Playing in pairs demands that each child listen carefully to his/her partner and check anything he/she does not understand, using, for example, 'Sorry, where is the cat?' or 'Can you repeat that, please?' The language used can be well within the child's limits, but it must be used flexibly and in response to what he/she hears from his/her partner. These games are not one-off experiences. You can probably find many opportunities to use different versions during your course.

Language pay-off from conceptual engagement

Many intelligence test puzzle-type activities also involve language use, or can be made to do so by the requirement that the 'answer' is expressed in English.

■ A simple reinforcement of time language involves giving students a series of pictures of clock faces (see Figure 1). In each face the time advances by a fixed number of minutes, quarters of hours or half hours or odd number of minutes according to the stage in the course. The final clock face is left blank and the students have to fill in the correct time completing the sequence and write or say it in English. Number progressions can be used in the same way.

Figure 1 A clock sequence.

■ Putting words into categories can produce useful vocabulary revision. An activity which allows latitude for imagination is one where students are given a grid of small pictures showing objects they know the names of and a number of place headings, for example a street, a garden, a house (see Figure 2). They are asked (alone or in pairs) to list under each heading the things they might expect to see in each place. Many objects could be found in more than one place, and such cross-categorisation not only means that they will repeat the vocabulary items several times but that they will also think about what is plausible in real situations. For example a chair will obviously be found in a house, but it might also be seen in a garden in summer or in a Mediterranean street when the neighbours sit out to gossip. Justifications for such choices may be made in the native language if necessary, since at least part of the objective of this activity is to develop lateral thinking, which goes beyond the expression of this thinking in English.

More formal categorisation activities might involve splitting a list of words into sub-sections of, for example fruit and vegetables or furniture and food, or putting names for family relationships onto a family tree diagram. A freer, more personalised activity of the same sort would be to give students a mixed list of words and leave them to find their own categories (for example 'Food I like, Food I don't like, Words beginning with "s", Colour words') as in Figure 3. Students could then compare results and learn from their fellows.

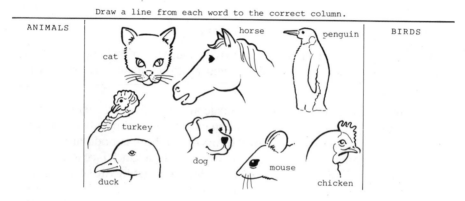

Draw a line from each word to the correct column.

Figure 2 Putting words into categories.

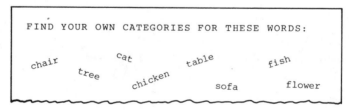

FIND YOUR OWN CATEGORIES FOR THESE WORDS:

chair   cat   table   fish
    tree   chicken   sofa   flower

Figure 3 Finding your own categories.

■ 'Picture dominoes' (see Figure 4) is a game which demands both lateral and logical thinking, together with an expression of that thinking in English. Students have to put a set of different picture cards into a chain in which each card has some link with the one next to it. The links may be obvious, 'They are both blue/both animals' or it can be the product of an individual child's imagination or opinion, 'They both hate the rain/They are both ugly'. The main point is that the link must be expressed in English before the move can be made. This game can be played using the normal rules of dominoes (one domino per turn, the first player to finish is the winner) but it works just as well or even better if students co-operate in building up the most satisfying chain, helping each other with ideas and language.

'The tree goes with the flower because you can see them both in a garden.'

'The cat goes with the dog because they are both animals.'

'The fish goes with the crocodile because they both live in water.'

Figure 4 A picture domino sequence with linking sentences.

Informal language analysis through puzzles and making activities

Some activities in which the child plays with or through the language provide him/her with an informal way of looking at the form or the system of the language itself. Many of the activities in this category are perhaps too much despised, because they look too simple and too much like the sort of puzzle that children enjoy in 'real life'.

■ A 'Find the word' grid may look easy and trivial but it can train children to recognise English spelling patterns, and if the words are all of one category, it can reinforce categorisation skills (see Figure 5). Look at the number of puzzle books for children (and adults) that are sold in most countries for leisure entertainment, and you will see how absorbing this simple, easily invented type of activity must be. A 'Word chain' in which the pupils have to separate out words from a string of unseparated letters is similar in function (see Figure 6).

FIND THE ENGLISH WORDS

H	A	M	B	U	R	G	E	R	U	N
B	R	U	X	M	X	A	X	I	M	O
T	I	M	E	B	I	R	D	Q	B	O
N	U	M	B	E	R	D	X	R	R	N
I	X	Y	E	S	O	E		S	E	D
C	X	L	E	M	O	N	S	N	L	I
E	X	L	O	T	M	E	T	A	L	B
P	Q	R	S	T	S	I	X	B	A	T

Figure 5 A letter grid with hidden words.

Figure 6 A word chain.

GRAPEARAPPLEMONIONCARROTOMATO

■ A 'Dot-to-dot' puzzle where the numbers are given as words or as letters of the alphabet (see Figure 7) can provide useful reinforcement for number and letter work. There is an additional language pay-off if the child then has to write under the solved puzzle, 'This is a . . .'.

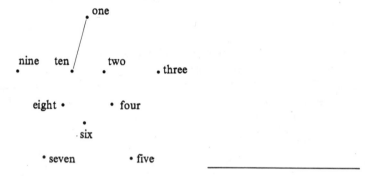

- one

nine   ten   two
                   . three

eight •   • four

        •
     . six

   • seven   • five
                              _____

Figure 7 Joining the dots.

■ Colouring puzzles, where the colours are given as codes, for example 'R = red', can be absorbing and exercise recognition and use of colour words. A more taxing version is a puzzle picture in which students are told, 'Colour all the small triangles red, and all the big circles green. What can you see?'

■ Model-making can be dangerously close to general artwork, with no linguistic base, if the instructions are too easy and obvious. If, however, you give oral instructions for making, for example, a simple paper jumping frog (see Figure 8), as the students watch and imitate they will be motivated to listen closely and perhaps to interrupt when a step is not clear. The motivation here is provided by the end-result – they will want to make the 'toy', which jumps when pressed. I have used this with up to a hundred giggling adults too. Simple models like this can be found in many L1 primary school resource books as well as in origami books intended for older people. Choose something simple to make and spectacular in appearance or performance and you will not go wrong. With very simple models you can give written instructions, supported by clear diagrams, as a start to 'Reading for information'.

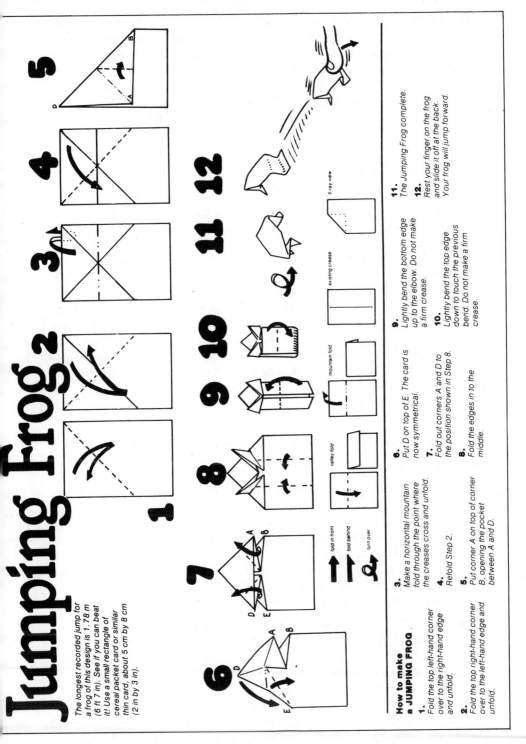

Jumping Frog

The longest recorded jump for a frog of this design is 1.78 m (6 ft 7 in). See if you can beat it! Use a small rectangle of cereal packet card or similar thin card, about 5 cm by 8 cm (2 in by 3 in).

↑ fold in front
↑ fold behind
↻ turn over

— valley fold
---- mountain fold
□ existing crease
X-ray view

How to make a JUMPING FROG

1. Fold the top left-hand corner over to the right-hand edge and unfold.

2. Fold the top right-hand corner over to the left-hand edge and unfold.

3. Make a horizontal mountain fold through the point where the creases cross and unfold.

4. Refold Step 2.

5. Put corner A on top of corner B, opening the pocket between A and D.

6. Put D on top of E. The card is now symmetrical.

7. Fold out corners A and D to the position shown in Step 8.

8. Fold the edges in to the middle.

9. Lightly bend the bottom edge up to the elbow. Do not make a firm crease.

10. Lightly bend the top edge down to touch the previous bend. Do not make a firm crease.

11. The Jumping Frog complete.

12. Rest your finger on the frog and slide it off at the back. Your frog will jump forward.

Figure 8 Simple but motivating origami.

43

A pleasant vocabulary revision activity is to make a mobile or a collage based on a theme. Pupils can work in pairs or groups to create elements of it. The sky or water provide good themes. You may need ideas from primary school resource books to help students make, for example, really good fish or three-dimensional stars or you may have excellent ideas of your own. They will certainly remember the word for 'their' object in English, and the hand-and-eye training is of undoubted general educational value.

Cultural dimensions

Overlaid on language pay-off and conceptual considerations we need to consider the cultural dimensions. Most of the activities mentioned above exist in real life as something that British children enjoy. Make sure that your students know this.

It is quite possible to invent simple games and write original stories, songs and rhymes with a pure language pay-off where you find a gap in your syllabus, but it is worthwhile also doing some research into fun and games activities which already exist in the culture of English-speaking children. Many of these activities are not confined to English-speaking cultures, but exist under other names in the native culture. Knowing that the story or game you are engaged in is one that English-speaking children enjoy must add to the satisfaction of playing it, and is an example of culture teaching at primary level.

Choosing or adapting activities for your situation

Going outside the classroom

Games convenient to the classroom tend to be static and word-based, for example 'I went to market', and there is a case for looking outside to playground games such as 'Mr Wolf' and 'Simon says' that may also exist in the native culture and at least introducing them in class and encouraging the children to try them in break-time. Teachers who can comandeer the school gymnasium or playground for a session of skipping rhymes and action games in English will add a lot to pre-fab learning and to the consciousness that children are much the same everywhere.

■ 'Simon says' is a listening game which is suitable for the classroom but is even better in a larger space. Students not only have to understand the commands, 'Simon says . . . Stand up!' but they must only obey commands which are prefixed by 'Simon says . . .'. You can do this in class with non-disruptive commands like, 'Touch your nose!', but in a gym or playground in which they can run around, you can add extra commands. Anyone who does the wrong thing – the wrong action in response to a 'Simon says' command – or who acts in response to a command without 'Simon says' is out.

Songs and rhymes

The choice here is tricky because many traditional songs and rhymes contain weird or archaic locutions that mystify even native-speaking children at first, but the range is large and from it can be recovered many real items that are simple in structure and vocabulary. 'If you're happy and you know it' presents few structural difficulties, but the popular skipping rhyme 'Apple crumble, Apple tart. Tell me the name of your sweet heart . . .' (then the children go through the alphabet until the skipper trips and they find a name beginning with the letter on which he/she trips) could present some difficulties unless the children are gourmets! An adaptation, 'One, two, three, four. Who's this at the door?' (children go through the alphabet and try to find a new skipper whose name begins with the letter on which the present skipper trips), is not traditional, but it might serve a purpose.

Less problematic is the traditional 'choosing' rhyme, 'One potato, two potatoes, three potatoes, four. Five potatoes, six potatoes, seven potatoes, more. O U T spells "out"' in which the 'chooser' hits fists with each candidate on each phrase and eliminates the one on which the 't' of 'out' comes, and then repeats with the remaining candidates.

Conclusion

Having started with a stern message about being systematic in your choices and your adaptations, I would now conclude with a message about how liberating such a systematic view can be. Provided you have established firmly in your own mind what you want to achieve (one eye on your coursebook or syllabus) and the different ways in which you might achieve it, there is a whole universe of resources open to you. Some ELT resource books will give you ideas ready made for the foreign language classroom, but by far the most inspiring sources are native language primary school resource books and books intended for children of eight to ten years simply to enjoy by themselves in their own time. Adapt the ideas you find. If possible, identify language points relevant to what you are doing and bend the activity to include them. But certainly, do not forget the value of extending pupils' experience in the fields of concept, culture and pure fun. Let the syllabus or coursebook be your backbone, but seek ribs to add to it. I hope the Bibliography will give you some starting points.

Appendix: A consumer's guide to the activities mentioned in this paper.

Activity	Cultural pay-off	Conceptual work	Fun/Motivation	Language
Pelmanism	Real game, played by native speakers	Spatial memory exercised – children have to remember position of particular cards	Competition. Satisfaction of making a successful match. Can therefore also be played alone	Pairing of word and image (vocab reinforcement) Other possibilities: matching of present and past tenses
'What's the time, Mr Wolf?'	Real game. Can be played with either native culture or British times for meals	Not much, except linking times of day with meal times	Running around, avoiding being caught. Quick reaction to dangerous times brings you an advantage	Pre-fab chunks *What's the time? It's . . . o'clock It's dinner/lunch/tea/breakfast time*
'I went to market'	Real game	Memory exercised. Perhaps students will use particular memorisation strategies for long lists. Discuss these in the native language	Satisfaction in remembering the whole list correctly. The desire to break the record	*Some/a* – practised Pre-fabs *I went, I bought* Food/market vocabulary revised
Song: 'If you're happy'	Real song	Not much!	Acting it out. Satisfying choral noise if children well trained to sing together	*If . . .* Vocab for different actions acted out and so more easily absorbed
Song: 'ABC'	Real song	Getting letters of the alphabet in the correct order. Realising that English may have more or fewer letters than native language alphabet	Good rhythm. Fun of trying to sing *LMNOP* very quickly	Fixes letters of the alphabet. Spelling games can now be played using the names of these letters
Story: *The Great Big Enormous Turnip* Story: *Chicken Licken*	Real stories	Practice in remembering a sequence and an ever-growing list	Fun and satisfaction of getting the whole list correct. Good story to act out	Past tenses *called, pulled, could.* Getting a good rhythm to the list is important
Find the difference	–	Developing the most efficient way of narrowing down the options in questioning in order to get the information needed as quickly as possible	Satisfaction in solving the mystery without looking at the pictures	*I can see a . . . . Have you got a . . . . ? Where is the . . . . ? and prepositional phrases Sorry! Can you repeat that, please?*

		Recognising patterns and sequences	Satisfaction in solving a puzzle	Time language *o'clock, past/to*
Clock sequences	—		Satisfaction in solving a puzzle	Time language *o'clock, past/to*
Category finding	Some possibility of comparison between cultures if, e.g., 'Food we eat for breakfast' is a category	Finding sets, according to either logical or personal criteria	Satisfaction in finding a group of items	Vocabulary is reinforced by being repeated in a different context, and understanding of it deepened by the new connections between the words that may be found
Finding pairs/Dominoes	—	Finding connections, logical or imaginative, between seemingly unrelated objects or ideas	Satisfaction in meeting the challenge	Language to express similarity *They are both . . . They both have . . .*
Word puzzles	—	Some visual discrimination practice	Satisfaction in collecting as many words as possible	Recognition of word patterns in English
Dot-to-dot puzzles	—	—	Curiosity about what is hidden in the picture	Recognition of correct sequence of letters in alphabet or of number-words
Colouring	—	Some, if the portions of the picture are to be coloured according to a code	Discovering what is hidden in the picture. Creating an attractive picture	Instructions and shape and size words, e.g. *Colour all the small circles blue*
Model-making	—	—	Creating an attractive object	Close listening, as well as watching, to find out how to make the desired object
Collage and mobile-making	Possible to create scenes reflecting life in the target culture, e.g. a street of shops	—	Creating something attractive	Vocab reinforcement if the mobile or collage is labelled. The instructions for the activity can be given in English
Game: 'Simon says'	Real game	—	Trying not to be caught out. An active game	Close listening to understand the orders, and to discriminate between *Simon says* . . . orders and others. Students perform actions and so learn the meanings of words involved
Rhymes	If real, interesting to children	—	The pleasure of speaking/chanting rhythmically	Good for rhythm and stress practice

Bibliography

Materials

PUZZLES AND SOLO ACTIVITIES

Granger, C. and **J. Plumb.** 1977. *Play Games with English.* London: Heinemann. A collection of games and puzzles which can be used for or adapted for young learners.

Rixon, S. 1980. *Fun with English.* London: Macmillan. Puzzles and games for young learners.

GAMES

Byrne, D. 19 . *Board Games.* London: Modern English Publications. A collection of board games, ready to play.

Lee, W. 1979. *English Teaching Games and Contests.* Oxford: Oxford University Press. A rich collection of drill-like and more communicative games for the classroom and playground.

Retter, C. and **N. Valls.** 1984. *Bonanza.* Harlow: Longman. A kit of classroom games for young learners.

Wright, A. *et al.* 1984. *Games for Language Learning.* Cambridge: Cambridge University Press. A collection of games and magic tricks for learners of English of all ages.

STORIES TO RETELL

Dunn, O. 1979. *Red Hen's Cake.* London: Macmillan. A retelling of the repetitive story of *Little Red Hen.*
Well Loved Tales. Ladybird Series. Beautifully illustrated stories, some with cassettes, including *Chicken Licken, Little Red Hen, The Three Billy Goats Gruff, The Enormous Turnip* and other traditional repetitive stories.

Oxenbury, H. and **A. Tolstoy.** 1988. *The Great Big Enormous Turnip.* London: Fontana Picture Lions. A delightful retelling of the turnip story.

MODELS TO MAKE

Jackson, P. 1988. *Tricks and Games with Paper.* London: Angus & Robertson.

Johnston, M.G. 1988. *Paper Sculpture.* US: Davis Publications.

SONGS AND RHYMES

Graham, C. 1978. *Jazz Chants for Children.* Oxford: Oxford University Press. Simple rhymes and chants for young learners.

Dakin, J. 1968. *Songs and Rhymes for Teaching English.* Harlow: Longman. A mixture of traditional and specially written songs for young learners of English.

VIDEO

Henny, L. and **S. Rixon.** 1990. *Look Alive!* London: Heinemann. Fifteen short episodes including stories, songs and games for young learners, with Activity book and Video guide.

Theory

Garvie, E. 1989. *Story as Vehicle.* Clevedon: Multilingual Matters. Inspirational! All you could ever need to know about the theory and practice of telling stories to young learners of English.

Opie, I. and **P.** 1969. *Lore and Language of Schoolchildren.* Oxford: Oxford University Press. The definitive collection of British children's games, rhymes, jokes and other traditional child culture activities.

Rixon, S. 1981. *How to Use Games in Language Teaching.* London: Macmillan.
Recipes for games and principles for creating your own games.

Rixon, S. 1987. 'Chicken Licken and other cumulative/repetitive stories.'
Papers of The British Council, Sorrento ELT Conference 1987 (Primary Teaching). London: Modern English Publications. Fuller account of suitable stories for young learners of English tried in Italy and suggested by teachers at the session.

Anne and Gordon Slaven, The British Council, China

4 'Ali, are you a boy or a monster?'

Drama as an English teaching aid with primary age children

This paper links drama activities with the tradition of roleplay and drama from adult EFL, and also ties in with the ideas discussed by Jackie Holderness and Shelagh Rixon. It provides a means for connecting play and activity with a serious analysis of the ELT situation in a particular country by making use of ideas drawn from needs analysis and functional syllabuses.

THIS PAPER aims to demonstrate that roleplaying, situational drama and other drama activities associated with communicative adult EFL teaching can be adapted for use with primary age children. All of the activities included in this paper have been used successfully with children in Africa and the Middle East.

Roleplay in the mother tongue has an important place in child development; helping children to relate others' experiences to their own lives and allowing them to assimilate a variety of thoughts and feelings unavailable to them in any other way. Mother-tongue primary drama techniques seek to extend a child's natural role playing in many directions: increasing body and space awareness with movement exercises, sense training and mimes; increasing language flow with choral verse speaking, roleplay conversations and improvisations; and combining all of these activities in extended improvisations and plays for performance.

The same techniques can be used with second language learners, providing language practice in a stimulating and entertaining way. These techniques are not intended to teach new language, but to allow the children to practise the language that they have already learned in a free, unstructured situation. The activities give the children a chance to explore and play with the possibilities offered by the new language, and provide situations where this new language can be related to the children's own experiences. The language thus becomes internalised and its value as a communicative tool is clear to the children at an early stage.

Initially activities are simple and the language used will be within the experience of most young learners. By increasing the language content and dramatic demands gradually, the children are drawn to ever more complex and demanding situations, and should continue to find the activities interesting, enjoyable and stimulating.

If some of the activities included in this article appear to have only a tenuous link with drama, that is because we have included any activity which stimulates the imagination, trains the senses or encourages the assumption of other roles. The activities are graded according to degree of complexity within each area. Simple listening and talking activities or improvisations with puppets can be attempted at an early stage of language learning, whereas a full scale play for performance will obviously require a considerable knowledge of English. Most of the activities are suitable for the classroom but some will be more successful in a club situation. At the beginning of each listening and talking activity there is a brief summary of age groups for which the activity is suitable, the best situation for the activity, whether class or club, and language practised. (A club situation may be more suitable for some activities: first, the children are there on a voluntary basis which may mean increased motivation; and, second, the atmosphere may be less formal than in a school classroom.)

Listening activities

Listening is a skill that many children find difficult, even in the mother tongue. The amount of concentration that a child can bring to a listening activity depends on his/her attention span and the stimulus given. With second language learners, difficulties with sound discrimination, speed of delivery, length of utterance and time allowed for assimilation make listening an even more demanding task. The activities that follow try to take these difficulties into account, while at the same time they challenge the children to succeed by demanding an active response.

Verbal response

RHYTHM AND SOUND

Ages: 6 – 10 years
Situation: Mainly in class
Language practised: Numbers, song titles and words,
other specific object vocabulary

1 The teacher shows the class a set of objects, for example a ball, a bell, a clock and a ruler. The children close their eyes while the teacher makes a noise with one of the objects, for example bounces the ball, rings the bell, bangs the ruler. The children identify each object as it is used.

2 The teacher now bounces the ball several times while the children listen and count with eyes closed. The children say how many bounces there were. This can be used for practising ordinal as well as cardinal numbers (for example 'When did I stop?' 'After/before the fifth bounce'). Different sounds can be used, including clapping, ringing, banging or stamping, and the children themselves can take turns to beat out the sound.

3 The teacher claps out the rhythm of a song that the children know. The children guess the title, then sing the song in time with the clapping.

SYLLABIFICATION

Ages: 11 – 12 years
Situation: Class only
Language practised: Voluntary revision, numbers

The teacher says a word, for example 'elephant', and the children say how many syllables it has. This exercise gives useful practice in distinguishing all the sounds of a word, and draws particular attention to unstressed syllables. It also ensures that the children listen carefully to the teacher's pronunciation and repeat it to themselves while they count the syllables. If they count wrongly, they will have to listen carefully a second time, making it more likely that they will pronounce the word correctly the next time.

Physical response

FOLLOWING INSTRUCTIONS

Ages: 6 – 12 years, depending on language ability
Situation: Mainly in class (mimes can be done in a club)
Language practised: Imperatives, classroom vocabulary, parts of the body, shapes, 'left/right'

1 Starting with simple instructions such as 'Sit down' and 'Stand up', the teacher leads on to 'Point to . . . / Look at . . . / Touch . . .'. After considerable practice at this, further instructions such as 'Pick up . . . / Put down . . . / Hold up a . . . / Show me . . . / Open/Close your . . .' can be given. Done quickly and with a competitive edge, these activities demand a great deal of concentration. They can be done with the children at their desks.

2 If there is scope for movement in the classroom and the numbers are manageable, these additional instructions can be included – 'Come here / Go to . . . / Walk/Run/Jump/Hop/Crawl to . . .'.

3 A similar activity is where the teacher gives instructions such as 'Wash your face / Brush your teeth / Put your jacket on', and the children mime the activity in response. Longer mimes can also be attempted, the children performing each new action as the teacher says it, for example 'Wake up, get out of bed, wash your face, get dressed, eat your breakfast, get your school bag, say "Goodbye".' or 'Get into the car, start the engine, drive away, you see a car coming towards you, you try to drive out of the way, you crash.'

4 When the children have got used to following instructions in this way, the teacher can make it more challenging by giving a series of instructions before the children start their mime. The first time the series has only two or three instructions together, for example 'Wash your face, get dressed, eat your breakfast.' The number of actions gradually increases until an entire scene, as in Activity 3 above, is mimed after the instructions have been given.

5 A series of instructions based on Activities 1 and 2 above can be given, but with the new challenge that they be completed in the correct order, for example 'go to the blackboard, write your name, run to the door, knock three times, go to your seat.'

6 The 'Robot' game is enjoyed by all children and can be done in pairs if there is enough space, or with individuals or small groups directed by the teacher. Directions are given, for example 'Walk three steps. Stop. Turn left. Run to the door. Stop. Turn right. Walk two steps. Turn left.' As the robots become more competent, the rate of giving instructions is speeded up and several instructions are given together.

Talking activities

Unlike listening, talking is something that most children need little prompting to do. Difficulties can arise when you are trying to promote free speaking in the second language. The activities under this heading try to provide an interesting stimulus, one that will encourage the children to speak by giving them something to say. For activities which involve only talking, the children need to have a reasonable command of English to verbalise what might be quite complex ideas. Where the talking goes together with a physical activity, however, gesture and expression can often overcome any language difficulties and enable a coherent conversation to take place with very limited vocabulary.

DESCRIPTION

Ages: 8 – 12+ years
Situation: Class/club
Language produced: 'He's/She's got a/some', adjectives, colours,
traits, present continuous

1 Either the teacher provides a set of cards with names of occupations on or the children think of an occupation themselves. One child mimes the activities associated with his/her given/chosen occupation, for example, a teacher. The mime could consist of talking and gesticulating, writing on the blackboard, marking books, telling a child off and so on. The rest of the class identify the activities first, then guess the occupation. Other occupations could include doctor, taxi driver, footballer, mechanic, bricklayer, police officer, soldier. Where the children are having difficulty guessing, the teacher can prompt, for example 'Is he inside or outside?', 'Is he alone, or with someone?'

2 Pictures are a traditional classroom aid for teaching and practising language structures and vocabulary. They can be further exploited as the basis for dramatic speculation: What are the characters like? Why are they there? What are they talking about? What has happened before? What will happen next? Such a class discussion could be followed by short improvisations in groups, based on the ideas generated.

3 Using hats, masks and clothes, some children dress up and the others describe what character has been formed: old/young, happy/sad, rich/poor, good/bad and so on. After the description is complete, one article of clothing is removed and the children explain how the character has now changed. After several different characters have been described, an imaginative class could invent a situation where all these characters would appear, and then attempt a short improvisation.

4 This idea can be developed with hand puppets. If no puppets are available, they can be fairly simply made by the children with odds and ends (see ideas on this in Appendix B). Each child takes a puppet, and the group describes its character. When several puppets have been brought to life in this way, the group works out and presents an improvised scene using the characters.

5 The teacher tells a short story involving several characters and a dramatic incident, for example, a motor accident. The children, in groups, each take a character and describe the incident from their point of view, perhaps in a court of law or as a newspaper interview. This, too, can be developed into an improvisation.

CONVERSATIONS
Ages: 6 – 10 (Activities 1 and 2), 10 upwards (Activities 3 to 9)
Situation: Class/club
Language produced: A variety of functional language at various levels of difficulty, stress, intonation

1 Younger children may have toys, puppets, construction bricks, a wendy house or class shop in their classroom. All of these can be exploited for practising functional language.
■ The class shop can be used for practising many items, from a simple '– Here you are. – Thank you' to more complex requests and replies, '– Have you got any . . .? – No, but I've got some . . .'.
■ The wendy house can also stimulate different levels of language, from a '– Please come in. – Thank you', to more complex interactions, '– Would you like some juice or some milk? – Some juice, please.'
■ Free play with puppets, dolls, toys or cars, or building with construction bricks can also stimulate the use of language. Puppets are particularly suitable here, because most children respond positively to them. Puppets can help to introduce other people to the classroom: other children, adults, the other sex in single sex groups, fictional characters and heroes. Shy children can hide behind the persona of their puppet and may be less reluctant to participate.

With all of these activities, the teacher has to judge the extent to which he/she can intervene to improve the quality of language produced, without destroying the children's sense of personal involvement.

2 'Foreign shopper' is a game much enjoyed by younger children. One child takes the part of the foreign shopper, who, by a mixture of gibberish and gesture, tries to convey his/her wants to the shopkeeper. The other assistants and customers all help to guess what the foreign shopper needs.

3 With older children, gibberish can be used to practise stress and intonation. Conversations in gibberish, in pairs or small groups, could involve one child relating a story while the others interrupt with questions. Alternatively they discuss in groups something they have found, or a sporting or other event. Gestures help make the meaning clearer. More able children can attempt an English translation of the conversation afterwards.

4 A set of old or toy telephones in the classroom provides many opportunities for pairwork practice. From simple 'Hello. This is . . . How are you? Goodbye.' conversations, the children can work up to longer conversations. Subjects include seeking information about buses or trains, inviting a friend to a party or a picnic, making excuses, apologising or thanking someone. A variation is to have a child hold one side of a conversation while the rest of the class or group guess what the person on the other end of the line is saying.

5 For children who can read, visually attractive workcards can stimulate improvised dialogues. Each workcard outlines a situation and gives suggestions for the dialogue (see Appendix A). Either the children perform the roles themselves or use puppets to represent the characters. Using puppets has two advantages – it takes some of the pressure off the individual and it enables him/her to see more clearly the character whose part he/she is taking.

6 'How to . . .' The robot game in the listening skills section is a simple example of this activity. An individual or group gives step-by-step instructions to another individual or group. More complex sets of instructions can follow from the robot game: how to make a milk-shake, ride a bicycle, make a paper plane. The giving and receiving of instructions usually involves considerable conversation ('– No, not like that. – But you said . . .').

7 'Desert island survival kit' is a roleplaying activity which can generate heated discussion among more able children. In groups of five or six each child takes an occupational role such as doctor, farmer, teacher, builder, carpenter. He/She is then given a list of 20 items which the teacher has prepared in advance from which to choose ten for his/her desert island survival kit. The teacher then tells the class that each group is going to a desert island, but they can still take only ten items per group. The members of each group must then negotiate and compromise until they all agree on what the ten items should be. Finally groups can compare their lists as a whole class activity, and each group must justify its own selection.

8 Questionnaires are a very effective device for generating language with children who can read. Each child is given a questionnaire – if possible, the teacher can prepare four or five different questionnaires to be distributed at the same time. Questions could include: 'Whose first name begins with B? Who was born in March/the same month as you? Who has been at this school since Grade 1? Who lives near you? Who is the oldest/youngest in the class? When were you born? How old are you? Where do you live?' The task is for each child to interview, say, five other pupils. Each child also has to answer questions about him/herself from other pupils. This will involve children moving freely around the classroom in order to interview others and be interviewed. This is a popular activity and the co-operation among pupils enables even the weaker ones to complete the task successfully. Follow-up work could include pooling results to prepare graphs of birthdays, heights, addresses and so on.

9 Interviewing in pairs is similar to Activity 8 above, but slightly more demanding. Each member of the pair prepares and asks questions to find out personal information about the other, including hobbies, favourite sport/colour/television programme and countries visited. Each child then presents a biography of the other either verbally or as a written exercise. Again this can lead to work on class statistics – how many pupils like football, how many have travelled abroad and so on.

Other activities

CHARADES

The complex conventions of this game are too difficult for most young children. With older children in a club situation it can become an enjoyable language activity. Divide the participants into teams. Choose an appropriate category, such as favourite characters from stories, titles of stories, names of foods or animals. Each group chooses a word in the category. They then decide together how to act out their word(s). In the adult version, syllables are acted out separately – this is only for the most sophisticated classes. Each group performs their word in turn – they can use mime or dialogue, props, a plot, and it can be as simple or as complex as they like. The rest of the class calls out guesses and suggestions, until someone guesses correctly. Their team scores a point. If nobody can guess, the team acting the word scores a point.

The language pay-off includes question forms 'Is it a . . . ?' and short answers, and the activity encourages pupils to scan through their mental vocabulary store for that particular category both when deciding on their own word and while guessing other groups' words.

RADIO SHOW

This could be the culmination of a term of talking activities such as those already discussed. The class prepares programmes, writes scripts and produces a half or full hour of recorded show. The preparation of the material produces the greatest use of language, but it is the show itself that the children enjoy. There could be a school news programme, a music request show, interviews with teachers or pupils, a 'how to' programme about a hobby such as collecting stamps and, of course, advertisements.

After brainstorming ideas for including in the show and agreeing on a shortlist, the children form small groups. Each group works on one item. Within each group, the children work out what they want to say, the questions they would ask if conducting an interview and research any background material. They can prepare a rough script based on these discussions and talk it through with the class teacher and the other groups. Problems are best identified at this stage, before final scripts are prepared.

Once scripts are finalised, the next stage is a practice read-through first within the group and then to the teacher and other groups. Advice on intonation and pronunciation can be given if needed. Sound effects can also be introduced at this stage, providing roles for those who are reluctant to speak.

The class can agree on the running order and the show recorded on cassette. It can then be broadcast to other classes or even the whole school.

Improvisations

Improvisation is defined here as any roleplaying activity which is centred around a dramatic incident or series of incidents as in a story. It presumes that the actions are worked out by doing and by class or group discussion, and that there is no script. This is a very wide definition, and the ideas for activities that follow can only provide a taste of what is possible.

No language practice summary is included, as the possibilities are limited only by the children's ability. The children will practise various levels of functional English and use pre-fabricated sentences from stories, songs or rhymes. Above all they can draw on their own linguistic resources to create original language. The ratio of pre-fabricated to original language will be determined by the children's experience with English and their general ability level. Whatever the level of language practised, improvisations show language at work, and provide the children with real communicative experience.

In the talking activities section, suggestions were made for improvisations based on pictures, the use of hats and masks, and a short story of a dramatic incident. In fact, any talking activity which involves roleplaying such as puppet shows, going to the shops, domestic scenes and telephone conversations, can be developed into an improvised playlet.

PUPPETS

Puppets provide good opportunities for developing improvisations and generating incidental speaking.

We have already suggested creating an improvised playlet using existing puppets and describing their characters. If children are allowed to make their own puppets, their sense of involvement and motivation will be increased.

If a group has enjoyed a particular story, for example, they can retell it as an improvised dialogue with puppets. Each child chooses a character and makes a paper puppet (see Appendix B), taking care that the face and clothing are appropriate. Avoid a script if possible. To give an air of authenticity, mock up a stage using a table set on its side or a curtain hung across a doorway at half-height.

STORIES AND FOLK TALES

The miming instructions activity included in the listening activities section can be extended to a story. The children can act out a story as it is told by the teacher. Familiar stories are best to start with. More complex stories can be chosen as pupils' competence increases. The teacher can check comprehension during and after the telling of a story with questions and paraphrasing, and also by getting the children to act out sections.

Folk tales from the children's own culture or from anywhere around the world are particularly suitable for this treatment.

Reading a story and simply telling the children to act it out is a recipe for frustration and failure. Steps for creating an improvised play from a story are as follows.

a) The teacher tells the story in a stimulating and clear way, using gestures, different voices, tones of voice and any other devices that will help to bring the story to life. If there are recurring phrases such as 'Fee Fi Fo Fum' in *Jack and the Beanstalk*, the teacher can get the children to chant them with him/her.

b) After the story, brief questions establish whether the gist of the story has been understood. This is not a comprehension test.

c) The children spread out. A hall is ideal, but a classroom with the desks pushed back is sufficient. The teacher goes through the dramatic points of the story and the children, alone, in pairs or in groups, act out the main points of the story. All the children should be actively involved, and the acting and language demands should be appropriate for their age and competence.

d) The children are divided into groups of a suitable number to act out the story, usually between six and ten. Either the teacher or the children themselves allocate roles within the group. Each group discusses their improvisation and all the groups act out their improvisations simultaneously. The teacher can circulate while the groups are working and note down important errors, but he/she shouldn't interrupt the flow of the acting.

e) An optional final stage is to have each group perform in front of the others, with some discussion about the strengths and weaknesses of each performance afterwards. This stage should only be attempted where the children have had considerable practice, and will not be upset by adverse criticism. See Appendix C for a brief summary of this type of improvisation at a fairly sophisticated stage, based on the *Story of the Goblin Spider*.

OTHER IMPROVISATIONS

1 Improvisations can also be built up from the children's own experience. With careful development, these activities can help children produce a great deal of original language. However, they cannot be forced to produce language. The teacher has to be aware of their linguistic and imaginative limitations, and should aim to extend each individual's range rather than make everyone produce language to a pre-set standard. The teacher's role is to stimulate the children's imaginations and to encourage them to relate his/her suggestions to their own experiences and feelings.

2 Whole class activities. Here the teacher takes the role of narrator and guides the class through a range of experiences, while they react accordingly. An easy way to begin is with the children as audience at, for example, a horror film, football match or circus. The teacher describes what they are watching and the crowd reacts: with fear or joy, talking/whispering to their neighbours, jumping up and shouting, and so on.

3 Whole class talking. The teacher tells the class they are in a busy place, for example the market, a toy shop at Christmas, the bus or railway station, the airport, zoo or park. The class then go about their business as individuals in, say, a large toy store. The teacher then stops the action and the children describe what they were doing at that moment. Some will be looking at model trains, construction bricks or other toys, some will be demonstrating clockwork animals, some will be serving and some will be taking money at the cash till.

The action restarts with each group now aware of what the others are doing. Queues form at the till, customers leave weighed down with packages, others need help from shop assistants. The teacher stops the action again and the children discuss what is happening. Suggestions are made for a suitable dramatic climax to the scene: a shoplifter, a tall display of boxes sent crashing to the ground by a toddler, two customers arguing over the last chess set.

The action starts again from the beginning and continues to the agreed climax. The improvisation will probably need polishing and the scene can be repeated several times. In improvisations like this, the children choose their own parts and decide for themselves how much talking to do. Although the extroverts may dominate, everyone has a chance to contribute as much as they feel able to.

4 Pair and groupwork. The activity described in 3 above can be adapted to smaller scale improvisations in pairs or groups. Following the example of the toy shop, pair and group activities based around a similar improvisation set in a bus station could include any of the following:

a) Arguments – over fares, seats, place in the queue, where the bus goes, change etc.

b) Questions – Which bus goes to . . . ? How much is it to . . . ? Where is the toilet? etc.

c) Chatting in the queue – about school, comics, plans for the weekend.

These could be integrated into the class improvisation again later.

Plays for performance

Plays for performance before an audience are not really drama activities. They have many drawbacks, not least of which is that a limited number of children are involved over an extended period, reducing the amount of time that the teacher can spend with others. Having said that, the fact remains that almost all primary schools throughout the world produce, at the very least, a year-end concert. The English department, or in the case of an English medium school, the drama department, is expected to provide a showcase for the talents of the pupils. This can range from a full scale play or musical to a brief, five-minute playlet in a variety concert.

The teacher responsible for preparing this play has to ensure that it generates language practice. Learning lines by rote and moving where pushed make for wooden performances. Most children enjoy acting and the fact that there will be an audience is an added stimulus to do well. Motivation is not, therefore, a problem. The language of the play itself provides a vehicle for understanding language in use, and the performance gives the audience some language practice as well. However, it is the rehearsal time that provides the greatest opportunity for the teacher to extend the children's use of language, in a situation where they are highly motivated and enjoying themselves.

AN IMPROVISED PLAY

1 This is the best kind of play. Using the improvisation techniques described in the last section, the result can be streamlined and polished until it is worthy of performance. This method keeps the participants constantly involved in developing and improving the end-product, as it is based on their own interpretation of the story or situation. Characters can be discussed, mannerisms developed and details added. In this way the children become involved in a much deeper way than if they were just following a script.

2 Improvised puppet plays can also be practised and polished for performance.

In some situations, for example if time is limited, developing an improvised play is impractical and a script is needed. This need not mean wooden dialogue without meaning, provided the teacher/director brings the children/actors along with him/her in his/her interpretation of the script. With children, the script should always be seen as a guide. Changes and paraphrases may be necessary to make the language sound natural and unforced. Cuts and additions may be needed to provide fluent action. This is true whether working from a published script or one written by the teacher for a specific group of children (see *The Strange Visitors*, Appendix D).

Once the teacher has cast the parts for his/her play, the rehearsals develop along the following lines, starting at least four weeks before performance:

a) The teacher tells the story of the play, indicating who will play each character as he/she goes along. He/She tells the story again, getting the actors to help out by saying what follows. The actors then tell the story, while the teacher acts out the dramatic parts. The scripts are taken away to be read.

b) The characters read the script, the teacher correcting emphasis/intonation and so on where necessary. The movements are worked out while reading the script. The characters move around while reading the script.

c) Rehearsal without the script. Full scale acting, stopped and changed where necessary.

d) Full acting of the play or scene, without a script, without stopping. Errors pointed out and corrected afterwards.

e) Full acting of the play or scene. Any errors, minor by this stage, mentioned only. Otherwise fulsome praise.

f) Performance.

Appendix A Two example workcards.

Appendix B Making paper puppets.

Materials: newspaper, string or cotton, scissors, coloured paper, papier-mâché or modelling clay if available, glue, paints, scraps of wool for hair, oddments of cloth.

1 Take two sheets of newspaper. Fold the first sheet lengthways four times, until it is about 5 cm wide. Fold the second sheet in half three times widthways.

2 Fold the first, longer roll in half and place the second piece inside it, as shown in A. Tie the shorter roll in place to form the arms and trim, as shown in B.

3 Stuff the space at the top with screwed-up paper to form the head.

4 Glue strips of white or coloured paper around the head.

5 Make a nose from papier-mâché or, for a quicker alternative, modelling clay. (Recipe for papier-mâché: Tear newspaper into thin strips approximately 3 cm wide and soak overnight in water. Mix flour and water to a thick paste. Build up shape required with strips of soaked newspaper coated in paste. Depending on thickness of finished work, this may take one to three days to harden. Paint.)

6 Paint features on the face, as in C. Wool can be glued on for hair. Clothes can be made from oddments of cloth and fitted on the puppet. Hair and clothes can more simply be painted on.

Appendix C Improvisation from a folk tale.

1 The Story of the Goblin Spider

Hokun was a town in Japan that was plagued by spiders. They were everywhere, in the houses, on the streets, in the beds, on the food, everywhere. One day, Talsin, the Samurai hero, and his friends came to Hokun and when they saw the spiders they decided to kill them all. So for three days and nights they went through the town, killing every spider they could find. When the last spider was dead the Mayor of Hokun called a feast in honour of Talsin and his friends. In the middle of the feast Talsin fell down, poisoned. He was taken to a room to recover, but in the morning he was worse. He told his friends that he started to feel worse when the boy brought him the medicine at midnight. His friends knew that no one should have brought any medicine and so they gave Talsin his sword and hid in his room that night. At midnight, the boy came to Talsin's room and Talsin cut him on the head with his sword. The boy jumped back and threw a web from his fingers which trapped Talsin and his friends. The boy escaped and the Samurai slowly cut themselves free from the web. They saw black bloodstains on the floor and knew that this must be the goblin spider himself. Although they were frightened, they followed the black blood trail out of Hokun and up the mountain. The trail led into a cave at the top of the mountain. When the Samurai entered the cave they saw a huge spider, as big as two men. It had a cut on its head and was surrounded by hundreds of other spiders. The Samurai fought the spiders, and when Talsin stabbed the Goblin spider in the eye it died, and so did all the other spiders. The Samurai returned to Hokun and another feast was prepared for them.

2 Improvisation, first stage

The children improvise the following points of the story. Class as individuals, pair and groupwork.

CLASS:	The townspeople are suffering from the spiders.
GROUPS OF 4:	Talsin and friends decide to kill the spiders, and then do so.
PAIRWORK:	The Mayor thanks Talsin.
CLASS:	The feast and Talsin's collapse.
GROUPS OF 4:	Friends carry Talsin to bed.
PAIRWORK:	The boy brings medicine to Talsin.
GROUPS OF 4:	Talsin tells friends about the boy and they decide to trap him.
GROUPS OF 4:	The boy comes, is cut, traps Talsin and friends and escapes.
GROUPS OF 4:	Talsin and friends escape, see the blood and decide to follow.
GROUPS OF 4:	At the mountain Talsin and friends are afraid but decide to continue.
GROUPS OF 8:	Four spiders fight Talsin and friends and are killed.
CLASS:	The final feast.

3 Group improvisation, second stage

Groups of about eight. Four are Talsin and friends, others take the parts of townspeople, Mayor, boy and spider.
All groups perform the improvisation simultaneously.

4 Performance, third stage

Each group performs its improvisation in front of the other groups.

Appendix D A scripted play – *The Strange Visitors*.

The following script was successfully performed as part of a year-end concert by 10- to 12-year-old boys, who had had 50 to 55 hours of English over a two-year period.

THE STRANGE VISITORS

[Stage bare. Backdrop of trees. Outdoors.
Enter stage left: ALI, MOHAMMED, AHMED *and* SAID]

ALI:	No, I don't think so.
MOHAMMED:	Yes, in the film *ET* the man from space was friendly.
ALI:	I don't think anything from space could be friendly.
AHMED:	I don't want to be friends with a thing from space, anyway.
MOHAMMED:	What would you do if some men from space came here now?
ALI:	Run away.
AHMED:	Fight them.
SAID:	What's that? [*Points to the sky. All look up.*]
ALI:	It's a star.
MOHAMMED:	No, it isn't. It's too big.
AHMED:	It's getting bigger.
MOHAMMED:	It's getting nearer.
SAID:	It's going to hit the ground over there.
ALI:	Is it men from space?
MOHAMMED:	It's landed over there. Let's go see.
ALI:	We must be careful.
AHMED:	We'll be all right.
SAID:	I think it's men from space. [*Exit stage right.*]

[*Re-enter stage left:* ALI, MOHAMMED, AHMED *and* SAID]

AHMED: Look – over there!

ALI: Shhhhhhh!

SAID: They *are* from space.

MOHAMMED: Let's talk to them – they've seen us.

AHMED: They're coming this way.

ALI: Let's go, quickly.

MOHAMMED: No, wait till they come.

[*They stand still. Four spacemen enter, stand and look.*]

ALIEN 1:   Brr Beep Beep?

[*All stand still.*]

ALIEN 1:   Brr Beep Beep?

MOHAMMED: Hello. My name's Mohammed.

[*Steps forward, holding out hand to shake.*]

ALIEN 2:   Bzeedoot! [*Shoots* MOHAMMED *with raygun.*]

[*Other boys start to rush forward and all are frozen by raygun. They are still awake, but cannot move.*

ALIENS 1–4 *put their guns away and walk round the boys – talking and pointing things out to each other.*

With gestures, they then indicate that they are going to take the boys onto their spaceship and take them away.]

ALI: Ohhhh! [*Pretends to die while still standing.* ALIENS *rush over to look at him.*]

MOHAMMED: Ohhh! [*As above. Aliens rush to him.*]

SAID: Ohhh! [*As before.*]

AHMED: Ohhh! [*As before.*]

[ALIENS *gather in front of them for talk. Shake/scratch heads, shrug shoulders. Each turns back and releases a boy from the spell. The boys grab the weapons from the aliens and shoot them.*]

MOHAMMED: Well done, everyone. That was clever, Ali, to trick them like that.

ALI: It wasn't a trick. I was so scared I fainted.

AHMED: Shall we kill them now?

SAID: Let's look at their machine.

MOHAMMED: I think first we should bring our fathers to see this – it might be important – maybe they are landing everywhere in the world.

ALI: Good idea.

AHMED: Shall we kill them first?

MOHAMMED: No, leave them. We must all go or no one will believe us.

SAID: Yes, you're right.

[*They leave the aliens frozen on the stage.*

After a few moments, one twitches and shoots the release into himself, then releases the others.

Talk talk . . . Follow boys? No, too dangerous. This world is no good, they are too clever, let's go. All agree. They leave. Roar of spaceship taking off.]

65

MOHAMMED:	[*Off.*] They're over here.
	[*Enter four boys and four men.*]
MOHAMMED'S FATHER:	I hope you are not tricking us, Mohammed.
SAID:	They've gone!
AHMED:	They were here.
ALI:	Maybe they're hiding.
ALI'S FATHER:	Oh, yes. Hiding in your head.
MOHAMMED:	They *have* gone.
SAID:	They *were* here.
AHMED:	Maybe we scared them away.
ALI:	*They* scared me.
SAID'S FATHER:	All right, boys, a good trick. We almost believed you.
AHMED'S FATHER:	But let's go home now.
BOYS:	But really, they were here. We saw a light . . .
	[*Exit*]

Ludmila Machura, University of Warsaw, Poland

5 Using literature in language teaching

In this paper Ludmila Machura gives a personal account of her use of children's stories. She links this with the theory and practice of reading, in a way which will be taken up later by Richard and Rona Parker in their paper on real books. This is the first of three accounts of personal experience in schools in Europe, and illustrates many of the principles already introduced in earlier papers. It is an extended version of the paper, 'The richest language: children's literature in ELT,' presented by the author and Dr Charles Mazer at the 22nd IATEFL Conference (Edinburgh, 1988).

TEXTBOOKS WHICH OFFER ADVICE on how to teach English can often be more intimidating than encouraging, especially to teachers who are about to take the first step in trying out something new. I assume that using children's literature with young learners will be for many teachers, as it was for me, quite a daring venture. I will present it as a story of discovery, told by a foreigner, a late language-acquirer and hence an inexperienced novice in the world of English children's fiction.

My encounter with children's literature started as it were through the back door – with no prior knowledge of children's stories, with a random selection of texts (often very poor ones), and with considerable distrust and apprehension stemming from a traditional approach to language teaching, which I believed should be hard work and not sheer enjoyment. Talking to a great many teachers of children in Poland I have learned that very few of them have ever been involved in extensive reading to and with children. I understand that the same may be true of other teachers throughout the non-English-speaking world. I hope that if I describe my experience as a process of learning to appreciate and use books, some of those teachers will find it convincing and stimulating.

The beginnings

At kindergarten level of age five to six (and this is the age group I started working with) most children do not yet write or read. There is no established tradition in Poland of teaching foreign languages to this age group. Some attempts to teach English and German have been made but most of them on a private basis, in small groups, usually within the family environment. Lack of formal support has meant a scarcity of materials and syllabuses. The few available guidelines recommend two ways of presenting material – either through grammatical categories such as nouns and verbs or narrow lexical areas such as toys, colours and numbers. Teaching at this level therefore requires a lot of initiative. It is practically pioneering work.

As I was lacking in formal preparation and training, I hoped that my enthusiasm and determination would stand me in good stead to meet the challenge of working with young learners. Yet having soon exploited my arsenal of basic rhymes and songs, I was desperately looking for help. Where to go from a limited number of words and phrases, from drawing and singing and playing the same games? I turned to picture books – any I could get hold of – and used them for demonstrating and practising colours, animals, plurality and so on – again segmented language items and concepts.

Then one day I brought with me to the classroom *Snow White* from Disney's Golden Series (one of the very few English books for children I had at home). I had planned to use it, like the others, as visual stimulus. But the children recognised the familiar story and asked me to read it. And so I did. After a line or two it was clear that my young listeners did not understand a word. If you look at any book from this series, you will see that the language is much too difficult not only for beginners but might also pose problems for some teachers. I felt stuck. Yet seeing eager faces, anxious to hear the story, I could not let my pupils down.

I tried to simplify the language, to repeat words and sentences, but the children grew impatient – the story either went too slowly or they did not understand much. Then I began to use Polish – translating whole phrases, then repeating them in English. I often referred to the illustrations and, pointing to familiar objects, I waited for someone to name them. Gradually I arrived at a combination of using both languages simultaneously with extensive contributions from the children. If someone had recorded our reading, the transcript would look like this:

TEACHER: Once upon a time. Dawno, dawno temu. Once upon a time.
TEACHER AND CHILDREN: Once upon a time.
T: There was a beautiful castle. Look, this is a castle (pointing to the picture of a castle). A castle.
C: A castle.
T: Do you like it? Podoba wam się? Do you like it?
C: Yes.
T: How big is it? Show me with your hands. Pokażcie.
C: (Stretch their hands and say) Big. Very, very big.
T: In this castle lived a beautiful queen. Queen.
C: Queen.
T: W tym zamku żyła piękna . . .
C: Queen.
T: Yes, she lived in this big castle.
and so on.

The children knew the structure of the story, knew that it should begin with 'Once upon a time', should have kings and princesses, good and evil characters, magic and fantasy. They also knew most of the story in Polish and, encouraged by my questions, were only too pleased to offer their own comments, guesses and interpretations. I soon realised that we were reading *together*. The pauses were frequent as the children often got excited and shared their experiences of what they had heard, seen, got – all in Polish; progress was slow – one or two pages per lesson, yet we had established the enjoyable habit of reading books. What is more, after only 40 hours of instruction, the children were 'reading' in English!

My meetings with the kindergarten children were short and infrequent – twice a week for 20, then 30, minutes. We used to begin the lessons by standing in a circle, holding hands, greeting one another and often saying a rhyme or singing a song. This had the dual effect of tuning the children in to English and helping them remember what they had learned. The middle part of the lesson varied from being quiet and easy-going to totally chaotic when some of the games or activities got out of control. I made extensive use of a complex system of rewards – singing songs, giving priority to start a game, sometimes distributing little gifts or sweets. My penalties were limited to making the child miss a turn or putting him/her in the corner. Yet both rewards and punishments were individual.

Discovering reading and the effect it had on the children showed me that I could make them more responsible for one another and for the whole lesson. A story was the ultimate reward, the long awaited and rightly deserved icing on the cake, provided the rest of the lesson had gone well. I made it a special thing, but not because I knew that it should be so. I know now. It was simply that I had only one or two books and very little hope of acquiring more, and I had to make them go a very long way.

The children would search my bag the moment I entered the room, making sure that their favourite story was there. So after some 'real' learning and when things had gone smoothly without any major catastrophe, we would all sit down to our five-minute reading ritual. I made sure that I sat slightly above the tight circle of eager faces so as to give the children a full view of the book. I glanced at it only occasionally, and my reading became more of an improvisation. This did not matter much as both children and I were creating the story anew.

School

Reading schemes

I kept on working with the same children, at the same time learning how to teach. *Play and Say with Pip and Paddy* (Books 3 and 4) and *Zig Zag I* saw us through the first two years of school (ages seven to eight). The children were growing more confident about reading and writing in Polish and were keen to do the same in English. A set of picture books, *Through the Rainbow*, that accidentally came my way proved very useful. Aimed at introducing English children to reading, the books contained sets of thematic pictures with captions, for example several drawings of different houses captioned 'a house' (Book I) or pictures presenting a woman carrying out different activities labelled as: 'Mummy cooking', 'Mummy washing' and so on.

The books helped us link the phonic and graphic systems and started children on writing by drawing pictures and copying the labels. As neither the texts nor the pictures contained a storyline, I devised a reading-guessing activity to exploit them further. I wrote fairly complex sentences, describing pictures and scenes, on strips of paper. I placed two or three strips in front of each child. As I turned the pages of the book the children had to match their sentences to the pictures. They scored points for correct identification (or guessing) and extra points for correct reading. The sentences contained clues and references to the pictures (place, objects, colours) but also new words, such as 'lying' and 'fire-place' as in the sentence: 'The brown dog is lying on the carpet in front of the fire-place.' The same type of exercise can be applied to any wordless picture book, provided the pictures are clear.

I went further in adapting available materials. I took some Polish books with nice illustrations and clear pictorial narration and translated the text. I then pasted English subtitles over the original script to simulate real English books.

Ladybird books

The next valuable step was provided by Ladybird books. Like most of my English acquisitions they came by chance. A parent suddenly remembered a set of books stored away in a cupboard and decided that I might put it to better use. The set contained about 30 books in six stages, including readers. I was delighted and determined to go through the 'teaching' books first – those practising spelling, reading and new vocabulary – before passing on to the fairy tales.

It was the growing restlessness of the children and their reluctance to proceed which signalled that something was wrong. There was no doubt that I was slowing my learners down, dwelling for too long on: 'This is Jane. This is Peter. Jane likes Peter. Peter likes Jane.' Designed for teaching reading to English children, the texts were already too simple both in terms of structures and general content for my learners, who were by now fully literate in their mother tongue.

I quickly sought rescue in the fairy tales I had been saving for later and we returned to the habit of reading together that had been suspended for nearly a year. This time our reading was real. The children still mainly looked at the pictures but there was no need to simplify the text or use Polish – they understood the English text. In this way I went through *The Gingerbread Man*, and *Snow White* again. Many of the traditional stories have very repetitive patterns, and halfway through a book the children would start to join in, chanting the words they had managed to memorise.

The next stage in fostering reading was to set up a small library and encourage the children to take books home. At first they would choose the stories we had already read. Gradually they started reading new ones, until finally they were familiar with all the books within a particular grade range. Too experimental, you might say, going from one extreme of slowed progress to pushing. Yes, that's how it was, especially since I always gave the children tasks to complete – to read aloud a favourite passage, to illustrate an event from the story or – but this was much later – to retell the story.

Graded readers

I was now coming into the fourth year of teaching. All this time I had been working alone with no help or guidance, not even from my colleagues – methodologists and teacher trainers who specialised in secondary school and adult learners. Those who had tried and failed to teach their own children discouraged me by emphasising how demanding and physically tiring it was and that linguistically it was not worthwhile. In this state of matters and mind – discouraged and doubtful – I came across a class set of L.G. Alexander's *Worth a Fortune*. Not only was it intended for adults and structurally difficult (Grade 2), it was available only on a short loan. Yet, for the first time, each child had a copy of the book for him/herself.

I asked the children to read one page at home before we went through it together in class. To understand the text they relied heavily on the illustrations, as if 'reading' the story from clearly sequenced, telling pictures. Some children also began to use dictionaries; some asked parents for help. The latter were puzzled and appalled and sent me warning messages asking how I could expect the children to understand 'have been' (or them, for that matter, to explain it), when I had taught only the present continuous.

The children, though, were delighted. After reading one-third of the book they already knew the whole story (guessing most of it from the pictures and reading ahead on their own). They got so involved in the story of a box of old Roman coins fished out from the sea that they suggested acting it out. And this is what we did. We modified the dialogues to make them pronounceable, prepared the props and invited the parents to admire not so much the quality of the performance as the enthusiasm of the young actors. And this I called my greatest success. Having captured the interest and motivation of my learners, I was confident that improvement in language ability would come with practice. Furthermore I had won parental approval and support for my undertakings.

I carried on with the reading programme, again groping in the dark for texts. I made some mistakes, for example going back to a Grade 1 Reader for children (L.G. Alexander's *In the Zoo*). I learned that once a certain level has been reached (for example Grade 2 stories), children feel undermined if asked to read below that level and their interest and motivation flags. It seems to me that formal marking of levels and grades on book covers, whether by number or colour, should be abandoned. It is too suggestive and colours children's attitude to the story from the start.

I stayed with the readers for another year. As we seldom had multiple copies of one title, I encouraged individual reading and our circulating library, set up the year before, flourished. Children often followed their friends' recommendations. Even if they did not manage to read much, at least they had regular contact with English books.

They were asked to keep some record of the stories they read – a list of characters, a favourite quotation, some illustrations. Every few weeks they all brought in their books and their experiences to share with each other. Some read aloud, some summarised the plot, others played recorded fragments. Those who were not ready (or willing) to do any of these could offer some comments or a summary in Polish. There was no need for me to check that these tasks had been done. Once something had been agreed upon by the class, the children themselves were their own monitors and assessors and showed they were capable of developing a great deal of independence and responsibility for their own learning.

Sources

The growing interest in teaching English to young learners has led to increased demand for English materials, especially for children's literature. Unfortunately, due to currency problems, the supply of English books is severely limited and they are practically unavailable in bookshops. The few books written and published in Poland are inadequate for present needs. In this situation it is only the British Council with its Resource Centre and the Lending Library that can offer considerable assistance. However, the library is geared mainly towards adult needs and stocks about 1,500 books for over 300 avid young readers. One is lucky to have 200 books to choose from at a time. One day I browsed through the shelves and was able to pick only 13 which were relevant for my students – short and appropriate for their age and language levels. Still, it was better than nothing, especially as I was once again faced with the question, 'What next?'

Real books

I was greatly aided by a course on children's literature offered at my Institute by visiting American lecturers. It was my first real encounter with English children's fiction. Enchanted by the magic of *Goodnight Moon, Frog and Toad, Make Way for Ducklings* and *Sylvester and the Magic Pebble*, I decided to share these books with my learners and was amply rewarded by their response. With the support and encouragement of the course lecturers to proceed with my attempts, I became fully converted to using original texts and, moreover, using them for sheer enjoyment rather than linguistic gains.

Ways and techniques

There are numerous teacher training books which offer sensible and workable suggestions about how to use literature and readers in English classes (see Bibliography). But it is one thing to know the techniques and another to apply them once you are confronted with a book. You can approach a new book in two ways. Either plan in advance how to exploit the story (for example, describe the plot or characters, continue the story, write letters or diaries, practise certain sounds or structures) or wait and watch the children's responses, and follow their reactions in setting activities.

I have often found that playing it by ear and inventing tasks by responding to children's needs and suggestions as they are reading is the most successful approach. Children want to do things and if you give them some independence, they will come up with the most ingenious ideas about how to use books. Instead of listing desirable techniques and exercises, let me share those activities that the books themselves inspired.

Frog and Toad Together

This was the first book written for English children that my students had read. To start with I selected *A List* (one of the five stories), as it naturally lent itself to writing our own lists of things to be done, for example '1 Get up, 2 Eat breakfast, 3 Go to school'. There is a lot of room here for children's humour and fantasy as well as opportunities for practising orders and the past tense ('I got up and had my breakfast'). Children so much liked the two friends, Toad and Frog, that they insisted on reading all the stories (some at home) and in a class vote chose *Cookies* as their favourite. We even coined a saying, 'You can have all your will-power and I'll have my cookies', which became proverbial with us.

Where the Wild Things Are

When Max is sent to bed without supper for his misbehaviour, he dreams of being King of the Wild Things.

The children were so stirred by the friendly monsters in the story who become rampant and wild and want to eat Max up that, when asked if they ever had similar dreams, they burst out and described their nightmares as if seeking comfort in sharing them. The ten-year-old beginners were struggling for words to relate their emotions in English and to make themselves understood to a native speaker, who was then with us. There was no consciously orchestrated activity here, but we needn't only measure the value of reading books in class in terms of language pay-off. The emotional responses triggered by some stories, as in this case, can be of great psychological significance, encouraging the children to associate reading in the target language with positive experiences.

The magic of the book lies primarily in the expanding and shrinking 'wild' illustrations. The small pictures which accompany the first few pages of text grow bigger as Max dreams his dream, encroach on the next page, and take up more and more space until they completely force the words off the page. As his anger recedes, so the images shrink to a more manageable size. But how powerful the book really is can only be discovered through several readings. Neither my university students (participants in the course for teaching young learners) nor I noticed at first that Max did to the Wild

Things what adults did to him – sent them off to bed without food. Nor were we fully aware of the implications of the reassuring ending, where Max returns home and sees his supper on the table. What children see in this book, according to T. Bradman, is '. . . that it is about overcoming and controlling the disruptive forces of your own anger.' (p. 29)

Bread and Jam for Frances

Frances, a little badger girl, will eat nothing but jam. So she is given jam for all her meals until she gets fed up and asks for normal food.
1 We talked about our favourite food and children wrote down what they liked/disliked. All of them liked jam and sweet things. And they also liked the book.
2 I found the story very didactic and useful with my own daughter. Instead of reprimanding her for eating too much jam I could just mention Frances and she understood.
3 The book is full of imaginative children's poetry. About eggs, for example:
   I do not like the way you slide,
   I do not like your soft inside . . .

Tell me a Mitzi

Martha asks her mother to tell her stories, 'Mitzies' (as they are about a girl called Mitzi), describing everyday activities.
   'Tell me a Mitzi,' said Martha.
   'Later I will,' said her mother. 'Now I've got a headache.'
   In a little while Martha asked her mother,
   'Mommy, now is it later?'
   'No,' said her mother. 'It's still now.'
   In a little while Martha asked her mother if she had a headache.
   'No,' said her mother, 'Why?'
   'Tell me a Mitzi,' said Martha.
   This was exactly my home scenario and I borrowed the idea of telling 'Mitzies' (or if you want – practising present and past tenses) of daily activities to my daughter. Later on I encouraged her to write her own Mitzies. From then on I often exploited the concept of 'readers' being also 'writers'.

The Very Hungry Caterpillar

This is the story of a tiny but very hungry caterpillar who eats his way through leaves and different foods (leaving real holes in the pages through which children can put their fingers) and turns into a beautiful butterfly. There is not a reader who will not succumb to its charm. My advanced 12-year-olds enjoyed it immensely.
   Ten-year-old students, in their fourth year of English (about 200 hours), read the book together, drew pictures of new foods, wrote down some phrases ('was born, looked for food, ate through, was still hungry, had a

stomachache, felt much better, built a house, nibbled a hole, pushed his way out') and then retold (re-read) the story several times.

Two months later, as a way of checking children's retention, I asked them to write the story of the hungry caterpillar. They were shown the book and could look at their notes. Figure 1 shows transcriptions of what they created.

I used the same book with eight-year-olds after ten hours of English.

1 We drew fruit and foods and practised new items in Bingo and Memory games.
2 We learned days of the week.
3 We talked (in Polish) about the transformation of a caterpillar into a butterfly.

After this preparation I read the book. First very slowly, pointing to the pictures of the moon, the leaves, the egg and so on, repeating the words, slightly simplifying the structures. When we came to fruit and weekdays – I waited for the children to say these words first. I encouraged them to repeat first after me, and then with me, the refrain, 'but he was still hungry'. When we looked at the drawings of other foods we talked a lot about what we like and dislike. I read the book several times and found that the children never tired of it. On the contrary, they seemed to enjoy it more and more and joined me in reading aloud.

The Twits

There is no need always to read the whole book. Extracts from longer books can provide more complex texts. Always give a full introduction and prepare the children for the activities you intend to carry out with the chosen fragments. One such example came from *The Twits*. Younger children were dictated two passages about ugly faces getting uglier with ugly thoughts or lovelier with lovely thoughts and were then asked to draw the faces before I showed them the illustrations from the book (see Figure 2).

Advanced learners heard the story of *The Glass Eye* and were asked to write their own version of *The Wormy Spaghetti* (the title of the next chapter), knowing that it would now be Mrs Twit's turn to play a nasty trick on her husband. Then they read their stories and the original text, only to find that they had all predicted accurately what the wormy spaghetti was.

Through the Window

The brewery horses gallop along the street, frightening pigeons and people. Jacob sees the commotion, but he is safe up in his room. And his mother will soon come up to make the tea.

Before reading, I asked the children to write down what they could see from their own windows and we shared our descriptions, talking about why we look out of windows, how often and if we like it. We read the book and then talked (partly in Polish) about the illustrations. They all seemed to like the dim colours, the drawings of the street, pavement and people, seen from

Once upon a time a very hungry Caterplillav
was born. He ate a lot of things:

The Very Hungry CATERPILLAR
At first day that was a very hungry
Caterpilar. On Monday he ate one apple
On Tuesday he ate too plums
On Wednesday he ate three pears
On Thursday he ate four strawberes
On Friday he ate five orange
but he hed was still hungry On Saturday
he ate a cake
      a water melon
      an ice cream
      a pickle
      a lollypop
      a cherry pie
      a sausage
      swiss chese
      a cup cake
      and sallamy
         and he had a stomacake
On Sunday he ate three hols in the
leaf but he still had a stomacake.
On Monday there wasn't a Caterpilar
but cocon and two weeks later became
a buterfly with a stomacake.
(Jurek, 10)

The Very Hungry Caterpillar
One day there was a very hungry Caterpillar.
He ate one leaf but he was still hungry.
He ate way through   1 Apple on Monday
      on Tuesday   2 pears,
      on Wednesday 3 plums,
      on Thursday   4 strawberies, and
      on Friday   5 oranges but he was
                    still hungry.

So on Saturday he eat through
one chokolate cake, one ice cream cone, one
pickle, one slice of swiss cheese, through salami,
one cupcake and one slice of watermelon,
and then he have a stomachache. Next
morning he ate some holes through the leaf.
Then he became a cocoon. After some
time he pushed his way out and the
caterpillar became a beautiful butterfly.
Kuba (11 years old)

But he was still hu

stomachache. When

a house and staye

nibbled a hole, pushe

a Butterfl

Once upon a time a very hungry Caterpillar
was born. He ate a lot of things:
– apples
– pears
– strowberis
– plums
– oranges
– cakes
– whater melons
– ice-creams
But he was still hungry. That's why he had a
stomachache. When he felt much better, he built
a house and stayed inside. Two weeks later, he
nibbled a hole, pushed his way out and then became
a B u t t e r f l y!
(Paula, 10)

Paula

Figure 1

Figure 2

above, through the lace curtains. They were moved by the atmosphere of mystery, some untold tragedy perhaps, and wanted to know why the street was 'all Jacob knew of the world', why Jacob's father was never mentioned, why the old woman was called 'Soap' and what happened to her dog.

These unanswered questions make the book very powerful. There is room for the children's own interpretations, and for them to draw on their own experience.

Group I: the children worked in pairs as Jacobs and mothers talking about what had happened in the street.

Group II: the children were writing letters to the father, telling him about the incident.

Why Mosquitoes Buzz in People's Ears

The iguana didn't greet the python, who thought that she was plotting some mischief against him. This misunderstanding started a chain of unfortunate events . . .

Before reading we made a list of animals which occur in the book and talked about their characteristics. I asked the children if they knew the answer to the title question.

The book is full of sounds and noises and the children loved hearing them.

77

They also enjoyed the darkened pictures of the dragging night. By the time it came to the meeting of all the animals in the jungle, the children were able to join in the chorus of the lion's accusations:

So, it was the iguana
Who *frightened* the python,
Who *scared* the rabbit,
Who *startled* the crow,
Who *alarmed* the monkey, and so on.

When a few months later I got hold of a cassette of the story, we all listened spell-bound to this captivating recording.

Teachers looking for a cumulative story with onomatopoeic sounds and a good moral thrown in ('There is never a quarrel without a reason, but seldom with a good one') will be happy with this one.

The benefits of reading

Nothing I could say would give justice to the feeling of accomplishment and satisfaction I had using books. By taking up reading children gain access to a richness and magic of language no coursebook can ever offer. They are also exposed to such issues as loss, death, friendship, responsibility, power and domination which can heighten their sensitivity and help them in the task of growing up. Furthermore the varied illustrations, which provide clues to the story, stimulate interest and pave the way for the text, in themselves develop children's artistic perception and imagination.

However, there are two other benefits which I value the most. One is seeing children at ease with English books, reading with great confidence, on their own, and enjoying it. The following incident best illustrates what I mean. Having heard that Paula (one of my ten-year-old pupils) had been learning English for four years now, her mother's friend gave the girl an English book to read to test her. Paula, instead of saying, 'Sorry, I don't know this book, I can only read my coursebook' (as most children would in this situation), actually opened the book and attempted to read it. The lady was utterly amazed. 'She really knows English!,' she exclaimed.

The second benefit is the integrating power of reading together. Sharing the same activities and experiences unifies the group, establishing closer bonds among children as well as between children and teacher. What is more, the joy that teachers experience in rediscovering the world of magic and beauty of childhood stories matches the benefit of doing it through the medium of English, thus expanding their own awareness of the language and culture. Reading together at home has enormous potential for involving parents in the development and education of their children. By showing interest and practising at home the skills first introduced in school, parents can further support and motivate their children.

Throughout my work with children I have learned to trust their judgement. And to them I would like to leave the final evaluation of books.

Books were arranged on the floor in a huge circle from picture books and readers on the left to longer, often pictureless, stories on the right. The children were invited inside and asked to take their time browsing through, reading, picking whatever books they fancied. I was sitting nearby observing their reactions, listening to comments. The children from eight to twelve, of elementary to lower intermediate level, totally ignored serious-looking, text-only, thick books. They spent some time with the books they had not read, leafing through rather than reading. What drew their attention was unusual format and graphics as well as novelty of approach. 'All books about Santa Claus are about how he brings presents. This one is different and I like it.' – about Raymond Briggs' *Santa Claus Goes on Holiday*. 'It's hard to imagine big numbers and here you can even see them.' – about *How Much is a Million?*

However, the most crowded space was where all the familiar fairy tales and picture books with short texts were displayed. Children swarmed around them, picking the same stories to read and re-read again and again, aloud, to their friends, sharing the humour, laughing together. Their choice confirmed the fact that when on their own, children need the reassurance of the familiar materials with which they feel confident and at ease. They also never tire of their favourite stories, adding new dimensions every time they read them.

Bibliography

Books with repetitive passages for interactive reading

Aardema, V. 1978. *Why Mosquitoes Buzz in People's Ears*. USA: Pied Piper.

Asch, F. 1984. *Happy Birthday Moon*. Sevenoaks: Hodder & Stoughton.

Carle, E. 1974. *The Very Hungry Caterpillar*. London: Puffin.

Gag, W. 1976. *Millions of Cats*. London: Puffin.

McCloskey, R. 1988. *Make Way for Ducklings*. USA: Scholastic.

Picture books

Briggs, R. 1975. *Father Christmas Goes on Holiday*. London: Puffin.

Brown, M.W. 1984. *Goodnight Moon*. Illustrator Clement Hurd. New York: Harper & Row.

Carle, E. 1988. *The Mixed-up Chameleon*. London: Puffin.

Hoban, R. 1977. *Bread and Jam for Frances*. Illustrator Lillian Hoban. London: Puffin.

Keeping, C. 1970. *Through the Window*. Oxford: Oxford University Press.

Kellog, S. 1977. *The Island of the Skog*. London: Warne.

Kraus, R. 1970. *Whose Mouse Are You?* Illustrator Jose Aruego. London: Macmillan.

Lobel, A. 1983. *Frog and Toad Together*. London: Penguin.

McPhail, D. 1987. *Pig Pig Grows Up*. London: Macmillan.

Schwartz, D.M. 1987. *How Much is a Million?* Illustrator Steven Kellog. USA: Scholastic.

Sendak, M. 1970. *Where the Wild Things Are*. London: Penguin.

Steig, W. 1969. *Sylvester and the Magic Pebble*. New York: Simon & Schuster.

Van Allsburg, C. 1984. *Mysteries of Harris Burdick*. Boston: Houghton Mifflin.

Varley, S. 1984. *Badger's Parting Gifts*. London: Fontana.

Poetry

Prelutsky, J. (ed). 1983. *The Random House Book of Poetry for Children*. Illustrator Arnold Lobel. New York: Random House.

Silverstein, S. 1964. *Giving Tree*. New York: Harper & Row.

Silverstein, S. 1984. *Where the Sidewalk Ends*. London: Jonathan Cape.

Fiction

Dahl, R. 1982. *The Twits*. London: Penguin.

Estes, E. 1979. *The Hundred Dresses*. Illustrator Louis Slobodkin. New York: Harcourt Brace Jovanovich.

Gorog, J. 1982. *A Taste for Quiet and Other Disquieting Tales*. Illustrator Jeanes Titherington. New York: Philomel Books.

Steig, W. 1988. *Abel's Island*. New York: Farrar, Straus & Giroux.

Townsend, S. 1982. *The Secret Diary of Adrian Mole*. London: Methuen.

Townsend, S. 1984. *The Growing Pains of Adrian Mole*. London: Methuen.

White, E.B. 1969. *Charlotte's Web*. Illustrator Garth Williams. London: Puffin.

Coursebooks and reading schemes

Alexander, L.G. 1968. *In the Zoo*. Harlow: Longman.

Alexander, L.G. 1968. *Worth a Fortune*. Harlow: Longman.

Bradburne, E.S. 1980. *Through the Rainbow*, Picture Books 1–13. Illustrator Trevor Stubley. Huddersfield: Schofield & Sims.

Byrne, J. and A. Waugh. 1979. *Zig Zag*. Oxford: Oxford University Press.

Ladybird: *Key Words Readers* (Series 641), 1a – 6a, 1b – 6b, 1c – 6c.
Read it Yourself (Series 777), Levels 1–5 'The "a" series gradually introduces and repeats key words, the "b" series gives further repetition in a different context, the "c" series supplies the link with writing and phonic training.' (1988 Catalogue)

Webster, D. 1974–77. *Play and Say With Paddy and Pip*. London: Macmillan.

Theory

Most of the books listed below refer to reading schemes in primary education in the UK and the USA. Undoubtedly similar guidelines exist in native languages in every country and teachers can draw on the general principles and ideas.

Bennet, J. 1987. *Learning to Read with Picture Books*. The Thimble Press Selection of 118 real books (not reading scheme material) and ideas to help young children become readers.

Benton, M. and G. Fox. 1985. *Teaching Literature Nine to Fourteen*. Oxford: Oxford University Press. Describes ways to teach various genre with bibliographies of fairy tales, myths and legends, science fiction and fantasy, stories, picture books, poetry.

Donaldson, M. 1978. *Children's Minds*. London: Fontana.

Dunn, O. 1984. *Developing English with Young Learners*. London: Macmillan. 'There are many beautiful picture books . . . which, although not graded, use simple language which makes them suitable for young learners.'

Egoff, S. *et al*. (eds). 1980. *Only Connect: Readings on Children's Literature*. Toronto: Oxford University Press.

Hedge, T. 1985. *Using Readers in Language Teaching*. London: Macmillan. For ESL and EFL teachers on readers and ways (with examples) of using them with adults and young learners.

Hill, J. 1986. *Using Literature in Language Teaching*. London: Macmillan.

Ingham, J. 1981. *Books and Reading Development: the Bradford Book Flood Development*. London: Heinemann. Books on behalf of the British National Bibliography. Appendix V lists favourite authors and titles in the programme, age 10 to 12.

Meek, M. 1988. *How Texts Teach What Readers Learn*. Stroud: The Thimble Press.

Reading for Enjoyment. 1987. Baker Book Services.
This is a set of four lists of recommended books for children ages:
0 – 6 (comp. Tony Bradman)
7 – 11 (comp. Vivien Griffiths)
12 – 15
16 – up

Signal – a thrice-yearly specialist journal devoted to children's books and the children's book world.

Stories in the Multilingual Primary Classroom. 1983.
ILEA Learning Resources. On the value and importance of stories for children. Very comprehensive, practical, well exemplified.

Sutherland, Z. *et al*. 1985. *Children and Books*. Glenview, Illinois: Scott, Foresman. The standard American guide to children's literature for teachers and librarians.

Teaching English as a Second Language to Young Learners: an Annotated Bibliography. 1988. The British Council Libraries Department. Very useful for teachers of young learners. The three main sections are: teachers' reference materials, courses, supplementary materials (readers, dictionaries, video and computer materials).

Trelease, J. 1985. *The Read-Aloud Handbook*. London: Penguin. Half of this book is devoted to an annotated bibliography of wordless books, picture books, short novels, poetry and anthologies.

Michel Trégret, Collège St Joseph, Savenay, France
Vincent Raymond-Barker, Wolverhampton Grammar School,
England

6 The Golden Diary Project

*This paper is an account of a joint project between schools in England and France.
It starts with an account of the project, but includes notes on procedures and ideas
which convey something of the excitement that teachers and learners feel when using
a new and creative approach to learning. It illustrates well the process of integration
that Jackie Holderness and Edie Garvie particularly discuss in this section of the
book.*

I N the mid 1980s the authors of this paper, living and teaching one in France and the other in England, began to exchange authentic teaching materials. We exchanged posters, leaflets and magazines for fruitful classroom use. It seemed natural to ask our pupils to join us in writing, and their photographs, bubble gum cards and inquisitive letters created an enthusiasm which delighted us as teachers and led us to a new view of language acquisition.

Writing simply to one another in their native languages, our pupils began to play a part in the teaching process. Just one letter provided so much – authentic handwriting, reinforcement of known language, a meaningful introduction to new language and a wealth of motivational background knowledge and colour.

We encouraged our pupils to use their letters as models to help them write in the foreign language, keeping the letters in transparent pocket display booklets. Pupils began to keep their pen-friends' letters and other documents from the country being studied alongside news sheets which they and their teacher had produced, creating colourful albums, with a fresh and original feel so often lacking in normal text and exercise books.

It seemed important to name and shape these stimulating folders, and we decided on the title 'Golden Diary'. This simple and punchy title defined the key qualities of the project – bright and durable as in 'golden', personal and informative like a 'diary'. A recent sixth-generation version of the title is 'Horizon 1992: A Golden Diary Project'.

We hope that some of our past pupils still use and value their Golden Diaries. Meanwhile the potential for new ideas to expand the project is healthy. We are blurring age and subject boundaries wherever possible, encouraging involvement from parents and other teachers. Audio and video messages strengthen the link between our pupils. Home-stay exchanges have been a natural outcome of the project.

Few would disagree that language is personal, precious, real and alive. In describing the Golden Diary Project, this paper offers practical advice for teachers wishing to nurture these qualities in their teaching.

Who does what? The different roles   *Aim*!

Pupils

It is important that pupils become involved with their counterparts and feel responsible for them. By writing in their mother tongue they can all become auxiliary teachers, some very consciously so. Poor handwriting can cause problems and we have found it helpful to insist upon printing. Pupils can record audio messages on cassette to provide their counterparts with pronunciation models. Some pupils find this easier than others. We try to encourage pupils to be clear, without interfering with local pronunciation patterns. Authenticity is desirable, but not to the point where it jeopardises communication.

When letters written in the target languages are exchanged, pupils may wish to correct their counterparts' mistakes. Negative feedback should always be avoided by a positive approach and constant encouragement.

Plenty of current news can be sent, birthday and Christmas cards exchanged, and progress can be acknowledged. Pupils become more self-aware as language learners by participating as teachers.

Teachers

The more contact a teacher has with his/her counterpart, the more successful an exchange is likely to be. Regular telephone contact need not be expensive if messages are well planned. Thanks for items received, intent to send particular items and definition of future needs should all form part of the telephone or letter dialogue throughout the school year.

Advanced pupils can be given considerable freedom to decide on the content of their letters. Pupils in the early stages of language learning can be given structuring devices such as 'letter menus': duplicated sheets for pupils to complete in individual ways but within a controlled lexical framework. Authentic communication is the target, but class sizes make control of vocabulary areas by the teacher a valuable asset in the exploitation of material.

Always check the quality of material before sending it. One way of encouraging a good standard is by awarding a mark to each piece of work before sending it. We have not always found this necessary – the motivation comes from the authenticity of the task itself – communicating real information to a real person.

If any pupils are absent when a package is prepared, you can provide a letter to the relevant counterpart(s) yourself or ask an able pupil to send two letters. No class exchange package should be sent incomplete; there should be something for everybody.

Teachers can exchange ready-to-use teaching materials such as cassettes, videos, worksheets and posters. School, local and national events can all be exploited. Realia such as leaflets and stickers can be exchanged and used as small prizes.

New material can be prepared even while waiting for a reply to a previous dispatch. The more quickly news is passed on, the fresher and more exciting it will be for the pupils. Counterpart teachers should be efficient in the practical matters of packaging and posting material.

Colleagues

As an exchange grows, other teachers can be encouraged to join in. Mother tongue teachers can help to prepare many kinds of material; accounts of recent events in the form of anecdotes are just one example.

Music teachers are often willing to provide material for tapes and games teachers can help by allowing their lessons to be filmed. The latter can even learn to give simple orders in the target language – words such as 'jump' and 'run' should not be learnt from dusty textbooks but in the open air on a games field!

Family

The more people involved in a Golden Diary exchange the better. Pupils' families can enjoy looking at photos from abroad and listening to messages received in their own language, even if they don't speak the foreign language. When they have photos developed, they could occasionally have a duplicate set made and put together a selection of good photographs to send to the counterpart, not just prints deemed unworthy of the family album!

Parents can help in other ways; allowing the family stereo equipment to be used, adding messages to letters and Christmas cards, providing money for postcards, cassettes and postage, and ultimately inviting the counterpart to be a guest in their home.

What do we send? A few ideas   *Shoot*!

The pupil-teachers may have practical ideas themselves about what to write/send, and we certainly encourage such initiative. It may be helpful, however, particularly at first, to suggest different subjects from which they can choose collectively or individually.

SCHOOL

a) The class timetable, with an accompanying worksheet to encourage counterparts to notice details (see Appendix A).

b) A map of the school, coloured and illustrated.

c) A list of teachers and other staff, with details of their different responsibilities.

d) A selection of pupils' end-of-term reports (names omitted).

e) School statistics, for example number of classes, pupils and teachers, numbers having school dinners, pupils' addresses and different means of getting to school.

f) Simplified extracts from the school rules; what is allowed and what is forbidden, what the range of punishments is.

CLASS LISTS

a) Dates of birthdays in chronological order, for use as a teaching stimulus and to ensure that each pupil receives a birthday card on time.

b) An individual characteristic for each pupil, for example 'SMITH, John . . . the tallest boy in the class', done tactfully, or a line written by each pupil describing their likes and dislikes (see Appendix B).

c) An event from each pupil's life, for example 'JONES, Gillian . . . broke her arm last year.'

d) Christmas presents hoped for or received by each pupil.

SPECIAL EVENTS

These can include accounts of school outings, sports events, charity fund-raising occasions, or perhaps an interview with a pupil who has distinguished him/herself in some way.

LOCAL, NATIONAL AND INTERNATIONAL CURRENT AFFAIRS

For example a newspaper headline with a brief summary of the event and, more importantly, a personal view, a pupil's reaction (see Appendix C).

So that comparisons can be made, give priority to events common to the two exchanging countries such as the Olympic Games, the European Elections or joint government assistance to countries in need.

CULTURE AND TRADITION

Set up surveys on topics related to culture and tradition, such as Christmas and the New Year in different families, pupils' views on religion, historical events or traditional celebrations. Pupils can exchange results sheets, possibly adding their own views. Prepare short pieces about local places of historical and geographical interest. Approach the subject from an unusual angle (see Appendix D).

INTERVIEWS

Arrange for the class to meet and interview native speakers of the target foreign language, for example language assistants, visiting pen-friends or even visiting professional sports or business people. Pupils can record the interview and photograph the event, sending cassette and pictures together with a report to their counterparts.

COLLAGES

Amusing and eye-catching collages with a theme can be made from an assortment of materials such as tickets, photographs, postcards, cutout drawings, cartoons and jokes.

SELF-EXPRESSION

Pupils can keep a daily diary for a week and illustrate it. Alternatively they can write about an important family occasion such as a wedding or the arrival of a new baby. Or they can write about their holiday plans and/or hopes for the future (see Appendix E).

ASSESSMENTS

Self-assessment sheets and assessments by teachers can make interesting reading.

The counterpart can become a sort of distant confidant, a faraway friend who gets closer with every photo, with every letter, with every cassette. With him/her comes the 'golden' gift of new language.

How to make a Golden Diary   *Bullseye!*

How do you enable each pupil to create a personal album of the highest standard?

Preparing the way

How you introduce the idea to pupils and parents is important. Simply passing round one of last year's Golden Diaries may be enough to generate admiration and enthusiasm. An A4 book of 20 transparent pockets filled with 40 attractive pages is quite impressive. If you don't have a completed Golden Diary to present, start with an empty book and explain how, little by little, it will be filled during the course of the year. Have a few model pages already prepared. As a general rule, the teacher does well to do something him/herself before asking his/her pupils to do it!

Insist on the *different* nature of the Golden Diary; an attractive piece of work, resembling a magazine more than an ordinary school folder.

Style and presentation

The style should not be uniform throughout and there should be no predictable chapter pattern. Instead we recommend plenty of variety. The following suggestions can help to achieve visual variety:

a) Titles of varying shapes and sizes, and headlines using different typefaces.
b) Carefully planned and well-filled pages – never only a few lines at the top of a page – with captions beneath photographs, newspaper-style.
c) Eye-catching colours – highlighting pens can be useful here.
d) A variety of illustrations including original drawings by the pupil or teacher, and press or personal photographs.

Appearance and quality of materials used are important to overall presentation: avoid lined or squared paper if possible in favour of better quality white paper. A plastic cover very quickly loses its attractiveness if it is carried around in a school bag every day. To be sure of a spotless, brand-new look at the end of the year, keep the finished pages in a temporary folder. At the end of the year pupils will know whether they need a book with 20 or 30 plastic pockets, according to how many documents they have produced. They can enjoy the final reward of inserting their work into shining pockets in a brand-new folder.

Content

Content is crucial: don't include grammar rules, homework or language exercises. Avoid stories from textbooks, which are studied by thousands of pupils and, however well chosen, lack originality. Include instead personal messages and reports of events unique to this year's class, all written in the foreign language.

The first page should be particularly striking as it sets the tone of what is to follow (see Appendix F). Help pupils to find an original title, preferably in the foreign language. Don't make it too academic – a little escapism and fantasy does everyone good. ('Golden Diary Project' or 'International Exchange Project' could appear as a subtitle.)

Pupils can work out a title page design. A logo combining the names of the two schools or towns could be part of this. (See Appendix F for an example of our logo for Wolverhampton and Savenay.)

An inscription can be included too, and we recommend a touch of humour. The 'HORIZON 92' cover featured this quotation:

After 1992 there will be one single market in Europe. It will be in
Amsterdam on Wednesday afternoons. *BBC Radio 4*

Each pupil adds his/her personal touch to the title page with his/her name and photo and choice of colours. The same title page design can be used for corresponding classes.

There can be other standard pages which pupils prepare together and copy for each member of the class:

a) An introductory page setting out the aims and contents of the project (see Appendix G).

b) A class photo, or photocopied photomontage of individual pictures, with an encouraging slogan such as 'All of us can succeed.'

c) A collage of packaging labels collected by pupils. The labels should include one or more words in the foreign language.

d) A list of school subjects.

e) A results page, with the number of points scored in different oral tests, personal comments from the teacher and self-assessment by the pupil.

f) The teacher's final message, with thanks to the people who have helped with the project.

g) A final blank page for people who have looked at the Golden Diary to write comments in the target language.

Completion and follow-up

It is a good idea to complete the Golden Diary Project several weeks or even a couple of months before the end of the school year. You can mark the completed diaries as they have not been done as an optional activity. Send two or three of the best Golden Diaries to the counterpart class so that they can see how their documents have been used.

Prepare pupils for an oral exam based on the Golden Diary Project. You could ask a native speaker to record a few of the pages common to the class. Pupils can use the cassettes to help them prepare for their exam, where they will be asked to talk about different parts of their Golden Diaries. (Let them keep the cassettes afterwards as personal souvenirs of the project.) The effort of memory will be considerably less if pupils have been encouraged to learn pages as and when they write or receive them, and if they have been trained to produce clear and simple work.

But what is the point of all this time spent on creating such a polished piece of work and learning it by heart? Pupils develop a fond, emotional attachment to their Golden Diaries, to their counterparts and to the foreign language and culture which they are studying. When pupils now meet a native speaker of the foreign language, they can discuss real events and people, they have the linguistic tools for real communication. They also have memories and souvenirs and human attachments to keep in the future – when the artificial characters and stories from standard textbooks have been long forgotten.

Exploiting exchange letters and cassettes in class

Many modern language teachers set up pen-friends and contacts with foreign schools. While the messages exchanged are often authentic, vibrant and instructive, they may not be fully exploited in the classroom. They are the icing on the cake, rather than the cake itself.

There are many ways of exploiting messages exchanged with a foreign counterpart. Here are three suggestions:

HOW TO MAKE USE OF LETTERS

Let us take the introductory letter as an example. It can become a sort of round, or musical score, for four voices.

Line 1   *The author introduces him/herself in his/her native language (say, English).*
Line 2   *The author's foreign language teacher (also English) corrects the letter.*
Line 3   *The receiving pupil translates the message into his/her language (say, French).*
Line 4   *The receiver's foreign language teacher (also French) corrects any mistakes in line 3, thus arriving at a translation which should now be perfect. (Line 4 may be unnecessary, but it is a worthwhile check.)*

At the end of the operation, the original message returns to its English author correctly translated into French. It is now up to him/her to benefit from it. If the French counterpart has also recorded the message on cassette, the English pupil now has at his/her disposal a unique tool to help him/her prepare for the oral examination.

AN APPROACH TO AUDIO CASSETTE MESSAGES

1 The message is recorded in the native language (say, English).
2 A transcript is sent with the cassette to the counterpart in France.
3 The counterpart's teacher gives the audio cassette to the appropriate pupil, but keeps the transcript.
4 The counterpart listens to the message and transcribes it.
5 The teacher gives the pupil the original transcript to compare with his/her own version.

How much of the message has been understood? If not 100 per cent, then why not? Excessive speed, poor articulation, complicated vocabulary, poor technical quality – or perhaps the receiving pupil is to blame. The sender's teacher can help to eliminate potential obstacles to understanding.

To reduce postage costs, four or five messages can be recorded on one cassette. If possible the counterpart teacher/pupils can copy the cassette so that each pupil can take home his/her own personal message. (See Appendix H for a way of advertising the cassette exchange.)

VIDEO EXCHANGES

If your school has video equipment, pupils could film messages for their counterpart class as an occasional rather than a regular event. Pupils will probably need to rehearse before recording, and will need to learn their messages by heart so that they can talk straight to camera.

A class video might include a brief tour of the school buildings and local area, an extract from a school play, part of a sports event, songs or even the class in action during a lesson. It is useful for the counterpart teacher if video material is recorded and sent early during the year and is then available for him/her to use with his/her class at the most appropriate time.

The video received could be used as an early introductory lesson, giving the counterpart class a clear mental picture of who they are writing to during the year, or as a reward lesson towards the end of the year.

Conclusion

The learning and teaching of a foreign language at school can only benefit from a letter-cassette exchange. For the writers of this paper, teaching a foreign language without such an exchange has become almost unthinkable. The exchange creates a motive for language acquisition more valid than the bestowal of marks out of ten.

This paper could serve as a basis for an exchange between you and your counterpart teacher. It is dedicated to Sheila Rowell, who introduced the authors to one another, and to Gail Ellis, who encouraged the completion of the first Golden Diary.

"Without my counterpart, I'm only half a person."

Appendix

Several sample pages from actual Golden Diary projects are included here to give a flavour of how the ideas described in this paper work in practice.

A Timetable and questionnaire
  Produced by the French half. Aim: resource material for pupils studying French at Wolverhampton.

B Classe de Quatrième A – 1989–90
  Text of a cassette message based on the class list.

C Hurricane Force Winds
  Produced by the French half of the exchange: Wolverhampton pupils answered French questions in English and returned the questionnaires to their French counterparts. Aims: vocabulary building and topical coverage.

D Ironbridge
  Produced by the English half. Aims: to introduce Savenay pupils to part of the Wolverhampton area; preparation for the homestay trip.

E Extracts from authentic letters
  Compiled by Michel Trégret.

F Horizon 1992
  Cover design by Michel Trégret for the 1989 Golden Diary Project.

G My Golden Diary
  An example introductory and contents page.

H Playing English is fun
  Illustration by M Gillet, art teacher at the Collège St Joseph, to advertise the cassette exchange.

A

		8.30 / 9.25 **1**	9.25 / 10.20 **2**	10.20/10.35 / 11.30 **3**	11.30 / 12.25 **4**	12.25/14.00 / 14.55 **5**	14.55 / 15.50 **6**	15.50/16.05 / 17.00 **7**
L		MATHS — Mle Lebastard	FRANCAIS — Mr Couëdel	ANGLAIS — Mr Lanoë	SC. PHYS. — Mle Lebastard	ALLEMAND — Mme Marchand	TECHNOL. — Fr. Jean	TECHNOL.
M		FRANC. (1 sem./2) / HIST-GEO	ANGLAIS	E P S — Mr Jouan / Mme Delagnes	E P S — Mr Jouan / Mme Delagnes	SC. PHY. (1 sem./2) / SC. NAT.	ALLEMAND	MATHS
J		CATECHESE — Fr. Jean	HIST–GEO — Mr Brény	FRANCAIS	SC. NAT. — Mle Fauchard	ANGLAIS	MUSIQUE — Mr Mordel	ALLEMAND
V		FRANCAIS	HIST.-GEO.	ANGLAIS	MATHS	DESSIN — Mr Gillet	ANGLAIS	EDUC. CIV. — Mr Brény
S		MATHS	E P S — Mr Delagnes / Mme Delagnes	FRANCAIS	4è			

29 élèves (11 garçons / 18 Filles)

COLLÈGE PRIVÉ SAINT-JOSEPH
10, RUE GENERAL-DE-GAULLE
44260 SAVENAY

4è D   88-89

COLLEGE PRIVE SAINT-JOSEPH
10, RUE GÉNÉRAL-DE-GAULLE
44260 SAVENAY
☎ 89.91.32

QUESTIONNAIRE SUR L'EMPLOI DU TEMPS DE LA QUATRIEME B (1988-89)

(entourer la bonne réponse
ou cocher la bonne réponse x)

1- A quelle heure commence l'école le lundi matin ?
à huit heures
à huit heures trente
à sept heures et demie

2- Combien de temps avons-nous pour déjeuner
au milieu de la journée ?
une heure quinze
une heure trente-cinq
deux heures
cinquante-cinq minutes

3- Qu'est-ce qui se passe à dix-sept heures ?
nous arrivons à l'école
nous arrivons à la maison
nous quittons l'école
nous quittons la maison

4- Chaque jour, il y a deux petites récréations d'un quart d'heure. A quels moments ?
l'une le matin, l'autre l'après-midi
toutes les deux le matin
toutes les deux l'après-midi

5- Chaque cours dure
une demi-heure
une heure
cinquante-cinq minutes

6- Quand commence le weekend ?
le vendredi midi
le vendredi soir
le samedi midi
le samedi soir

7- Quels jours n'avons-nous pas d'école ?
le lundi et le mardi
le jeudi et le vendredi
le mercredi et le dimanche
le samedi et le dimanche

8- Combien de cours avons-nous au total dans la semaine ?
vingt-deux
vingt-cinq
trente et un

9- Quelle matière compte le plus d'heures de cours par semaine (5 heures) ?
L'EDUCATION CIVIQUE   L'HISTOIRE ET GEOGRAPHIE
LES SCIENCES NATURELLES   L'ANGLAIS
LES SCIENCES PHYSIQUES

10- Que signifie E P S ?
Ecole Primaire et Secondaire
Education à la Politesse Stricte
Etablissement Politique et Social
Etude Paresseuse et Sage
Education Physique et Sportive

11- Le Frère Jean, professeur principal, enseigne 2 matières. Lesquelles ?
Technologie et Dessin
Technologie et Musique
Technologie et Catéchèse

12- Comment s'appelle notre professeur d'ALLEMAND ?
Madame Marchand
Monsieur Couëdel
Monsieur Rocard
Monsieur Lanoë

13- Dans quelle matière avons-nous deux professeurs ?
(l'un pour les filles, l'autre pour les garçons)
Education Physique et Sportive
Mathématiques
Education Civique

(suite)

14- Les diagonales, dans la ligne du MARDI, signifient que les cours alternent
                un mois sur deux
                une semaine sur deux
                un jour sur deux
                une année sur deux

15- Dans la classe, les FILLES sont-elles   PLUS nombreuses   que les GARÇONS ?
                                      MOINS nombreuses
                                        AUSSI nombreuses

16 à 20   **FAIRE CORRESPONDRE CHAQUE COURS AVEC LA SALLE APPROPRIÉE**

Education Physique et Sportive	SALLE DE LANGUES (dans la salle de..
Sciences Naturelles	GYMNASE (au gymnase.)
Allemand	ATELIER (dans l'atelier)
Histoire et Géographie	SALLE DE PERMANENCE (dans la salle de
Technologie	LABORATOIRE (au laboratoire.)
En cas d'absence d'un professeur	SALLE AUDIO-VISUELLE (dans la ...)
Travail personnel de recherche	CENTRE DE DOCUMENTATION ET D'INFORMATION (C.D.I.) (au CDI)

Comparez avec votre emploi du temps. (les matières ....   les heures ... etc...)

exemple : Je fais plus de Maths, moins de Dessin ... que les élèves français.

-
-
-
-
-
-
-
-
-
-

B

COLLÈGE PRIVÉ SAINT-JOSEPH
10, RUE GÉNÉRAL-DE-GAULLE
44260 SAVENAY
—

Classe de QUATRIÈME A   Année scolaire 1989-90

Premier contact avec une classe de WOLVERHAMPTON GRAMMAR SCHOOL
15 septembre 1989

ANEZO	Delphine	Je m'appelle Delphine Anézo. J'aime beaucoup la danse.
BEZIER	Annabelle	Je fais de la gymnastique.
BLOYET	Audrey	J'aimerais bien avoir une correspondante
BRIANCEAU	Sandrine	J'aime faire du sport.
BRONDY	Régis	J'aime le football
CHASSELOUP	Eric	Je joue au football
DELASALLE	Jean-Marc	J'ai treize ans et je suis en Quatrième.
DUCLOYER	Xavier	J'aime le vélo et la lecture, mais pas le football ni le tennis.
GERGAUD	Frédéric	J'aime le vélo.
GUERCHET	Nathalie	J'aime beaucoup la musique.
GUICHARD	Stéphanie	J'aime beaucoup le basket.
GUINE	Gaëtan	J'aime les motos.
JEAN	Bertrand	J'aime pratiquer le sport, en particulier le football.
LABARRE	Anthony	J'ai passé trois semaines en Angleterre l'été dernier.
LE DU	Laurent	J'aime beaucoup le rugby.
LE MAO	Fabien	J'ai treize ans. J'aime le tennis ainsi que le football.
LOREAU	Yann	J'aime beaucoup le cyclo.
MACE	Nathalie	J'aime beaucoup la musique rythmée.
MAILLARD	Marina	J'adore le New Circus
MOINE	Ludovic	Je fais la collection de pièces étrangères.
NEVOUX	Catherine	J'adore le twirling.
OILLIC	Valérie	J'ai déjà correspondu avec un Anglais l'année dernière.
PERCHAFFE	Laëtitia	J'aime tous les sports.
POTIRON	Gaëtan	J'ai treize ans et j'adore le basket.
FRIZET	Nathalie	J'adore les animaux domestiques.
RIALLAND	Cécile	Cet été, j'ai communiqué avec une Anglaise, et cela m'a beaucoup plu.

Combien y a-t-il d'élèves dans la classe ?   Combien de filles ?
Combien de garçons ?

Excusez-nous, l'enregistrement n'est pas très bon. Cela prouve cependant que nous existons et que nous avons envie de vous connaître. Au revoir !

NAME

"BY RETURN OF POST SHEET"
"EXPRESS SHEET"

HURRICANE FORCE WINDS 25th JANUARY 1990

B.B.C. NEWS : Storms and hurricane force winds from the Atlantic have been sweeping across Western Europ, causing casualties and widespread damage and dislocating communications. Britain was worst hit with nearly 40 people killed and many injured...Shipping in the English Channel was severely disrupted. On land, many of those who died were in vehicles hit by trees brought down by blasts which reached more than 100 miles an hour. Most train services to and from London stopped for several hours...

COULD YOU, PLEASE, ANSWER THESE QUESTIONS IN YOUR MOTHER TONGUE. BUILD SENTENCES. THANK YOU

1- A Wolverhampton, y a-t-il eu beaucoup de vent, de pluie, de grêle, de tonnerre ou d'éclairs ?

_ _

_ _

2- A ton avis, y a-t-il eu beaucoup de dégât dans ta région ?

_ _

3- Y a-t-il eu une coupure de courant ou une panne d'électricité ?

_ _

4- A-t-on demandé aux gens de ne pas sortir de chez eux, sauf en cas de nécessité ?

_ _

5- Si tu as voyagé, as-tu été retardé à cause de la tempête ?

_ _

6- As-tu vu une inondation ? (une rue inondée, un jardin inondé, un terrain inondé)

_ _

7- As-tu vu

- un arbre déraciné ? _

- le toit d'une maison emporté ? _

- des tuiles arrachées ? _

- une antenne de télévision abattue ? _

- une clôture démolie ? _

- autre chose endommagée par la

_ _

8- Connais-tu des gens qui ont été

9- Connais-tu des gens dont les bi

_ _ _ _ _ _ _ _ _ _ _ _ _ _ _ _ _ _ _ _

10- Cela a-t-il été la pire tempêt

11- As-tu un commentaire, une réa

_ _ _ _ _ _ _ _ _ _ _ _ _ _ _ _ _ _

_ _ _ _ _ _ _ _ _ _ _ _ _ _ _ _ _ _

MERCI BEAUCOUP D'AVOIR REPONDU A CE

D

birthplace of the
Industrial Revolution

Ironbridge Gorge

IRONBRIDGE

Shropshire

It was Sunday, it was a lovely day, and my wife and I decided to go to Ironbridge. After church we didn't stay for coffee; instead we went straight home and gave our daughter Rebecca her lunch. We made a bag of sandwiches for ourselves, got into the car and set off. After a week in the town, it was a joy to be out in the green, sunny countryside. We were soon on the outskirts of Telford, and we followed the signs to Ironbridge Gorge. We drove through Ironbridge and parked in the free carpark on the banks of the River Severn. Then we walked back along the main street, which runs parallel to the river. On our left were the steeply sloping little paths of the town, leading to picturesque houses overlooking the river. We got to the famous bridge (built in 1779, the

Ironbridge Gorge Youth Hostel & Walker Study Centre

Telford
Ironbridge

Shrewsbury B4380

Cannock

Museum
Visitor Centre Ironbridge

Museum Offices

Wolverhampton Walsall

Ironbridge
power station

River Severn

BIRMINGHAM

The Iron Bridge & Tollhouse

Scale 15 miles
24 kms

Urban area

first cast-iron bridge in the world) and crossed it. We went into the Toll House (people used to pay there to cross the bridge) and looked at the exhibition. Then we walked back over the bridge, and down the road to the carpark. On the way we shared an icecream and saw two colourful canoes on the Severn. On the way home, my wife said: "People who say the south of England is best don't know what they are talking about!"

Ironbridge Gorge

94

E

1- My hobbies are looking after a pony and swimming.
   I am not keen on school.
2- We have two pets : a dog called Sabre and a cat called Fluffy.
3- My name is Sara. I am 13. I was born on the 19th of December 1971.
   I am 158 cm tall. My Dad is a teacher of Physics, my mum works in
   a shop. I have a guinea-pig called Patch.
   I like playing badminton...
   I don't like going to bed early.
4- I have blonde hair and blue eyes.My father's name is Roy and his
   occupation is a veterinary surgeon. My mother is called Patsy and
   she is a veterinary nurse. My favourite sport is football.
5- My mum hasn't got a job.
   I don't like being disturbed when in bed.
6- My height is 1 metre 58. My father works at a milk factory.
7- My mum is a housewife. I hate wearing a tie.
   My dad is an engineer.
8- My dad's occupation is a carpenter and joiner.
   My mum's occupation is a cleaner at Camelford Primary School.
9- I enjoy all kinds of music, including a bit of jazz.
10- My weight is 8 stone. At school I like P.E. art and drama.
   I live in a little village near the sea. My father is a decorator
   and painter. I like riding my bike. I collect stamps, posters of pop
   groups. I also like sport and modern dancing. I have no brothers or
   sisters. I travel to school by bus. My favourite pop star is
   George Michael of WHAM, he is lovely. My house is quite big, it has
   a quite large garden.
11- I like listening to music and watching tele.
12- My dad drives a petrol tanker and my mum is a secretary at the
   District Education Office. My pastime is scouting and sports
13- My dad runs a post office and my mum runs a shop.
   I like chicken and stamp collecting.
   I dislike fish and school.
14- My dad is a clay-worker and I have no mum as she died.(quarry worker)
15- I also have one sister, Valerie, who is 19 and is married.
16- I live in a tiny village near the sea. My dad's occupation is a
   milkman and my mum helps him.
   I do not like people smoking
17- My dislikes are vegetables.
   My interests are astronomy, american football. I am also a scout.
   I also like old forms of writing which I copy.
18- My dad works as a cook in our cafe and mum serves in our cafe.
   I live in a small village near the harbour.

What do yo
when.

How do you
What is you
My pet hat

How old are you ?
What is your likes and
dislikes ?

What are your likes and
dislikes ?
school subject
female singer
actor actress
male singer
pop group
sport
What is your favourite food :

What are your pastimes ?
What are your hobbies ?
interests ?
pastimes ?
Have you any pets ?
What are your parents' occu-
pations ?
What are your religion ?
What's your religion ?
What's your nationality ?
When is your birthday ?
Where do you live ?
What's your name ?

F

G

```
┌─────────────────────────────────────┐
│  I n t r o d u c t i o n    t o       │
│  M Y   G O L D E N   D I A R Y        │
└─────────────────────────────────────┘
```

WHAT IS IT ?

    - a personal dossier, something unique,
        the only one in my life,
        it has never been done at the college so far.

    - a masterpiece, everything will be well set out.
        I'll be proud of it,
        I will not get rid of it at the end of the
                      school-year.

    - a souvenir, something precious and valuable.
        I'll keep it all my life,
        it will remind me of the "good old days"...

HOW TO USE IT ?

    - If I go to Great Britain, I'll show it to the British
        family who welcome me.
    - If I meet British people in France and invite them to
        call on me, I'll be able to show it to them,
        to introduce myself.
    - In both cases, it will be an interesting talking point.

CONTENTS :

1- a British calendar (school-year 86-87)
    on which I can write important personal events.
2- lovely stickers encouraging me to communicate in English
    with native-speakers.
3- news of the world, accounts of current events
    (mainly of Great Britain)
    with personal reactions.
4- information about myself for a pen-friend,
    a counterpart, or another teacher (oral-test).
5- authentic materials, with English written on them
    collected in France,
    sent by my counterpart in WINTON SCHOOL BOURNEMOUTH.
6- my form register with the words I taught my school-
    friends and the phrases I learnt from them.
7- self-assessment after taking oral-tests :
    What did I do well ? What did I do badly ?
    Comments written by the examiner.
8- personal comments : events in my own life and in my
    family.
    Developments in my hobbies and interests.
9- ...   .

    N O   G R A M M A R   R U L E S   !

96

Leonora Fröhlich-Ward, Munich, Germany

7 Two lessons: five-year-olds and seven-year-olds

This paper draws upon experience in Germany. Two lessons for beginners are described, one for five-year-olds and one for seven-year-olds. Some of the teaching methods are more formally structured than the work outlined in previous papers. It is worth considering these ideas against the discussion of different cultural expectations in the general introduction to this book.

ACCEPTING THE FACT that young children are able to learn foreign languages more naturally and therefore to some extent more easily than older learners, the question arises from what age foreign language teaching is a feasible project for a school, education authority or group of parents to undertake. While the teaching of a foreign language can never match the natural acquisition of the mother tongue from birth, it seems reasonable to suggest that children start learning a foreign language as soon as they are old enough to accept the social requirements demanded by group teaching. In European society the age of five is generally accepted as being an age at which children can be expected to play together, for example in play school, kindergarten, école maternelle.

Together is the operative word when we are talking about foreign language learning for young children. A graded course with a child-centred approach is the only way to achieve marked progress in the short time usually available. Group learning enables children to learn from their peers, and group play can positively support learning.

The earlier the better may be the ideal answer to the question of how early to start foreign language learning, but in practice it will turn out to be as early as possible. In order to give viable suggestions to anyone planning to set up a course for younger learners, I offer examples of teaching units for beginners aged five to six and beginners aged seven to eight.

Happy birthday to you!
A lesson theme for five-year-old beginners

Children aged five to six often begin to learn social behaviour at play school or kindergarten and to gain from social interaction in groupwork. The

97

generally accepted purpose of such institutions is to prepare children for real school, and to help children to appreciate, for example, spatial relationships, concepts of time, colour, size and distance, and audio, visual and tactile sensations.

The planning of a foreign language course for this age group should take into consideration the points listed below to make teaching as effective as possible. The term 'effective' applies not only to the structure of the course and the language to be taught, but also to the way the course is taught and the circumstances in which the children are learning. The points are listed in order of importance:

a) THE TEACHER

Long years of experience have shown that the most important factor is the teacher. Without a suitable teacher, teaching young children becomes impracticable. A teacher of young learners first of all has to have the ability to communicate with them – this seems to be an instinctive skill which some people have and some don't. The other essential skills, which can be acquired, are competence in the foreign language and teaching experience. It is a common mistake in looking for a foreign language teacher for young learners to look for competence and teaching skill first, before investigating communicative skills. The most highly motivated, highly qualified teacher sometimes simply fails to get on with the children!

b) THE SIZE OF THE GROUP

The size of the group is an important factor. Ideally, it should not exceed the physical reach of the teacher – sitting in a circle this will mean ten, at the most 12, children. This low teacher:pupil ratio causes some teachers of older children and education planners to shake their heads in horror, but it seems entirely natural to a teacher of young children. In reality, of course, numbers may be far greater.

c) THE LENGTH OF THE LESSON

Lesson length is another crucial factor. It is well known that young children cannot concentrate for long periods and that forcing them to work for longer results in them learning nothing at all. A maximum 20 minutes active teaching at a stretch has been proved to be acceptable for both teacher and children.

d) MOTIVATION

Young children do not usually ask to learn a foreign language. From their position in society they are not often confronted with problems of communication with speakers of other languages. They are not motivated to learn another language in the way that older learners might be. If they are to take part in a foreign language course with success (i.e. they really learn something), the motivation has to come from another source. First it comes from their parents who enter them for the course, but above all it comes from the enjoyment and pleasure experienced in the learning situation. The only way to teach a foreign language to young learners is in a childlike fashion, in a course full of play; play combined with structured teaching so that the children are only aware of the play content and learn the foreign language almost without noticing.

A course for young German learners, *English for Mopsy and Me*, was developed and piloted between 1970 and 1972. Some of the then current theories about teaching young children were tried out and found wanting, for example:

1 that children from the age of two can learn foreign languages. This proved to be impracticable in a group teaching context because children under the age of four have not yet developed the social skills they need to work within a group.

2 that group choral work, for example chanting, was a useful method for teaching young children a foreign language. It was found that five-year-olds wanted to speak individually and be praised for their efforts.

Others were shown to be true, for example:

3 that if children are taught in small groups, personal contact takes place and language acquisition benefits from peer teaching.

4 that teaching units must be short to reflect the limited concentration span of young children.

5 that the whole child should be catered for with singing, dancing and attractive visual materials as well as work with pen and paper.

The authors tried to incorporate all the good points into their course – they produced a structured handbook for inexperienced teachers and designed play and work material for a group of young learners. The sample teaching unit for five-year-olds below is taken from this course.

Class profile

The five-year-olds have been learning English in a play programme in their kindergarten for almost five months and can understand everything their English teacher, Joan, says to them within the narrow field of their English experience. The programme has involved three 20-minute periods a week – Joan has taken the children out of their kindergarten group for their play-English. They think Joan can't speak German because she only speaks English in their presence and has told parents not to speak German to her when the children are there.

Everything they have learnt in their English group has been connected to some sort of play activity which requires the oral/aural use of language. Up to now they have learnt to say their name, ask somebody else's name, describe various objects, parts of the body, animals and so on, using adjectives and prepositions. They know how to express likes and dislikes, to ask for something and to give somebody something he/she asks for, to ask and answer various quiz questions. They can count up to ten at least and use the plural of most nouns they know. They have learnt the feminine and masculine possessive pronouns and the names of family members.

Meeting 1

This morning Joan brings the hand puppet, Mopsy the dog, with her to the playgroup. He is wearing a colourful bow around his neck. He says good morning to the children, who naturally want to know why he is dressed up. They probably make some remark about it in their mother tongue. Joan takes this up without speaking their mother tongue:

JOAN:	Oh, good morning, Mopsy.
	You've got a lovely scarf on today.
	Look, children, what colour is Mopsy's scarf?
CHILD:	It's green!
JOAN:	Yes, it's green. And it's very soft/shiny/long . . . isn't it? (She encourages the children to describe the scarf.)
	And do you know what day it is today? (Possibly one child will guess in the mother tongue.)
	Yes, it's Mopsy's birthday.
	Shall we sing him a song? (She starts singing *Happy Birthday*.)
ALL:	(Sing) 'Happy Birthday to you' (Some children may know the song, but not the correct version, so Joan will have to check that they learn it properly.)
JOAN:	How old are you, Mopsy? One? . . . two? . . . three? (She counts and the children join in.)
MOPSY:	No . . . no . . .
ALL:	Four? . . . Five?
MOPSY:	Yes, I'm five, I'm five!
JOAN:	Oh, Mopsy is five. And how old are you? (to one child)
CHILD:	(with Joan's help) Five, I'm five.

The same question is now asked of the ten children, all of whom are five or six years old. Joan then gets Mopsy to go around the group asking in the same way. Each child takes Mopsy on his/her hand in turn and asks his/her neighbour the target question. This type of exercise is used frequently in the play programme. So in this case Joan holds Mopsy and speaks to her neighbour:

JOAN:	(as Mopsy) I'm five. How old are you, Frieda?
FRIEDA:	I'm six.
JOAN:	(as Mopsy) Oh, I see. (as Joan) Now you take Mopsy and ask Michael.
FRIEDA:	(holding Mopsy, in Mopsy's deep voice) I'm five, (with Joan's prompting) how old are you, Michael?

Each child now has a turn at saying his/her age, then being Mopsy, saying Mopsy's age and asking the age of the next child. By the time everybody has

said 'How old are you?' once correctly, Joan can be sure that most of them will recognise the question when it is next used in the same context. She now puts Mopsy away, since he is very tired!

At this point in the 20-minute period Joan changes the activity, for example to a card game which is already known to the children. The lesson ends with a song or dance game.

Meeting 2

Joan revises the question, 'How old are you?' at the beginning of the next meeting with Mopsy, still wearing his bow. Joan has a picture of Mopsy's birthday party with a cake and candles and some presents. She may have a real cake (perhaps it is one of the children's birthdays and a parent brings a cake) or just some real candles in a play-dough cake. The candles are described and counted:

JOAN:	Look, this is a candle. Can you say it?
CHILD:	This is a candle. (Each child takes the candle and names it.)
JOAN:	What colour is it?
CHILD/ALL:	It's blue.
JOAN:	There are more candles on the cake.
	How many candles are there?
ALL:	(Count the number of candles) Five!
JOAN:	Yes, they're Mopsy's candles.

Now Joan shows the picture of Mopsy's birthday and gets the children to describe what they can see. They might be able to suggest what is in the parcel on Mopsy's table. They usually have good ideas, for example 'dog cake!' Finally Joan tells the children to turn to page xx in their workbooks. Some children will need help to find the right page. There is a picture colouring exercise, and Joan goes around talking to them while they work. She makes sure that everyone uses the word 'candle' again and answers the question 'How many candles are there?' The words for describing each child's picture will vary according to what colour they are making the cake and the candles, the ball and the parcel.

In this way the children learn to use the language they have just been taught in a communicative and natural way – telling Joan about their pictures. Later they will be able and keen to tell her about their own birthday party and what colour their candles were. The language learnt in this theme will be used again and repeated in different contexts. Although there is no written consolidation, the children become accustomed to talking about their pictures and will happily explain them to an 'English' visitor who comes to the class.

Five-year-old children can talk about birthdays because they are within their experience. They have not yet learnt, however, to comprehend time according to the clock, weekdays, months, the future and the past. These concepts usually develop during the fifth year but not to the level where they can be dealt with in a foreign language.

Future meetings

The theme will be revised in new contexts. The children will learn to say how old their brothers and sisters are. When there is a birthday in the class, they will enjoy singing 'Happy Birthday', and asking about and describing their cakes.

The birthday party
A lesson theme for seven-year-old beginners

How would I approach teaching English as a foreign language to seven- and eight-year-old beginners? I would only speak English to them from the start, even if they knew I could speak their mother tongue. If I was their class teacher, I would wear a visual device, such as a Union Jack badge or a particular scarf, during English lessons. This would be a signal that I had become the 'foreigner' and could only speak and understand English. I would have a hand puppet, perhaps a dragon, as an assistant who could always help out in real trouble. This helper, Drago or Mopsy, would be able to translate a word into the mother tongue for a child if he/she really needed to know it. It is important not to let children feel inadequate during the lessons or they will never learn to accept the foreign language. Another idea would be to give every child a Joker card at the beginning of the course. Whenever a child needed particular help, he/she could show his/her Joker.

Skills development

Among the first utterances that children need to learn are how to introduce themselves, how to ask somebody else to come and play and how to get something to eat. All these themes can be taught without written work. There are many coursebooks available today full of ideas for transmitting language in the context of play. A newly introduced structure, for example 'Good morning, what's your name? My name's John,' might be repeated in a coursebook where the seven-year-old pupils have to fill in missing information, such as writing the owner's name on an object, or draw a line to join an object to its owner.

For vocabulary work the teacher can make Lotto or Quiz games with pictures of the target items. Such games provide a source of great enjoyment and effective revision for young learners. Another vocabulary revision and alphabet teaching aid is a picture dictionary, which each pupil can start to compile long before he/she learns to read or write in English. Allow a few pages for each letter of the alphabet. As new words are learnt, pictures drawn by the children or cut from magazines can be stuck into the book under the appropriate letter. If individual picture dictionaries are too time-consuming to produce, set up a class or group dictionary as an ongoing project.

Towards reading and writing

The emphasis on visuals as teaching aids in this paper is indicative of the fact that learning to read and write English as a foreign language poses a real problem for many young learners. As neither meaning nor intonation are conveyed by the written word, the young learner must base his/her attempts at reading and writing English on his/her experience of learning these skills in the mother tongue. Even adult learners who are more conscious of the difficulties, have problems in this field; how much more dangerous for the young learner who transfers an immature knowledge of mother tongue writing, spelling and pronunciation rules to the unknown foreign language. Reading and writing should therefore be kept to a minimum at the beginning. Most lexical items should be introduced in picture form and children should be encouraged to tell stories with the help of picture cards or sequences in their coursebooks.

As reading and writing become an integral part of the teaching, the children should always hear and say lexical items before they learn to read and then write them. This objective can be easily achieved if the course workbook only revises and recycles known language in new contexts and constellations.

The birthday party

After approximately eight weeks of two 40-minute lessons a week, the theme of the birthday party is introduced. A real birthday would be the best starting point – it is always a good idea to incorporate real-life situations into the teaching theme. Alternatively a picture showing a birthday table (as here, using a picture of Mopsy's birthday party) provides the initial stimulus.

STEP 1

As nearly all the vocabulary will be known (perhaps 'candle' will be new) and it will be obvious that it is Mopsy's birthday, the children can now describe the picture in much the same way as the five-year-olds would do.

STEP 2

The picture is for colouring. While the children colour the picture, the teacher goes round the class talking to them about what they are doing. The teacher asks, 'What's in the parcel/box?' to set their minds working on this theme. After five or six minutes some of the children tell the class about their pictures:
Mopsy's cake is pink./It's a chocolate cake.
His ball is green and blue. The candles are red.
There are five candles on the cake. (This is quite difficult.)
There is a basket/bed/baby dog in the parcel.

STEP 3

The teacher asks how old Mopsy is, if this question hasn't already been asked and answered right at the beginning, followed by:
How old are you? I'm seven.
This language will be expanded in a later unit, to involve all members of the class, the family, friends and so on. One idea is to get the children to interview each other in pairs. One child from each pair reports to the class about his/her partner. If half the children in the class can be made to speak individually during each lesson, all the pupils will see that great progress is being made. The teacher can note down who has spoken in each lesson and make sure everybody gets a turn.

STEP 4

Over the period of days when the teaching theme is the birthday party, the teacher provides a current calendar showing every day of the year. While teaching the names of the months, which need to be clearly shown on the calendar, the teacher tells the pupils to come and write their name against their birthday on the calendar (they will know when their birthdays are). Each child then says:

My birthday is in February.

A nursery rhyme or a song such as 'January brings the snow' will help children to have fun while learning the months of the year.

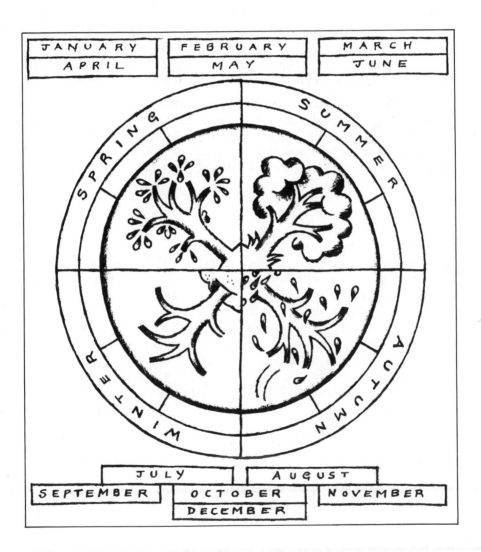

STEP 5

What day is your birthday this year?
The children can answer this question using the calendar if they already
know the days of the week in the foreign language. If not, the days can be
taught at this point.
Revise language for describing activities and add the weekday name, to
make new, true sentences:
When do you play football? I play football on Saturdays.
When does Linda go swimming? She goes swimming on Thursday
afternoons.

STEPS 6, 7, 8

The teacher asks questions in the mother tongue about traditional ways of
celebrating birthdays, whether children have birthday parties, whether they
receive presents, what sort of presents and so on. Care should be taken not
to offend poor/rich children and not to embarrass anyone in the group.

A celebration at the school might enable the teacher to lay on a simple party
– not necessarily a birthday party – where all the children have something to
eat or drink. This occasion then provides an opportunity to practise phrases
for offering/accepting/requesting such as:
What do you want/would you like – a slice of cake or a biscuit?
I want . . . /I'd like . . . Thank you.
Please can I have . . . ? Thank you.

STEP 9

A further step in this theme can be a discussion about the seasons. This
theme should be dealt with according to the local climate. In a country with
only two seasons – wet and dry – this picture would only be useful to
explain what the climate is like in other parts of the world. Here the single
disciplinary approach is broken open to admit the themes of geography,
geology, nature study and so on. In a country where all four seasons exist
within the children's experience, all sorts of vocabulary dealing with
weather and clothes can be introduced. This is a marvellous opportunity for
a class teacher to interweave information about the world at large into the
foreign language context and for the children to appreciate the foreign
language as part of real living.

A model lesson

This model for teaching the birthday party theme is not intended to be
exhaustive or binding in any way. It is just a description of one way in which
the theme can be handled so that the children will actually learn the foreign
language. The steps above are not designed to be taught undiluted one after
the other, but rather built into lessons alongside other themes where

language is being repeated and revised. This example lesson plan shows how part of the theme might be incorporated into a 40-minute period:

Introduction: Greeting. A song: 'Good morning to you.'
'Good morning, good morning, good morning to you.
Good morning, everybody, and how do you do?'
Young children will quickly pick up the tune and words of songs. The teacher starts the singing with the hand puppet. The children join in with the repeated words, and later more complicated groups of words. Here, the words 'everybody' and 'how do you do?' can be practised separately after the children have clapped and sung their way through the first line.

Small talk: Is everybody here today? Who's missing? Is he/she sick? Have you got your English notebooks? I can't find my pencil case. Where's my pencil case? (You have hidden it somewhere and get the children to guess where or look for it.) Where's Mopsy? (Also to be looked for and found, wearing the big bow or other festive decoration.)

Step 1, Step 2, Step 3 as above.

Relaxation: A theme taught some time ago is now revised, for example prepositions of place are used in a group or team activity.

The class is divided into teams. Each team chooses an object to hide. The first team hides their object, for example a doll, while the others close their eyes. Several members of the team move around the class noisily while the object is hidden. The teacher or a team member says, 'Open your eyes', and asks, 'Where's the doll?' The class now tries to find the object by asking questions and without moving from their seats. The second team has one guess, for example, 'Is it under the book cupboard?' If the answer is 'No', the third team has one guess. And so on until the answer is 'Yes, it is.' The team that guesses correctly scores a point and the second team then hides their object and so on.

Quiztime: Using pictures from the picture library or workbooks, vocabulary related to a particular theme is now revised. Even if the children are not writing yet, it is important to make them aware of sounds. Three or four consonants are chosen and put on the board, for example d, t, b, p (consonants which are often confused). The children try to pick out words related to the theme which begin with these consonants. After two or three minutes, the teacher asks children in turn, 'Tell me a word beginning with b.' When a child answers correctly, the picture can be put on the board under the appropriate letter. The child then asks the next question, with help if necessary.

Homework: If the teacher wants to set homework, it could be: 'Draw four things beginning with b.'

Thus a complete lesson involves the learning of something new, the revision of something well-known and a period of consolidation of items already learnt but needing more practice.

There are practically no limits to what the children are capable of learning, but a useful guide for the teacher is to try and keep sentence patterns and vocabulary to a small number and make sure that what is once learnt is repeated and reused in many and varied contexts.

Conclusion

While the lessons described here show that seven-year-olds can apparently learn more than five-year-olds in a similar period, because they can concentrate for longer and because they learn more consciously, it has yet to be proved that the intuitive way in which the very young acquire a foreign language is less successful in the long run. If children can be given the opportunity to start their involvement with a foreign language at the age of five, and gradually change from a play-centred approach to more conscious and cognitive learning at a later age, it will be a most valuable experience for them. Not only will their foreign language competence improve, but other more idealistic and immeasurable advantages, such as greater tolerance and understanding between people of different races and tongues will develop.

Bibliography

Clyne, M. 1986. *An Early Start.* Melbourne: River Seine Publications.

Dunn, O. 1983. *Beginning English with Young Children.* London: Macmillan.

Fröhlich-Ward, L. 1979. in Freudenstien, R. (ed). *Teaching Foreign Languages to the Very Young.* Oxford: Pergamon Press.

Garvie, E. 1989. *Story as Vehicle.* Clevedon: Multilingual Matters.

Holden, S. (ed). 1986. 'The younger learner.' Papers of the 1985 British Council Conference, Bologna. London: Modern English Publications.

Lado, R. 1967. *Moderne Sprachunterricht.* Munich: Hueber.

Mackey, W.F. 1969. in Stern, H.H. (ed). *Languages and the Young Schoolchild.* London: Oxford University Press.

Schmid-Schönbein, G., L. Fröhlich-Ward and H. Feder. 1982. *English for Mopsy and Me.* Oxford: Pergamon Press.

Ray Tongue, formerly The British Council, Singapore, Hong Kong and elsewhere

8 English as a foreign language at primary level: the search for content

This is a reprint of a paper by Ray Tongue, who had the original idea for this book, and who started off the planning and editorial process. It is based particularly on experience in Hong Kong and Singapore, and establishes links between primary practice and EFL theory, while at the same time addressing a particularly important practical problem for curriculum planners.

THE TITLE OF MY PAPER is, I fear, rather an unexciting one. May I, then, add a couple of subtitles which I hope will make sense in the context of what I shall have to say later on? The subtitles are 'You can't speak speaking' and 'Siu Leng is younger than her mother'. The first is an adaptation of the title of a well-known article written some years ago by Wendell Johnson, of the University of Iowa. The second is an authentic quotation from a primary school textbook which is still in use.

In my lifetime, foreign and second language teaching has tended to concentrate on the *forms* of the target language. This concern with form has shown itself in two quite distinct ways. Historically first has been the approach to language teaching which aims at having the learner *know about* the language being taught, this information normally being supplied in the mother tongue of the learners. Such a traditional method accounts for my own knowledge of the grammar of the French language together with my inability to use French for any meaningful purpose. This way of teaching, or failing to teach, foreign languages was succeeded by the audio-lingual, oral-structural and structural-situational methods, the principal aim of which is to have the learner *practise* the language forms.

In spite of the fact that the proponents of these two approaches disagreed, sometimes violently, with each other, we can see now that they had a number of important things in common. First, both approaches tended to take the sentence as the unit of instruction. It is true of course that the sentence is the largest unit of language structure describable in formal terms. Nevertheless, the exemplification and practice of the grammatical system mainly through isolated and uncontextualised sentences has had some harmful effects on language learning. All over the world, learners of English as a second or foreign language have difficulty with such features as the article system and anaphoric reference generally, the sequence of tenses, connectives and stylistic choices. These are, of course, intersentential features; they belong to the whole text, not to the individual sentence. They *cannot* be taught by an approach which focuses almost exclusively on the sentence.

The second point which the traditional and the structural approaches shared was even more important; they both paid very little attention to language function, and equally little to the purposes for which the language was being learnt. *Meaningful use* of language, using language for purposeful communication, was neglected with the result that much language teaching became formal to the point of sterility. Most of the instructional materials linked to these formal approaches, especially at the beginning and early intermediate levels, were of the utmost dullness. And not only dullness! Since the writers of materials were using language forms as their starting point, their task as they saw it was to demonstrate how these forms operated as linguistic units or language items. The sociolinguistic dimension was often forgotten, authenticity was lost, and meaning was subordinated to form (and frequently ignored altogether); the medium became the message, with a vengeance! As a result, one finds textbooks full of sentences like the one I have used as my second subtitle, 'Siu Leng is younger than her mother'. Grammatically correct, yes. A possible sentence outside the Theatre of the Absurd, no. Sentences like this abound in teaching materials which take language items as their point of departure; some of them are very funny, but one's laughter comes, or should come, through tears! The effect of teaching materials of this kind on the interest and motivation of the learners requires no emphasis.

A further consequence of this commitment to formal approaches to language teaching has been that the aims and objectives of language teaching programmes, when they have been defined at all, have been described in linguistic terms, either of language content or of language skills. This has resulted in a great deal of language teaching being circular in nature, language being used solely for the purpose of teaching language; the pupils are being asked, in fact, to speak speaking! But, as my first subtitle asserts, 'You can't speak speaking' you have to speak *about* something, you have to speak (and write, read and listen) to some purpose.

The effects in the classroom of the approach described, of English being presented as a series of strictly sequenced formal items, has been (in my view brilliantly) described recently by a primary school teacher of English in Hong Kong in the following words:

> . . . pupils learn their English by picking up spare parts of the language machinery each year, and what is more disastrous is that the parts they keep on collecting for one whole year are only good enough to assemble a bigger component. Thus, instead of enjoying the success of possessing a miniature train, the child has to be satisfied with all the screws and bolts and maybe a couple of wheels and axles to play with over again. It

would be miraculous for him/her to talk about fun or interest in learning the language at all. If the lower primary teacher wants to amuse his/her class with a little story in English, he/she cannot find enough words to use from the lists. There is no 'rabbit' or 'fox', 'fairy' or 'giant' in them. And when there is 'cat', there is no 'kitten', or 'puppy' for 'dog'. Then the language he/she uses should also be drawn from among the forms 'a', 'an', 'It is a . . .', 'I am', 'You are', 'This is', 'He is . . .', 'What is this?', 'Is it . . . ?', 'Yes/No' and a few simple orders, movements and colours. What a boring story that will be.

Such is the result of focusing on the language and ignoring the learner.

The essential point which I attempt to make in this paper is that the purposes of second and foreign language programmes need to be determined in other than formal, linguistic terms. One way of achieving this is to set up performance objectives, to attempt to specify what the learner should be able to do with the target language at different stages of the programme. When language courses are being designed for specific purposes, it is almost axiomatic that the more precisely the objectives of a course can be defined, the greater the likelihood that the course will be successful. The setting up of tightly specific performance objectives in the early stages of a general English programme, however, is an extremely difficult task, especially in situations where, as in Hong Kong, the later applications of the language learning are different for different groups of learners. The converse of the axiom suggested earlier is that the less precisely the objectives of a language course can be defined, the smaller the likelihood that it will be successful. This is a situation which has been jocularly given the acronym TENOR: Teaching English for No Obvious Reason. TENOR to some extent represents the situation of primary English in Hong Kong – not *no* reason, be it noted, but no *obvious* reason. In the past, the obvious reason was the need to pass in English at the Secondary School entrance examination but this situation no longer obtains. But to move away from Hong Kong for a moment, and to take a wider view, I believe that this problem of defining suitable objectives for general English courses is the key issue in ELT worldwide at the present time. I think that insights from ESP (English for Specific Purposes) will help; I believe that every teaching/learning situation, however, has got to be looked at on its own merits.

Within the general framework of performance objectives, an extremely attractive idea is the study skills approach. If there were a universal switch to English as the medium of instruction, a study skills focus could be given to English which would give much greater purpose to primary English than it has at present. This is not possible, of course, since a substantial minority of pupils continue their education in Chinese at secondary level. Study skills, however (it seems to me), show promise of providing a kind of activity where language has some purpose to perform outside itself, even perhaps for pupils who will be studying in Chinese later.

In the present situation it can be said that, as far as primary English in Hong Kong is concerned, there are no objectives (other than the language skills themselves) and no content (other than grammar and vocabulary).

The difficulty of establishing credible performance objectives has been considered above. Can we find more grounds for optimism if we turn to the question of content? I believe we can.

I shall describe briefly four possible approaches to primary English in Hong Kong in which content rather than language forms would be paramount. We need at the outset to look at the other parts of the primary curriculum as a source of content for the English programmes – the 'search for content' begins.

It has been pointed out by S. Gopinathan of Singapore that 'the content of language courses has to be organised in relation to the functional range of the language in question in the society concerned'. The 'functional range' of English in Hong Kong is not altogether easy to determine. Worldwide, however, English is pre-eminently the language of science and technology. Science is international; English is the leading international auxiliary language of wider communication. Furthermore, in many languages the scientific vocabulary has borrowed widely from English. My first suggestion, then, is for the syllabus in science (or substantial parts of it) to be taught in English from Primary I. The new bilingual education policy in the Philippines has been designed along these lines, with science and maths being taught in English from the first year of Primary, with all the other subjects taught in Pilipino. I should like at this point to give a couple of examples of what this approach via content might mean in terms of language teaching materials.

Here is a typical extract from an English language textbook:

LANGUAGE ITEM has, have

This is a cat.
It is black.
It has legs.
It has a tail.

And here is an extract from a primary science text:

PLANTS

This is a balsam plant.
It is red.
It has leaves.
It has a stem.

Note that the first extract does no more than demonstrate how some elements of the English language work. The second extract does precisely the same *and* tells the learner something he/she did not know before. Language is not being drilled, it is being used for the communicative purpose of conveying some new information. Here is the second example:

LANGUAGE ITEM can, cannot

Peter, can you touch the door?
Yes, I can.
Can you touch the ceiling?
No, I cannot.

MAGNETS

Here are some things: a piece of chalk, a paper-clip,
an eraser, a stone, a nail.
Can a magnet attract a paper-clip?
Yes, it can.
Can a magnet attract a piece of chalk?
No, it cannot.

Here again the first extract is an exemplification of language forms. In the second extract, in which the same grammatical feature occurs, language is being used for a communicative purpose, namely, talking about a simple scientific experiment. That the content-based extracts offer materials of greater interest to the learner seems to me beyond dispute. If science continued to be studied in English by all pupils in lower Secondary, a study skills element could be introduced into the teaching in Primary V and VI which would add greater relevance to the language work.

A second approach would be to scan the rest of the primary curriculum for appropriate English language teaching content. Cantonese and English are both very much present here in Hong Kong; each language performs a different set of functions, the former broadly 'integrative' ones and the latter broadly 'instrumental'. It might be possible to argue, then, that the Hong Kong child, after exploring the world through his/her mother tongue, should be encouraged to have a second look at appropriate parts of his/her world (the 'instrumental' parts) through English. Certain sections of the social studies curriculum, for example, seem eminently suitable for such treatment. Topics such as public transport, clothing worn in other lands, countries of the world, postal and telephone services, sea and air transport, newspapers, TV, the UN and the Commonwealth lend themselves well to being taught through the 'instrumental' language. Other parts of the primary curriculum can offer useful content too.

A third approach particularly suitable perhaps for the first years of primary, is to put the teaching of English into a 'language and other arts' framework, with a concentration on games, puzzles, verses, stories, competitions, quizzes and simple dramatisations, together with songs and music, drawing, colouring, tracing, composing pictures and other 'pre-artistic' activities of various kinds. In such an approach, language use would be much less tightly controlled than it is at present. The excessively strict control of language is, in my view, the main reason for the dull and uninteresting nature of much primary language teaching material.

Finally, a combination of all three approaches sketched above might offer an attractive body of content for primary English. In fact, this eclectic approach is the one widely adopted by writers of English coursebooks, especially at the secondary level. Since, however, these books tend to adhere strictly to the sequence of language items given in the syllabus, it is the language which determines the content of the lesson and not vice versa. But now that there is no public examination in English at the end of primary school, we have a chance not-to-be-missed of establishing the principle that content and/or purpose should be paramount in determining the items of language to be taught.

I have recently been rereading Michael Halliday's fascinating study of a child's acquisition of language, *Learning How to Mean*. If many of our primary school children fail to learn 'how to mean' in English, this may be related to the fact that, at the present time, so much of the English they encounter is essentially meaning*less*. In conclusion, then, may I state again my conviction that considerations of learner interest, enjoyment and successful use of language for particular communicative tasks should have priority over structural grading and other matters related to linguistic form. Unless content or purpose (or both) are identified and stated for the primary English programmes in Hong Kong, the enormous number of hours of pupils' time devoted to English lessons will continue to produce results which no one deems to be satisfactory.

Bibliography

Johnson, Wendell. 1962. 'You can't write writing.' in **S.I. Hayakowa** (ed). *The Use and Misuse of Language*. Greenwich Cann.: Fawcett.

Halliday, M.A.K. 1975. *Learning How to Mean. Explorations in the Development of Language*. London: Edward Arnold.

Edie Garvie, Peterborough, England

9 An integrative approach with young learners

Edie Garvie's paper returns to the themes of the earlier papers in this section, but links them together systematically to provide a rationale for integrative work. This paper is a clear and practical statement of methodological principle which provides a context for the more detailed discussion which follows in later papers.

THE MOST EFFECTIVE METHODOLOGY in English Language Teaching (ELT), will be one which is firmly based on an awareness of the important issues in language, learning and teaching. What is language? How is it acquired? What then is the most appropriate provision that can be made by the teacher for whose pupils English is a new language? In a brief paper justice cannot really be done to these immense questions. There is a vast literature about them and some references are to be found at the end. What *will* be attempted is selective mention of one or two of the issues, followed by some definition of what I am calling an integrative approach to ELT in the primary school. This is the content of the first part. In the second part aspects of a methodology are considered. In other words, bearing in mind the issues, certain classroom options will be suggested.

Selected underlying issues

Language
Under this heading I select two.

The first concerns two ways of looking at language, broadly speaking. It can be seen in terms of structure and it can be seen in terms of use. There is the linguistic picture concerned with such things as the sound system and the grammar, and there is the communicative picture where the components are function and purpose. These two sides of the language equation with vocabulary straddling them both, should be constantly in the teacher's mind. They run through every aspect of the methodology.

The second issue to highlight is the matter of language skills. There are the four basic ones, sometimes called modes – listening, reading, speaking and writing. And of course within each there are many sub-skills. It is useful to think of the basic modes in groups: listening and reading as receptive and speaking and writing as productive; listening and speaking as modes of oracy and reading and writing of literacy. The learner reveals his/her language competence through his/her handling of these modes, from the physical use of ear, eye, tongue and hand to the skills of interpretation and construction.

Learning

Three issues are highlighted here.

The first is the important link between language, thought and experience with particular reference to young children learning another language. They are still developing their concepts of the world about them, both physical and social. A new language suggests a new culture and a new life view. How far can the new be accommodated into that which is already developing? There is a strong challenge here for the teacher, a challenge which is at least different from if not greater than the one the teacher of older learners has to meet. The very young are as yet 'unformed' in any language.

The second important issue concerns different kinds of learning. There is the discovery type, well supported by many primary teachers, where the pupil is exposed to an experience and acquires what he/she can from it. There is the kind where the teacher or the learner him/herself focuses and the learning is conscious. This notion of *acquisition/learning* is useful to bear in mind. It is something which people do anyway – acquire unconsciously and learn consciously. The teacher needs to match this with his/her methodology.

Still with types of learning and especially language learning, we speak of *fluency* and *accuracy*. Learners have to be able to give their messages smoothly and clearly without being too conscious of the structure and they need to understand others easily without the form of the utterance or written text getting in the way. At the same time they have to be knowledgeable about the way words are put together or they cannot hope to be really fluent. Here is another learning issue which has many implications for the teacher.

Third, I wish to focus briefly on *progression* of learning, bearing in mind the point about language and thought being closely linked. There is concept getting and concept using and language which goes with them. The baby developing his/her first language or L1, seems to go through stages I have labelled with five key words. I have always found these helpful when considering teaching programmes, though I say this warily because it is dangerous to push the analogy too far. The acquisition of L1 and the learning of L2 or 3 or more languages can never be the same by virtue of the fact that the learner is a different being each time. His/Her experience of life and his/her conceptual framework have grown. However, with this reservation in mind, let me share my key words.

The first is *Identification*. This is the naming of objects, people, events. What/Who is it? What is happening? The learner must be able to give labels, first at a simple perceptive level. The next key word is *Qualification*, by which is meant the ability to describe attributes of colour, size, shape, purpose, location in time and space and so on. What colour is X? What is Y for?

When/Where is the event? Then, having identified and qualified, can the learner now compare and contrast? Can he/she see *Relation*, my third key word? Does he/she notice samenesses and differences? If things are different, how do they differ? Is this one bigger? Is that the smallest? Is X on the table and Y under it? Is X happy and Y sad? A wider understanding of relation leads to the fourth key word, *Classification*, the matter of putting into sets or categories, an important part of the primary school child's mathematics programme. These go together because of X or Y, they share one or more attributes.

You will notice that all my key words end with 'tion'. These first four 'tions' represent for me the *getting* of concepts. The fifth, *Manipulation*, refers to their *using*. By this time the learner can leave the here and now and move into the past, future or possible. He/She can understand and express cause and effect and make hypotheses. In other words he/she has reached the higher order thinking skills.

Here then is a progression of developing thought, however simplistic. It may help us to focus on the learning journey and to consider the kind of experience we need to offer in our language teaching. This, taken with the other issues of learning we have looked at and those of language itself, suggests a flexible teaching methodology, one which can incorporate the various dichotomies and their progression.

Teaching

The issues here are by implication, some already suggested. They will be taken up again in the methodology section. For now, three in particular.

First, the teacher's approach must be a kind of double bill, to use jargon from the world of entertainment. In teaching language he/she must cater for both the linguistic and the communicative, the form and the use. While in practice it is difficult to separate the two, the teacher must know where his/her emphasis lies at any given point in time. Linked to this, he/she must vary the regime from one of direction and instruction to one where the learners have free rein to make their discoveries and to use the new learning gained. This double role of instructor/facilitator is important whatever the age of the pupils, but especially so when they are young.

The skilful teacher makes the two sides of the double bill work together. The work on language structure will be contextualised meaningfully while the needs and purposes for English will be catered for and their expression given structure. What happens in the periods of directed teaching should have relevant effect in the times of more flexibility and what may arise more spontaneously in these latter sessions should be picked up by the teacher and focused upon later.

The notion of 'focusing' within a recognised 'field' of operation is relevant to my second teaching issue, that of *progression* of learning, this time from the teacher's standpoint. The teacher must be able to think globally about the total learning context while at the same time concentrating on a specific piece of learning. But, in addition, he/she must be aware of some kind of going forward. In facing children with something very new like an L2, I believe the field in the beginning should be fairly limited. After exposure to this where some learning may have been acquired, there should be focusing in order to make firm. Better equipped as it were, the children can then go on to a wider field and use their new learning productively. Then comes more focusing and a widening of the field. And so on in circular fashion. Children need experience to acquire and develop language. They also need language to cope with new experience. But there is nothing new in this. The good teacher has been following such a pattern for a long time. It is interesting now to recall the five 'tions'. It seems to me that in the initial presentation of the limited field, the first four – Identification, Qualification, Relation, Classification – should be catered for. This is the time of concept getting. They are made sure, along with their expression, in the following focus sessions. As the field widens, the fifth 'tion' – Manipulation – comes to the fore with concept using. So there is a double bill which progresses and does so it is hoped in the way that people learn.

The third teaching issue which I wish to highlight at this point is the matter of moving from the known to the unknown in the child's general experience, again something which all good teachers do. It is of particular significance, however, in an L2 learning situation. Even very undeveloped young children bring with them to school a competence in their L1 and they have already gone some way along the concept learning journey. But what the teacher has to remember is that this learning has come about in a particular culture with its own special way of looking at the world. How much does the teacher understand of this? He/She may be of the same culture him/herself and his/her own bilingualism the same as that of his/her developing learners. This is ideal I believe, and the teacher should make full use of his/her own experience in helping the children to use theirs. I am speaking of moving from one set of particulars to another, of understanding perhaps what might be universal, of helping children to switch codes and to know when to do so, of knowing just where children are in the developing thought process so that a new language and culture can be used to advantage and not to confusion.

The exciting matter of having more than one language with which to understand and confront the world is another vast subject which can only be touched on here. It is something which the language teacher should try to be knowledgeable about, but lest non-bilingual teachers in particular should feel depressed at the enormity of the task, let me remind them that to some extent we are all bilingual and we all code-switch. Even within one language there are varieties of one kind or another and most of us are adept at changing our style of speech, depending on the circumstances. The main point to take from all this is that the teacher should, by whatever means he/she has, cash in on the assets the children bring so that they can be used to enhance the new learning.

The approach

Focus on integration

With this field of issues as context I would like now to focus on one or two facets of an integrative approach. First, a general point about primary teaching. Most teachers of young children are child orientated rather than subject orientated. They are concerned with the development of the whole child rather than with his/her learning of history or mathematics. The 'integrated day' became an important approach in Britain and other places many years ago. So the integration of subject areas in the curriculum is no new thing for the teacher of young learners.

Related to this is another kind of integration which has become normal procedure, particularly in infants classes, and that is the linking of language work with all the other work. The idea that language for the young child *is* what it *does* has prompted teachers to look at the actual curriculum needs and to foster the development of the relevant language *in situ* as it were. So, for example, the child needs to cope with order in mathematics. The words 'first', 'next' and 'last' would be given where they were required in the real situation. Experience and language are made to march together. The total view of the child, including the development of his/her language, enables the good professional to use the whole curriculum for each child's benefit. He/She can take the child's growing awareness in one direction to assist that in another. This is made easier in most primary schools because the same teacher takes the majority of subjects. Language across the curriculum, a kind of catchphrase originating I think from the famous British Bullock Report of 1975, is fairly widely known in other countries too. In primary schools at least teachers seem to be trying to put it into practice.

Where does the teaching of an L2 fit into this picture of subject integration and language? This question itself raises one or two further interesting questions. But first it is necessary to speak to two different situations of L2. There is the one where the children are learning it as a *foreign* language, as would be children learning English in Germany for instance. English is not one of the principal languages in the community. The children are probably not hearing it used much around them and all the rest of their school learning is conducted in the L1. In this English as a Foreign Language (EFL) situation, it is likely that the lessons would come in 20- to 30-minute periods, perhaps daily or less frequently. The teacher of English may not be the one who teaches other subjects and he/she is likely to use an ELT syllabus and/or commercial course.

A very different learning situation is that in a British or Australian school perhaps where children of immigrant background are being educated alongside children whose L1 is English. Here the language *is* important in the community, it is the main one used. For the L2 children it is a *second* language (ESL). They need it for living and learning. They may have special help with a syllabus and/or course, but often as not they have to glean their knowledge of English from the tasks which are set across the curriculum as they share lessons with their L1 classmates, and of course from the everyday exchanges in classroom and playground. There are, however, situations in the world where the distinction between EFL and ESL is not quite so easily defined. In Malaysia, for example, English is an important second language in the country but the teaching medium throughout is Bahasa Malaysia. So the children learn English as a subject only, and the situation could be called EFL. In Zambia, English, virtually a foreign language in the country, is the chosen medium of instruction from the start because of the vast number of indigenous languages. No one of these could be selected for political reasons. So in this situation all the pupils are ESL learners. Here there *is* a syllabus/course in English. And there is the situation as in black education in South Africa, where the children start their schooling in their L1 or perhaps the wider community language and then at a certain point, about the fifth year of school, change to English medium. In the way I am defining the terms here, EFL becomes ESL.

But lest I digress too far into the complications of world diversity, let me return to integration. The terms EFL and ESL are not important in themselves. They are not perhaps very useful or definitive. I use them only to make a point about L2 and its link with the rest of the curriculum. They are a kind of shorthand. Children in an ESL situation need to have help with their language across the curriculum. Their second language is their tool of learning so everything that has been said above about the language of the subject areas being focused upon for children in general, is of special importance for the ESL learner. If there is also an ELT syllabus/course, then the teachers must see that this serves the curriculum, that the focus is done within the field.

What of the EFL situation? How significant is the wider curriculum here? It may appear at first that an English class could survive quite happily in isolation from the rest of the school, and many do. The English syllabus/course becomes the total field of learning and the focus is restricted to the items within it. Reacting to this, can I refer back now to my last teaching issue? I spoke of cashing in on the assets the children come with. In a sense, we have here another opportunity for cashing in. Could the teacher of English not make use of the children's growing awareness in other subjects? What is already comprehensible in another subject could be put to good effect in the English class I believe. The teacher could be easier in his/her mind about the underlying understanding. The important implication is of course that he/she must *know* the wider curriculum as well as his/her own English work. He/She must be able to work with other teachers so that the EFL class is not a kind of carbuncle on the body of the school.

My own experience of both ESL and EFL situations in many parts of the world suggests that integration of subject content and L2 is often more possible than people realise and, when done appropriately and well, is an undoubted asset to the learner. Sometimes there needs to be a kind of redress of balance. The ESL learner needs more focus on structure within the lively, communicative regime of the primary classroom perhaps, particularly where there is no ELT syllabus. And, in the EFL situation, the focus on language structure which is sometimes emphasised overmuch in syllabuses, needs to be relevantly contextualised.

So much for integration of subject and language. It seems to me that yet another kind of integration has now been implied and that is one between L1 and L2. I believe that a school should be concerned with the total lingualism of its pupils. The L1 and every further language learnt constitute this lingualism. Every language developed should be enhanced by the one or more further on. The child as a being is not only the sum of these parts but greater than that. If this is true, schools must have policies on language. All teachers are concerned because all teachers are teachers of language, though the specialist language teachers may have a particular interest and role to play. I cannot linger on this wide topic. Suffice it to say that an integration of the work in L1 with that of L2 and L others in these school policies would appear to be desirable.

We move on now from this glimpse of a general approach to focus on a methodology which for me has three main functions. First, it is a stimulus and motivator. Second, it is a vehicle capable of carrying all the issues of language, learning and teaching discussed and probably many more. And last, it is an instrument of integration, again in the ways we have looked at and more. I refer to the use of topic or theme across the curriculum.

The methodology

In general

First catch your theme. A careful selection has to be made and this is often best done by the children themselves. It may arise from the children's 'news' or from something buzzing in the wider community; it may come from a subject other than English, from discussion or reading. Whatever it is and wherever it comes from, the teacher or better still the teaching team has to make decisions about which parts of the curriculum are to be pervaded and about how long the work should go on. If several teachers are involved, it is necessary to work out who does what and what exactly *is* to be done. How is the theme to be presented and how followed up? How can individual differences be catered for? If there are children in the class whose L1 is English along with those for whom it is a second language, is the work of the theme catering for both? If there is an ELT syllabus/course, are items from it being 'loaded' into the vehicle along with those from subject areas if the situation is ESL? Are ideas from these same subject areas to be used in *some* way if the situation is EFL? And so on. There is much to do at the planning stage. Let us consider this a little further in the light of what was said in the first part of this paper. The theme must provide for the two sides of the language equation. There should be activities which concentrate on the form of English and those which emphasise its use. There should be activities to promote listening and speaking out of which come those to develop reading and writing. The learners should be free some of the time to enjoy, acquire and put into practice and at other times the teacher should have a group round him/her and draw the learning together. With each activity the teacher must make sure that there is a progression in the learning, that the 'tions' are covered and revised and that there is a leading on from initial, perceptual work to manipulation of concepts. If possible the L1 should be made to *help* the L2. An activity could be conducted in L1 first and later in the second language. A story told in Polish today could be repeated in English tomorrow.

Mention of story suggests organisation of theme. There must be some way of structuring the work. The value of story as a theme in its own right is that it has a beginning, a middle and an end with lots of other staging-posts in between, at each of which learners and teacher can pause on the learning journey and assess where they have got to, go over old learning and perhaps have new introduced. At the various stages too the teacher can load the language from the syllabus/course and/or that from the curriculum areas. I have found the story kind of theme to be particularly helpful.

But, whether or not story *is* the theme or just one activity amongst others in a different kind of theme, these staging strategies should be able to work. For example, a 'doing' kind of theme like 'looking after pets' or 'caring for my bicycle' could be organised into a number of sub-activities. Each of these could be divided yet again and the whole arranged perhaps in an order of activity. Or if the theme is of the 'knowing' variety like 'people who help us', 'kinds of buildings' or 'colours', then a descriptive kind of categorisation has to be imposed. The stages would be used in the same way as those of story, the field being focused upon in an organised and progressive way, language being developed *in situ*.

Just a brief word here about teaching materials. The kind of theme selected suggests its own activities and the teaching aids to match. Most primary teachers are trained to use these imaginatively, very often making their own. A particularly useful gadget is the magnetboard or old-fashioned flannelgraph with figurines for the children to manipulate. The retelling of a story for instance can be very well done by this means, the visuals being much more flexible than the pictures in a book. Various kinds of games and materials for group tasks are another helpful aid. The notion of prototype should be borne in mind. More will be said about this and about the collecting of materials in a kind of resource bank, materials for both the initial presentation of the theme and for its follow-up across a wider curriculum. Meantime I hope that the above has given some idea of the value of theme in general. It carries the learners along by its interest and appropriacy and it is a vehicle offering options to match the issues with which we are concerned. It also integrates so many components in the learning/teaching scene.

A particular example

It is hoped that the hypothetical situation to be described now will be capable of generalisation to others. Let us imagine an EFL class of about 25 children in the lower primary, say eight to ten years. They have 20 to 30 minutes of English on three schooldays a week. The teacher comes in specially and she is bilingual in the children's languages. She has a good relationship with the rest of the staff and with the parents. It is a caring school, lively and communicative in the L1, with a fair degree of integrated activity and a quite generous allowance for materials. What the school cannot itself produce, the parents are prepared to supply. There is no commercial course being followed but the teacher herself has worked out an English syllabus, guided by her reading, by the outlines of several printed courses and of course by the needs of the children in her care. This then is the scenario.

A baby has just come to the home of one of the children. All are interested in this news, many already having experienced the same and some about to. There is lively discussion in the L1 with the teacher beginning to think that the theme could be useful for her English work. 'Families and babies' is launched. Surreptitiously almost the teacher begins to use English words. Next day she comes armed with a story which she first tells in the L1 and later in the second language. The story is well illustrated with figurines for retelling on the magnetboard. The children are asked to bring photographs and pictures from home, including ones of animal families and their young.

At this stage, once the teacher has been able to assess the interest and to plan for how long she wants the theme to operate, she approaches her colleagues and draws them into her planning. Would they be willing to use the theme in other subjects? Could geography for instance look at family life in other lands? Could some appropriate work be done in art and craft, music and drama? In return could she, the teacher of English, pick up something of the essence of all this work being done through the medium of the L1? She even gives up some of her free time to sit in on a few of the L1 activities so that she can better understand where the children are.

Meantime, interested parents have been asking about the work. They are invited to come to the school, not only to observe but to participate if they wish to. A typical scene is groupwork using classroom, corridor and playground. The teacher has one group round her in the room. After a magnetboard retelling of story in which the teacher has allowed 'helpful' error, the kind which the learners have to make as part of their developing language, she concentrates on accuracy with some special focus and leading questions. The work is easier because the theme has made the vocabulary exciting and familiar.

Another group, also in the room, is doing a graph, transferring information from lists to a chart. This is a mathematics activity suggested by another teacher. It is something the children would have been doing in any case. Now the 'Families and babies' theme is allowed to pervade it. The activity is supervised by a parent and is conducted in English. A third group with a child as appointed leader is playing a board game, Bingo. The pictures are of various members of a family and the teacher has already covered the first four 'tions' in her discussions on these pictures. The basic perceptive work has been done. These children, a more able group in the class, are now quite capable of playing the game, of monitoring each other in English, and of manipulating and using the concepts embedded in the activity. Group Four is in the playground, playing at 'Hunt the Baby'! A doll has been brought by one of the children. Another parent is helping here, having her work cut out to change the excited L1 chatter to English! The teacher has given some ideas, especially concerning the use of prepositions and question forms. A fifth group is making a scrapbook, labelling their pictures in English and writing short sentences. Again this is one of the more able groups, child-led after some initial help from the teacher. They are out in the corridor where a collage is being prepared by the class as a whole. It lies on a trestle table. The scrapbook group are also labelling the collage as they go along and will later talk to their classmates about it. This is only a very brief look at the possible. I hope it speaks for itself. Instead of further comment I shall now try to put together a few reminders for the teacher using the methodology of theme.

Reminders for the teacher

BUILD UP A RESOURCE BANK

a) of potential themes

Though the alert teacher is always ready to pluck ideas out of the air as it were, it is wise to build up a collection of potential themes of all kinds including story. They must obviously be relevant and of interest to the learners *and* to the teacher. A bored teacher is a bad one. And these should be sought from a variety of sources as has been suggested. It should be recognised that some themes are good for carrying certain issues, others for different things. And the notion of a typical or prototype theme should be borne in mind, such as certain kinds of story, of 'doing' topics or descriptive ones.

b) of potential materials

Prototype materials should also be banked. There should be real objects to see, pick up, play with, the realia of the here and now, there should be pictures, models and other representational material, and there should be ideas for moving the children on to more abstract and challenging thinking. There should also be materials for variety of emphasis and degree of direction and for difference in size of learning groups. The four modes have to be catered for. Prototype materials for the development of these are a useful aid. Finally there should be lots of varied materials not only at different levels of difficulty but also at the same level, suitable for all kinds of groupwork.

HAVE A STRATEGY

a) Know your field

This applies not only to the items of the English language which may have to be covered but to the syllabus as a whole and also to the curricular subjects.

Obviously one cannot hope to know all this in every detail but a global and comprehensive view of the field ensures more judicious and careful focusing and more effective guidance for the learner. Knowing your field can also apply to what the children bring with them in L1 competence and general concept development. The more understanding of this the better for progress in L2.

b) Pervade the field with your theme

Not only does theme motivate in an overall way, but it also helps to integrate all the subjects so that the learning is generalised. The whole curriculum, even in an ESL situation, may not need to be used for every theme. The teacher should be selective and sensitive to what is most expedient for the learning, matching concepts and language.

c) Find skilful ways of loading

L2 development will go forward more effectively if the work is carefully planned and organised. The learning journey must be broken down into stages where theme, curricular needs and English can all meet and learning points be made firm. There must be skilful loading of the learning vehicle. The theme must be properly used.

'PACKAGE' YOUR THEMES

My final point concerns teachers working together. As a profession we are notoriously individualistic, keeping our ideas and materials to ourselves, sometimes jealously guarded in locked cupboards. If a particular theme works well, why not share it? Try to package it in some way so that it can be used again not only by yourself but by others, even in other schools. Teachers who can work as a team all stand to benefit. There are different strengths and weaknesses on a school staff and we should allow ourselves to be led as well as to lead. Ideally the use of theme should be a team effort from the start with some kind of record of events being kept of both the activities and the materials. Notes should include the age and stage of the learners the theme was used for and the particular English language items being covered in the parts of the curriculum pervaded. They should also indicate the progression of the work and perhaps some ideas which were not tried out but which could have been. However it is done, effective work should be husbanded and made available for further use in comprehensible packages.

It should also be constantly revised and brought up to date. The powers that be make changes in the curriculum or English syllabus perhaps. New materials come on to the market and new ideas are given on in-service courses. Above all, history is constantly being made in the world outside school. What are today's themes for today's pupils? What is today's curriculum for the themes to pervade? Indeed, what is today's English language for the themes to carry? We sometimes forget that the latter changes too. The teacher must keep an open mind and be aware of the current issues as he/she seeks for classroom options.

Conclusion

I began by suggesting issues of language, learning and teaching of which the English teacher in the primary school should currently be aware. I hope that what has been outlined subsequently in approach and methodology illustrates at least some of the options which can cater in practice for these issues. It is recognised that many teachers in various parts of the world are not able to work with others, for whatever reason. This and other constraints may make the use of the methodology difficult. At the same time, where there is the will the way can often be found. Let me hope at least that there is *something* here for every teacher of English to young children to explore for him/herself.

Bibliography

Some useful reading.

Bullock Report. 1975. *A Language for Life:* Report of the Committee of Inquiry appointed by the Secretary of State for Education and Science (UK) under the Chairmanship of Sir Alan Bullock, FBA. London: HMSO.

Dunn, O. 1984. *Developing English with Young Learners.* London: Macmillan.

Edwards, V. 1983. *Language in Multicultural Classrooms.* London: Batsford.

Every Child's Language. An in-service pack for primary teachers. Multilingual Matters and the Open University.

Garvie, E. 1989. *Story as Vehicle.* Clevedon: Multilingual Matters.

Holden, S. 1980. *Teaching Children.* London: Modern English Publications.

Hawkins, E. 1984. *Awareness of Language: an Introductory Guide for Teachers.* Cambridge: Cambridge University Press.

Houlton, D. and R. Willey. 1983. *Supporting Children's Bilingualism: Some Policy Issues for Primary Schools and Local Education Authorities.* Harlow: Longman.

Wright, A., D. Betteridge and M. Buckby. 1984. *Games for Language Learning.* Cambridge: Cambridge University Press.

Meriel Bloor, University of Warwick, England

10 The role of informal interaction in teaching English to young learners

Meriel Bloor's paper extends the process begun in other papers of systematically addressing the principles of primary teaching. She also draws on practical experience in a number of situations. In particular she provides reasons, based on language principles, for encouraging informal interaction, and these reasons are linked clearly to practical illustrations.

THIS PAPER looks at the role of informal interaction in the teaching of English. By informal interaction is meant the exchange of ideas, using spoken English, between teacher and learners and among the learners themselves.

Billows (1961) was one of the first language teachers to stress the fact that a language has no life in itself. 'It must live,' he wrote, 'in the mouth of the teacher in relation to the activity and situation of the classroom. It is a social skill. In other words, the teacher must really be himself (or herself), talking to real people about real things and then training the pupils to talk to one another about real things.'

The concern here is not with interaction that may be part of the formal, planned part of the lesson (although any lesson with young learners is likely to include interactional activities like games or drama) but with ways in which the use of English can be encouraged for real communication outside the main pedagogic events of the classroom. The proposal is that it is the job of the teacher to provide learning experiences that will help the children to use spoken English for real communication about matters of interest.

What do we mean by informal interaction?

A number of studies of classroom language have shown that in most native-speaker classrooms language is used for functions other than direct teaching. These extra functions include such matters as greetings, discussing health, attendance, the weather and so on. Barnes (1969), in his description of classroom language, labelled these functions 'Social'.

Social interaction also takes place in foreign language and second language classrooms, but in many such classrooms the native language is used for this purpose.

Fanselow (1977) attempted to set up a system for observing and recording different types of communication in the language classroom. He established five headings, in the form of questions:

- Who communicates?
- What is the pedagogical purpose of the communication?
- What mediums are used to communicate content?
- How are the mediums used?
- What areas of content are communicated?

All of these questions are of interest to language teachers who wish to think about how language is used in their classroom, but it is the last of these questions that is the main concern of this chapter. The question is concerned with these crucial areas: what the teacher talks about to the children, what the children talk about to the teacher.

Fanselow found that there were four main content areas in most lessons:

LANGUAGE	PROCEDURE	SUBJECT MATTER	LIFE

The first of these areas, *Language,* concerns those times when a teacher is explaining or illustrating the language, or when the pupils are asking questions about the language, or practising pronunciation or structures. In most English classes nowadays, this part of the lesson is conducted in English.

The second, *Procedure,* concerns those times when the teacher is managing the class, explaining what to do next, how to do it and so on. Some teachers use English for class management and others use the children's mother tongue, at least in the early stages.

The third of Fanselow's categories, *Subject Matter,* concerns those times when the language is being used to convey some specific topic as part of the lesson. For example, if the teacher tells a story called *The Frog Who Got Lost,* the subject matter is the frog and its adventures. In this case the teacher's intention might be to illustrate the use of the past simple tense, but the content area of language used in that part of the lesson is not tenses but the tale of the frog. In the language classroom, this part of the lesson would be conducted in English.

The final content category identified by Fanselow, *Life,* concerns communication between teacher and pupils about real life matters – not directly about the lesson. This category embraces the type of questioning Barnes called 'Social' as well as any other type of communication about the real world. Thus, for example, if the teacher directs a particular student to 'Open the window', or asks another, who has nothing to write on, 'Where is your notebook?', or genuinely asks another, 'Is your brother playing in the football match on Saturday?', he/she is using language to talk about the real world that is part of the learners' direct experience. In the majority of foreign language classrooms, this type of informal interaction is conducted in the mother tongue rather than in English.

It is the intention of this paper to encourage teachers of young learners to extend the use of English to include all four of Fanselow's categories of communication and, in particular, to suggest ways in which the Life category can be conducted in English.

Why should we encourage informal interaction in English?

There are four main arguments for encouraging informal interaction in English as part of the language teaching process:

1 Children learn languages best in situations where their attention is focused on meaning rather than on language. This argument is based on research into the way in which infants learn their mother tongue and the ways in which foreign language learning parallels first language learning. The younger the learners the more they will benefit from the experience of hearing the target language in appropriate situations.

2 Since the main purpose of teaching English is so that our students will be able to use the language in real situations, we must at some stage provide the opportunities for appropriate practice. The earlier we introduce realistic practice the better.

3 Meaning is communicated more directly in informal settings. Unfamiliar vocabulary is more easily understood when the objects under discussion are present in the surroundings and the speaker's emotions and attitudes are more clearly identified with real experiences.

4 Children naturally seek and need human interaction. Linguistically this normally occurs through the medium of the mother tongue. If we want English to come naturally, we must demonstrate to the children that English is a means of communication in the same way that their mother tongue is a means of communication: that the context, the child's knowledge of the world, the child's natural curiosity, and such factors as gesture and facial expression can all help in the process of communicating in English.

Some applied linguists have suggested that natural communication through language is the basis of all successful language learning. Such a position is taken by those who accept what is known as the *Interaction Hypothesis*.

The Interaction Hypothesis was proposed by Allwright (1984a, 1984b) as a contribution to discussion of the question, 'Why don't learners learn what teachers teach?' This question is a common cry among teachers who have struggled to teach aspects of the language to the best of their ability but find that many of their students continue to have serious problems with what has been taught.

Allwright's suggestion was that what happens in language lessons has a very powerful effect on how and what children learn and, moreover, that what children *can* learn is limited by the learning opportunities that are made available to them. The Interaction Hypothesis states that the nature of the linguistic interaction a learner engages in will affect the speed and quality of the learning. What is interesting to find out is how far interaction in English is possible with young learners, and what types of interaction help children to learn more quickly. In order to test the Interaction Hypothesis and to find answers to these questions, we need to provide varied learning opportunities where interaction in English can take place.

There is some evidence that different learners require different types of interaction in order to succeed to the best of their abilities. That is to say that although some children will learn better if they are given the opportunity to speak in the language, others will learn just as well if they spend most of their time listening. There is little doubt that many children make their breakthrough into the language with non-speaking activities, such as reading stories. We must beware of assuming that if children engage in spoken communication all their language problems will be solved. Such an assumption would raise false expectations and lead to disappointment. Allwright's own research confirms that we cannot make simple generalisations about how people learn languages.

Nevertheless, engaging in spoken interaction is a necessary stage for all learners who hope to use the language for speaking outside the classroom, and the next part of this paper describes some of the ways in which this can be done.

How can we encourage informal interaction?

Teachers who wish to encourage spoken interaction sometimes fail to find opportunities in a busy school day. This section concerns such matters as how teachers can recognise and create opportunities for interaction with the children, both inside and outside the language class, and how children can be encouraged to use English to interact with each other. The problem of how to maintain communication with reluctant speakers is then discussed in the light of classroom research.

Opportunities for interaction

Children naturally use their mother tongue with any other person who knows it. When children find themselves in the company of others, particularly their peers, who speak other languages (or other dialects of their own language) then they will make an effort to understand and use the new language. In an ideal world, we would be able to arrange regular meetings between our language learners and children who were native speakers of the target language. This is sometimes possible through exchange schemes and school trips but for most children it is at best a rare event.

In the absence of regular meetings with English speakers, the foreign language teacher has to establish him/herself as a speaker of the target language who uses that language to communicate, at least part of the time. Otherwise the children are unlikely to use the language freely in real interaction with the teacher or each other.

Learners with a teacher who uses English freely and easily in informal situations will have the advantage of a proper model of language use. Although this situation may develop more naturally if the teacher is a native speaker of English, it may be even more effective when the teacher is bilingual because the children will see their teacher as a more precise role model. Here is a speaker of their own language – Italian, Spanish, Greek, Kiswahili or whatever – who uses English for certain communicative events: exactly what they themselves are aiming to achieve. The teacher who only tells the learners *about* the language, guides them through a coursebook and helps them to read or write, may be an excellent teacher in many ways, but he/she will fail to demonstrate how real human interaction takes place in the language.

In order to establish him/herself as a speaker of English in the eyes of the class, the teacher must use the language for specific communicative events and create opportunities for those events to take place; they can be part of the language lesson or even take place outside class.

The types of event that are suitable for informal interaction depend very much on the age and interests of the children, but there are certain principles that apply with children of any age:

1 Informal interaction is incidental, not central, to the lesson, i.e. only a very short time in any lesson need be taken up with this type of interaction. The teacher may make a few simple remarks in English at the beginning of the lesson, for example, with beginners, commenting on unusual weather conditions ('Phew! It's hot today,' perhaps fanning his/her face to help comprehension), or saying 'Happy Birthday' to a child in English. Class management may also take place in English, of course.

2 It is not necessary for all the children to be directly involved in the interaction. Remarks addressed to individuals or small groups can be just as useful as remarks addressed to the whole class. They all help to establish an English-speaking atmosphere in the classroom.

3 Where possible, the remarks should be made meaningful by context, helped by gesture or facial expression, but total comprehension of every part of the interaction is not an absolute necessity. (What happens when communication breaks down is discussed below.)

There are a number of topics that are particularly appropriate for informal interaction. Many teachers keep their own check-list of topics as a reminder. Here are six categories that could provide the basis for such a list:

1 *Life events*: birthdays, weddings, a new baby, anniversaries, illness, hospital visits
2 *Festivals*: holidays, the religious calendar, seasons
3 *Entertainment and sport*: games and toys, TV programmes, local theatre and cinema, local sports events
4 *The natural world*: the weather, the night sky, plants and animals, science
5 *The local scene*: markets, workplaces, other schools, churches, geographical features (rivers, hills, the beach, beauty spots)
6 *The school*: teachers, other subjects (e.g. history, geography), buildings, the school day, school events

Much of the vocabulary surrounding such events will be included in the language taught formally as part of the course. The sensitive teacher will be able to recyle this vocabulary in informal interaction.

In some countries it is normal for children to bring objects from outside the classroom into school. For example children bring flowers for the teacher's desk or interesting objects like rocks or shells to place on a nature table. These objects provide an ideal stimulus for an informal exchange.

The teacher who receives the gifts can thank the children in English and make an appropriate comment: 'What interesting shells! You can put them on the nature table.'

Even beginners will respond appropriately, although not necessarily verbally, when the meaning is clear from the situation.

An English teacher who enters the classroom later in the day might look at the flowers on the teacher's desk and comment on them, 'What lovely yellow flowers!', thereby making use of an informal opportunity to reinforce colour words in a meaningful context and to display natural language use. With more advanced learners more complex exchanges can take place: 'Who brought the shells? Where did you find them?'

Notice that the questions here would be genuine: the teacher asking these questions does not know where the shells have come from. These are functional as well as formal questions. Many of the questions used in normal language classes are demonstrations of *form* but not of *function* because the teacher already knows the answers and the children know that the teacher knows the answers.

If the English textbook contains a story about a boy named Pablo who took some shells to school and the teacher asks the class, 'Who took the shells to school?', the children know that the teacher is just checking on whether they have understood the story; he/she already knows the answer. Similarly, if children practise asking and answering questions about a specific picture (a common interactive exercise), they usually have the same information in front of them and no genuine exchange takes place. It is more like a quiz (where the questioner already knows the answers). There is an important place for quizzes in language practice and the teacher must, of course, check learners' understanding, but the object of informal interaction is to extend language use to real situations where questions are used for the actual purpose of acquiring information. Other utterances, like greetings, requests or commands, similarly take on their true functions in a meaningful context.

Extending the language lesson

One way of extending opportunities for natural language practice is by extending the contexts for interaction that are outside the normal English class.

Some teachers have used English very successfully as part of other lessons in the curriculum where appropriate. For example in one Spanish school, a geography lesson on Spanish exports involved the children discussing the English words for such items as the fruit and vegetables that are normally exported to Britain. The teacher (who taught a number of subjects, including English, to the same class) came to Britain for a summer school and made a collection of English advertisements for Spanish holidays and Spanish products on sale in Britain. She planned to use these informally in her geography lessons.

Another teacher, who taught English to near beginners in an African primary school which was very short of books and equipment, used to take the children on nature walks in the local countryside and use the opportunity for conversation, in English, about the places they saw and the insects and plants that the children collected. Situations such as this, where communication can take place outside the classroom on a variety of topics, are the nearest we might get to opportunities for 'natural' language practice.

Other opportunities can be devised for using English in wider contexts. In a German school, each class prepared a Christmas reading and a carol for the December concert for parents. In the English language classes, the students learned an English carol and prepared their reading in English. This type of activity can prove attractive and involving, particularly to young learners. As Allwright (1984) says, 'in general the central point is well established that the communication of ideas that matter to the learner is likely to aid learning through getting learners more deeply involved in what they are doing.'

Another way of involving learners in English as a means of communication is to make sure that the uses of the language outside the classroom are acknowledged as relevant inside the classroom. Prodromou (1988) from his experience in Greece points out that many school classrooms are drab places, 'with nothing on the walls – no sign that there is a world outside the classroom.' Learning English, he claims, is often a case of playing 'let's pretend', where the speech acts of the language lesson are based on situations that most pupils will never have to function in. Yet, in Greece, English does have a significant social role, often appearing in signs, on T-shirts, in shop and brand names, and as the language of aspects of international culture, of some popular music and sports. English is even used in job advertisements in local newspapers when English-speaking applicants are sought. The major task here for the teacher is to find ways of establishing links between the real uses of English in the environment and what happens in the classroom so that the learners will recognise and understand the English they see around them. Prodromou suggests encouraging the learners to bring samples of English they have seen in their towns or villages into the classroom where they can be discussed and maybe used as the basis for communicative activities.

The object of extending the use of English beyond the language class is to make learners aware of the potential of the formal instruction for actual communication outside school. This is becoming more and more possible with the increase in international tourism and trade, but of course opportunities vary considerably from country to country.

Interaction between children

Children interact freely in their own language. Traditionally it has been one of the teacher's main jobs in the classroom to curtail this chatter and to get the children to 'keep quiet and listen'. In recent years in some countries, however, some types of interaction between children have been encouraged, both as a means of language development and to help children learn in a co-operative way. Phillips (1985) summarises the position in British schools:

> During the seventies, a highly significant change in attitude to children's talk occurred, a change which moved talk from something to be forbidden to something to be encouraged at all costs. As part of that change, many teachers had moved away from the dominant position in front of the classroom, which research had shown them inhibited children's talk, and had set up situations in which the children could talk to each other freely.

This move has prompted some teachers of English as a second or foreign language to set up similar situations (usually around problem-solving tasks or other communicative activities) in their classrooms. Where these activities are developed as part of the formal class they can encourage interaction effectively, but many difficulties can arise, particularly where the children share the same first language. The main problem of course is that when the children become involved in and excited about the tasks they are performing, they naturally revert to the mother tongue for communication. Spontaneous interaction in English between such children is a rare occurrence.

Nevertheless, children can be encouraged to speak to each other in English. Little research has been undertaken into spontaneous informal language use between children in a second or foreign language. Some observations have been made which indicate that children's first use of the target language between themselves involves stock phrases or expressions embedded in conversation in the mother tongue. I myself have heard children using their mother tongue intermixed with the names of games and song titles in English. The name of the school English textbook is often the first English expression the children use freely.

The same phenomenon of the use of standard expressions has been observed in children (by Prodromou among others) in the unfortunate habit of using English as the favoured medium for graffiti. French and Greek children often use English for their messages of love ('Pascal loves Marie') and exhortations to football teams ('Go home Juventus'). In spite of the anti-social aspects of such behaviour, the activity provides evidence that children will use a language other than their mother tongue for spontaneous informal expression. The task of the teacher is to develop in the children the ability and desire to express themselves in English, but to channel the activity into a more socially acceptable form.

Perhaps the main proposal for encouraging informal spoken interaction among children has been to promote roleplay as a classroom activity. The principle behind roleplay is clear: providing children with the chance to use language in specific situations (the shop, the doctor's or more exotic places) prepares them for using it in a wider context than the classroom. Furthermore, children naturally adopt different roles in their play (using their own language) and these classroom activities imitate natural learning processes.

There are, however, widely differing interpretations of what roleplay in the classroom means. At one extreme, roleplay can involve little more than practising dramatic dialogues. Many textbooks contain dialogues matched to specific situations. An example follows (from Bloor *et al.* 1982):

In the shop *Mr Mohapi is the shopkeeper*

T'SEPO:	Good morning, *Mr Mohapi.*
MR MOHAPI:	Good morning, *Tsepo.* How are you?
T'SEPO:	I'm very well, thank you. Can I have *a box of matches,* please?
MR MOHAPI:	Here *are the matches.*
T'SEPO:	Thank you. Here's the money.
MR MOHAPI:	Thank you. Goodbye, *T'sepo.*
T'SEPO:	Goodbye.

In the teacher's guide the teacher is advised to read the dialogue aloud, explain the meaning and then teach it through repetition until the class can practise it in pairs. When most of the children know the lines, they can play shop, arranging the desks to make a counter, using real objects and changing the italicised words for their own names and their own choice of purchases.

Many teachers today would reject this approach completely, believing that for the experience to be of real value, the speakers must create meaning through their own consciousness by constructing their own utterances to express what they want to say. These teachers would set up the play situation and let the children use the language as they wished without much concern for language accuracy. Two children in a shopping situation produced the following conversation:

BOY SHOPPER:	I want to buy rice.
GIRL SHOPKEEPER:	What you want?
BOY SHOPPER:	Give me rice.
GIRL SHOPKEEPER:	Here is the rice. You pay two shillings.
BOY SHOPPER:	Here is the lot of money.
	(*laughter*)

In some ways this is a very satisfactory piece of interaction. First, the girl spontaneously asks for clarification when she fails to understand the boy's opening statement – something that is not likely to happen in a learned dialogue. Second, the management of the financial transaction, with the shopkeeper making first mention of money, seems more appropriate than T'sepo's 'Here's the money' in the textbook dialogue, where the price is not mentioned.

However, there are also problems with this conversation. For instance, the girl makes a serious grammatical error when she omits 'do' in the question 'What you want?' The boy uses unidiomatic English when he fails to use a determiner like 'some' with 'rice' and uses 'the' in place of 'a' with 'lot of money'. Moreover, most of what is said is inappropriate because the children have not mastered the polite forms of English. While this type of activity has the advantage of allowing free expression in English, it does nothing to *teach* the forms that the children need to express themselves correctly and appropriately.

Some teachers have tried to resolve this paradox by providing both activities in the school week. Dramatic dialogues are used for learning correct forms actively, and at a later stage the children have an opportunity for free interaction. They are still likely to make mistakes in the free situation, of course, but there may be a gradual move towards accuracy.

Another approach is to provide the linguistic input or situational models via film, radio or video. The children watch a dramatised or real, documentary scene of people using language for specific tasks. For the children this is a fairly passive activity. The teacher might help the learners to observe specific features of the interaction such as the use of 'please' and 'thank you', perhaps comparing such words with politeness markers in the children's mother tongue. At a later stage, the free roleplay takes place. Theoretically the children will draw on the model they have seen to help them structure their language in the roleplay, but research is needed to establish whether or not all children can actually exploit what they have seen in this way. It would be difficult to establish how far such activities led to spontaneous use of English between children in their own play.

As yet we have no definite evidence of which approach is likely to produce the best results in the long term. It may be that different children learn better with different methods or that all children would benefit from experiencing a combination of approaches.

There is some evidence that what is known as 'structured play' in pre-school years helps native speakers to achieve better results in school. In structured play an adult (parent or teacher) talks through how the child is going to spend his/her time in a particular session. Thus, the teacher might run through the main stages of the particular game or activity, illustrating new words with objects, pictures or demonstration. This approach might be of value with language learners – it would provide them with some of the language they might need to talk about the tasks they were performing *in English*. Once more, however, the research is in the early stages.

The maintenance of communication between teacher and pupils

Far more is known about how children can be encouraged to use English with the teacher. Many teachers use what is known about interaction in order to help maintain communication with the class.

As learners gain more confidence in using the language, they begin to respond in a variety of ways to the teacher's attempts at interaction. At the early stages of language learning some children will remain silent when the teacher talks to them in English. Others will often respond in the home language. A few will try to use English, even if only to repeat the teacher's question or parrot a few of the teacher's words. These different responses are all quite natural and care must be taken not to make children feel foolish if they don't respond in the way the teacher expects.

It can be very helpful if a teacher trains learners early in the use of such expressions as: 'I'm sorry, I don't understand'; 'Would you please repeat that?'; 'I'm sorry. Let me try again.'

The teaching of such expressions 'gives permission' as it were for the children to be honest and admit to non-comprehension. For some children, this prevents a great deal of the worry and tension that can arise from not knowing how to respond. Partial comprehension can also be accommodated if children learn formally in the language class how to express such ideas as, 'I don't understand "*shells*" '; 'Please explain "*fish bone*".'

Incidentally this training also prevents the development of common errors such as, 'What means "shells"?', a badly formed question often heard from the lips of more confident speakers who try to use what they know. Teaching the correct expressions is one way of helping learners survive in communicative situations.

Unless children are taught how to respond politely in English when they do not understand, their reaction will usually be puzzled silence. Inexperienced teachers may in turn react to such silence by giving up all attempts at natural communication with the learners in English. There are, however, resources that the teacher can call on to help maintain communication when a child fails to respond appropriately to a remark in English.

Oduol (1985) studied the way experienced teachers reacted to a breakdown in communication between teacher and students in primary school. The classes he observed (and recorded on cassette) were of children aged between nine and eleven years in Kenyan primary schools, who had been learning English for three years, but not in ideal circumstances.

In his recorded corpus of lessons, there were many occasions when the children did not respond appropriately to the teacher's questions or directives. He found that there were four different ways in which the teachers responded to children's silence and re-established communication:

a) Repeating what he/she has said using the same words.
b) Re-wording what he/she has said.
c) Saying something different.
d) Translating what he/she has said into the children's first language.

One of these four strategies often helped to get the conversation going again. In the following exchange we can see an example of a teacher using both a Type (a) strategy and a Type (c) strategy:

TEACHER: 'Next'. What is the meaning of 'next'?
STUDENT: (no response)
TEACHER: Now, who is sitting next to you?
(pause)
Who is sitting next to you?
STUDENT: It is Gatei.

The teacher's first question is an extremely difficult one to answer. Many native English speaking children would find it difficult to explain the meaning of 'next', not least because 'next' has a number of different meanings and uses in English, some concerned with time and some with place. When the child does not reply, the teacher realises that her question was too difficult and changes it to a completely different question, 'Who is sitting next to you?' This question tests whether the child understands the meaning of the word 'next' used in context, which is all the teacher needs to know. Here the teacher has used the Type (c) strategy.

When she still doesn't get an immediate response, she uses the Type (a) strategy and repeats the second question. This gives the learner time to understand the question and to formulate an answer. The expected answer ('It is Gatei') does not give a definition of 'next', but it shows just as conclusively that the learner understands the meaning of the expression 'next to', which is what the teacher actually wanted to find out.

An example of the Type (b) strategy is seen in the next exchange, where the teacher is talking about pieces of rock:

TEACHER: Okay now. Why can't they change?
STUDENT: (no response)
TEACHER: They cannot grow bigger. They cannot grow smaller. Why?
STUDENT: Because . . . because they are non-living.

The teacher here seemed to sense that the children did not understand the word 'change' in this context. Quite correctly she predicted that they would know 'bigger' and 'smaller', and communication was re-established.

In the next exchange we see the teacher using a Type (c) strategy to keep the communication going:

TEACHER: I told you that a knife can be very dangerous if you do not use it properly. What other things can hurt us?

STUDENTS: (no response)
TEACHER: There is something that we use when we are cooking, and this can be very dangerous. Who can give me the name of this thing that we use when we are cooking?
STUDENTS: Fire.

In this example of Type (c), the teacher moves from a general question with many possible answers to a specific question that refers back to something discussed in a previous lesson. This reminds the children of the earlier discussion and, even though the teacher's language is quite complex, the words 'cooking' and 'dangerous' trigger the correct reply, 'fire'.

These examples illustrate the fact that simple English does not necessarily consist of fewer words or shorter sentences. Some types of supposed simplification can actually make comprehension more difficult because the grammar is more complex or because clues that would help understanding are omitted. This can be a particular problem with inexperienced teachers because there are few general principles that can be taught about what is easy or difficult to understand in natural language. What is easy depends on the experience of the learners in question.

In one of the classrooms studied, for example, the teacher was asking some questions relating to the story of a thief. The teacher asked, 'Was he caught?', but none of the children responded. The teacher then re-worded the question with the longer and superficially more complex, 'Did the police catch him?' and the children immediately responded correctly. This may have been because the learners were not familiar with the passive voice or the irregular past participle ('caught') in English, or it may have been because the reference to 'the police' helped them to understand the question. Whatever the reason, the re-wording had the desired effect.

Oduol's research showed that the Type (d) strategy, resorting to the first language (or 'code switching'), was a device commonly used by experienced teachers, as in this exchange where the teacher uses Kiswahili:

TEACHER: Now, they are divided into two groups, and the groups are animals *with* a backbone and animals *without* a backbone. Where is the backbone?
STUDENTS: (no response)
TEACHER: Backbone *ni huu mfupa uko hapa kwa mgongo* (*is this bone here at the back*). It is this bone here at the back. Can you feel it is hard here?
STUDENTS: Yes.

It is clear from this and many other examples in the recordings that the most efficient teachers use the more familiar language briefly to make a particular point, but discourage the learners from maintaining the communication in that language. After using the more familiar Kiswahili, the teacher immediately reverted to English. She repeated the information in English, asked the question in English and expected a response in English, which is what she got.

In all the examples of re-establishing communication given here from Oduol's research, the questions are classroom questions – that is to say, the teacher knew the answers and the children knew that the teacher knew. They were not *real* questions from the functional point of view. Oduol's recordings of primary classrooms reinforce the view, also established in other research, that real questions in the target language are actually very rare. Nevertheless, the strategies for the maintenance of communication are just as valuable with real interaction as they are with the make-believe of the Kenyan classroom, and teachers who wish to train their students to be confident in communicative situations will develop their strategies for maintaining communication in English.

Conclusion

Many years ago Michael West (1960), language teacher and author of children's extensive reading books, expressed his concern at the way teachers were judged by their success in passing pupils on to the higher stages of education. He regretted that exams were often measures of fitness for further study rather than measures of whether the learner knew anything of use to him/her at that time. He was concerned that language learning should, like a good insurance policy, have a 'high surrender value' even for those students who did not go on with their English studies up to university or college level. Every learner, he believed, should be able 'to go on talking after he/she leaves school. If he/she does not go on speaking the language, he/she will not go on learning: on the contrary, he/she will soon forget that which he/she has learnt'.

In many countries the examination system has not changed; it is geared to the most successful learners and their higher ambitions. Prodromou, (op. cit.) refers to what he calls the 'great Greek paper chase', the hunt for qualifications that naturally only the best succeed in achieving. The good teacher, however, will not be misled into merely coaching for examinations that will be of advantage only to the few but will teach in such a way that all learners, even from the earliest stages, are able to make the most of their limited linguistic knowledge to interact with others in the language. Early practice in interaction will not hinder those who are able to reach the highest levels of language study, and it will certainly build the confidence and skills of the majority.

Allwright (1984) argues that an important aspect of interaction is that it must be 'managed' by the learners as well as by the teacher. That is to say that the learners must be confident enough to initiate communication in English, not merely respond when they are addressed by the teacher. A learner who has something to say, an apology or a request to make, a question to ask, a greeting to give, should be encouraged to express him/herself in English. This is particularly important in places where young learners have the chance to study English. If resources are not to be wasted and opportunities missed, children must learn English in the way that they learned their own language, as a living language that can be used for active communication and for establishing personal relationships.

Bibliography

Allwright, D. 1984a. 'Why don't learners learn what teachers teach? – the interaction hypothesis.' in **Singleton, D.M.** and **D.G. Little** (eds). *Language Learning in Formal and Informal Contexts.* Dublin: IRRAL.

Allwright, D. 1984b. 'The importance of interaction in classroom language learning.' *Applied Linguistics* 5/2: 156–171.

Allwright, D. 1988. *Observation in the Language Classroom.* London & New York: Longman.

Barnes, D. 1969. 'Language in the secondary classroom.' in **Barnes, D., H. Britten** and **H. Rosen.** *Language, the Learner and the School.* London: Penguin.

Billows, F.L. 1961. *The Techniques of Language Teaching.* London: Longman.

Bloor, M., T. Bloor, L.L. Masuka and E. Simelane. 1982. *New Primary English for Swaziland.* Grade 1 Teacher's Guide. London: Longman.

Fanselow, J.F. 1977. 'Beyond Rashomon – conceptualising and describing the teaching act'. *TESOL Quarterly* 11/1:17–39.

Oduol, C. 1987. Maintenance of communication in primary classrooms: some evidence for the role of elicitation and code-switching in English medium schools in Kenya. PhD Thesis. Birmingham: Aston University.

Phillips, T. 1985. 'Beyond lip service: discourse development after the age of nine.' in **Wells, G.** and **J. Nicholls** (eds). *Language Learning: an Interactional Perspective.* London: Falmer Press.

Prodromou, Luke. 1988. 'English as cultural action.' *ELT Journal* 42/2: 73–83.

West, Michael. 1960. *Teaching English in Difficult Circumstances.* London: Longman.

Julia Khan, University of Warwick, England

11 Using games in teaching English to young learners

Julia Khan takes up the theme that Shelagh Rixon has already addressed from a practical perspective. She draws on research in psychology and game theory and leads us towards the more formal analysis of principle found in Section Two of this book, while at the same time continuing to provide practical examples and illustrations.

CHILDREN PLAY and children want to play. Children learn through playing. In playing together, children interact and in interacting they develop language skills. Games provide contexts for play, reasons for playing and routines for playing.

This article explores the basis of these assertions in order to argue the importance of giving games a place amongst activities used in teaching English to young learners. It then considers how games might be categorised and how teachers might use and maybe develop them with confidence as part of their methodology. The different roles of language practice games and communicative language teaching games are considered in the context of current thinking on syllabus and methodology for ELT. Finally, some common misgivings about using games in the classroom are discussed and defused.

Why use games?

Characteristics of games

What is a game? Everyone feels intuitively that they know but definition is elusive. Perhaps we can say that, 'A game is played when one or more players compete or co-operate for pay-offs according to a set of rules' (Jones 1986). Alternatively, 'Gaming is competitive . . . rule-governed . . . goal-defined . . . Gaming has closure . . . gaming is engaging' (Rodgers 1981). The games of young children have their own special qualities: 'A true game is one that frees the spirit. It allows of no cares but those fictitious ones engendered by the game itself . . . Play is unrestricted, games have rules. Play may merely be the enactment of a dream but in each game there is a contest . . .' (Opie, I. and J. 1969).

The key characteristics for our purposes are these: games are activities governed by *rules*, which set up clearly defined *goals*. The achievement of these goals signals the end of the game. Games involve a *contest* either between players or between the players and the goal, and games should lead to having *fun*. Games are for playing, and this element of *play* is crucial.

Ground rules must be set for how games are played. The authority behind the rules and the contest lies in the game itself rather than with the player or teacher and the authority must be acknowledged if the game is to be played fairly. Children are usually very concerned with fairness and with preventing others from breaking the rules.

Children's games

Games are activities that children naturally and universally engage in. There is a certain timelessness in the pleasure children find in games and in how the nature of the games they play changes as they develop, ranging through fantasy, ritual, competition and luck.

Generations of children rediscover the same games and delight in playing them. Games may be seen as a route by which children come to terms with their social environment, presenting as they do a social situation which is firmly governed by rules but whose outcome is unknown. Piaget (1967) saw children's games as, 'the most admirable social institutions. The game of marbles for instance . . . contains an extremely complex system of rules . . . a code of laws, a jurisprudence of its own . . . If we wish to gain any understanding of child morality it is obviously with the analysis of such facts as these that we must begin. All morality consists in a system of rules . . .' It is of course not our present concern to explore morality but to remember that children play games, and to take account of these natural tendencies when developing teaching strategies for young learners.

Children want to play

It is clear then that games – since children naturally want to play them – can be motivating. In pedagogical discussion of motivation for foreign and second language learning in general, emphasis is often put on the sometimes conflicting forces of 'instrumental' motivation and 'integrative' motivation (McDonough 1981). A learner of a foreign language who is instrumentally motivated is concerned to develop competence in the language for reasons such as passing an examination, improving job prospects, gaining prestige or needing to study in the medium of the target language. A learner who is integratively motivated is committed in some way to establishing closer links with the language community within which the language is used. Sometimes a learner's strong desire to pass an exam or to get a new job will create enough motivation to lead to success in language learning even if the teaching leaves much to be desired. The same may also be true of integrative motivation for the mature learner. But for the young learner, motivation deriving from factors outside the classroom, such as parental and social attitudes, is likely to be weaker than that created by events in the classroom itself. Children need to be involved and even excited in order to learn effectively.

Some of the recent major advances in educational psychology focus on the need that children have to be actively involved in whatever they do in order to succeed in learning. Bruner (1983) speaks of the need for teachers to engage in a 'battle against passivity'. Donaldson (1978) argues strongly that all children have the right and the capacity to succeed and that schools must offer all children opportunities to succeed if they are to educate them effectively. She quotes Bruner – 'We get interested in what we are good at' – as a central truth. Burstall (1974) reported that the major finding of a project in Britain on the teaching of French to young learners was that 'Nothing succeeds like success.'

The discriminating use of games in the young learners' classroom can help in creating, on a small scale, opportunities for involvement and excitement, for achievement and success. And children who are eager to take part in playing a well chosen game will want to master the language necessary for doing so.

Developing language through interaction

Games usually lead to social as well as intellectual involvement since players need to communicate in order to compete or co-operate, to organise or argue.

Wells (1981), in working on first language acquisition, found clear evidence that a child who has a lot of opportunities for negotiating meaning – for making sure that he/she has properly understood what is being said – develops language skills more rapidly than a child who does not. Games can create these opportunities in the foreign or second language classroom by setting out situations where children urgently need and want to communicate in order to have a turn at playing, to point out the rules, to challenge another player and so on.

Games and the communicative approach to English Language Teaching (ELT)

Many of the points made about games hitherto echo the fundamental principles of communicative approaches to language teaching. A brief exploration of how the two correspond will clarify some of the reasons for using games.

It is a principle of communicative approaches to ELT that task-based activities enhance learning. In language learning, task-based activities are those which stimulate effective use of language but involve no conscious analysis of language. An exercise which instructs learners to change the tense of verbs is not task-based because it is language-focused. Getting learners to listen carefully to instructions in order to draw a picture, make a model or play a game are examples of a task-based approach. The purpose perceived by the learners is non-linguistic. The understanding and use of language is necessary but the analysis of language is not. Some of the most powerful ideas developed recently on syllabus and methodology for language teaching derive from this central notion of the importance of task-based work (Breen 1987, Nunan 1989, Prabhu 1987). It is argued that if tasks are identified as the main elements of the syllabus, then syllabus and methodology will control each other. Getting learners involved in tasks will thus be a catalyst for language learning.

It is a *sine qua non* of a game that it has clearly defined goals – that these are motivating and provide the 'purpose' of the game. To play a game is to enjoy competing alone or in groups against other players, against time or against the challenge of the game, and not to think consciously about the language involved in doing so. In other words, games may be seen as tasks. If they successfully engage the learners' attention as a proper children's game should, then learning will be supported. Young (1983) describes the use of specially devised communication games and out-of-classroom games to supplement a traditional syllabus in primary schools in Hong Kong; using games in this way as a supplementary activity in order to give children the opportunity to use language purposefully and playfully may be a comfortable and sensible route to follow.

The interactive principle is also central to communicative approaches to ELT. Work on second language development echoes findings about the way in which negotiation and interaction help first language development (Ellis 1985). Opportunities for using a language in order to interact effectively – even if inaccurately – with someone else, help learning to take place. It was assumed for a long time that such opportunities would occur naturally only outside the classroom and, for the foreign language learner, only during visits overseas. But the creation of social contexts inside the classroom where interaction needs to take place in the target language is an important part of any communicative methodology. If a learner can be put into a situation where sheer need to use the language makes him/her strive to do so as effectively as possible, that experience contributes to language learning. Using the language is the best way of learning to use it. Involving children in games which they are very eager to play may be a good way of creating a powerful need to use the language.

A third important principle of communicative methodology is that the teaching situation must be learner-centred. Learners' needs both as future language users and active language learners should be the chief criterion for assessing how appropriate syllabus and methods are. We can relate this principle to what we have already said about motivation, involvement and the need for success. Krashen (1982) applied several of these principles to the field of second language teaching and one of the concepts he developed was that of the 'affective filter'. He sees the affective filter as being the emotional disposition of an individual which acts upon learning processes. A high affective filter causes the learner to be a relatively inefficient learner and is likely to result from anxieties, disturbances or inhibitions. A low affective filter which may result from feelings of relaxation, well-being or success maximises learning efficiency. If it is a condition of games that they contain an element of fun and that they absorb the interest of the learner, it seems clear that using them in the classroom will produce a low affective filter in participants. Accordingly, the capacity of learners to learn should be acknowledged and brought out. Teachers of young learners may find acknowledging the natural tendencies and desire of children to play and incorporating games into classroom activities in a well-ordered and purposeful way to be an effective strategy.

The arguments for using games run parallel with and indeed are simply a part of the broader arguments and theoretical justifications of adopting a communicative approach to ELT.

Which games?

Children may wish to play games for fun. Teachers, however, need more convincing reasons! We have explored the general pedagogical justification for using games. We now come to the classroom specifics. Teachers need to consider which games to use, when to use them, how to link them up with the syllabus, textbook or programme and how, more specifically, different games will benefit children in different ways.

This section builds up a system for identifying the procedures and characteristics of different games, which should indicate whether a game is useful and what demands it makes.

Most textbooks published for young learners in recent years incorporate some games. A useful selection of resource books and teachers' books is also available, providing ideas for a range of games for young learners (a brief list is provided at the end of this chapter). There are also a number of games referred to in other chapters of this book. Our purpose here is not to duplicate any of those but to create an analytical framework suggesting ways of selecting games to suit particular contexts and learners. Games referred to are explained in the appendix to this paper.

The pedagogical focus of games

Games to be used for ELT must in some way be language dependent. The specific language focus of a game could be items of vocabulary or particular structures or functions. The language skill focus could be any one of the major skills of listening, speaking, reading or writing, with a narrower focus on, for example, spelling or pronunciation. 'Simon says', for example, uses a range of language including the function of giving instructions, imperatives and vocabulary for parts of the body. The leader of the game has to produce all these items orally and the players have to listen and respond with understanding. The teacher could therefore justify the game as consolidation of the language items or as listening practice.

Another example is 'Spelling bee' which focuses on whatever vocabulary items the teacher selects. The skills involved are very restricted – listening and speaking – with all the emphasis on accuracy of spelling. The teacher could justify the game as vocabulary development, or listening or spelling practice.

At the pedagogical level then, the focus of the game should match what the teacher wants to teach. This formula may not be as simple as it sounds, however. Focusing on specific language items may be one dimension of language learning, but learners also benefit from being put into situations where they are very eager to communicate but have to manage with what language they have. In the previous section we noted that task-based activities are not normally language-focused. We shall consider these points again below in discussing features of language practice games and communication games.

Young learners often find it is worth learning language in order to play a good game! The involvement and enthusiasm generated by the game itself may give an important boost to children's motivation. And playing the game is for the children an authentic opportunity for language use.

Patterns of organisation

The way in which games are organised varies a great deal. Some games are played in pairs, some in groups, some in teams, some with the whole class playing against the teacher or one leader. This factor may help the teacher decide whether a game is suitable. Is it going to lead to 'dangerous' situations where learners are outside the immediate control of the teacher? Is it going to involve moving a lot of furniture? Are frequent changes of place going to disrupt the class? Is it going to lead to noisy, excited competition between teams?

The pattern of organisation has clear implications for the sort of language activity that a game will engender and is itself controlled by the rules and closure or outcome of the game. A game played in pairs may involve more children in oral interaction for longer than a teacher-led game. 'Find the difference', for example, played by negotiating pairs, involves extensive oral interchange. 'Vocabulary snap', on the other hand, is played in groups and involves reading practice of a limited number of words, repeated oral production of 'Snap' and perhaps some oral negotiation relating to dealing cards, taking turns and who said 'Snap' first! Each game has its own characteristic range of language activity.

Materials and equipment

Teachers may also be strongly influenced in their choice of game by the nature of the materials needed. Computer games, board games, card games, box games, paper and pencil games, blackboard games, question and answer games . . . the level of materials and equipment involved varies considerably. Availability and expense will be major factors in selection as will the effort of organising children's groups, and conservation and storage of materials.

'Ludic' principles

We have already discussed the nature of games. Here we can usefully identify characteristic differences between games in terms of game-related or 'ludic' principles, providing the teacher with another way of defining what is being undertaken and whether it is appropriate. It will also be a way of approaching the invention of games to suit particular purposes, a way perhaps of turning other activities into games.

The ludic principles or playing spirit of a game may derive from a number of elements which give a game its particular tone. For example, different games involve different combinations of the conflicting forces of chance and skill. On the whole young learners like games which have an element of luck because it can add to the excitement and reduces the socially divisive nature of 'clever' games. For teachers with a wide range of ability in the class, an element of luck is very important in a game. Games entirely dependent on skill have the tiresome habit of producing the same few winners repeatedly and thereby rapidly reducing the level of involvement of the majority of the players. Games with a powerful element of chance include guessing games, games with a dice or randomly dealt cards.

Other ludic principles are those of competition and co-operation. One game may be driven by competition between players; another game may require co-operation in order for play to proceed. Some games of course involve both. Whilst every game has within it an element of competition, it may be that players need to co-operate with each other in order to compete against the challenge that the game sets up. 'Describe and draw', for example, involves players in co-operative negotiation in order to beat the challenge of transferring information orally from one given graphic to another. If either one of the pair did not co-operate, the game could not proceed. 'Find the difference' similarly requires co-operation.

Co-operation in a game therefore encourages verbal negotiation. Many games are purely competitive of course and winning may be the perceived objective of an individual, a group or a team. With young learners it is important for winning to come everyone's way at some point in order to maintain involvement and enthusiasm. Using teams and groups also helps to reduce the individual pressures of competition.

Uncertainty, caused by demands made on memory, is another ludic principle, important in some types of game. 'Grandmother went to market', for example, is a game because players' memories will fail at some stage; the excitement comes from the challenge of uncertainty!

Bearing in mind these principles – chance and skill, competition and co-operation, uncertainty – that are at the heart of many games may help a teacher to turn a textbook-led language exercise into a game. Introducing an element of competition into a language activity is something teachers often do in order to stimulate effort ('Who can finish first?') Sole use of that ludic principle can, however, be discouraging.

Subtler approaches may be more effective. Straightforward question and answer activities between teacher and pupils ('Where is the pen? It's next to the rubber/on the book/behind the cup') can be livened up for example by introducing the memory principle ('Look at the things on the table. Now turn round ... Where is the pen? Where is the cup? ...). Possible adaptations are many.

Finally and most importantly perhaps in identifying the characteristic features of games we must consider the ways in which the procedures of games, by setting up particular patterns of activity, offer different kinds of opportunity for language development.

Language practice games

We can define language practice games as those which involve repeated use of particular language items, where the language form is given and controlled and where accuracy of reproduction or spelling is required in order for the player to succeed. Games of this sort are in many ways like language drills; they offer opportunities for repetition of language items that are intended to be learned because it is assumed that engaging in such repetition will lead to learning of the language. Rixon (1981) refers to such games as code-control games.

Using games may certainly be an effective way of making repetition of language natural and purposeful for young learners. Many games involve routines and repetitive formulae, which may be part of their charm for young children who often relish the familiarity of favourite activities. The formulae involved in 'I spy with my little eye' or in 'Happy families' are the routine of the game itself and very much a means to the end of playing the game. Such games might be considered as the palatable side of behaviourist ideas of how language is learned by repeated imitative use and reinforcement. Language practice games might thus be seen as fulfilling a useful role amongst the 'pre-communicative' activities of a broad communicative approach to language teaching (Littlewood 1981).

Second and foreign language development probably owes no more than first language development to behaviourist patterns of learning by stimulus, response and reinforcement. Equally however it is clear that much authentic first language use amongst young children involves repetitive language routines in play. Activities in the classroom which draw upon this natural predilection are unlikely to be rejected if they are used with restraint. They will never on their own be capable of creating in learners a capacity for communicative use of language but they may be a very valuable technique for familiarising children with new language and giving them the confidence to produce that language. Such games may, arguably, still be seen as 'tasks'.

It is worth remembering that a lot of negotiating often goes on in these games as part of managing the game. While the formal focus of the game may appear to be tightly controlled and accuracy- and practice-orientated, incidental discussion goes on about whose turn it is, whether the rules have been broken, or about someone who isn't paying attention and doing what they should be. This is a valuable part of the activity in the English language classroom where the medium is also the message.

Communicative language teaching games

Within a communicative language teaching game the emphasis is on the message being transmitted by the medium of the language rather than on the language itself.

According to Palmer and Rodgers (1983), there are six features which can be seen to greater or lesser extent in communicative language teaching games: the players have to interact; they have to deal with some unpredicted information; they have a clear purpose; the context of the activity is clear; players have to be actively involved; they are given a particular role to play.

More simply, communicative language teaching games can be seen as pair or group games where the need to communicate is powerful and urgent but no fixed language formulae are available or adequate for doing so. The game is the task which sets off the search for the necessary language. The theory of language development underlying the use of such games for foreign language teaching is that language development ensues when learners are put into an interactive situation with which they can just about cope by drawing on language resources and communication strategies. The situation is the game.

'Find the difference', for example, is a communicative language teaching game insofar as the routine, rules and objective of the game make it necessary for information to be transmitted from one player to the other. Hadfield's imaginative collection (1984) offers a range of games within which players, often using cue-cards, seek their partners, plan days out, try to work out routes, transmit information to each other about bus times, shopping lists, family members, items in pictures of rooms and so on. Such games can provide excellent models on which the teacher can base other games in his/her own particular context.

In brief, then, in deciding which games to use a teacher has to bear in mind a number of points. Does the game focus on appropriate language items and skills? Can it be organised within his/her classroom? Are materials available or 'makeable'? Are the learners going to find the degree of competitiveness or co-operation stimulating? Is the balance between skill and luck right for the class? Are the children at a stage where they will benefit from familiarisation through repetitive practice? Do they need the stimulation of situations where they have to struggle a little but which are fun because of the challenge, and can they cope with them?

The questions are many but may be quickly dealt with by the teacher who has begun to use games as a teaching technique and resource. The appendix at the end of this paper presents all the games referred to and indicates how their key features may be identified in terms of the analytic framework laid out in this section.

Meeting the critics

There are numerous misapprehensions about the use of games in the language teaching classroom. An effective way of synthesising what has been said so far and of focusing on some of the uses of games for teaching English to young learners is to identify and discuss some of these misapprehensions.

'Games are not serious and cannot therefore be treated seriously as part of a methodology for teaching English.'

It is true that many games are seen by the players as fun rather than work. A serious objective can be approached by many routes, however, not only those which preclude fun. A teacher perceives classroom objectives differently from children. Statements of syllabus (the teacher's perception) are not intended as a means of explaining to children the purpose of their activities.

'Games can only ever be decorative extras – time-fillers perhaps.'

This attitude builds upon the previous one, implying that worthwhile learning takes place only when teaching activities are declared to be such to the learners. Krashen and Terrell (1982) would claim the opposite: '. . . experienced instructors who work with children know that they become more involved more quickly within an activity if it is presented in a game format.' Our earlier discussion of the nature of tasks identified the fundamental principle of communicative approaches to language teaching that using language to succeed in a task is one of the most profitable ways of developing competence. A game is, for young learners, a task.

'Games belong outside the classroom.'

It is sometimes argued that classroom games lack authenticity – children only really believe in the games they organise for themselves in the playground, the street, the home. To set up such a divide between children's lives outside school and in the classroom seems to ignore the intense importance to children of their school relationships and involvements. Breen (1985) argues that learning activities are fully authentic for eager learners (more so in the classroom than imported, simulated situations can be). The classroom is a social context with as much reality for those participating in it as any context outside the classroom. For young learners who enter into friendships, enmities, arguments, sulks, resentments, fears and excitements with such very real passion and involvement in the classroom, it is very unconvincing to argue that appropriately managed games cannot engender as much involvement inside the classroom as outside.

'If children get involved and excited in playing games, they will use their first language and gain no benefit in English.'

It may indeed happen where children are playing games in groups or pairs that breakdown in communication or eagerness to finish a game tempts them to switch languages. Persuasion is always worth trying. Children are quite able to understand that if their lesson is intended to help them learn English, they should use English. It is also worth remembering the power of the rules of a game; if the rule is to conduct as much of the game as possible in English, that has some authority.

We should also bear in mind, however, that switching between languages is a recognised communication strategy resorted to by many efficient language learners when faced with communication breakdown. For young learners striving to become efficient learners, the strategy will be a natural resort. Occasional use of it is an indication of normal learning processes in operation. They can be encouraged to switch back to English once the immediate problem has been solved. The attentive teacher will be able to observe and remedy the cause of breakdown.

'Games are noisy and therefore disruptive.'

Games may focus on oral or written language, use a wide range of patterns of organisation and procedures, focus on a vast selection of activities. Certain activities will be potentially noisier than others; certain procedures will be more difficult to organise with a large or boisterous class than others. But the most powerful threat to good order in the classroom comes from lack of learner interest in what is going on. High levels of motivation are conducive to good order. Purposeful and involving games may be a strong support to motivation. The promise of play becomes an effective way of maintaining order.

Conclusion

We have discussed why games might be used in teaching English to young learners and tried to indicate clearly the many dimensions that need to be taken into account in selecting and organising games if they are to become an important part of a teacher's repertoire. Once teachers have discovered the enthusiasm they can engender in children, they are not likely to be deterred by the classic misapprehensions outlined above. It remains a powerful truth that play is in the essential nature of the child. The teacher who has the confidence to recognise that and to direct and exploit it for language learning purposes will soon reap the benefits in the classroom.

Appendix

This appendix describes all the games mentioned in the chapter. Many of the games are quite well-known and many are played outside the classroom as well as being useful in it.

Each game is classified in terms of the categories identified in the paper. The playing rules (procedure) are also described for each game.

Simon says

Teaching focus:	Instructions, imperatives, parts of the body, action verbs
Organisation:	Whole class v. leader
Materials:	None
Ludic principles:	Competitive (individuals), skill
Game type:	Language practice
Procedure:	The leader instructs the players to perform actions. The players only follow the instructions if they are preceded by, 'Simon says . . .'. e.g.

Simon says sit down (players should all sit down)
Simon says put your hands on your head (everyone should do so)
Clap your hands (nobody should clap).

The leader can 'mislead' players by demonstrating all instructions as he/she calls them out. Players who make a mistake and follow instructions without 'Simon says' are eliminated from the game. The winner is the last remaining player, who then becomes 'Simon'.

Spelling bee

Teaching focus:	Spelling of vocabulary items
Organisation:	Two teams and questioner/leader
Materials:	None
Ludic principles:	Competitive (in teams), skill (and luck also, depending on choice of words)
Game type:	Language practice
Procedure:	Both teams stand up. The questioner asks one player at a time (alternating between teams) to spell a word. If the player succeeds, he/she remains standing. If he/she fails, he/she sits down and the next member of the other team answers. The *losing* team is the one where everyone is sitting down first.

Describe and draw

Teaching focus:	Function of describing with particular emphasis on prepositions relating to position; vocabulary items according to the drawing
Organisation:	Pairs
Materials:	Drawable pictures or diagrams
Ludic principles:	Co-operative
Game type:	Communicative
Procedure:	Child A has a picture which he/she must not show to his/her partner, Child B, but must describe so that Child B can draw a version of it. Child B can ask as many questions as he/she likes but must not peep at Child A's original picture. Child A can watch Child B drawing and can explain mistakes but not redraw. The game closes when A decides that B's drawing is close enough to the original *or* when time is finished.

Grandmother goes to market

Teaching focus:	Items that may be bought (allowing a little fantasy!)
Organisation:	Whole class and leader
Materials:	None
Ludic principles:	Competitive, memory-based
Game type:	Language practice
Procedure:	The first player says, 'Grandmother went to market and she bought a . . . (any item).' The second player continues, 'Grandmother went to market and she bought a (first player's item) and a . . . (any other item).' The sequence continues, each player having to reproduce the whole list thus far. When a mistake is made, that player is out and the next player starts a new list. The winner is the last remaining player.

Find the difference

Teaching focus:	Asking for and giving information, describing; vocabulary as indicated by pictures
Organisation:	Pairs
Materials:	Pairs of pictures which are similar but not identical
Ludic principles:	Co-operative, luck and skill
Game type:	Communicative

Procedure:	Each member of the pair has one picture. They must not look at each other's pictures but must ask questions in order to identify a given number of differences. The game ends when they have found all the differences *or* when a given time ends.

I spy

Teaching focus:	Vocabulary relating to items in the room; spelling – initial letters; Question, 'Is it a . . . ? Yes, it is/No, it's not.'
Organisation:	Whole class v. one player
Materials:	None
Ludic principles:	Competitive, luck
Game type:	Language practice
Procedure:	The first player stands at the front, silently selects a visible item in the room, and declares, 'I spy with my little eye something beginning with _____ (initial letter).' The other children raise their hands to volunteer suggestions (the player at the front selects one at a time). 'Is it a . . .? Yes, it is/No, it's not a . . . .' Whoever guesses correctly changes places with the player at the front and declares, 'I spy with my little eye . . .' and the game proceeds.

Happy families

Teaching focus:	Polite requests 'Please have you got . . .?' and answers 'Yes, I have/No, I haven't.'
Organisation:	Groups of four to six
Materials:	Playing cards containing families of four cards – Mr, Mrs, Master and Miss + names + professions or country of origin. Total of 40 to 48 cards.
Ludic principles:	Competitive, luck, memory
Game type:	Language practice and communicative
Procedure:	The whole pack is dealt out equally. Players look at their own cards and sort them into families. The objective is to collect families. Whole families are placed on the table. Players ask each other in turn for the cards they need to make their families complete and the player asked must give up the card he/she has been asked for if he/she has it. The winner is the player who collects the largest number of families.

Vocabulary snap

Teaching focus: Reading of vocabulary (as it appears on the cards)

Organisation: Groups of four to six

Materials: Playing cards with single words written on them. There should be four or five cards with the same word and a total of about 50 or 60 cards.

Ludic principles: Competitive, luck, skill (in reading)

Game type: Language practice

Procedure: The cards are dealt out randomly to all the players in the group. They are dealt out face down and the players hold them face down. In turn, each player turns a card and places it in front of him/her to form his/her own pile. When the cards at the top of the two piles are the same, any member of the group may call, 'Snap'. The first player to do so collects all the cards in those two piles. The winner is the player who collects all the cards.

Bibliography

Resources

Byrne, D. 1980. *A First Book of Board Games.* London: Modern English Publications.

Carrier, M. and **The Centre for British Teachers**. 1980. *Take 5.* London: Nelson.

Dorry, G.N. 1966. *Games for Language Learning.* London & New York: McGraw-Hill.

Hadfield, J. 1984. *Communication Games.* London: Harrap.

Lee, W.R. 1986. *Language Teaching Games and Contests.* Oxford: Oxford University Press.

McCallum, G. 1980. *101 Word Games.* Oxford: Oxford University Press.

Retter, C. and N. Valls. 1984. *Bonanza: 77 English Language Games for Young Learners.* Harlow: Longman.

Rixon, S. 1981. *How to Use Games in Language Teaching.* London: Macmillan.

Rixon, S. 1983. *Fun and Games.* London: Macmillan.

Wright, A., D. Betteridge and M. Buckby. 1984. *Games for Language Learning.* Cambridge: Cambridge University Press.

References

Breen, M. 1985. 'Authenticity in the language classroom.' *Applied Linguistics* 6/1.60–70.

Breen, M. 1987. 'Contemporary paradigms in syllabus design Part II.' *Language Teaching* 20.3 157–174.

Bruner, J.S. 1983. *In Search of Mind.* New York: Harper & Row.

Bruner, J.S., A. Jolly and K. Sylva (eds). 1976. *Play – its Role in Development and Evolution.* London: Penguin.

Burstall, C. et al. 1974. *Primary French in the Balance.* Slough: Nelson/NFER.

Donaldson, M. 1978. *Children's Minds.* London: Fontana.

Ellis, R. 1985. *Understanding Second Language Acquisition.* Oxford: Oxford University Press.

Hadfield, J. 1984. *Harrap's Communication Games.* London: Harrap.

Jones, K. 1986. 'Games, simulations, Wittgenstein.' *Simulation/games for learning – The Journal for SAGSET* 16/2. 47–54.

Krashen, S.D. 1982. *Principles and Practice in Second Language Acquisition.* Oxford: Pergamon Press.

Krashen, S.D. and T.D. Terrell. 1983. *The Natural Approach.* Oxford: Pergamon Press.

Littlewood, W. 1981. *Communicative Language Teaching: An Introduction.* Cambridge: Cambridge University Press.

McDonough, S. 1981. *The Psychology of Foreign Language Teaching.* London: Allen & Unwin.

Nunan, D. 1989. *Designing Tasks for the Communicative Classroom.* Cambridge: Cambridge University Press.

Opie, I. and P. 1969. 'Street games: counting-out and chasing.' in Bruner, J.S. *et al.* 1976. London: Penguin.

Palmer, A. and T.S. Rodgers. 1983. 'Games in language teaching.' *Language Teaching* 16/1 2–21.

Piaget, J. 1965. 'The rules of the game of marbles.' in Bruner, J.S. *et al.* 1976. London: Penguin.

Prabhu, N.S. 1987. *Second Language Pedagogy: a Perspective.* Oxford: Oxford University Press.

Rixon, S. 1981. *How to Use Games in Language Teaching.* London: Macmillan.

Rodgers, T.S. 1981. 'A framework for making and using language teaching games.' in *Guidelines for Language Games* 1–7 Singapore, RELC.

Wells, G. 1981. *Learning through Interaction.* Cambridge: Cambridge University Press.

Young, R. 1983. 'The negotiation of meaning in children's foreign language acquisition.' *English Language Teaching Journal* 37/3 197–206.

Jean Brewster, Ealing College, England

12 Listening and the young learner

This paper addresses the theme of listening from a practical perspective. There is plentiful illustration of the principles outlined, but the emphasis is on linking theory to practice.

Listening in the primary EFL classroom

Listening in a foreign language is hard work. Our work as teachers of young children is much easier if the learners are motivated and enjoy what they are doing. It is up to us to ensure that the activities they are engaged in are interesting and/or fun. We also have to be clear about how much we want our children to listen in English and whether we expect them to understand everything they hear. This last expectation is of course unrealistic, yet teachers frequently behave as though it were possible. We should provide purposeful and carefully directed listening activities where learners are asked to focus on specific points. We must ensure that the children's learning is supported wherever necessary. Learners will also of course sometimes listen just for fun, without having to do anything with what they hear.

Studies of classroom interaction show that children spend a large part of their time listening – listening to the teacher, to each other or to pre-recorded material. Each time the teacher uses English to explain something, give instructions, tell a story or praise someone, he/she is making listening demands on the pupils. Problems are likely to arise if teachers do not teach children *how* to listen, so that they can cope effectively with these demands. All too often listening tasks ask children to demonstrate their understanding in question and answer sessions. This kind of activity simply encourages children to remember what they have just heard and tests recall rather than understanding, as McDonough (1981) writes, 'It is a truism to point out that the technique of asking questions after a reading or listening task is a testing technique and not a teaching technique.'

Preparing pupils for listening

To prepare pupils for the kinds of listening that are demanded in the classroom, teachers must develop a greater awareness of the kinds of listening demand they make on their pupils and set up a learning environment which makes easier the children's task of meeting these demands. This can be achieved in several ways:

a) By making explicit the reasons for listening to something – if the children know what they will be expected to do while or after listening, they can focus on the most important part of the message or simply listen for gist. This will normally be achieved by setting a specific task which may contain written or visual support and which allows the children to show their understanding by producing a 'product'. Such a product might be a drawing which is labelled while listening to explanations or instructions or a chart which is filled in while listening to descriptions.

b) By being aware of the most common listening demands they make on their pupils teachers can equip their pupils with specific strategies for different listening purposes, such as listening to follow instructions, explanations or descriptions.

c) By emphasising that children are not expected to understand or remember every word of a spoken message, teachers can build up their pupils' confidence in listening.

d) By encouraging pupils to exercise 'intelligent guesswork', using their background knowledge or context clues, such as pictures, to make sense of what they hear.

Thus teachers need actively to support their pupils' understanding of the spoken word and to equip them with a range of strategies on which they can draw.

Listening as part of the teaching programme

Teachers tend to take one of two approaches to the place of listening in the teaching programme. The first considers listening as part of a set of activities which is integrated with other skills work. For example the children might listen to a dialogue with a clear grammatical focus on tape or read aloud by the teacher as preparation for reading it themselves to practise specific grammatical patterns. Anderson and Lynch (1988) refer to this type of material as 'ancillary' listening, since it is normally linked structurally, functionally or thematically to the planned language learning focus of the lesson. The second considers listening as part of a set of activities which may not necessarily be closely integrated with the children's other language learning. This is referred to as 'autonomous' listening practice and may take the form of specially produced listening exercises, such as those in Scott (1980).

Listening as part of language acquisition

Whether listening is viewed as ancillary or autonomous the importance given to listening derives from the teacher's view of how children learn a foreign language. We can look at three approaches:

a) One view springs from the idea that language is a *linear* process and that listening provides the learner with confidence in speaking. These two skills – listening and speaking – together provide a backdrop for the subsequent teaching of reading and writing skills. The language content of the listening activities is closely monitored so that it is at the current level of the children's language learning.

b) The second view sees language learning as a *comprehension-focused* process where listening may be regarded as the primary source of language experiences. The first exposure to the L2 thus aims to provide learners with success in understanding the spoken language but not in producing it. Some of the language content in this case might be pitched at a slightly higher level than the stage which the children have reached.

c) The third approach regards language learning as an *integrative* process where from the outset all four skills are developed in parallel. In this method, learners are encouraged to make connections between skills, so that practice in one can reinforce another. They also develop thereby a more holistic view of how the L2 is used.

The first two approaches appear limited; (a) implies that listening can only be linked to speaking, while (b) implies that listening is linked only to the performance of certain actions. Teachers can most easily provide their learners with suitable frameworks of support and a variety of outcomes when listening by using other skills. Developing an awareness of the processes involved in comprehension necessarily invites us to see the links between reading and listening. Furthermore, the current focus in language learning on developing learners' ability to interact with one another meaningfully leads us to draw together the skills of listening and speaking. And one of the many ways in which children can demonstrate their understanding of a spoken text is through simple writing activities, such as labelling or chart-filling. The integrative approach to listening (c) appears to make a lot of sense for the primary classroom.

What is effective listening?

Language comprehension is generally seen as part of an interactive process arising from the complex interplay of the three main dimensions of interaction; the social, the cognitive and the linguistic. The social dimension takes account of the fact that interaction between people is the chief means of maintaining relationships and exchanging information. The cognitive dimension refers to the relationship between interaction and ideas; children hear ideas, suggest their own ideas and develop new ideas through talking and listening to others. The linguistic dimension refers to the ways in which participants interpret, predict and summarise components of the spoken message. As Smith (1975) writes, 'comprehension means relating new experiences to what is already known.'

Research into the ways in which children acquire listening skills and perform as listeners in their mother tongue is generally acknowledged to reveal useful insights into comprehension processes in foreign language learners (see Anderson and Lynch 1988). Studies of young learners' comprehension skills show that many aspects of listening are mastered at an early age, particularly in supportive, conversational contexts where social skills are highlighted. However, when the listening focus involves more demanding cognitive skills, such as processing information or monitoring the adequacy of a message, children frequently encounter problems. Training studies directed at improving the information-processing skills of children have been found to improve their performance.

All of these studies show that it is possible to improve children's ability to listen with understanding to their mother tongue. It seems, therefore, even more important to train children to listen with understanding in a foreign language. The question is, how feasible is it for children to develop strategies for listening to a foreign language which might draw upon what they know about their mother tongue?

Many authors currently take the view that there are several parallels between the processes involved in L1 acquisition and L2 learning (see Krashen 1981, Ellis 1986). It is felt that children, who already have experience of drawing upon different kinds of information source in understanding their first language, have the ability to transfer some of these skills and strategies to second language learning. The kinds of information source used in comprehension can be summarised under two main headings (adapted from Anderson and Lynch 1988 p.13):

a) Knowledge about the content of the spoken message

  - general knowledge to do with facts and information
  - sociocultural knowledge to do with topics, settings and participants in interaction
  - procedural knowledge about how language is used, for example, knowing that questions generally demand responses

b) Knowledge about the language used in the spoken message

  - recognition of items of vocabulary and sentence patterns
  - understanding of phonological features such as stress, intonation and sounds

While they are drawing upon these kinds of knowledge listeners are engaging in the process of constructing a coherent interpretation of the spoken word. This process, which involves selecting, interpreting and summarising input, emphasises the active and personal nature of successful listening. Thus it is not appropriate to describe listening as a 'passive' skill; listeners are just as much active participants in interpreting a spoken text as readers are active when making sense of a written text. These links between listening and reading are crucial in understanding comprehension processes. Another important link is that between talk and listening. In order to be an effective participant in interaction, the L2 learner has to develop skills in both speaking and listening. This interdependence means that learners need to be given opportunities to develop, practise and integrate both sets of skills.

The role of the teacher, therefore, is to encourage children to draw upon different information sources, skills and strategies in order to learn how to help themselves understand. Once teachers are aware of these processes, they will be able to include in their planning interactive or specific listening tasks focusing on one or more of these strategies. Six types of strategy are given below, described in the context of listening to a story.

1 Getting the general picture

This strategy is used when children are being encouraged to listen to a story simply for pleasure. In this case the learners do not attempt to focus their attention on or remember details but to listen for gist to get a general idea of what the story is about.

2 Predicting

This strategy is useful when children are trying to follow the sequence of events in a story. If the children are motivated and have some support for their understanding, they can be encouraged first to predict and then to check whether what they hear matches their expectation. This is an example of a learning context where knowledge of the language system and general knowledge based on previous experience of L1 stories work together to facilitate comprehension.

3 Extracting specific information

The focus here is on recognising specific components of the language system, such as selecting relevant adjectives to describe particular characters in a story to fill in a tick-chart or recognising specific verbs and nouns when matching pictures with events in a story. If the aim of the activity is listening comprehension rather than memory testing, for this strategy to work the learners need to know beforehand what kind of information to listen out for. The support materials (pictures and charts) help the learner distinguish relevant from irrelevant parts of the message.

4 Inferring opinion or attitude

An awareness of stress and intonation, combined with knowledge of lexical items and grammatical patterns, enables the learner to determine whether a character is happy, angry or sad and therefore to work out some of the context of the story.

5 Working out meaning from context

It must be made clear to children learning English that they will not be able or expected to understand every word in a story. Thus the teacher needs to develop their confidence in facing texts with new vocabulary. Key words may be glossed beforehand while visual support or written frameworks (for example charts) will help the learners understand detail. Some learners might be able to draw upon their knowledge of the language system. For example in the story, *The Very Hungry Caterpillar*, which describes the life-cycle of a butterfly, some learners might be able to work out that the use of the verb 'live' with the noun 'cocoon' must refer (in very simple terms) to a place where the caterpillar stays for some time.

6 Recognising discourse patterns and markers

Every story will have certain story-telling conventions, for example an introduction beginning, 'Many years ago there was a wicked witch . . .'. The recognition of discourse markers used in logical relationships, as well as the use of appropriate intonation, will help learners to work out some of the storyline. Examples are the use of 'but' and fall-rise intonation to express contrast, and the use of 'so' followed by falling intonation to express a result. Stories often include repeated sequences; these help learners to predict from the discourse markers what might happen next. Other sequence markers, such as 'first', 'then' and 'next', also enable learners to recognise and follow the stages in a story.

Developing a task-based methodology with children

The notion of 'task-based' learning in which there is a current growing interest is based on a learner-centred view of education. It is seen by many teachers as a means of creating purposeful contexts for learning which provide children with a more varied learning environment. It is also thought to be more motivating than traditional teacher-centred classrooms. Many courses such as the innovative *Jigsaw* (Abbs and Worrall 1980) have given recognition to this idea. However, the term 'task' has until recently rarely been defined, since its meaning is generally assumed to be obvious. This non-definition may have concealed some of the differences between various task types.

In examining the notion of 'task' many authors emphasise the requirement that it should involve some kind of cognitive process and should lead to very definite 'products'. This is neatly described by Ur (1981) who writes, 'each task consists of a thinking process and its outcome in the form of a tangible result. It is not enough just to think out a problem, or explore the ramifications of a conflict: the results must be written down, ticked off, listed, sketched or tape-recorded in some way.' (p.13)

This is a very clear working definition which sees tasks as process-outcome orientated. This view is echoed and taken to its logical conclusion by practitioners such as Prabhu (1983) who is best known for his development of the 'procedural syllabus' for language teaching. He takes the view that a language teaching syllabus should not contain a specification of language items, but rather the kinds of classroom activity which will cause 'genuine deployment' of language. This reflects an emphasis on creating active learning contexts where the child is engaged in purposeful activity. The language focus in this case has as its starting point the task itself rather than the strict specification of context-free language items which is determined beforehand. Not all teachers will feel comfortable with this kind of methodology or indeed feel free to adopt such procedures. However, it is worth considering a range of approaches and activities which might be used to facilitate and support children's comprehension skills in a way that fits in a wide variety of classroom contexts.

It is important to make a distinction between the teaching and testing of listening. The practice of asking children to listen to something with no support other than questions to answer after listening has many drawbacks. It concentrates too much on the testing of comprehension or memory rather than encouraging children to develop strategies for coping with the spoken message. This kind of methodology tends to overload the child's capacity for processing and retaining information. Thus the emphasis is placed on assessing what the children have understood rather than in supporting their understanding so that they can show that they have understood.

It is only when teachers direct the children's attention to the purpose of the listening task beforehand and provide a suitable framework for providing access to the spoken message that they can be said to be teaching listening. Possible frameworks to be used can take the form of pictures, charts or questions which aim to create interest and supply motivation and support for the successful completion of the task. This kind of methodology reflects the view that the listening process is a form of interaction between the listener and the text. The meanings which learners construct in this interactive process depend on the one hand on their 'set' to the text and on the other hand on the content and the language contained in the text. The 'set' can be described in terms of what the learner brings to the text, that is, the schematic knowledge described earlier such as background knowledge and feelings, attitudes or interest. The content of the text will of course draw upon linguistic items such as vocabulary and grammar as well as discourse features such as reference, lexical relations, logical connectors and intonation. This linguistic content may serve to refer to events, people, animals, places, objects, feelings, attributes, concepts and so forth. With the help of the teacher, who creates a context and a purpose for listening, the focus of the comprehension activity can be on any of these aspects.

Creating a listening purpose

The purposes of listening tasks which incorporate all the linguistic, social and cognitive dimensions discussed so far are summarised in Figure 1.

The role of the teacher in planning and setting up listening activities is thus to draw upon these different aspects to allow for the kind of interaction between listener and text referred to earlier. Such interaction is generally

Listening purposes

Listening to develop general 'language awareness'	listening for enjoyment, listening to improve concentration, attention span, attitude etc.
Listening to reinforce conceptual development	listening to stories, descriptions etc. to develop concepts of e.g. size, shape
Listening to develop specific language points and interactional skills	listening and pronunciation including recognition of sounds, stress and rhythm, aspects of intonation
	recognising and selecting words, grammatical patterns, or discourse features
	listening to understand specific language functions such as descriptions, descriptions of processes, explanations and instructions
	listening to collaborate with peers, i.e. interpreting others' points of view, negotiating meaning by asking for clarification, checking information etc.

Figure 1 The purposes of listening tasks.

achieved by thinking of the teaching of comprehension as having three phases; these are usually described in terms of pre-, while- and post-listening activities.

The first stage is an introduction or orientation to the text during which the teacher might elicit what the children already know about a topic by asking them questions, or create interest by relating aspects of the content to the children's own experiences. The teacher might use the L1 at this stage but, depending on the listening purpose, might need to move on to English to introduce, for example, the key vocabulary or grammatical items contained in the spoken text. The second stage involves an explanation of the purpose of the listening task so that the children are quite clear what their role is and whether they need to focus on specific aspects of the text. The purpose may be simply to listen and enjoy a story, song or rhyme in which case they can participate if the teacher wishes. If the listening purpose is to extract specific information it 'is at this point that the teacher will explain the task and refer to any visual or written support he/she has planned. The learners will then listen to the text, which may be pre-recorded or spoken by the teacher or another child, and complete the activity. The stage after this is then concerned with checking information by asking questions (oral or written) or by asking for feedback on any other outcomes the learners may have produced, such as completing a game, finding the correct sequence of events or drawing and labelling a picture.

The four types of listening purpose outlined above are looked at here in more detail:

Listening and language awareness

There has been much interest recently in creating learning contexts where the focus is not only learning the language for its own sake but learning about language. This kind of 'language awareness' (often referred to as 'metalinguistic awareness') is thought to have an important relationship with children's developing cognitive abilities. Pratt and Grieve (1984) argue that, 'the development of metalinguistic awareness in the pre-school and early school years is closely related to the child's developing ability to reflect upon the products of his own thought processes and apply his cognitive skills in a wide range of contexts.' (p.128)

Indeed, recent research points to the view that one of the positive effects of being bilingual is that it leads to an increase in such metalinguistic awareness.

In relation to listening comprehension it may be useful to encourage children to reflect on the skill of listening itself, including the kind of things they listen to and different listening purposes. Children could be encouraged for example to reflect on the listening they do in their L1 and draw parallels with the listening they carry out in the L2. Activities such as asking what the children would miss most or would be unable to do if they were deaf might include some of the following:

I like listening to / I need to listen to:

stories, jokes, songs
the television and radio
friends giving me information about a birthday party

From this activity the children can deduce that the main listening purposes in their lives are based on enjoyment or on receiving information of various kinds. The teacher might like then to ensure that his/her learners are able to enjoy listening to a similarly wide range of listening material with a variety of purposes in the L2 also. This would be in addition to activities which focus on learning linguistic items.

The children might like to carry out a survey (in their L1) on what television programmes their friends and family watch and listen to. This might take the form of a simple checklist containing questions such as:

How often do you watch television? (every day, four times a week etc.)
How long do you watch television for? (one hour a day etc.)

This would make a suitable homework task. The children could then write the questions in English (thus encouraging them to focus on 'Wh-' questions) and report back in English. This could be followed up by making charts and graphs to illustrate their findings. The repeated patterns in relaying the information gained would consolidate the children's use of question forms, past tense and adverbials. They would also be able to integrate the skills of reading and writing as well as the concept of using and interpreting charts. This is an especially useful set of activities if the teacher views language learning as an integrative process, as outlined earlier. The general aim of carrying out this type of work would also be to improve children's attitude to listening work.

Listening to reinforce conceptual development

Stories are a rich source of listening practice and for very young learners especially often involve the reinforcement of concepts of time, number, colour, size or shape. Published stories which are aimed at English-speaking children, that is, 'real' books which are not especially written for language learning purposes, can frequently be adapted for young bilingual learners. Examples of popular stories which could be used to develop concepts of time, number and size are *The Very Hungry Caterpillar* and *You'll Soon Grow into them, Titch*. Books such as *Dear Zoo, Rosie's Walk* and *Where's Spot?* reinforce children's spatial concepts and practise the use of prepositions. In addition, the repeated patterns of stories like these frequently provide an opportunity for children to listen carefully and predict the next part of the story. For further details of how to use stories see Hester (1983), Ellis and Brewster (1991) and other papers in this book.

Listening to develop specific language points and interactional skills

LANGUAGE AND PRONUNCIATION

This kind of focus is appropriate if the teacher sees pronunciation as a separate skill that is practised independently of other language learning. It could also be integrated into activities where songs, rhymes and stories are being used. The kinds of while-listening exercise used here are based on the skill of discriminating between sounds and patterns. Listening to songs and rhymes, for example, can be used to develop a sense of rhythm by encouraging children to clap to the beat or to underline the stressed words in a song. The rhyme might also focus on a particular sound, as in the example below.

In this case the children could be asked to identify how many times they hear the / tʃ / sound.

Charlie has a cheerful face,
He loves to chatter, chuckle, chase,
The children come to watch him too,
For Charlie Chimp is in the zoo.

Action rhymes encourage young learners to listen and mime an activity. Useful sources of action rhymes are Beck and King (1985), Brown (1987) and Dakin (1968).

167

The use of stories which contain a lot of direct speech helps the learner develop a sense of how intonation is used to express attitudes and feelings. The children can be asked to identify who is happy, sad, angry and so on. In their own acting out of a story (either themselves or using puppets) they can be encouraged to use the appropriate intonation patterns. Other activities which focus on ear-training skills are:

- Recognising whether two sounds or rhythm patterns are the same or different.

- Finding the 'odd one out' in a sequence of sounds or rhythm patterns.

- Recognising mistakes in a form of dictation game called 'Correct me'. Here the teacher reads out a story or short description where words with an incorrect vowel or consonant are substituted for the correct word. The children have to listen carefully, recognise the error and provide the correct word, for example:

    One sunny gay two boys went for a walk in the good. They met their friend John and thought they would climb a free. When they were at the top John was very hippy and said, 'Shall we build a tree mouse?'

In listening to 'catch the teacher out' the overall aim of this activity would be to improve children's attention span and concentration.

Listening to develop knowledge of vocabulary, grammar, language functions and interactional skills

There are many activities which involve young learners in recognising and selecting specific vocabulary items or grammatical patterns. Games provide a rich source of such practice and can be played with the whole class, in pairs or in groups. Guessing games can be used to practise different kinds of question form, while memory games where the children repeat sentences and add extra items or modify them are useful for practising new vocabulary items. There are many sources of games such as Carrier et al. (1980), Retter and Valls (1984) and Wright et al. (1984).

The games and other activities included in this section provide examples of eight kinds of 'while-listening' task. These can be labelled in the following way: performing actions, drawing, guessing, matching, sequencing, transferring information, predicting and problem-solving. Each of these is described below with examples of the language focus they might provide:

1 Performing actions

This is likely to take the form of listening to action songs, rhymes and games in which the children are required to follow instructions. Young children usually enjoy songs and rhymes, especially those which encourage them to join in. 'Heads, shoulders, knees and toes', for example, invites the children to listen carefully and while singing or listening to touch the appropriate part of the body as it is named. This clearly provides a meaningful context for reinforcing lexical items to describe the body. Many published versions of action songs and rhymes are available (see Bibliography).

An example of a game in this category is 'Simon says' where the teacher gives instructions; if he/she prefaces the instruction with the words 'Simon says . . .', then the children must do the appropriate action, otherwise they must stay still, for example:

'Raise your left arm.' (children stay still)
'Simon says put your hand on your head.' (children put their hands on their heads)

2 Drawing

There are numerous examples of activities which encourage children to draw while listening to a description. A simple task is 'Dot-to-dot' where children listen to instructions to join up dots to form a picture. In this case the numbers or letters do not occur in sequence so that the children have to listen carefully.

Another while-listening activity involves the children listening to a description and drawing a picture of what they hear. For instance the children could draw shapes in the correct position and colour them in according to instructions given by the teacher. Modified versions of this activity include providing a picture with details missing which the children complete while they listen and asking the children to label a picture as they listen. A more difficult task would be to draw a monster or robot as it is being described or to give the children a variety of shapes to begin drawing the parts of the body and let them select one which they think fits the description, adding their own details. This could be linked to the telling of a story about monsters, especially if the story is pre-recorded; a group of children could have control of the tape recorder and stop and start the tape to work at their own pace. The children might like to make their own book to accompany their drawings by adding speech bubbles which retell the story in their own words.

This kind of listen and draw activity can be done with the whole class listening together, with groups of children working on pre-recorded material or with the children working in pairs, taking turns to describe and draw. In this last case one of the children in the pair would need to have their picture hidden from the second child. Written prompts could be provided for the child describing the picture, as this is the most difficult part of the task.

3 Guessing

There is a wide variety of games which encourage learners to listen for clues in order to work something out. An example for use with the whole class is 'Guess the animal' where the teacher gives one child a picture and the other children have to ask questions to find out which animal it is. Only 'yes/no' answers can be given, for example, 'Does it have four legs? Does it have stripes?'

The picture given to the student could provide certain key prompts on the back to help him/her reply. The language focus of this activity is practice in listening for details and inferring information; it also provides a 'disguised drill' in practising 'yes/no' questions.

Another guessing game involves a 'feely bag' full of objects which children feel without seeing. They describe an object they can feel while the rest of the class try to guess what it is.

4 Matching

Another game where the children must listen carefully to match items is the old favourite, 'Bingo'. The bingo cards can take the traditional form of numbers (in numerals or words) or can use pictures or words for other vocabulary development. The words can either be matched directly or can be words which have the same meaning or even an opposite meaning. There is also 'Sound bingo' where pre-recorded everyday sounds are played; the children match each sound to a picture of what makes the sound, for example a clock alarm going off and a picture of an alarm clock.

Other matching activities, this time connected to stories or descriptions, include selecting pictures of the items described. For example, a spoken text (live or pre-recorded) describing a visit to the zoo might include a selection of animals; in this case the children are asked to select the appropriate picture of the animal and put it in the correct cage on a zoo plan while they listen. This would focus on adjectives and nouns for describing parts of animals' bodies and prepositions for describing location. The children can also practise literacy skills while listening to a story by matching written speech bubbles containing the characters' direct speech to pictures of the characters.

A more difficult task for slightly older children is to match items expressing relationships of cause and effect in a story or description of a process. This is most easily done if the text is pre-recorded so that the children can start and stop the tape as they wish. An example from the story *Rupa the Elephant* involves matching pictures to show how Rupa wanted to adopt the characteristics of other animals to make herself more beautiful, for example:

She wanted to look like a tiger   so she covered her body in stripes.

She wanted to look like a peacock   so she stuck on a lovely tail.

Here the children can listen and either match a picture of a tiger to a picture of stripes or can match parts of written sentences.

5 Sequencing

Stories or short descriptions have so far proved a rich source of listening activities. An obvious activity for this section is sequencing the events of a story, either in pictorial form or by listening to and reading sections of the story to order the events. Sound effects could be used, with the teacher making up his/her own tape of everyday sounds for the children to order.

Another useful text type is a set of instructions for making something which the children have to sequence while listening.

6 Transferring information

In this case the children listen to a set of information, for example descriptions of people, animals and places, and either complete a tick-chart or matrix, fill in details on a graph or fill in boxes on a flow-chart. This can be done in an interactive way, with pairs of children asking each other questions and listening for the answer or as a whole class or group activity with pre-recorded material.

A tick-chart (see Figure 2) can provide practice in using and understanding 'yes/no' questions with different tenses. ('Have you ever . . . ? Did you use to . . . ?')

	Manuel	Jean	Mohammed	Luigi
Can you swim?	✓	✗	✓	✗
Can you ride a bike?	✓	✓	✓	✓
Can you skate?	✗	✗	✗	✓

Figure 2 An example tick-chart.

Matrices are useful for describing and classifying; the matrix in Figure 3 can be completed while listening to descriptions. It then provides a useful framework for further talk or writing.

	4 legs	2 legs	no legs
striped	zebra		
spotted			
with a long neck		ostrich	
with a long tail			

Figure 3 An example matrix: Describing animals.

7 Problem-solving

Problem-solving is best done in pairs or groups of four, either with pre-recorded material or after the teacher has read out a short story or description. Examples include:

- Listening to a story and choosing the written statement from a set of four which summarises the story most accurately.

- Listening to a description and choosing four or five items from a list which you would need, for example if you were visiting an imaginary planet to make a film of the wild animals there. In this case the children would select from a list including a boat, food, oxygen, water, rope, matches and so on, those items that match details given about the climate, food and oxygen supply.

- Predicting the next item in a story or description from a set of choices. Here the text is split up into sections which the children listen to one at a time. They are given a set of written statements from which they predict the most likely outcome, the next part of the text is then read out and the children verify their choices and go on to predict the next part.

Many of the activities described above which are used with pairs or groups will develop children's skill in interacting with others. All of these activities can be developed as ancillary material to link in with the current linguistic or thematic focus of the classroom, or can be used independently to practise specific skills and strategies.

The role of the teacher in supporting listening with understanding

It requires patience, imagination and skill to create an interesting environment for young learners to develop confidence in listening. The teacher's role in this respect is fourfold: planning for listening work; choosing relevant texts and tasks; providing appropriate support; varying the learning context.

Planning for listening and choosing appropriate texts and tasks

Listening provides a wealth of practice in specific language points, for instance pronunciation, vocabulary, grammatical patterns and discourse. The activities chosen may also enhance thinking skills and concept development, for example when matching or predicting items. Certain activities, for example information transfer and problem-solving, are suitable for children who can already read and write in English, while others such as the use of songs and rhymes and pictorial matching or sequencing are suitable for children who are at an earlier stage of language proficiency.

To promote effective listening the teacher needs to develop an awareness of the listening demands and purposes of different text types and tasks. At the same time the teacher needs to widen his/her repertoire of the types of spoken text used to develop listening as well as the type of listening skills practised. Some text types such as stories provide a rich vein of language learning material and can provide a focus for all of the strategies mentioned above. Others such as tightly controlled language games or songs and rhymes have a more limited focus. The teacher's choice of text will, therefore, be influenced by the children's age, language level and interests, the specific language and listening focus he/she wishes to provide and the degree to which listening is integrated into general language learning or regarded as a more separate activity.

Some of the skills involved in the tasks described so far include listening for gist, listening for specific information, predicting, inferring attitude, working out meaning from context and recognising features of discourse. The teacher needs to develop a feeling for the kind of task which 'fits' a certain text type. Developing a wide repertoire of activity types which are then selected indiscriminately can lead to ineffective or unsuccessful results. A description of people, for example, generally fits in with a tick-chart activity or a listen and draw activity more naturally than sequencing. This in turn fits more comfortably with a story containing several events.

It is equally important to be aware of the level of difficulty of task types. Listening to label a picture, for instance, is easier than completing a matrix, sequencing statements or selecting the best summary of a story.

Providing support and varying the learning context

We have seen that support can be given simply by telling the learners what their listening focus should be before they listen to a text and by other pre-listening orientation activities which arouse interest and introduce key language items or concepts. In addition, it is important that teachers provide young learners with as much visual support as necessary.

We have seen that much listening work can come from teacher talk with the whole class. Independent visual support can be provided with real objects, magazines, published material and the teacher's or pupils' drawings. Written frameworks such as maps, plans, tick-charts, flow-charts and matrices will support the slightly older, literate child; these frameworks can be put up on a blackboard, flipchart or overhead projector beforehand or can be written up while the teacher talks.

Published material may include dialogues, songs and stories or specific while-listening activities such as drawing and completing exercises. These can be used with the whole class or in groups. It may be possible to set up a listening corner in the room where one group at a time works with this material on a rotating basis. In this case it would be important to provide appropriate instructions before the task and feedback after the task. Afterwards there needs to be a record of the activities the children have completed. This record could be completed by the teacher or by the pupils themselves.

One of the qualities a teacher needs is creativity. If there is little published material available or simply to provide variety, the teacher can record material onto a cassette him/herself, varying the sex and age of the speakers recorded. Another advantage of teacher-made listening material is that it can be tailored to the children's experiences or interests. They will always enjoy stories written about them, especially if the tape is accompanied by a written version with the children's own drawings or even photographs. When the children are working more independently in this way it is worth scripting careful instructions on the tape, either in the L1 or L2, which ensure that the children have all the materials they need – worksheets, coloured pencils, pictures and so on – and are clear about what they have to do. It is always useful to have one example as a model, for instance the beginning of a flow-chart completed or the first item in a sequencing exercise already given. It is usual practice to have the spoken text recorded in its entirety first; the children listen all the way through without stopping. Depending on the focus of the activity it may then be useful to record the text again, this time divided into sections. If the teacher builds in a sound signal on the tape – a spoon tapped on a glass, for example – the children can be trained to stop the tape upon this signal to complete a part of the activity. The children can then take their time to select the appropriate picture in a matching exercise and so on. This takes the pressure off learners who may experience difficulty in extracting information within the given time-limit when teacher talk with the whole class is used. Wherever possible a completed version should be available so that the children can immediately check if they have worked out the exercise correctly.

An example of teacher-made material which could be recorded onto cassette is shown in Figure 4. It is based on *Rosie's Walk* (op. cit.), a simple picture book useful for teaching prepositions. The example contains four listening activities: listen and point, listen and match, listen and sequence, listen and retell a story. We shall assume that the children are familiar with the content and key language of the story, have been trained to work independently in pairs and have been taught to understand simple instructions in English. Before the children begin the activity the teacher explains the task, probably using the pupils' mother tongue. The taped instructions in English are deliberately short and simple and encourage independence with techniques such as checking the pupils have the equipment they need and self-checking 'solutions'.

Notice how the teacher breaks up the text using a sound signal to give children time to complete the activity, how she recycles the meaning of the story in feedback and encouragement and the way the instructions are clearly signalled by using 'first', 'next' and so on.

Figure 4 Transcript of a listening activity devised by a teacher.

Rosie's Walk

To do this work you need the folder with pictures from *Rosie's Walk* and the chart with eight boxes.

Have you got these? Good. Now listen carefully.

First of all, look at the picture of Rosie and the fox. Point to the picture of the farmyard; point to the picture of the pond, (PAUSE) the mill, (PAUSE) the beehives, the fence and last of all the haycock. (PAUSE) Done that? Good.

Now listen carefully to the story. As you listen find the right picture. Put it in the right box on the chart. The first one is done for you.

Rosie the hen went for a walk across the yard.

Point to the picture of Rosie in the yard in box number one. (PAUSE)

'Ah ha!' said the fox. 'Now I've got you!' But oh dear, there's a rake. 'Oh no!' said the fox, 'My nose!'

Find the picture of the fox with the rake and put it in box number two. **

It looks very painful, doesn't it? Where did Rosie go next?

Well, she walked on and went around the pond. 'Ah ha!' said the fox. 'Now I've got you!' But oh dear! He's fallen in. 'Oh no!' said the fox, 'I'm all wet!'

Find the picture of the fox in the pond and put it in box number three. **

Done that? Good. He's very wet, isn't he?

But Rosie didn't see him and walked over the haycock. 'This time I've got you!' said the fox. But oh dear! He slipped and got stuck.

Now find the picture of the fox in the haycock. **

He looks very unhappy, doesn't he?

But Rosie still didn't see him and walked past the mill. 'I've finally got you now!' said the fox. Find the picture of Rosie walking past the mill and put it in box number four. **

It looks like trouble, doesn't it?

'Oh no! I'm all white!' said the fox And oh dear! There he was, all covered in flour.

Find the picture of the fox covered in flour and put it in box number five. **

Next, Rosie thought, 'I'm in a hurry. I'll go through the fence.' 'I'm so hungry,' said the fox. 'Now's my chance!' So he jumped over the fence and landed right in a cart. 'Oh no!' said the fox. 'I'll hit the beehives!'

Find the picture of the fox in the cart and the picture of the bees chasing him. Put them in boxes number six and seven. **

Rosie was a very lucky hen. 'I wonder where that fox is,' she thought and got back just in time for dinner.

Last of all, find the picture of Rosie safe and sound and put it in box number eight. **

I hope you've got all of the pictures in the right order. Check your picture with the one in the folder.

Now see if you can use the pictures to tell the story again yourselves.

Note: ** denotes the sound signal where the learners stop the tape and carry out the instructions. The children switch on again when they are ready.

This activity would be particularly suitable for slower learners, who may not have grasped all of the details of the story when working with the whole class and are now able to listen to the tape again and again. The taped material can of course be produced by the children themselves; this might include the retelling of stories, new stories, radio plays, simple interviews, descriptions, instructions for how to do something and so on. The benefits of this kind of learning include:

- helping the children develop autonomy and a sense of responsibility for their learning.

- letting children work at their own pace.

- providing variety and interest.

- providing extra work for those children who are always racing ahead and finishing activities very quickly.

- providing extra support for children who learn more slowly and may need to recap an exercise or try a different or easier activity with the same listening text.

A final variant of the learning context is pair or groupwork. Examples of tasks have already been provided such as surveys, problem-solving and describe and draw activities where it is useful to encourage a more interactive learning style. In this case the children are both speaking and listening to each other, which more closely mirrors real-life communication.

Thus we can see that activities based on listening provide a wealth of possibilities not only for developing listening skills as an end in themselves, but also for providing a springboard for supporting development in talk, reading and writing too.

Bibliography

Abbs, B. and A. Worrall. 1980. *Jigsaw.* Harlow: Longman.

Anderson, A. and T. Lynch. 1988. *Listening.* Oxford: Oxford University Press.

Beck, I. and K. King. 1985. *Oranges and Lemons: Singing and Dancing Games.* Oxford: Oxford University Press.

Brown, M. 1987. *Hand Rhymes.* London: Collins.

Carle, E. 1982. *The Very Hungry Caterpillar.* London: Puffin.

Carrier, M. 1980. *Take 5.* London: Harrap.

Dakin, J. 1968. *Songs and Rhymes for the Teaching of English.* London: Longman.

Ellis, G. and J. Brewster. 1991. The Story-Telling Handbook. London: Penguin.

Ellis, R. 1986. *Understanding Second Language Acquisition.* Oxford: Oxford University Press.

Hester, H. 1983. *Stories in the Multilingual Primary Classroom.* London: Harcourt Brace Jovanovich.

Hutchins, P. 1977. *Rosie's Walk.* London: Puffin.

Krashen, S.D. 1981. *Second Language Acquisition and Second Language Learning.* Oxford: Pergamon Press.

Matterson, E. 1969. *This Little Puffin.* London: Puffin.

McDonough, S. 1981. *Psychology and Foreign Language Teaching.* London: Allen & Unwin.

Pratt, C. and R. Grieve. 1984. 'Metalinguistic awareness and cognitive development.' in Tunmer, W., C. Pratt and M. Herriman. *Metalinguistic Awareness in Children: Theory, Research and Implications.* Germany: Springer Verlag.

Retter, C. and N. Valls. 1984. *Bonanza: 77 English Language Games for Young Learners.* London: Longman.

Scott, W. 1980. *Are you Listening?* Oxford: Oxford University Press.

Smith, F. 1975. *Comprehension and Learning: a Conceptual Framework for Teachers.* Eastbourne: Holt, Rinehart & Winston.

Ur, P. 1981. *Discussions that Work.* Cambridge: Cambridge University Press.

Wright, A., D. Betteridge and M. Buckby. 1979. *Games for Language Learning.* Cambridge: Cambridge University Press.

Richard Parker, University of Western Sydney, Macarthur, Australia
Rona Parker, Nicholson Street Public School, Balmain East, Australia

13 Real reading needs real books

In this paper, Richard and Rona Parker take up some of the themes already explored in Ludmila Machura's paper on using literature. They also look at some of the theoretical bases for a real books approach to reading, and support their proposals with practical suggestions.

THE SIX-YEAR-OLD has returned from school, and is sitting in one of her grandmother's lounge chairs reading a book. Her grandmother enters, bearing afternoon tea.

GRANDMOTHER: What's that book you are reading, dear?
CHILD: (somewhat disparagingly) That's not a book, Grandmother! That's my reader.

The story may be familiar, but the point is worth restating. Children know the difference between *real books* and *reading books*. They know that you find real books in libraries and in children's bedrooms. They know that they are the ones to read on a winter's day or, better still, to present to an adoring adult with the request, 'Please read me a story.' They also know that reading books are the books they take out of their desks or bags whenever the teacher says it is time for a reading lesson.

Unfortunately, many teachers do not view real books and reading books with the same clarity. Reading books, frequently in large sets and accompanied by a host of support materials, are seen by many teachers as the most reliable path to reading development. Real books, on the other hand, are seen as educational frills and are used as a reward for children who complete the reading lesson quickly or are read aloud to the children late in the school day when the teacher has exhausted his/her energy or ingenuity.

It is our view that real books are the foundation of an effective reading programme for first and second language learners alike. In classrooms where real books abound we have observed an enthusiasm for reading that is rarely evident in classrooms where contrived reading materials are used. Numerous teachers have said to us, 'I used to worry because the children in my class would not read. Now that I base my reading programme on real books, my problem is that I have to stop them from reading in order to cover the rest of the curriculum.'

Reading instruction in the first language classroom

The last three or four decades have seen a number of approaches to reading instruction. Common to the earlier approaches was the assumption that children should be presented with small words initially and be permitted to progress to longer (and, by definition, more difficult) words as they became more competent.

One approach placed great emphasis on the sequential mastery of a set of discrete phonic rules. Texts were created using words which contained the same sound, so that cats sat on mats, dogs rolled off logs and fish were put on thick dishes. Where teachers were enthusiastic and committed to the approach, many children mastered the mechanics of reading, and in the initial stages even showed some excitement over their growing control of the reading process. However, such excitement tended to be short-lived and few children displayed a long-term love of the texts which were the centre of attention in the reading lesson.

Another approach which captured the support of many teachers featured those familiar characters, Janet and John. The aim of this approach was to establish a basic sight vocabulary by introducing words gradually and repeating them frequently. Each new word was drilled extensively before the pupils were permitted to encounter it in the text. Children spent long periods of time staring at flashcards and barking the appropriate responses. Children from literate backgrounds must have spent equally long periods of time wondering why the central characters in the book before them devoted so much of their time to looking upwards and saying, 'Look, Mummy, look!' This second approach was no more successful than its predecessor, and there were few children who sneaked home copies of their school reading books for inclusion in their treasured personal libraries.

In many parts of the world, reading schemes were replaced for a time by boxes of colour-coded workcards, machines which emphasised the speed of visual processing and schemes of various types which owed their existence to the 'science' of programmed instruction. Children obediently completed the almost endless sequences of carefully graded exercises which were thought to promote reading comprehension. Reading comprehension was seen as quite distinct from reading for enjoyment by children and teachers alike.

More recently there has been a major focus on using children's literature (or what we refer to as real books) as the basis of classroom reading programmes. Children who are fortunate enough to be in classrooms where reading at home and reading at school are seen to be the same thing are frequently observed sharing their reading experiences with one another and with their teachers.

Reading instruction in the second language classroom

Similar trends to those outlined above can be observed in second language classrooms. Second language classrooms where the teaching of discrete grammar items predominates parallel classrooms where phonics instruction is common. Situational syllabuses are based on similar ideas to those that led to the creation of Janet and John, while the audio-lingual approach emphasises technology in much the same way as do programmed reading kits.

Learning to read and reading for enjoyment are also separated in the same way. It is common in second language classrooms to talk of *intensive reading* and *extensive reading*. Intensive reading consists essentially of reading practice, often practice in reading aloud. We do not find the intensive/extensive distinction at all useful and prefer the notion of a wide range of reading experiences which together contribute to the child's developing competence.

Recent influences on reading instruction

It is worth considering briefly the influences that have led to the current focus on using real books as the basis of classroom reading programmes.

Among them has been the work of theorists such as Frank Smith and Ken and Yetta Goodman, all of whom have stressed the centrality of meaning in reading. The goal of reading is reconstructing the ideas of the writer. The skilled reader interacts with the text using existing knowledge, as well as the information on the page, to approximate the author's intended message.

Meaningful texts are essential for this type of reading to take place. Texts in the 'real' world are usually meaningful, but many of the reading materials that teachers place before children are not. Where reading for meaning is emphasised, reading silently is the preferred mode – oral reading makes additional demands of the person reading, resulting in a loss of meaning.

Accounts of the reading process (such as those referred to above) have also pointed out the importance of prediction in reading. Earlier approaches to teaching reading tended to emphasise accurate word identification, but teachers are now beginning to realise that children need to be taught how to build up hypotheses about what the writer will say next. Texts which have been contrived in order to provide children with some form of reading practice are notoriously difficult to predict, whereas well-written stories are relatively easy to predict.

Another major influence has been a concern for the development of life-long reading habits. Increasing numbers of teachers are not content to produce children who are capable of reading, but who do not choose to do so unless forced. These teachers provide genuine purposes for reading, not the least of which is reading for enjoyment. And because the purposes are genuine, the materials are real or at least based upon the real materials encountered by adults in the course of their day-to-day activities. Just as adults spend a good deal of their reading time on fiction, and rarely any time at all on materials designed to turn them into better readers, so children should be given ample opportunity to interact with real books.

These influences are evident in many first language classrooms. Second language learners have just as much to gain from similar influences, and we would argue that a literature-based reading programme should be a feature of all second language classrooms.

A framework for reading development

Recent approaches to second language teaching and learning have emphasised natural acquisition. Such features as 'a stress-free learning environment', 'minimal correction' and 'provision of comprehensible input' have been suggested as necessary for language acquisition.

A more detailed analysis of the conditions under which children naturally learn to listen and speak has been described by Brian Cambourne (see Butler and Turbill 1984). He summarises his position thus:

> The evidence is, I believe, conclusive: in order to learn to talk one must not only be human, but certain conditions must operate to permit that learning to occur. These conditions are many and complex but, I believe, there are seven that stand out. I also believe that these seven conditions are relevant to all kinds of language learning, e.g. learning to read, write, spell; learning a second language. Furthermore, I believe that these conditions are transferable to classroom practice. (p.6)

The seven conditions identified by Cambourne are:

IMMERSION	APPROXIMATION
DEMONSTRATION	EMPLOYMENT
EXPECTATION	FEEDBACK
RESPONSIBILITY	

Cambourne's discussion is largely in terms of children's initial acquisition of oral language, and as such, may have relevance beyond the particular focus of this chapter. However, the seven conditions will be described here in terms of their relevance to learning how to read.

IMMERSION refers to the importance of surrounding the child with language. Successful classrooms are filled with real books and the school day is filled with opportunities for children to read. Some of these opportunities are planned; others are spontaneous.

DEMONSTRATION refers to the importance of appropriate models of language use. Teachers need to demonstrate reading to their pupils. They need to demonstrate the fact that they themselves enjoy reading and that they know books. They need to demonstrate what books are used for and how readers can make best use of them.

Successful classrooms are filled with the sound of real books being read aloud, usually by the teacher; the hesitant oral rendition of a less-developed reader is unlikely to sustain the interest of the other children. Reading aloud to children is one of the most effective ways of exposing children to the features of standard English and, later, to the distinctive features of different types of text. Sharing good stories with children is probably the most effective way of demonstrating why it is worth becoming a proficient reader.

Cambourne points out that parents and teachers frequently communicate to children a strong EXPECTATION of what those children are likely to achieve. Where these expectations are positive, children tend to succeed, but where the expectations are negative, children are more likely to fail. In turn, children who have failed begin to expect to fail and invariably do.

The teacher in the reading classroom needs to make it clear that learning to read is natural, easy and inevitable. An expression such as, 'I have some hard work for you in our reading lesson today!' might be better replaced with, 'We are all going to enjoy the reading I have ready for you today.' Clearly teachers will need to have a wide range of books available (this is part of what is implied by 'immersion') if they are realistically to expect children to succeed. They will also need to develop a range of before-reading strategies to reduce the distance between some children and the text. One good way of doing this is by first reading the text or story to children on one or two occasions before expecting them to control their own reading of the same text or story.

In the natural process of learning to speak, children assert the right to choose the contexts in which they will speak. Cambourne suggests that without the opportunity of taking RESPONSIBILITY for the aspects of language they use at any one time, they will not develop into competent language users. The skilled teacher of reading will encourage children to choose what they will read, perhaps even when they will read. The skilled reading teacher, having first demonstrated a variety of meaning-gathering strategies, will encourage children to experiment with them and assess their usefulness under different conditions. When learning to speak children are encouraged to try, even if their efforts at pronunciation or sentence construction fall short of perfect. They are, in other words, encouraged to APPROXIMATE the language that surrounds them. Teachers need to be aware that it is far preferable for children to make an effort and be partially correct, than to make no effort at all. Teachers also need to be closely attuned to the language behaviour of the children in their classroom; it is only through careful observation that teachers will be able to detect small, yet significant, improvements in the way children are dealing with texts.

Many teachers have found it useful to conduct reading conferences with their pupils. A reading conference consists of a short period of consultation with a child (or even a small group of children) during which the teacher explores issues by asking questions such as:

> What was the last book that you read? Can you tell me about it? What did you like most about it? Was there a character you didn't like? Would you like to read me a section that you really enjoyed?
> (After the reading) When you came to this word (pointing at a word that caused the child some difficulty), what did you do? How did you work it out?

Cambourne notes that young children are given a great deal of opportunity for EMPLOYMENT of the language. Becoming proficient in anything requires regular sustained activity. Reading is no exception. All of us have been in classrooms where organisational matters take up several minutes, after which children are ordered to prepare for the reading lesson. More time is devoted to having children take turns in reading small sections of a text aloud to the rest of the class. It is not uncommon for children under these circumstances to spend less than one minute actually interacting with the text. If children are to become competent readers, they need to spend a large part of every day actively engaged in reading.

The final condition, FEEDBACK, refers to the way in which significant people respond to the child's use of language. When children are developing control over oral language, it is rare for parents to correct the form of the language (though serious errors of fact are often corrected). Instead, parents affirm what has been said and then model a more accurate form (Butler and Turbill 1984):

TODDLER: Dat cup.
ADULT: Yes, that's a cup. (p.9)

When children are gaining control over their reading, they benefit from affirmation of the strategies which they have employed for making meaning. They also benefit from modelling of even more refined or appropriate strategies. This presupposes that teachers are themselves familiar with an extensive range of meaning-making strategies which are based on a sound understanding of the reading process.

Cambourne argues that when these seven conditions are present, language learning may occur as naturally as learning to speak occurs for the vast majority of children.

What the research says

Considerable research has been done in first language classrooms to support the value of silent reading of real books as the basis of reading development (Allington 1977, Gambrell 1978). Some research done in second language classrooms confirms that similar conclusions apply.

Aranha (1985) examined the influence of a sustained silent reading programme in a fourth grade class in an Indian school. She found significant gains in reading achievement for the experimental group, though the gains were much greater for the girls than for the boys. This latter conclusion may have been a result of the range of books made available.

Perhaps the most striking study is that of Elley and Mangubhai (1983). These researchers compared the effectiveness of two classroom approaches using real books with a well-established structural and audio-lingual approach. In some primary classrooms in Fiji, children were given a 'shared book experience' using a collection of 250 books, including some large format books. In other classrooms there was a 'flood of books' but the emphasis was on sustained silent reading. The control classrooms retained the normal audio-lingual programme, and in all classrooms the time given to language was held constant.

The results indicate that both of the book-based approaches were clearly superior to the audio-lingual approach, and confirmed the hypothesis that, 'exposure to large numbers of story books will have an effect on general language competence.' (Elley and Mangubhai 1983). The gains persisted over time and pervaded the whole school curriculum. The complete study is worthy of careful examination.

Other studies to provide support for a literature-based reading programme for second language learners include the work of Spack (1985) and Carrell (1985).

Selecting books for the classroom

Using real books in the language classroom is not only educationally sound but is fun and rewarding for both teacher and pupils. Special qualifications in children's literature are not essential for teachers who want to use literature in their classrooms, just a willingness to take the plunge and get started.

Perhaps your experience of children's books is limited to those you remember from your own childhood, and maybe even these were from another language background. If you have a library nearby with a good children's section, then your task of beginning is not so difficult. Go to the library, browse through the books and choose some titles that you think both you and your class will enjoy. If the library has limited borrowing rules, then seek the assistance of a senior librarian to enable you to borrow in bulk. Start reading yourself, but don't take too long before you start sharing these books with your students. If a library is not at your disposal, then some persistence and ingenuity may be required in order to get the books you need.

The following guidelines may be useful in selecting books, but bear in mind that there are really no firm rules for book selection. When you get to know what is available and what your pupils will enjoy, you will intuitively know what to select.

A book needs to be 'a good read'; one that both children and teacher will enjoy again and again. It needs a good storyline, in which the children will become actively involved as they silently anticipate and predict what will happen. In John Burningham's *Avocado Baby*, for example, right from the start we know that there is something special about this weak baby who will eat only avocado. Our wondering and anticipation are built up as the baby does a lot of extraordinary things leading up to the story's climax, where the baby deals with some big bullies in a most decisive fashion. We cheer, good has prevailed yet again and the story leaves us feeling satisfied.

The language used may range from simple to complex, but it should leave the reader with the feeling that the author's words could not be improved. Marjorie Flack and Kurt Wiese do just this in *The Story About Ping* using language that is restrained and delicate, yet painting an eloquent picture of life on the Yangtze River.

> Ping knew he would be the last, the very last duck if he crossed the bridge. Ping did not want to be spanked. So he hid. Ping hid behind the grasses, and as the dark came and the pale moon shone in the sky Ping watched the wise-eyed boat slowly sail away down the Yangtze River.

Illustrations are crucial to books for young learners, particularly those for whom English is a second language. They do not need to be large and colourful, but should support the text and stimulate the reader. Good illustrations will enhance children's understanding of the text, and promote lots of excited discussion.

Children's interests and taste in books change as they get older, and the language teacher needs to develop an understanding of what books will appeal to different age groups.

Four- to five-year-olds, while still fairly egocentric, are beginning to realise that other people have feelings and needs. Books dealing with topics that are part of the child's immediate experiences of life and family such as being sick, starting school, coping with a new baby, getting lost and feeling scared, are important and enjoyed at this age. Shirley Hughes' stories about Alfie and Judith Kerr's tales about Mog the cat and her human family are two fine examples. Children are very attuned to the rhyme and rhythm inherent in language and enjoy simple poems, rhymes and songs, particularly those that are a little absurd and humorous. Traditional tales such as *The Gingerbread Boy* and *The Little Red Hen* are also favourites at this age and have the additional advantage of existing in a number of different cultures.

Six- to eight-year-olds, while still needing security and warmth from their important adults, are developing more confidence as they accomplish new skills and strive for greater independence. They have a growing sense of justice and empathy with others, and a keen interest in the world around them. Their sense of humour is developing; they are beginning to see humour in incongruous situations and in others' misfortunes. They are also more able to distinguish fantasy from reality, and this is the beginning of the wonderful age of 'Let's pretend'; children really know that animals can't talk and that cars don't fly, but they can still imagine, 'Could this really happen?' and 'What if . . . ?' Poetry is still a source of delight.

Nine- to twelve-year-olds are developing their ability to appreciate other viewpoints. At this age stories about family and friends should not only reassure children about themselves but provide them with new insights into how other families and children cope with various situations. Children at this age enjoy stories that extend their experiences. Adventure or mystery, fantasy or reality, the important feature of these books is that they contain a well-developed plot and credible characters. Poetry remains popular, provided it is read for enjoyment rather than literary study.

Choosing books for the second language classroom requires careful consideration of the language as well as the supporting illustrations and the likely interest appeal. This does not mean that language always needs to be very simple. Rather it needs to be understandable, enjoyable and memorable. When this is the case, students will be able to cope with and remember the odd complicated word or phrase, and their language will be extended.

There are many books that cross the broad age/interest categories discussed above, and these are superb resources for the second language teacher who is anxious to find titles that appeal to a particular age group *and* contain language that is appropriate to the students' level of language competence.

Eric Carle's *The Very Hungry Caterpillar*, which tells the life story of a caterpillar, appeals from babyhood to at least the age of ten. Although the caterpillar eats some unusual food, the story is supported by excellent illustrations and a predictable text which employs some repetition and some very memorable language. There are a number of language activities that can be based on this delightful story. Many children will commit the story to memory because they like it so much, and the words and phrases will then be part of their developing language repertoire.

John Burningham's *Would You Rather . . . ?* contains a hilarious, sometimes scary but always funny series of important decisions for the reader to make. This book could even be used with adults and is guaranteed to produce a lot of discussion. A number of enjoyable language activities can be based on this story, which children will clamour to read again and again.

'Big Books' are just what their name implies, and they are an invaluable resource in any language classroom. Children who go to school having been read to by a loving adult on a daily basis, are well on the way to becoming readers. Unfortunately, not all children experience this important preschool activity. Big Books were developed to help classroom teachers reproduce as closely as possible the ideal conditions for developing language and literacy. The teacher can place the Big Book on a stand or easel, and because everything about the book is big, the whole class can see the text and be actively involved in the discussion. There are many published titles available which meet the interest demands and language levels of second language classrooms too.

Often language teachers perceive a need for books that more closely reflect the social and cultural experiences of their particular students. This need can be met by getting the class to make their own books. Class books can be based on a familiar story, and are probably best suited to the Big-Book format. If books are made in small groups, children whose written development is not particularly advanced can be involved in discussion of the story and in its illustration.

Lorraine Wilson, a teacher in Melbourne, Australia, saw the need to write books for her class of ESL children. She wrote about experiences the children could relate to such as having a haircut, losing a bus fare and getting a new teacher, and she used the everyday language of the children. These 'home-made' books caught the eye of a publisher and the *City Kids* series was born. Although originally intended for younger children, the humorous and age-ambiguous illustrations make the series suitable for much older children as well. The books have been printed in several languages, and the 'no-text' versions enable teachers and children to write their own captions and stories. *Country Kids* has been equally successful. While the books deal with issues related to living in Australia, the universal themes of family, friends and school cross many cultural barriers.

Using books in the classroom

A language classroom needs to have a class library to which children have regular and frequent access. Don't hide the books away in your cupboard and only produce them for special lessons. Children learn a lot about language, literacy and books when they are allowed a daily time of free-choice reading, so make the books available to the children. Read yourself during this reading time. It's an excellent chance to familiarise yourself further with children's literature, and you will be demonstrating to the students that you consider reading enjoyable and important.

Set aside some time each lesson or day to read aloud to the children. This activity is not only fun for everyone, but immerses children in the world of books and demonstrates a number of very important aspects of language learning. Reading aloud engages the children's interest in language and books. It exposes them to good models of standard English, and to the sounds of written language in all its richness and variety. It helps children to become better readers, writers and users of language. Choose from the wide variety of picture books that are available, both fiction and non-fiction, and don't forget a poem or two. As the children's attention span lengthens and language competence develops, try serialising longer stories.

Book-based activities

Ideas for language activities based on particular books will quickly spring to mind, perhaps coming out of children's enthusiasm for and reaction to the story. Good language activities have no age limits; an idea which works with five-year-olds will, with some minor adaptations in content and presentation, probably work equally well with much older learners.

Many of the activities outlined below are presented in *Literacy Through Literature* (Johnson and Louis 1985) and *Dimensions – Teacher's Book* (Nicol, Unsworth and Parker 1985). In this latter book, literature-based activities are placed in the three broad groups detailed below:

Getting ready for the book

This may take the form of a discussion in which children are encouraged to look at the cover and make predictions about content based on the illustration and title. This could lead on to a brief discussion about pupils' related personal experiences or to the first part of an activity that the children will return to later in the session.

For example, in introducing the story *Naughty Nigel* by Tony Ross, children could suggest in discussion or write for themselves what they think Nigel will do. These ideas could be briefly reported and after the reading, children could tick off the items that were mentioned in the story. Other pre-reading tasks could include instructing children to look out for various characters or to take particular note of certain details or pieces of information that they will need later.

During the reading

Teachers should be careful to ensure that the flow of the story reading is not lost during the first reading at least. One or two well-timed questions are much better than ten that spoil the story. Questions should be open-ended, and all feasible responses should be warmly accepted. Children could also engage in further predictions about the story.

After the reading

Activities here may be as exciting and as varied as the books themselves. Many books will immediately beg a second reading, which could include audience participation; the children could be invited to 'help' read the repetitive parts or to make appropriate noises.

'Can't you read?' is the question often asked of Thomas in *The Tale of Thomas Mead* by Pat Hutchins. The same question is echoed by enthralled listeners, who also like to play the part of Thomas, as he replies, 'Why should I?'

Some ideas to help you get started

- Children could make or paint a wall-sized very hungry caterpillar and all the food he eats through, organising the food in the correct order, and labelling it with appropriate parts of the text.

- Pupils could help illustrate a class Big-Book version of a story.

- Pupils could contribute to a class version of *Would You Rather . . . ?* by John Burningham, making up their own funny or scary situations.

- The same strategy of making additions works well with many poems. Michael Rosen's *This is the hand* or *I know someone who . . .* are ideal for this.

- *The Lighthouse Keeper's Lunch* by David and Ronda Armitage leads very naturally into writing and illustrating favourite lunch menus for the

Grinlings or snack recipes for Mrs Grinling's recipe book. Perhaps some of the snacks could be made in class; cooking activities are excellent language learning situations.

- Children could make puppets and, in pairs or small groups, plan and perform a retelling of the story *Goldilocks and The Three Bears* or other familiar story. The puppets can be simple cardboard cut-outs, attached to sticks.

- Many stories lend themselves to story-mapping. Children decide on the main features of the story, and then draw a map indicating who the characters were, and where and when they appeared in the plot. They should then take a partner (or the class) on a walk through their map, retelling the story. Older children are able to point out significant features and justify the inclusion or exclusion of various details.

- Other activities focus more clearly on the characters. Wanted or Missing Person posters featuring a character from a story require lots of careful thought, re-reading of the text and discussion of which characteristics should be included.

- The personal qualities of the characters can be rated on a continuum, for example kind to unkind, clever to stupid, thoughtful to selfish. Children can then compare their ratings and justify them with evidence from the text.

- Children can write literary letters for a variety of purposes. After reading *The Lighthouse Keeper's Catastrophe* (David and Ronda Armitage), they could write to Mr Grinling and suggest another way he could have got into the lighthouse.

- Diary writing can be fun too. Children can write about a day in the life of Snow White, Naughty Nigel's mother, Thomas Mead or Ping.

Although children may need to try each type of activity several times before they begin to exploit fully its learning potential, it is essential that activities be varied, so that the learning environment is stimulating, exciting and unpredictable. It is also important to plan each activity beforehand. Remember to give clear instructions and to communicate to the children what is expected of them. This will often involve a demonstration of the activity by the teacher with the whole class watching, discussing and participating. When the children know exactly what to do, and how to go about the task, they can work on the activity in small groups, in pairs or individually. When they have completed the activity, a brief report-back session provides children with some feedback on their success.

Teaching language using real books is challenging for the teacher, but a classroom full of motivated children, excited by their encounters with real books, will be ample reward.

Bibliography

Allington, R.L. 1977. 'If they don't read much, how they ever gonna get good?' *Journal of Reading* 21, 57–61.

Aranha, M. 1985. Sustained Silent Reading Goes East. *The Reading Teacher* 39, 214–217.

Armitage, D. and R. 1977. *The Lighthouse Keeper's Lunch*. London: André Deutsch.

Burningham, J. 1984. *Would you Rather . . . ?* London: Collins.

Burningham, J. 1986. *Avocado Baby*. London: Collins.

Butler, A. and J. Turbill. 1984. *Towards a Reading-Writing Classroom*. Rozelle: Primary English Teaching Association.

Carle, E. 1974. *The Very Hungry Caterpillar*. London: Penguin.

Carrell, P.L. 1985. 'Facilitating ESL reading by teaching text structure.' *TESOL Quarterly.* 19 (4), 727–752.

Elley, W.B. and F. Mangubhai. 1983. 'The impact of reading on second language learning.' *Reading Research Quarterly* 19, 53–67.

Elack, M. and K. Wiese. 1968. *The Story about Ping*. London: Puffin.

Gambrell, L.B., R.M. Wilson and W.N. Gantt. 1981. 'Classroom observations of task attending behaviours of good and poor readers.' *Journal of Educational Research.* 74 (6), 400–404.

Goodman, K.S. 1985. 'Unity in reading.' in Singer, H. and R.B. Ruddell, *Theoretical Models and Processes of Reading*. Newark, Delaware: International Reading Association.

Hutchins, P. 1980. *The Tale of Thomas Mead*. London: Bodley Head.

Johnson, T.D. and D.R. Louis. 1985. *Literacy Through Literature*. North Ryde: Methuen Australia.

Nicoll, V., L. Unsworth and R. Parker. 1986. *Dimensions Teacher's Book*. North Ryde: Methuen Australia.

Rosen, M. 1981. *You Can't Catch Me*. London: André Deutsch.

Rosen, M. 1983. *Quick, Let's Get out of Here*. London: André Deutsch.

Ross, T. 1982. *Naughty Nigel*. London: Anderson Press.

Smith, F. 1985. *Reading*. Cambridge: Cambridge University Press.

Spack, R. 1985. 'Literature, reading, writing and ESL: bridging the gaps.' *TESOL Quarterly.* 19 (4), 703–725.

Wilson, L. 1979. *Having a Haircut*. Melbourne: Thomas Nelson Australia.

Wilson, L. 1979. *Our New Principal*. Melbourne: Thomas Nelson Australia.

Wilson, L. 1979. *The Day I Lost my Bus Fare*. Melbourne: Thomas Nelson Australia.

Gail Ellis, The British Council, Paris, France

14 Learning to learn

Gail Ellis concludes Section One by providing an argument for teaching the processes of learning, and linking that with specific experiences of innovation in classrooms in France. The practical illustrations given serve to pull together the themes of this section, as well as giving some pointers to the more abstract themes of Section Two.

THE IDEA of learning to learn is not new, but there has been a revival of interest in this area among language teachers and learners; witness recent ELT course materials, Whitney 1984, Hutchinson 1985, Ellis and Sinclair 1989 and Whitney and Samuel 1990. However, in many education systems the curriculum still concentrates on the traditional targets of 'useful knowledge' and 'basic skills' rather than on learning to learn. This paper will suggest that in order to develop an awareness of learning and learner responsibility, learning to learn should be built into the curriculum in an explicit and systematic way. This can be done by introducing it in the context of conventional subjects such as foreign language learning. Major factors will be discussed, guidelines for lesson planning given and procedures suggested.

When to introduce learning to learn

In France in a recent project to promote learner awareness and responsibility with pupils aged between 11 and 14, I experimented with ways of integrating learning to learn into English language classes on a systematic basis. The 11- to 12-year-olds, who were mostly learning English for the first time, were highly motivated, while most of the third year 13- to 14-year-olds had become demotivated and experienced little success with their English. Many of them had already acquired limited learning strategies, and viewed English as product-orientated, whereas the natural enthusiasm and relative open-mindedness of the first years produced a greater willingness to experiment. Project evaluation focused on pupil feedback and showed that the 11- to 12-year-olds were more receptive to learning to learn than the 13- to 14-year-olds. The following comment comes from a 12-year-old at the end of Year One, 'I have learnt things that I didn't know about myself and English.'

It was sometimes difficult to convince the third years of the benefits of learning to learn. This may have been because they were pressurised by syllabus demands to move up into the next class, and they may have perceived learning to learn as time lost for language learning and gaining the necessary marks. Peer group pressure may also have been a factor inhibiting experimentation.

The project, however, confirmed an overall positive response in terms of changes in attitudes to language learning, improved motivation and an increased awareness of the learning process. It also established that it was possible to introduce learning to learn in the context of conventional subjects, and that 11- to 14-year-olds could express their opinions about language learning if and when asked. They were not only capable of taking responsibility for their own learning but also enjoyed it. The increased motivation and interest in language learning were also seen as positive outcomes.

This led me to hypothesise that learning to learn might be introduced earlier, for example in the later stages of primary school (eight- to ten-year-olds) when pupils are beginning to develop greater self-awareness. The following guidelines may be of interest to teachers wishing to introduce a learning to learn component into their English language classes with younger learners.

Factors to be considered

a) *Time*. If the teacher is working with an imposed syllabus, decisions will need to be made about which language learning activities in the coursebook or syllabus will be cut in order to accommodate the learning to learn.

b) *Using the mother tongue*. Some learning to learn may need to be carried out in the mother tongue, especially with lower level pupils. For example, questions about the language or language learning may need to be asked in the mother tongue, but this will not affect the learning to learn benefits.

c) *Syllabus*. If the syllabus takes priority, the learning to learn can only constitute a fairly small proportion of the course. It will have to be subordinate to the language learning aims of a lesson so that it will not override these and disrupt the syllabus.

d) *Educational context*. Many classrooms emphasise accuracy and teacher control rather than opportunities for reflecting on the learning process. Learning to learn will need to be introduced in a way that will conform to the expectations of both teachers and pupils so they understand its rationale and do not perceive it as time lost for language learning.

e) *Transferability*. It is important that learning to learn is developed concurrently with the experience of learning and does not degenerate into tips for coping with the system. Too often it can become an 'add-on' element in the curriculum, taught out of context and, therefore, less likely to be applied in practice. On the other hand, integrating learning to learn in the context of regular subject teaching may tie it too specifically to the subject and hide its potential for transfer. For example, the self-testing strategy demonstrated in Figure 1 for practising times tables may not be perceived by

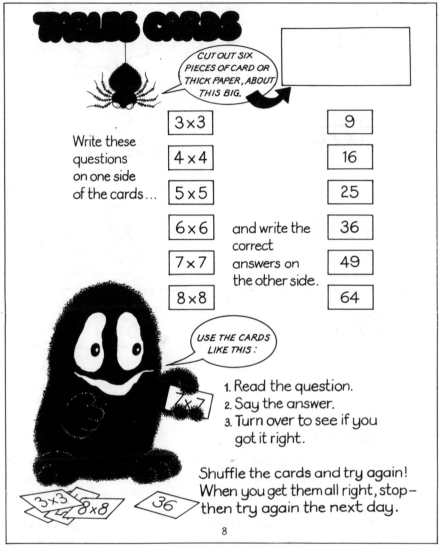

Figure 1

learners as useful for English vocabulary, see Figure 2. For learning to learn to be effective, it needs to be introduced explicitly in a meaningful context and demonstrated with transfer in mind. From the learners' viewpoint, this represents a switch of emphasis from specific skills connected with school subjects towards an approach which aims to help them to understand and to develop a conscious awareness of their own learning strategies.

It can be seen that there are a number of factors to be considered when introducing learning to learn. However, once the teacher is aware of what learning to learn involves, this task need not be any more daunting than introducing other components. It simply becomes another element to be woven into the fabric of a lesson.

Figure 2

Lesson planning

This section describes a technique for lesson planning which I used in France. As I had to cover a syllabus in a limited amount of time, I needed a technique which would allow the learning to learn to be integrated without causing disruption.

On the lesson planning sheet in Figure 3 the objectives are ordered so that learning to learn is the last item to be considered, thus preventing it from overriding the language learning aims. The ordering of the other objectives may vary according to the organisation of the course materials being used – whether they are structurally, functionally or topic-based.

The starting point is the aim of a unit, here 'Future: going to' or 'talking about plans', which is then considered for its learning to learn potential. The learning to learn can thus be naturally derived from and incorporated into the language learning work. The next step is to select learning to learn components which can be integrated into the language learning and do not distract from it, here setting short term aims, 'What am I going to do next? I'm going to learn ten new words this week', so that the pupils also use the structure presented to focus on the learning process. Figure 4 shows the worksheet used in this lesson at the practice stage.

LESSON PLANNING SHEET

Class: 6^e (11-12 yrs., 1st year of English)

Date: 14th April

Materials: Imagine you're English 6, Unit 17

Objectives

STRUCTURAL	going to
FUNCTIONAL	talking about future plans
SKILLS	All
PHONOLOGICAL	going to : stress on go + weak for to (tə). Falling intonation "What are you going to do this evening?" "I'm going to watch TV."
LEXICAL	pastimes : write letters, play cards, watch TV etc.
LEARNING TO LEARN	Setting short term aims I'm going to .....
ANTICIPATED DIFFICULTIES	- a lot of new vocabulary ie pastimes - listening to each other.

EVALUATION: Becoming more familiar with pair work. Setting short term aims arose nicely out of structural aim of the lesson

---

Figure 3 Learning to learn integrated in the lesson plan.

Similarly, learning to learn can be introduced on a topic basis. Figure 5 shows how the learning to learn derived from a gap-filling exercise was integrated into a topic-based lesson on pop music.

I have found that this lesson planning technique, because of its flexibility, allows learning to learn to be integrated into different syllabus types without causing any major disruption. It also provides the teacher with systematic records of learning to learn covered, as well as opportunities for ongoing evaluation of their lessons.

<u>Talking about Plans</u>

1. What are you going to do this evening?   Please tick (✓)

I'm going to	YOU	YOUR PARTNER
write some letters		
play cards		
watch TV		
listen to music		
go to the cinema		
see friends		
learn some English		
other?		

Now ask your partner.

2. What English are you going to learn or practise this week?

	YOU	YOUR PARTNER
I'm going to learn 10 new words.		
I'm going to		
....		
....		
....		
....		

Figure 4

Procedures

There is a variety of familiar procedures that can be used for helping pupils learn to learn, as they provide opportunities to think about learning and to experiment with different learning strategies.

a) *Elicitation:* for example the teacher asks his/her pupils, 'How do you learn new words?' The following are some of the strategies used by a class of French 11-year-olds in their own words:

LESSON PLANNING SHEET

Class: 4e (13-14 yrs., 3rd year of English).

Date: 22nd March

Materials: Topic-based lesson on pop music

Objectives

STRUCTURAL	Simple present: Wh questions. Identify the. Look for...
FUNCTIONAL	Understanding questions. writing instructions
SKILLS	All
PHONOLOGICAL	/ei/ make say. awareness of syllables
LEXICAL	Vocabulary associated with pop music
LEARNING TO LEARN	Becoming aware of contextual and linguistic clues. Guessing & Predicting
ANTICIPATED DIFFICULTIES	Will probably need to ask questions about gap filling exercise in French

EVALUATION: Pupils became really involved in the activity & liked the problem solving aspect. Had to ask some of the questions in French. Teacher-guided so control of class was good but suggestions came from pupils. Good preparation for listening stage.

Figure 5

'I keep a vocabulary book which I organise alphabetically, for example, "floor" I put under F.' (Grouping alphabetically)

'I write the word and then draw the thing.' (Visual reinforcement)

'I write the words on my blackboard and learn them, then I rub them out and try to rewrite them.' (Written repetition and self-testing)

'I try to use the word in a sentence.' (Contextualisation)

Figure 6

This procedure of elicitation can help pupils become aware of the strategies they actually use, of possible alternatives which they may not have previously considered and of individual differences.

b) *Suggestion:* learning strategies can be suggested by other learners. Figure 6 shows how Nathaniel learns English vocabulary by collecting realia containing words in English and making them into a collage. Presenting learning strategies through other pupils can add a humanising element to learning to learn, take the focus off the teacher and show pupils that they too play an important role in the teaching and learning process. A teacher could use data on learning strategies in this way as a starting point for discussion.

c) *Demonstration:* this procedure requires the teacher to determine which strategies are required, to explain why a particular strategy can be effective, to demonstrate how it can be applied and, if necessary, to offer students a framework within which to operate. For example, the strategy of self-assessment needs gradual introduction. First the teacher would need to explain why it can be useful.

Figure 7 shows a framework for self-assessment which was used in the initial stages with 11-year-old beginners. It includes a self-rating of their performance in class, an opportunity to review work covered and a further self-rating for general achievement. When possible, time can be allocated to discuss self-assessment in class. Later pupils can be encouraged to use their self-assessment charts as a basis to set short term aims.

For a further example of this procedure see Figure 1 where Inky, a spider, and Splodge, a friendly monster, demonstrate a self-testing strategy for times tables. This material could be used in the English language classroom to provide practice in numbers.

d) *Modelling:* the teacher can question the learner's basic assumptions and premises about learning and probe weak areas. Through this form of interrogation the teacher is modelling self-questioning strategies for the learner.

e) *Discussion:* this can be informal or formal and can encourage learners to speculate on their attitudes and learning strategies, exchange points of view about language learning and reflect on their own performance. If the discussion can be conducted in the target language, it provides pupils with extra opportunities for fluency practice.

In my own teaching context in France, demonstration and modelling tended to be the most appropriate procedures, although the others were used from time to time. They tended to conform more to the pupils' expectations being more teacher-guided and quick and efficient in a context where time was limited and classes were large.

These familiar procedures are probably already part of many teachers' repertoires. The common element of these procedures is a concern with the processes rather than the products of learning. They also allow learning strategies to be integrated into normal classroom activities. It is for each teacher, however, to experiment with them and to select the ones most appropriate for his/her own context.

The above guidelines offer a starting point for teachers who would like to introduce learning to learn in the context of English language teaching. To do this in a way that encourages transfer to other tasks and subjects assumes that teachers themselves know how to speculate on their own cognition, examine their own strategies for tackling tasks and reflect on their own performance. Bearing this in mind, teachers may like to ask themselves the following example questions about what they do in the classroom and why:

1 Why do I use gap-filling exercises?
2 What is my objective?
3 How do I present the exercise? Why?
4 Could I do this differently? How?
5 How did the pupils react? Why?
6 Shall I do it the same way again? Why/Why not?

SELF-ASSESSMENT   Name Denizon Valérie Date 20/04.187

How did I do in class today?

A C T I V I T Y	Good	OK	I must try harder
SPEAKING	X		
LISTENING		X	
GRAMMAR	X		
VOCABULARY	X		

Vocabulary: I learnt ..8... new words in English today.

the boss   to carry   the file
Spy   to use   busy
Sorry   to visit

Grammar: I learnt ... the future

Speaking: I learnt how to say " fruit juice ", " busy "

Give yourself a score out of 10

10 = highest
0 = lowest

| 1 | 2 | 3 | 4 | 5 | 6 | 7 | 8 | 9 | 10 |

Figure 7

Bibliography

Dickinson, L. and D. Carver. 1980. 'Learning how to learn. Steps towards self-direction in foreign language learning in schools.' *ELTJ.* 35, 1: 1–7.

Ellis, G. and B. Sinclair. 1989. *Learning to Learn English.* Cambridge: Cambridge University Press.

Hutchinson, T. 1985. *Project English.* Oxford: Oxford University Press.

Whitney, N. 1984. *Checkpoint English.* Oxford: Oxford University Press.

Whitney, N. and J. Samuel. 1990. *Adventures in English.* Oxford: Oxford University Press.

Section two

Background papers

This section contains eight papers.
Between them they survey the major foundation theories.
They explain why primary teaching is as it is,
and why language learning is as it is.

Marion Williams, University of Exeter, England

15 A framework for teaching English to young learners

In this first paper in Section Two, Marion Williams examines a linked framework for considering language teaching and primary level teaching together. Subsequent papers will develop many of the themes of this paper in more detail.

R ELATIVELY LITTLE ATTENTION has been devoted in ELT literature to the teaching of English as a second or foreign language to young learners. In fact the prevailing fashion in ELT methodologies, whether it be dialogues, substitution drills or roleplay, has generally been applied in the same way in coursebooks irrespective of whether they are for adults or children.

In this paper I will argue that it would be fruitful if teachers and writers of materials for young learners turned their attention instead to the field of education, for example, how children learn, conceptual development and motivation theory, for a basis on which to build an approach and methodology. This approach should be informed and fed by current wisdom from the world of ELT and applied linguistics.

In the first part of the paper, some relevant aspects of applied linguistics and education are surveyed briefly in order to produce a theoretical rationale for an approach to teaching young learners. It is argued that an activity-based or content-based approach provides a suitable framework within which knowledge from both fields can be incorporated. In the second part, a framework for teaching young learners is outlined and some guidance is given for designing suitable activities.

Theoretical background

The ELT world

I will now consider some aspects of applied linguistics and ELT that are relevant to the formulation of an approach.

First, a clearer picture of the way in which a learner learns or acquires a second language is beginning to emerge. It is also becoming apparent that teachers need to take note of these learning mechanisms.

An important mechanism for learning a language appears to be one of hypothesis forming and testing, or 'creative construction' (Dulay and Burt

1978, Littlewood 1984). This means that learners make hypotheses about how language works, based on evidence from input of language, and try out their new hypotheses. If we then deny the learner the opportunity to experiment with language and consequently to make mistakes and learn from them, we may be denying him/her an important learning strategy. In fact, by guiding and encouraging learning strategies, learner-active processes, rather than relying on feeding in structures for children to practise, we may be providing them with a far more valuable tool for self-learning.

There is now a fair degree of evidence that what is taught does not necessarily equal what is learnt, and that teaching a form does not automatically assist the learning of the form. It seems that the way classroom learners learn a language may have some similarities with the way learners pick up a language in a natural learning environment with no lessons. (Pica 1985, Felix and Hahn 1985, Lightbrown 1985, Ellis 1985 etc.)

The extent to which instruction does help children to acquire rules is still in question, and opinion is divided between those who maintain that instruction can assist acquisition, and those who believe it cannot. Results from researchers such as Ellis (1984) suggest it may be that instruction helps only when the child is ready to acquire the form, that is when the form is in 'the zone of proximal development' of the child (cf Pienemann's 'Teachability Hypothesis' 1989).

There is also a certain amount of evidence of a 'natural order' of learning; that is, all learners learn a language very broadly along the same route or in the same order, whether they are learning it as their first or second language (see for example Littlewood 1984 for details). Those who subscribe to what is known as 'the strong hypothesis' maintain that teaching cannot alter this order (Dulay and Burt 1973, Krashen 1982, Felix 1981). This of course could have serious implications for how we teach. Krashen and Terrell (1983) follow this strong hypothesis.

What seems to emerge then is a picture of the learner taking some measure of control over his/her own learning, regardless of what the teacher does, and the role of the teacher being to facilitate the development of the language and the learning strategies. This does not imply a throwing out of grammar and explicit focus on language, but rather a reassessment of how and when to teach it, and an awareness of learner mechanisms so that they can be allowed to operate and encouraged to develop within an approach to teaching.

What appears to be unquestioned in the literature is the crucial role of language input – input of language through listening and reading – for the learner to act on in order to activate and develop his/her own learning mechanisms (Krashen 1982, and others).

The development of these learning processes, then, is a factor which must be taken into account when developing an approach and a methodology of classroom practice.

As Sharwood Smith (1985) writes, '. . . No applied linguist can begin to propose principles of language planning, classroom methodology, or pedagogical grammar . . . before informing himself or herself on what second-language researchers have so far uncovered about the *real* process of acquisition.'

The second aspect I would like to consider briefly is the role of grammar in teaching, what grammar to teach, and the communicative approach to teaching.

Current approaches to language teaching tend to be versions of a structural (and synthetic) approach (presentation – practice – free practice), or of a communicative approach. Briefly, in a communicative approach learners use language for a real purpose in order to communicate something to someone, in the process of learning the language. This therefore simulates real, life-like reasons for using language. The communicative approach provided a refreshing and welcome shift from the teaching of grammar (a grammatical approach) or the practice of structures (a structural approach). But there is considerable confusion as to what a communicative approach actually means.

Some proponents of a communicative approach, like Dr Prabhu of the Bangalore Project in South India, hypothesise that we learn a language when our attention is focused on meaning rather than form. In his methodology there is no explicit focus on form at all, but rather the learners focus on the task to be completed.

Some develop these ideas into a task-based approach, where learners engage in carrying out tasks, and through doing the tasks they acquire the language (for example Willis 1983).

Other advocates of the communicative approach, however, see communication as a sort of extended free-practice stage for practising particular language items (sometimes called the 'weak version'), which is in fact not very different from a structural approach.

These represent fundamentally different views of the place of grammar within the methodology. A problem can arise when taking the second approach with children; the learners soon realise what form they are supposed to practise and over-use it in the lesson, but still have little idea of how to deploy the form in real communication.

I will propose that language can be explicitly focused on, but as and when the learner or the teacher perceives that the learners need the focus or an explanation to help them to further their goal of completing the task. This is unlikely to be at the initial stage (as in a presentation-practice methodology), and is more likely to be after the learner has begun the task. This language focus can be tackled in various ways as will be discussed later.

A further question arises; if we do teach forms, how do we select and sequence them? Gibbons (1983) and others have argued that there is no definite way of sequencing forms according to traditional categories such as simplicity, teachability and so on. This leaves us with the question of how to sequence, if at all, in our methodology. I shall argue then for sequencing according to pupils' needs and the demands of the task as and when the need arises, so that language is taught within a framework where the language is a means to an end (the task), rather than an end in itself. We shall see later how a checklist can be used to keep track of what is covered.

The communicative approach has in practice given us a set of techniques or recipes; and the question that arises is whether these are the best or the most appropriate techniques for teaching children. And if not, whether we can find any more suitable ones that are perhaps more child-centred or more motivating. We will pick this point up later.

Third, I would like to consider the powerful argument for the need for authentic language. Sinclair, Willis (1990) and others have suggested that many of the rules we teach are far from watertight or correct, for example rules governing 'some/any', reported speech and conditionals. We simply do not have an adequate description of the English language to explain it properly. The language is so complex that we can only ever present an approximation of it or over-simplified rules, from which no one could ever hope to speak the language correctly. Input of authentic language then becomes important so that learners are in fact exposed to the true complexities of the language.

The education world

I will now look briefly at the field of primary teaching, and what goes on in a good first language primary classroom.

For a number of years various premises have underpinned primary classroom practice. The belief that children learn by doing, by being actively involved in their learning, and a belief in the process of learning being as important as the content, have given rise to discovery methods and activity-based learning. Learning how to learn has been a key principle. In the classroom we see children involved in doing activities through which their concepts and their language can grow.

Most popular has probably been the project or thematic approach, where children explore a theme across the curriculum and use the theme to develop maths, science and language, as well as reference skills, conducting mini-surveys, questioning, observing, recording, thinking out how to find out rather than waiting to be told.

There are many links between this approach and a communicative approach to teaching a language, and this paper proposes that a content-based approach best combines the two. If language is to be used for a purpose in the communicative approach, then the thematic or content-based approach provides a very real purpose for using language.

Here, a distinction is made between *meaningful* and *purposeful*. The communicative approach has yielded a set of techniques such as information-gap exercises, and these activities entail the use of meaningful language. But I would seriously question whether these activities have any purpose to a child, or belong within a child's world.

In a content-based approach, the purpose is learning other things (other than language), exploring the world, finding out information, recording it or participating in activities for sheer enjoyment; stories, songs, drama and so on, activities that belong to a child's world. And in order to participate in these things in a foreign language, certain language and language skills will be needed.

A further key issue in the literature on teaching children is that of attitude and motivation. Children will learn better if they have a positive attitude towards what they are doing and if they are motivated or want to do it. Interest becomes a crucial factor in deciding on classroom practices for teaching children. It has been proposed that motivation is more important that aptitude or method (Gardner and Lambert 1972). A good illustration is provided in the account by Burstall *et al.* (1974) of the primary French project in the UK, where lack of motivation appears to be a key factor in pupils' lack of achievement.

The brief survey above has, I hope, highlighted a few current issues, enough to begin to point the way towards an approach and a methodology for teaching young learners. The next section of this paper describes an activity-based or content-based methodology that has been in use in Singapore for the past few years. (This was proposed by The British Council Primary Project, Singapore.) I would not like to give the impression that this is the only way to teach children. Rather, if the teacher takes due consideration of the collective wisdom from the fields of second language learning and primary education, then he/she is at liberty to decide on his/her own methodology.

A framework for a methodology

If we now pull together knowledge from both fields, we can represent the situation diagrammatically (see Figure 1).

Applied linguistics
- how language is learnt
- creative construction
- learner strategies
- input
- authentic language
- the place of grammar
- language to communicate

Education
- language to learn
- discovery methods
- language as a means
- motivation and attitude
- projects and thematic approaches
- enjoyment

Activity- or content-based approach to ELT

Figure 1

I would argue that we can start with the children and what interests them, stretches them and motivates them, and design appropriate materials that will allow them to use language in order to explore their interests. We can then feed in an explicit language focus as and when necessary or appropriate, and use our knowledge of how language is learnt and of applied linguistics, to organise a suitable language focus in terms of analysis, awareness or explanation. I will call the approach a content-based or activity-based approach to ELT.

The main organising tool becomes, then, not form, not functions, not techniques but content, so that children now have something to talk about, something to learn about, rather than spending many hours in the classroom uttering such nonsense as, 'Is John running? Yes, he is running', or to use Ray Tongue's well-known example, 'Siu Leng is younger than her mother', guaranteed to demotivate any child.

Let us now summarise what happens in an activity approach. The children (or teacher) decide to explore something or to do something. This can be a project, an activity, an enquiry or some other task designed to stimulate and motivate the children. It could also be imaginative. The children need to use language in order to carry out the activity. The teacher gives help with the language as needed. Accuracy is achieved through a desire to do something well rather than because the teacher demands it. And finally, through doing activities, the children's language and skills develop.

The teacher or materials writer, then, needs to exercise a degree of judgement as to suitability when designing activities. The following seven criteria are suggested:

1 INTEREST

The activity should be exciting, interesting and motivating to these children. If they do not like the chosen activity, change it. With the students' interest aroused we have a good starting point for learning.

2 CHALLENGE

It should provide a suitable challenge for the age group. It should stretch them a little without being too difficult, but not falling into the trap of being too simple.

3 PURPOSE

The children should focus on getting the task done, rather than practising a language item.

4 LANGUAGE USE

The pupils will need to use language, receptive or productive or both, in order to complete the activity. There is often a language aim to the activity (for example giving clear instructions) or a particular language skill (for example a reading skill) to develop, but the pupils are never confined to this language.

5 LANGUAGE INPUT

There will generally be oral or written language input at an appropriate level and in context, but this is not a 'presentation-practice-production' situation.

6 CONCEPTUAL APPROPRIATENESS

The activity should be within the conceptual ability of the pupils. They cannot do things with language that are outside their conceptual grasp. If we are looking at the development of the whole child, we will design activities that help to develop his/her thinking and his/her concepts too.

7 PROMOTION OF LEARNING

If possible, it should promote learning other than language. One of the most successful ways of combining interesting activities for children is by following a theme or topic, around which reading, writing, drama, games and so on are centred.

There are many types of activity suitable for children that are motivating and involve language use. The following list gives a few that we have found successful, but there are many more:

doing puzzles and solving problems

writing and solving riddles

using maps

measuring and weighing things

conducting surveys (e.g. food, birthdays, traffic survey)

growing plants

following and writing recipes

interviewing people (e.g. parents, people in the neighbourhood, different occupations)

making things (e.g. masks, aeroplanes, puppets)

pretend play and drama (e.g. witches, spacemen, stranded on an island)

inventing and designing things (my ideal . . . , a machine to . . . , fashions)

planning things (e.g. an outing, a party)

inventing games (e.g. board games, writing the instructions)

choosing (e.g. films, clothes)

writing letters (for real purposes)

reading and designing brochures

designing and recording a TV programme

finding out (e.g. what things are made of, what materials are used for, how things grow, whether objects float or sink)

filling in forms

studying the local environment (e.g. plants, birds, buildings)

making charts and graphs

using songs and rhymes

listening to stories (a particularly motivating form of language input, and recommended as a daily activity)

painting, drawing and talking about what we are doing

It must also be remembered that the language should be used for sheer enjoyment. Regular reading aloud of interesting stories to the class, singing songs, learning rhymes and playing games are all valuable parts of daily classroom practice.

Particularly in the school situation where reading and writing are considered important, the children should also be involved in purposeful reading and writing activities. Most projects lead nicely into purposeful writing; letters, brochures, instructions, recipes and so on.

And all classrooms should form stimulating reading environments, with authentic reading materials and classroom libraries. Reading is discussed in detail in other chapters and is therefore not discussed here, save to say that frequent and regular reading provides invaluable input of language.

Lesson planning

Let us now turn to the question of how to plan a series of lessons based on a theme. This can be broken down into two stages.

STAGE ONE

First decide on a theme which will motivate and interest the children. Take Hallowe'en as an example. 'Brainstorm' and write down ideas for possible activities leading from it as in Figure 2. This particular theme leads to imaginative work rather than learning about the world. Both types of theme have a place.

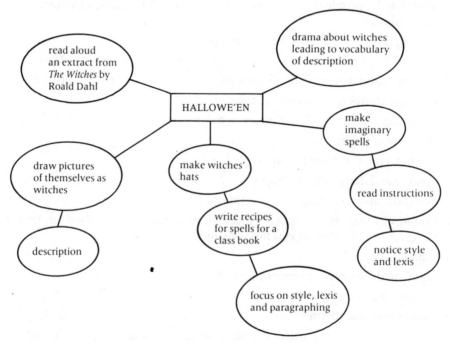

Figure 2 Ideas for activities based on a theme.

The next stage consists of making a selection of activities using the criteria listed above. Check that there is a good balance of input and output, oral work, reading and writing. There should also be a range of techniques such as drama, poetry, stories and discussion.

STAGE TWO

The next stage involves planning the series of lessons on a chart as in Figure 3 – part of the Hallowe'en theme is taken up here.

Activity	Materials	Language, Skills	Comments
1 Pupils read instructions on how to make witches' hat and follow them, working in pairs. T. helps where necessary	Black paper, scissors, pencils	Exposure to language of instructions	*Instructions needed repeating several times*
2 Exercise to analyse language of instructions: sentence length, lexis	Exercise	Layout of instructions: short, clear sentences, imperative form, linking words 'then', 'next', 'after that'	*Pupils recognised linking words well*

Figure 3 Extract from a lesson planning chart.

1 Notice that the activity comes *first*, and the language arises because of the activity. Language is therefore sequenced according to the needs of the task.

2 The teacher may or may not predetermine *which* language items or skills will be focused on, according to his/her view of learning and the situation that exists in the school. He/She also decides *when* they are focused on and *how*.
   For example the teacher may wait to see what items the pupils need help with, give help when needed and complete the 'language' column after the lesson.
   It is not necessary to pre-teach the items as in a presentation-practice methodology. They can be focused on at a later stage of the lesson when the children see that they have a need.
   And moving on to the question of 'how', the teacher may use a language analysis method, 'Notice how speaker X said something or how writer Y expressed something', which will enhance the pupils' ability to analyse language, an important strategy for language learning.

3 Rather than using one language form at a time, several skills and forms will be used at once, which is what happens in real life.

4 The 'Comments' column provides a record of work and can contain information about how something went, what needs further work and so on.

5 For teachers who have a syllabus to cover, a form like this can be used as a checklist to show which syllabus items have been covered.

6 There is space within this format for explicit and fairly formal language focus if the pupils are making a common error or have a common need. But this focus or mini grammar lesson arises out of the needs of the pupils rather than the syllabus specification or the teacher's whim.

Conclusion

In this chapter I have described a way of working that has been successfully used with foreign language and second language learners. I have also attempted to outline some of the theoretical considerations that might underlie such an approach.

The classroom teacher will find her own way of working; no one format will be suited to everyone. However, I hope I have provided something that the teacher can start with and I hope ultimately develop in his/her own way to suit his/her own purposes.

Bibliography

Burstall, C., M. Jamieson, C. Cohen and M. Hargreaves. 1974. *Primary French in the Balance.* Slough: NFER.

Dulay, H. and M. Burt. 1973. 'Should we teach children syntax?' *Language Learning* 23: 245–58.

Dulay, H. and M. Burt. 1978. 'Some remarks on creativity in language acquisition.' in Ritchie, W. (ed). *Second Language Acquisition Research.* London: Academic Press.

Ellis, R. 1984. 'Can syntax be taught? A study of the effects of formal instruction on the acquisition of WH- questions by children.' *Applied Linguistics* Vol. 5, 2.

Ellis, R. 1985. *Understanding Second Language Acquisition.* Oxford: Oxford University Press.

Felix, S. 1981. 'The effect of formal instruction on second language acquisition.' *Language Learning* 31, 87–112.

Felix, S. and A. Hahn. 1985. 'Natural processes in classroom second language learning.' *Applied Linguistics* Vol. 6,3.

Gardner, R. and W. Lambert. 1972. 'Attitudes and motivation in second language learning.' U.S.A.: Newbury House.

Gibbons, J. 1983. *Sequencing and Language Syllabus Design.* RELC Conference, Singapore.

Krashen, S. D. 1982. *Principles and Practice in Second Language Acquisition.* Oxford: Pergamon Press.

Krashen, S. D. and T. Terrell. 1983. *The Natural Approach.* Oxford: Pergamon Press.

Lightbrown, P. 1985. 'Input and acquisition for second language learners in and out of classrooms.' *Applied Linguistics.* Vol. 6,3.

Littlewood, W. 1984. *Foreign and Second Language Learning.* Cambridge: Cambridge University Press.

Pica, T. 1985. 'The selective impact of classroom instruction on second language acquisition.' *Applied Linguistics* Vol. 6.3.

Pienemann, M. 1989. 'Is language teachable? Psycholinguistic experiments and hypotheses.' *Applied Linguistics* Vol. 10,1.

Sharwood Smith, M. 1985. Preface to *Applied Linguistics* Vol. 6,3.

Willis, D. 1983. The implications of discourse analysis for the teaching of spoken English. (Unpublished PhD thesis, Birmingham.)

Joan Tough, formerly of Leeds University, England

16 Young children learning languages

Joan Tough draws upon a lifetime's experience of research and practice in language work. She examines the process of language development in young children, relating the mother tongue context to second language development.

A N INTRIGUING PARADOX in the development of young children is their ability to establish their first language at a time when they are unable to understand anything about the system which they come to use with such competence. Nor is this capacity for learning language limited to the first language. There are many documented cases of young children learning to use a second language when they are in close contact with a speaker or speakers who use it. There are also reported cases where children develop the use of two languages almost simultaneously in a home where two languages are in daily use between members of the family (see Grosjean 1982).

From experiences of learning other languages at later ages there is much that indicates that learning language is not easy. Yet young children the world over persist with what later appears to be a difficult, tedious and protracted task, and almost all are remarkably successful. Such observations, supported by research and theoretical deduction, have led to a view that the early years of childhood provide an optimum period for learning languages and many argue that it is indeed a critical period.

The fact that young children learn their first language with such speed and competence must mean that if the process can be better understood it should be possible to design experiences through which children learn a second language in much the same way as they learn their first language.

It is the potential for social and cognitive development during the early years to which we must look in order to explain the drive towards competence in using language. Both social and cognitive development depend upon children being drawn into interaction with others and both are set on course in the very early days as parents and other carers talk to children while attending to their needs. Physical handling is generally accompanied by aural and visual stimulation. The parent's voice, facial expression and gestures in time call out responses from the baby and these in turn provoke responses from the adult. Within a short time the sound of the parent's voice alone draws the baby's attention. As the baby turns towards the source of the sound the speaker's face comes into view. The movements of the speaker's face, and particularly of the eyes and mouth,

213

attract the baby's attention and the speaker's face is brought into focus. In this way parents and others become familiar and recognition is evident in the baby's responses. Research and observation show that babies distinguish between pleasant and disapproving tones of voice and facial expressions, responding to the former by smiles and happy vocalisations and to the latter by signs of distress and crying. So social interaction is established and communication is underway.

Research has examined the emergence of babies' smiles and vocal responses to parents' talk, showing the way in which a conversation-like quality in the exchanges develops and how such 'conversations' gradually extend. Research also shows how the spontaneous playing with sound, which develops around the third and fourth months of life, begins to die away around the sixth and seventh months, as babies apparently begin to concentrate on the production of a smaller range of sounds. This indicates growing control over the mouth, tongue and throat and gradually the baby produces the articulation controls needed for the production of speech. At this stage we can see the pleasure babies find in being able to produce particular sounds at will and how the obvious pleasure of those around them encourages them to repeat sounds deliberately and spurs them on to further accomplishments.

Important too is the interaction that takes place through gesture and facial expression and through deliberate action. Young children communicate their wants by reaching and pointing, by pushing away and rejecting, by smiling, frowning and crying, and in this way influence the responses of others. Parents also use facial expressions, gesture, action, tone of voice and stress intuitively to support the meaning of what they say. It is through such interaction that meaning becomes attached to a small range of sounds a baby can produce at will, forming first 'words', and so the conditions for the development of the first language are established.

As children's physical development goes apace, more and more of the concrete world around them comes within their grasp and investigation as they begin to crawl or shuffle and then to walk. More and more information becomes available through sight, hearing and touch. Expectations build up about the way the world is through interaction with the concrete and social world around them and new 'meanings' are established as they become aware of different attributes. The human potential for setting structure upon experiences gives impetus to development. As children seek to impose structure on their world, words not only serve to encapsulate meaning but when used by others also direct attention to aspects of experience not yet differentiated, thereby promoting concept formation. Inherent in this development is the urge to impose structure on the language they hear, which is reflected in the language they attempt to use as they begin to talk.

Most children establish a small range of first words between the ages of about 12 and 18 months, and respond appropriately to a wider range used by others, suggesting that they too have attached meaning. From the age of about two years they begin to put words together and so move towards discovering the system of their first language.

The sequence of development of the first language

There is now a considerable body of research that has examined aspects of the development of the first language. During the 1960s a number of longitudinal studies of individual children produced evidence of the sequence in which the use of particular features of the first language appeared. When these words were compared it was seen that some features were common to all the children studied, and attempts were made to identify these and to describe strategies that were characteristic of the speech of young children. For example, the early stages of language were found to be characterised by one-word utterances used to communicate a range of meanings that were differentiated by intonation and gesture. As two-word utterances appeared there were found to be regularities that could be identified in the utterances of all the children in the studies. These early speech patterns were described as being *telegraphic* by Brown and Fraser (1963). Braine (1963) recognised two classes of words in two-word utterances which he described as *open* and *pivotal* according to the way in which they were related to one another, and which indicated that already rules of word order relating to meaning were being applied. Even in these very early stages it seemed learning was not haphazard, common characteristics of order could be identified and Bloom (1970) produced evidence to show that this reflected deliberate attempts to express structural meanings.

Several studies have attempted to describe aspects of the development of language during the early stages. The majority of these studies focused on the emergence of grammatical structures and many were concerned with the kind of errors that children made as they moved towards grammatical competence. Although it is clear that children's development of grammar moves across a broad front, studies tended to focus on one or two grammatical features, for example the use of negatives and questions (Klima and Bellugi 1966), the responses to questions (Ervin-Tripp 1970), the development of verb and noun inflections (Cazden 1968), and the development of locative terms (Clark 1973).

A further development was to examine the use of particular morphemes (that is grammatical elements from which words are constructed, for example, in English 's' added to nouns to indicate plural, and 'ed' added to verbs to indicate past) and to identify the order in which they appeared. Roger Brown (1973) examined the use of 14 morphemes and showed that although the rate of development varied between children, the route through which they developed was common to all. A later study by de Villiers and de Villiers (1978) confirmed a similar order of appearance of morphemes in the speech of 21 children.

Alongside the above research, which had examined the development of language in English-speaking children, research was being undertaken into similarities that occur whatever language is being acquired. In one study the early stages of language development in 40 different languages were examined and similarities were identified which supported the view that all children adopt similar principles in their attempts to differentiate the rules of

TEACHING ENGLISH TO CHILDREN

the language they are acquiring (Slobin 1973). Generally it seems that children use certain structures before others, that there are similar stages in the development of many structures, and that there are common features in the development of a first language whatever the language being acquired.

The evidence of such common features in early language learning led to the theory that young children's ability to develop the use of language is a result of innate cognitive and linguistic abilities which together operate as a Language Acquisition Device and account for common characteristics in early language learning, whatever the language used, whatever experiences are available to the child, and whatever the context (Chomsky 1966, McNeill 1966). Support for this theory came from research that showed that the frequency with which children were exposed to particular structures was not a predictor of the order of appearance in children's talk (Brown 1973). Such a theory aroused interest in the experiences of language that children meet and focused attention on the use of language by those who care for children during the early stages of development.

Children's experiences of the use of language

During the 1970s a number of studies examined the way in which parents and others talked to young children in their care. Generally these produced evidence to show that talk is based on something in the immediate environment that takes children's attention or to which their attention is drawn. Thus parents' talk most frequently refers to objects present and to distinctive action, so the language used has a present context and reference has concrete illustration. Other characteristics are often the use of a higher pitch of voice, slower and more clearly articulated speech, grammatical modification or simplification, frequent repetition of a phrase, repetition of what the child has said, often in a corrected form offering a model to the child, and often with an expansion of or an elaboration on what the child has said. Such behaviour, it is suggested, helps the child to identify the 'adult' form. 'Motherese', as such behaviour has been termed, operates as a set of intuitive language lessons for young children and urges them towards communicative competence (Snow 1972, Snow and Ferguson 1977, Nelson 1973 and Newport 1976).

The evidence from a study by Bloom (1970) gives further insight into the way in which competence develops. This study found that changes in a child's competence in using language were accompanied by changes in the adult's talk, so that as children matured the adults adjusted their own use of language accordingly, thus providing a model that was just ahead of a child's competence.

It seems, then, that parents look intuitively for signs from which they can judge what a child is ready for and is able or soon will be able to understand.

Learning to communicate through talking

An important question, then, is whether parents' responses to children's talk are concerned with helping children to establish correctness in the use of particular linguistic structures or to help effective communication through the use of language. Recent research supports the view that it is the latter that provides the basic motivation, and that the intuitive help with acquiring linguistic structures is the result of attempts at *negotiating* meaning rather than any determination to *correct* the child's use of language.

A closer examination is needed of the characteristics of interaction between parents and their children in order to identify the intuitive strategies that enable children to learn to operate rules governing the language they are acquiring.

A number of studies have focused on the patterns of interaction between adults and children and have concluded that it is through the construction of conversations in which both child and parent strive to communicate particular meaning that children become competent in using language.

In an analysis of such conversations Bloom, Rocissano and Hood (1976) identified a number of strategies used by children which took information from an earlier utterance by the adult in order to take a turn in the conversation. They suggested that in the early stages of using a first language children imitated words and structures in the adult's speech which they had already partly or fully acquired. Later they repeated the verb used by the adult and incorporated words or phrases used earlier in the conversation. In this way it seems children are helped to expand their repertoire day by day and learn about the lexical and syntactical function of verbs. A study by Scollon (1979) confirmed that such a process of *incorporation* was a regular feature in conversations between adults and children and provided important information which helped to extend children's knowledge of the language. Bruner (1978) has also concluded that it is through established routines of carrying on conversations about here and now events that children are helped to recognise how talk relates to what is seen and touched and how linguistic structures are used to discriminate variations in meaning.

Substantial support has been given to this view by a longitudinal study of children between the ages of 18 months and ten years carried out by Gordon Wells and his team at Bristol University between 1972 and 1981. The project recorded samples of children's talk at home with parents on a regular basis and followed up with studies of their responses to school and educational achievement at the age of ten. Interestingly it was found that, although there were differences between children in the rate of language development which related to certain characteristics of talk in the home, it seemed that language development followed the same stages whatever the rate of development (Wells 1985).

An important finding was that certain characteristics of interaction in the home were closely related to aspects of children's subsequent use of language and level of achievement in school. Two particular approaches were distinguished. In one parents interacted with their children, helping them to express their thinking by as it were a series of negotiations in an attempt to make clear the meaning intended to be communicated. In this the adults showed sensitivity to children's interests and focused attention, and helped them to develop ideas arising from those interests by clearly valuing children's contributions, and adding to their ideas by offering relevant information. Such interaction was described as *supportive*. In contrast a second pattern of interaction was characterised by greater imposition by the parents of the topic under discussion, with little recognition of the children's attempts to contribute to the exchange and revealed that the parents were intuitively assuming a *tutorial* role. It was found that those children who experienced interaction in the home that was categorised as supportive tended towards greater achievement in school at the age of ten (Wells and Montgomery 1981).

From this and other studies of interaction Wells concluded that the most important experience for children is for carers to be sensitive to their interests and stage of development, to find their attempts to communicate of interest, and to help them make their meanings clear (Wells 1985).

It is the search for regularity, for common features, and the impetus towards the formation of concepts that provides the possibility for language to emerge and it is the urge to communicate differences in meaning that makes parents intuitively give attention to helping their children to recognise the part that structures of the language play in conveying particular kinds of meaning.

A longitudinal study of children's use of language between the ages of three and seven years undertaken by the author also has some relevance here (Tough 1977a). In this study it was found that children developed a disposition to use language which was related to the way in which parents interacted with children in the home. The purposes for which children readily used language in school related closely to the way in which parents viewed their children, and were themselves disposed to use language when talking about their children. For example, where parents readily turned to look for related and causal explanations for their children's development and behaviour so it seemed that their children were disposed to use language for similar purposes in their approach to activities in school. By the age of seven it seemed that children's use of language reflected a disposition to think in particular ways and this influenced their use of language. From this study it was concluded that interaction with adults through talk involves children in the adults' ways of thinking and that children's efforts to understand lead them to attempt to express similar meaning.

Research into classroom interaction, however, has generally shown that teachers' talk predominates and that opportunities for children to communicate and extend their ideas are limited (Tizard, Philps and Plewis 1976). The studies referred to above give some insight into ways of talking with young children in school that teachers should adopt if they are to extend children's thinking and the range of purposes for which they use language, and so their competence in using language.

Young children learning to use a second language

During the last 20 years interest has developed in the way in which young children learn a second language in natural situations and much has been found to be held in common between learning the first language and learning a second language. The appearance of 'errors' of grammatical structure in the early stages of learning first and second languages, and the emergence of specific structures, for example the use of question forms, have been compared. Generally similar patterns have been found when children are learning English as a second language as when younger children are acquiring English as their first language. Studies of the development of the use of morphemes, referred to above, conclude that there is a natural order through which grammatical structure develops (Slobin 1973).

From such studies many researchers have concluded that there are some universal processing strategies that are used both in learning to use the first language and in learning to use a second language. They suggest that children gradually reconstruct rules for a second language that is becoming familiar, by imposing rules from their first language on what they hear, and then try to produce talk in the second language guided by those rules. The responses they then receive from adults gradually help them to recognise that the rules are different, and to recognise different regularities, which they then seek to impose until the problem of communicating meaning successfully is resolved (Dulay and Burt 1978).

Other research, however, has questioned this conclusion. Several studies have found that the same sequence of development did not necessarily take place, and that differences were dependent on the child's first language. However, generally researchers agree that children have a predisposition to use language and that there are common characteristics between learning the first language and learning to use a second language, with some variance that relates to established expectations about the use of the first language.

The kind of interaction and contexts from which young children will receive the most effective support for learning a second language has not yet been the subject of much research but it would seem that present knowledge of first language learning provides insights which can guide those who seek to help young children learn a second language.

Becoming attuned to a second language

Although children between the ages of three and seven, that is during their early years in school, generally have more skills than two-year-olds, particularly in their use of language, they still share some important characteristics. They are now aware of 'talking' but they are still unable to conceive of language as a system that conforms to a set of rules that can be learned and applied, even though they are applying intuitively many of those rules. Nor are they likely to have a commitment to learning a second language because of some advantage this might bring in the future, motivation that would be understood, if not embraced, by older learners. And there is still only one medium through which they can learn language; since generally they are unable to read and write they are still wholly dependent on learning language through talking.

Children's experiences during the period before they begin to acquire their first language, that is up to 18 months to two years old, have been shown to be crucial in preparing the essential basis for the development of language. During this period the necessary relationships are developing between parents and their babies, and communication is established through gestures, facial expression, actions and vocalisations. The importance of parents talking to young children, even though what is said carries meaning for them only through tone of voice and accompanying gestures and facial expression, cannot be overemphasised. From such experiences young children develop skills and expectations which, when intellectual development makes it possible, lead to the development of language. It is essential, then, to consider whether such conditions will also be needed in an environment created to give optimum support to children when they are learning a second language.

Clearly the pre-linguistic period has already provided the preparation necessary for learning any language. By the age of four most children are already communicating well in their first language, the articulation mechanisms are already well developed and conceptual development is way ahead of that required for acquiring the first language. So the long period of preparation before any words are produced, essential for learning a first language, would not seem to be necessary before learning a second language becomes possible. Nor would the long period of producing single words before longer utterances are produced seem to be required since articulation is generally well under control. Nevertheless children will need time to adjust to and become familiar with the environment in which the second language is used and form friendly relations with others in the group. They will need to feel at home, welcome and secure, and have established trust in the adults who have taken over their care. The use of their first language with other children and adults can provide the support they need for quickly becoming confident and able to take part in activities. Research has shown that where such support is available during the early years in school, learning generally goes ahead more quickly and progress in learning a second language is sustained.

Even though young children have a remarkable potential for learning language this potential can only come into play if they are immersed in experiences of the language being used. So it is just as essential for children to see and hear the second language being used, with much of it being directly addressed to them, as it is for babies to experience the first language being used before they can acquire it themselves. Since children already use a first language, the conditions for acquiring the second language should resemble as far as possible those of living in a family where two languages are in daily use, and where the children themselves are frequently involved in using both.

When speaking to children in a second language it is important, as it is when they are learning their first language, to support communication through the use of gesture, facial expression and action because this gives children clues to the meaning of what they hear and so draws their attention to and helps them to become familiar with the sounds, rhythms and stress of the second language which are different from those of their first language.

So it will be essential for teachers of young children and assistants to use the second language, addressing children directly as individuals when they are engaging in activities in small groups, in the way that parents would with children in a family. They need to adjust their own talk intuitively to come within the capabilities of the particular child they are addressing, encourage children to respond by whatever means they can, and respond to them with talk and accompanying gestures and non-verbal signals that support communication and give essential information, not only to the child who is being directly addressed, but also to others who are present and are hearing what is said.

Strategies that parents use intuitively to draw children into the use of the first language must be used deliberately by teachers to draw children into using the second language. Research, referred to above, indicates that parents generally speak a little more slowly, articulate more carefully, and use gesture, facial expression and tone of voice when talking to young children to aid their understanding and to encourage them to respond. Only with frequent experiences of this kind, which must be pleasurable so that children do not try to avoid such encounters, can children become familiar with the sounds, rhythms and stress of the second language and be motivated to try to use some elements of it to communicate.

Again, research indicates that parents intuitively recognise when children are ready to take new steps. It is through frequent interaction with individual children, even when they cannot respond in the second language, that teachers will be able to judge when each child is ready to take another step forward, taking clues from each child's behaviour as to what that new step will be. This includes recognising when a child is attempting to use some element of the second language for the first time and offering responses that will help and encourage further attempts. Such attempts will be an indication that the child is becoming adjusted to the new environment and attuned to the second language and is ready to take further steps in using the second language. It is a process that requires great sensitivity on the part of the teacher and it is important that children's attempts to communicate are rewarded with obvious pleasure on the part of the adult, adding to the pleasure in the activity itself.

The period of such adjustment and attunement will vary as it would for all children beginning school, regardless of the language being used. Some children may require only a week or two before they are attempting to communicate in the second language and for others the period might extend to two or three months and, in a few cases, longer.

From first to second language

At whatever age children begin to use a second language we know that they will have developed skills and strategies in learning to use their first language that can be drawn on to aid learning the second language. Unlike younger children developing their first language, where concept development and language development are largely interdependent, they will have established a wide range of concepts and well-developed meanings that they are able to express in their first language. This means that once they try to use elements of the second language to communicate they will intuitively be looking for a means of expressing already established meanings.

Intuitively children will be looking for evidence from the sounds they hear, from the gestures and actions of speakers, and from the objects and materials being used to help them identify 'words' and their reference as they would in their first language. Children may also, without any awareness, be trying to apply intuitive knowledge of the structure of the first language in order to bring some order to what others are saying.

In the past it seems to have been agreed that what had been established in learning a first language was likely to 'interfere' with learning a second, since languages have such different structures. There is some evidence that children may intuitively be seeking for structure characteristic of their first language and this may cause frustration when it fails to bring a solution. One of the most outstanding characteristics of first language learning, however, is the trial and error character of children's attempts to use language, and their ability to use responses from competent users of the language to amend their intuitive search for regularity in structure. More recent research supports the view that where two languages are being acquired simultaneously there will be parallel development. Where one language is established before acquiring a second, then strategies developed in learning the first language will transfer to the process of learning subsequent languages and be a positive aid to learning. Such transference seems more likely to take place when the experiences through which the second language is learned are of a similar nature to those through which the strategies have been developed in the first place.

Children, then, are already experienced language users, and have well-developed strategies for learning language to assist them in acquiring a second language, although they may have some expectations that might take some time to be amended. Knowledge of the children's first language should alert teachers to features of the second language that are contrary to the children's expectations. They might then deliberately offer appropriate information through their responses, repeating phrases that give clues to the different structure, as parents do in first language learning, in order to help children change their expectations and more quickly identify the different regularities of the second language. This would also apply to sounds used in the second language that are not part of the first language and so may go unnoticed or present difficulties of articulation. Teachers' responses might then include slightly exaggerated articulation, making sure that children see the movement of the mouth, as parents would use when children are learning their first language, in order that children might have clearer information about the production of the particular sounds.

When children are learning a second language it is clear that it will be some time before the second language will become adequate for expressing ideas commensurate with their intellectual and social development and before the second language can be effective in promoting conceptual development. The importance of children continuing to have appropriate experiences of using the first language during this period should not be underestimated, both for cultural reasons and for promoting intellectual development and learning, which will ultimately contribute to their competence in using their second language. Studies of young children becoming bilingual suggest that the contexts in which each language is used should be clearly differentiated, either by association with particular adults or with particular situations, so that children build up expectations about when each language will be used.

Children's strategies in learning language

From studies of first language learning, then, it is clear that both children and parents intuitively develop strategies that promote acquisition of the first language and there is also some evidence to suggest that young children will apply the same strategies when learning a second language.

In the early days of language study the view that language was learned mainly by *imitation* and *repetition* was widely accepted but the theory more recently put forward by Chomsky and others, referred to above, that innate mechanisms are the main source of learning, has led to the role of imitation and repetition being accorded less importance than formerly. More recently the closer examination of interaction and the nature of talk to and with young children, and of children's responses, has led to a re-examination of the role of imitation and repetition by children when acquiring both first and second languages (Clark 1978, Hatch, Peck and Wagner-Gough 1979).

From studies of both first and second language learning it is clear that the very first attempts to produce speech are attempts to imitate single words used by others. As meaning becomes attached children go on to use them frequently, repeating them as though practising using them. Children then begin to combine words learned in this way, showing creativity in the production of 'telegraphic speech' referred to earlier. In first language learning parents often respond by filling out their child's telegraphic utterance, which the child often imitates before the parent responds to the

223

child's meaning. Often children respond to a parent's comment by repeating what has been said before going on to formulate a response. Through such imitation and repetition it seems children are helped to recognise the way in which utterances are structured.

Children also imitate and repeat short phrases attached to particular kinds of situation in the same way. Through frequent imitation such phrases are learned and continue to be used as unanalysed wholes and so have been termed *formulaic*. There is some debate about the nature and role of such formulaic speech. According to Wong Fillmore (1979), formulaic speech is central to the development of language in the early stages but once children move into creative production of language and intuitively recognise underlying rules they become less and less dependent for communication on the strategy of formulaic speech. Others argue that although formulaic speech remains as unanalysed wholes for some time, eventually the structure within is recognised and so makes an important contribution to the development of the intuitive application of rules.

All recognise, however, that there are many utterances that are learned as wholes in both first and second language learning and these generally have a grammatical complexity that will not fit the intuitive imposition of structure that children are attempting in their creative utterances. Phrases like 'I don't know', 'It doesn't matter' and 'That's no good' are used frequently and are attached to types of situation rather than to particular objects or activities. They serve well in conversation and give children a means of responding to and initiating talk even when they rely mainly on gesture and action for communicating about specific objects, actions, needs and intentions. Children's use of formulaic speech, then, is a valuable strategy to be recognised and encouraged by those who seek to promote children's learning.

Recent studies of young children learning a second language have confirmed that imitation, repetition and formulaic speech are the first strategies to be used. In summarising evidence on second language learning, Hatch (1983) places importance on such use, not only for children's first steps in learning the second language, but for their continuing progress.

The responses of others to children's attempts to communicate through the use of imitation, repetition and formulaic speech when learning a first language lead to the development of a fourth important strategy, that of *incorporation*. As children's use of repetition proceeds they begin to put such learned components together to express meaning. Often this takes the form of repeating a word or short phrase used by the adult and putting it in some sequence with elements already established. They incorporate an element heard in the present situation into an already established phrase or one that is being produced creatively from elements already established, or by imitating an utterance used by the adult and adding to it elements established previously. In this way, it is argued, the learner is moved towards recognising rules that underlie the language used.

The teacher's role in promoting second language development

Research, referred to above, has revealed much about the role that parents intuitively play in promoting children's development of a first language. From this research it is clear that there are certain characteristics of parents' talk with children that provide children with essential information about the language they are using and motivation to persist in their efforts to use language and to develop strategies for learning language. Young children who are learning a second language in school will need support of a similar kind if the strategies for learning language are to be brought into play. Teachers need therefore to use deliberately strategies that parents generally use quite intuitively. Those strategies have already been discussed and a summary only is needed here.

Generally parents' talk to and with children is about a concrete present situation in which children's interest is held by their own involvement in the activity and talk adds to their interest and enjoyment. Talk is essentially used to communicate about aspects of the activity.

In the early stages much of parents' talk is paralleled by gesture and action so that reference is established for objects and distinctive actions. Parents tend to speak a little more slowly to young children and with a higher pitched voice signalling that talk is addressed to them individually. Parents tend to articulate more clearly, often repeating single words as they indicate objects and actions, and often follow up by using those same words in simple, well-formed, colloquial utterances long before children begin to produce elements of the language themselves.

As children begin to talk, at first with single words and then combining two or more, and using formulaic phrases, parents respond to the meaning, or what they think is the meaning, of what children are trying to express, but at the same time intuitively provide models for children to hear.

Parents frequently repeat single words clearly, often several times and at a level at which the child can see the movements of the mouth, in order to help a child with reference or with articulation, and encourage the child to try again, by facial expression and tone of voice which the child soon comes to recognise as a signal to imitate what the parent has offered.

Once children begin to produce single words as reference to objects and actions parents delightedly repeat the word often several times, and often then incorporate the word in a colloquial complete phrase that is generally used for making such reference. If a child wrongly names an object or action, parents will quickly give the appropriate name, repeating it several times and often indicating the object to which the word the child used refers. They join in the child's activity accompanying their own actions and the child's with appropriate simple utterances, intuitively emphasising words carrying reference but, also intuitively, letting the child hear them in well-formed colloquial structures. Parents encourage children to talk, are prepared to listen and give them time to complete what they are trying to say and use gesture intuitively to help children understand what they are trying to communicate.

When children begin to use telegraphic utterances parents essentially respond to children's meaning, but intuitively first fill out the telegraphic phrase the child has used to a well-formed phrase with the same meaning, and then address the meaning of what the child has said, so that children frequently hear their telegraphic phrases expanded to a well-formed version.

Parents often begin a response to children's talk with a reformulation of their ill-formed utterances before proceeding to extend meaning and stimulate children to think and communicate further ideas. Once children show that everyday references and simple colloquial structures are being established, intuitively parents begin to introduce alternative structures and ways of expressing similar meaning, preceding them or following them with forms their children are already using. Intuitively parents recognise when what they have said is beyond their children's understanding and seek to express the same ideas in language forms with which they are familiar to help them recognise that meaning is similar. In this way parents intuitively give impetus to children's acquisition of more complex structures and vocabulary that allow greater differentiation of meaning.

Above all parents involve their young children in conversations about what they are doing very frequently and often for sustained periods.

Teachers and others who are involved in helping young children to acquire a second language need to examine their talk with young children and consider to what extent they are providing children with conditions similar to those through which the first language develops. Conditions in schools cannot be the same as those at home, if only because of the greater number of young children with whom they must talk. However, teachers involved in the final phase of the Schools Council Communication Skills Project found that it is possible to create environments that support children's development of English as a second language by following principles drawn from studying the way in which first languages are learned, and by using quite deliberately strategies that parents generally use quite intuitively. Publications from this project (Tough 1977b, 1977c, 1985a, 1985b) indicate how such principles might be carried into practice in schools for young children in order to promote more appropriately the learning of English as a second language.

Bibliography

Bloom, L. 1970. *Language Development: Form and Function in Developing Grammars.* Cambridge, Massachusetts: MIT Press.

Bloom, L., L. Rocissano and L. Hood. 1976. 'Adult-child discourse: developmental interaction between information processing and linguistic knowledge.' *Cognitive Psychology* 8, 527–552.

Braine, M. 1963. 'The ontogeny of English phrase structure: the first phase.' *Language* 39, 1–14.

Brown, R. and C. Fraser. 1963. 'The acquisition of syntax.' in **Cofer, C.N.** and **Barbara S. Musgrave** (eds). *Verbal Behaviour and Learning.* New York: McGraw-Hill.

Brown, R. 1973. *A First Language: the Early Stages*. Massachusetts: Harvard University Press.

Bruner, J.S. 1978. 'The role of dialogue in language acquisition.' in Sinclair, A., R.J. Jarvella and W.J.M. Levelt (eds). *The Child's Conception of Language*. New York: Springer-Verlag.

Bruner, J.S. 1981. *Under-Fives Research in Britain*. London: Grant McIntyre.

Cazden, C.B. 1968. 'Acquisition of noun and verb inflections.' *Child Development* 39, 433–448.

Chomsky, N. 1966. *Aspects of the Theory of Syntax*. Cambridge, Massachusetts: MIT Press.

Clark, E. 1973. 'Non-linguistic strategies and the acquisition of word meanings.' *International Journal of Cognitive Psychology* 2, 161–182.

Dulay, H. and M. Burt. 'Some remarks on creativity in language acquisition.' in Ritchie, W. (ed). *Second Language Acquisition Research*. New York: Academic Press.

Ervin-Tripp, S. 1970. 'Discourse agreement: how children answer questions.' in Hayes, J. (ed). *Cognition and the Development of Language*. New York: Wiley.

Fillmore, L.W. 1979. 'Individual differences in language ability and language behaviour.' in Fillmore, C., K. Templar and W. Wang (eds). *Individual Differences in Second Language Acquisition*. New York: Academic Press.

Grosjean, F. 1982. *Life with Two Languages*. Cambridge, Massachusetts: Harvard University Press.

Hatch, E. 1983. *Psycholinguistics: a Second Language Perspective*. Rawley, Massachusetts: Newbury House Publishers Inc.

Hatch, E., S. Peck and J. Wagner-Gough. 1979. 'A look at process in child second language acquisition.' in Ochs, E. and B. Schieffelin (eds). *Developmental Pragmatics*. New York: Academic Press.

Kilma, E. and U. Bellugi. 1966. 'Syntactic regularities in the speech of children.' in Lyons, J. and R. Wales (eds). *Psycholinguistic Papers*. Edinburgh: Edinburgh University Press.

Krashen, S.D. 1981. *Second Language Acquisition and Second Language Learning*. Oxford: Pergamon Press.

Krashen, S.D., C. Madden and M. Bailey. 1975. 'Theoretical aspects of grammatical sequencing.' in Burt, M. and H. Dulay. *Second Language Learning, Teaching and Bilingualism*. Washington DC: TESOL.

McNeill, D. 1966. 'Developmental psycholinguistics' in Smith, F. and G.A.

Miller (eds). *The Genesis of Language*. Cambridge, Massachusetts: MIT Press.

Nelson, K. 1973. 'Structure and strategy in learning to talk.' Monograph of the Society into Research into Child Development, 38 (1–2, 149).

Newport, E.L. 1976. ' "Motherese": the speech of mothers to young children.' in Castellan, N.J., D.P. Pisoni and G.R. Potts (eds). *Cognitive Theory*. New York: Lawrence Erlbaum.

Rees, O. and B. Fitzpatrick. 1981. 'Mother tongue and English teaching project.' Summary of Report Vols 1 & 2, Bradford College.

Scollon, R. 1979. 'A real early stage: an unzippered condensation of a dissertation on child language.' in Ochs, E. and B. Schieffelin (eds). *Developmental Pragmatics*. New York: Academic Press.

Slobin, D.I. 1973. 'Cognitive pre-requisites for the development of grammar.' in Ferguson, C. and D. Slobin (eds). *Studies of Child Language Development*. New York: Holt, Rinehart & Winston.

Snow, C.E. 1972. 'Mothers' speech to young children learning language.' *Child Development* 43, 549–565.

Snow, C.E. and C.A. Ferguson. 1977. *Talking to Children: Language, Input and Acquisition*. Cambridge: Cambridge University Press.

Tizard, B., J. Philps and I. Plewis. 1976. 'Staff behaviour in pre-school centres.' *Journal of Child Psychology and Psychiatry* 17, 21–23.

Tough, J. 1977a. *The Development of Meaning*. London: Allen & Unwin.

Tough, J. 1977b. *Talking and Learning*. London: Ward Lock Educational.

Tough, J. 1977c. *Talking and Learning*. A set of ten video tapes. Cardiff: Drake Educational.

Tough, J. 1985. *Talk Two: Children Using English as a Second Language*. London: Onyx Press.

Tough, J. 1985. *Children using English as a Second Language*. A set of ten video tapes. Cardiff: Drake Educational.

de Villiers, J. and P. 1973. 'A cross-sectional study of the acquisition of grammatical morphemes in child speech.' *Journal of Psycholinguistic Research* 2, 274.

Wells, G. 1981. *Learning through Interaction: the Study of Language Development*. London: Cambridge University Press.

Wells, G. and M. Montgomery. 1981. 'Language learning and education.' in French, C. and M. Maclure (eds). *Language at Home and School*. Slough: Nelson/NFER.

227

Roger Beard, University of Leeds, England

17 International perspectives on children's developing literacy

Roger Beard addresses one of the key aspects of early schooling. For most children, this is their first major introduction to literacy, and he examines the research bases for the development of literacy. Understanding this may be a key to an important agent of language learning.

To SUMMARISE the general development of literacy in children in one short paper is clearly a difficult undertaking. However, it is important that such attempts are regularly made because of the perennial need for everyone involved with the development of children's reading and writing to be as well informed as possible. The international goal of universal literacy is still a long way off and it is important to recognise that each country in the world has its specific demands and constraints. Furthermore, any discussion about the teaching of reading and writing needs to be coupled with a note of caution because no panacea yet exists, and at times debates in the literacy field become unduly polarised. I shall try to provide a sense of balance and ensure that discussion of possible routes into literacy are not omitted just because they do not fit a certain ideological mould. In the light of the British government's current initiative to introduce a national curriculum, I shall also mention some of the programmes of study and attainment targets which have been adopted; these make useful points of reference in the evolving debate about how literacy develops in primary school children. At the same time I shall draw upon significant publications from a number of different countries, including the USA, Canada, Argentina and New Zealand.

As well as tracing the development of literacy, this paper will identify some of the recent developments in the teaching of early reading and writing and some of the current tensions and uncertainties in studying them. First, it is useful to remind ourselves of the changing social context of the uses of literacy in the world around us; this brief survey can help place evidence and debate about growth and development in a broader and more critical context.

The literacy demands of contemporary life

It is easy to overlook how far the literacy demands of modern industrial society are increasing. Continuing research and publication, for instance, is leading to an inexorable increase in society's knowledge base of great magnitude; one eminent university vice-chancellor recently suggested that human knowledge is currently doubling every four or five years. This has enormous implications for the ability of people to use information retrieval strategies in making efficient and effective use of the available data banks. Whether it be about the purchase of a new washing machine or a package holiday, there are many choices in everyday life which require a great deal of thoughtful decision-making and a critical weighing up of information and implication.

Over the past 15 years or so there has been a range of educational developments reflecting and recognising these changing demands, and recently the plans for a national curriculum in England and Wales continued this trend. The first report of the working party on *English for Ages 5 to 11* (DES 1988b) suggested that there be attainment targets and programmes of study in reading for both 'the ability to read, understand and respond to all types of writing' and 'to develop reading and information retrieval strategies for the purpose of study.' In fact these two targets have since been merged into one by the National Curriculum Council (DES 1989) but the terms of reference for information retrieval have been retained, thus continuing the trend toward the growing recognition of the *functional reading* demands of contemporary life.

There is more to functional reading than information retrieval, of course, and the first of the targets mentioned above indicates the crucial importance of recognising the role of response in reading. Many studies have shown how many seemingly commonplace texts do not simply reproduce reality but instead provide a carefully filtered or selected representation of it. Advertisements are a case in point: some use subtle association techniques in text and illustration to imply status or romance ('As the meal ended, the evening began' Courvoisier cognac); some make ingenious use of various syntactic devices, such as simple, emphatic clause structures, questions and commands or figures of speech ('Classic British footwork' Church's shoes); others again may take their ingenuity to the point where they mislead or misinform, leading to reprimands from the Advertising Standards Authority, as was the case with the claims of several motor car manufacturers about their 'environment-friendly' products in July 1989 – the ASA concluded that no car could justifiably be described in this way.

Of even more concern for many commentators is the insidious distortion to be found in some newspapers, in their trivialisation of events, their sensationalist style and their political bias. While these traits are much documented, it is chastening to read of the relative lack of awareness among regular readers of popular newspapers of this print prejudice (Butler and Kavanagh 1980). As the Kingman Report from the Committee of Inquiry into the Teaching of English Language (DES 1988a) reminds us, comparison of newspaper headlines or reports of the same event from different papers shows that newspapers can obscure truth as well as reveal it. It is a significant indication of the growing public unease about British journalistic standards that in April 1989 the British government announced that it was giving the popular press a year in which to 'prove itself' before considering taking legal action.

The world of leisure reading, especially of literature, has long been held up as a legacy of civilising values to help counter such excesses in the written language of the modern world. Here there are some encouraging signs that commerical enterprise is seeking to inject the field of adult leisure reading with greater publicity and renewed promotion through other media such as newspapers and television. The publicity surrounding the annual Booker prize is a good example, with the announcement of the winner now being televised live. These new developments have tended to create more of a climate of cult authors and titles, reflected, for example, in a trend in total sales of popular paperback books. More books sell over 100,000 copies in their first year of publication than a decade ago, although the total sales of the most popular 100 books is less than was the case ten years ago.

Considerably less is known about the general patterns of writing in everyday life. One attempt to sample this is reported by Griffiths and Wells (1983) who record their surprise at the frequency and 'range of function' of the writing being reported by a sample of 133 people in the Bristol area. Writing seemed to play a significant role in the lives of the majority, although for some it was clearly not a frequent activity and the researchers were disturbed by the number who said they were uncomfortable about their basic capabilities. Griffiths and Wells also warn of the difficulties of categorising writing types and of the unsatisfactory nature of the 'poetic-expressive-transactional' model adopted by the Bullock Report (DES 1975).

There are a number of other major aspects of the literacy demands of the real world within which educational institutions have to operate: the technical reading demands of the world of work, the recent arrival of teletext in thousands of homes, the use of public libraries, the leisure reading of local newspapers which increasingly include 'free' editions, the light reading of magazines (the sales of which, together with those of newspapers, amount to four times the total sales of books) and the almost subconscious reading of the environmental print which is all around us. This kind of print scenario is a complex and bewitching world in which there is entertainment and information, expression and argument, innumerable contexts and settings. It is in this multi-layered context of written language in use that recent studies of young children's early development of literacy have been located.

The early years

The 1980s saw a growing interest in the way in which young children can make sense of the world of written language and how by identification, imitation and roleplay, their awareness and skills in literacy will emerge over time. Particular impetus to this view of early literacy has come from sociologists who have adopted an ethnographic approach to research. In a collection of conference papers about developments in this field of literacy studies, Bloome (1987) asks a number of key questions to remind us that the use of literacy is part of a wide range of social and cultural processes which influence how reading and writing are used, how these uses are defined, and how uses of literacy in schools are related to those in the real world outside.

One of the most practical spin-offs from this perspective is a great deal of interest in the kinds of literacy experience which young children can bring with them from home and from the world around them. Children's 'emergent literacy' can evolve from a whole range of contexts in which they attempt to make meanings with written language. The various ways in which they can do this are well reviewed by Hall (1987), who warns against over-simple generalisations about how little many young children appear to know about literacy and who stresses how children are influenced by seeing people participating meaningfully in literacy for real purposes and with enjoyment. He emphasises that children can be motivated by having their child-centred efforts welcomed and taken seriously. Hall draws his evidence from a variety of sources, including Heath's study of the literacy practices and 'acts' in two different communities in the USA (1983), Ferreiro and Teberosky's studies of emergent literacy in South American children (1983) and the parallels drawn between learning to talk and learning to read by, among others, Kenneth Goodman (1986).

Ferreiro and Teberosky have been especially influential in drawing attention to the ways in which children construct their own hypotheses about the nature of the processes of reading and writing. They suggest that the natural order of learning how to read and write varies from child to child, although they argue strongly against the assumptions that reading is essentially deciphering and that learning to write is largely a matter of copying an external model. They argue that children will gain from being encouraged to write from the beginning so that they can discover that their own system of letters and spellings is not the conventional one and that there are valid reasons for substituting their own hypotheses with conventional ones. They refer approvingly to the possibilities of children inventing spellings as in FES SOWEMEG EN WOODR (accompanying a picture): 'fish swimming in water'. Clearly these suggestions will appear controversial to many teachers and parents and they do raise certain doubts which will be discussed later. First though, there are clear implications from these sources for playgroups, nursery schools and reception classes.

Perhaps the most immediate one is that the context of young children's learning should reflect a genuinely meaningful approach to print and the uses made of it. Opportunities should be taken to show print in action in notices, labels, instructions, announcements and 'news' of all kinds, so that children can be helped to become more aware of how written language is created and used. The effectiveness of this environmental print is likely to be greater still if teachers and parents also talk informally about it and how it helps us in day to day activities. This need for reflection on language use is in fact an important part of the recommendations of the Kingman Report referred to above.

The importance of reflection on language use is identified in a slightly different way by Wells (1985) whose longitudinal study of children's language development, based in Bristol, is now internationally known. Wells reported that of all the factors which were associated with reading attainment at the age of seven, the most significant was the child's knowledge about the conventions of reading at the time of entry to school; this in turn was associated with the extent to which parents encouraged an interest in books and literacy and in particular by the frequency with which they read stories to the child, as well as the quality of their conversation with their offspring. Indeed, the power of story experience on the development of early language and literacy has become increasingly recognised in recent years.

Stories are now widely seen as contributing to children's development in a number of important ways. Teachers have been very influenced by the suggestion that narrative is a 'primary act of mind'; children do seem naturally to use narrative to order their thoughts in 'pre-sleep monologues' (Applebee 1978) and seem to identify readily with the 'story grammar' of setting, main character(s), plot and denouement in early experiences of books and literacy, reflecting the strength of the influence of narrative in our oral culture (Wade 1984). Two further developments have added to this recognition. First, Wells has stressed the importance of stories in helping children to think and use language in a 'disembedded way', projecting their understanding of characters, situations, events and emotions onto different and imaginative contexts, beyond their immediate circumstances and experiences. Second, there has been a widespread recognition of the current 'golden age' of children's picture books, whose ingenious and compelling uses of illustrations, word-play and 'child-appeal' provide remarkably compressed and self-contained experiences of literacy (Beard 1990). Eminent examples of the underestimated 'teachers of literacy' who have made these experiences possible are Allan and Janet Ahlberg (for example *Each Peach Pear Plum*), Quentin Blake (for example *Mr Magnolia*) and Pat Hutchins (for example *Rosie's Walk*).

Emerging doubts about 'emergent literacy'

There are, however, also a number of doubts about the adequacy of some of the main perspectives currently being used to discuss early literacy. For example if literacy can 'emerge' so naturally from interactions with environmental print and having stories read, as some writers argue, there needs to be some explanatory framework for why in some instances this emergence does not take place. Does potential literacy competence lie submerged? What is the nature of the link between experience and the development of literacy? Tizard's recent research in inner city schools (1988) offers a warning against any view that children learn to read by a kind of osmosis:

> All the nursery classes had a plentiful supply of books, and the staff read regularly to the children. But simply introducing children to books in a happy atmosphere does not ensure that they will make a connection between meaning and print, or have any understanding of written language. We found that on leaving the nursery less than half of the children understood that in a picture book it is the print that is read, rather than the pictures. (p.169)

Second, there are uncertainties about how far it is possible to generalise from learning to talk to learning to read in the way Goodman has increasingly suggested as part of a 'whole language' perspective. Margaret Donaldson (1989) has been particularly concerned to raise this issue, arguing that in fact literacy learning differs profoundly from the learning of the mother tongue. As part of a general discussion of current debates about learning to read and the kinds of text used to promote this, she outlines some of the biologically based differences between the nature and uses of spoken and written language. She goes on to suggest some of the means by which bridges can be established between spoken and written language; by shared reading, by helping children to produce written language, by the use of environmental print, and by the use of the patterns of children's speech when producing texts for them. She goes to some lengths to illustrate the very special qualities of written language, particularly its capacity for generating systematic thought.

A third set of doubts about the natural emergence of literacy has been expressed by researchers into early writing skill. After many years of studying children's spelling, for instance, Margaret Peters (1985) warns against any suggestion that children will 'catch spelling' through the use of their inventive spelling. She is concerned that this 'nebulous' concept can distract teachers from the clear implications of her own research that ultimate success in spelling in the primary school depends more on what the teacher does than any other factor. The influence of teaching is likely to be particularly significant in helping children to attend to the structure of words and in helping them to learn words by imaging them, attempting their spelling and comparing their versions with the conventional ones ('look, cover, write, check'). The teacher can also help promote spelling skill by encouraging a swift, well-formed style of handwriting from an early age, a skill which Peters suggests is of cardinal importance in fostering spelling ability, because of the 'feel' for the patterns of the English spelling system which it promotes.

Support for this kind of specific skill-training has also come from Rosemary Sassoon (1989) who has specialised in the educational and the medical aspects of handwriting. In supporting the decision to assess handwriting separately in the National Curriculum Attainment Targets, she wrote:

The importance of training the movement is so fundamental that it must be separated from the literary aspects of handwriting and cannot be child-led. Reception teachers must not be encouraged to ignore movement errors that soon become automatic, leading to serious problems. This vital early teaching should start as soon as children try to write. It can be done imaginatively and need not inhibit creative writing.

Furthermore, in a range of seminal studies in Canada, Carl Bereiter and Marlene Scardamalia (1987) have argued that many children may need specific assistance in learning how to write extended texts, whose structure and style are less familiar. This research is focused on the psychological shifts which children have to accommodate in making the adjustment between 'conversation and composition', especially in learning to 'go alone in language' and to create texts without the interactive support of a conversational partner. This adjustment may be helped by a number of 'facilitative procedures', such as brainstorming, wordlisting, planning final sentences in stories or key points of a report. Bereiter and Scardamalia suggest that children tend to rely too much on 'knowledge-telling' strategies in writing, a kind of unstructured outpouring, when for many kinds of writing, 'knowledge-transforming' strategies are needed. This is especially so for non-narrative and discursive tasks whose written discourse structures are not so likely to be related to a supportive chronological sequence. While facilitative procedures can play some part in fostering such development, the latter are likely to evolve over a long period of time as children learn to read with a 'writer's alertness to technique'.

Finally there are doubts about the influence of a well-meaning but possibly over-optimistic child-centred ideology in the study of early literacy development. From the publication of the rather romantically inspired Plowden Report (CACE 1967) onwards, there have been recurring reservations about the adequacy of projecting the informal contexts of children's early, pre-school learning upwards into curriculum planning for the succeeding school years. Even in the year of Plowden, a group from the University of London Institute of Education (Peters 1967) warned that, 'It may well be that a very bad way of developing autonomy, independence and "creativeness" is to give children too many opportunities for uninformed "choices" too young.' (p.11)

Twenty years later Alexander (1988) was to note, a little sardonically, that

> Never properly defined, yet ever suggestive of ideas and practices which were indisputably right, 'informal' was the flagship of 1960s Primaryspeak, whose vessels, somewhat tattered now, are beginning to disappear over the educational horizon: spontaneity, flexibility, naturalness, growth, needs, interests, freedom, the whole, the seamless robe . . . and many more. (p.148)

Alexander is referring not only to the specific demands of the National Curriculum but also to the accumulated evidence which suggests that in the primary age range, the teacher's structure, lesson overviews, recapitulations and 'audits' seem to have a major influence on children's academic attainment in the core curriculum areas (for example Bennett 1976, Galton *et al.* 1980, Mortimore *et al.* 1988).

The new National Curriculum in England

The National Curriculum Attainment Targets and programmes of study seem to have tried to make appropriate concessions to the emergent perspective but have also built in more orthodox demands and benchmarks. First of all, though, it is worth making some reference to the general background and framework of the proposals.

The National Curriculum has been introduced partly to fulfil a political pledge to raise standards, but also as a response to a concern shared by all the main British political parties to make the curriculum more consistent. In primary schools this concern can be traced back at least to the report over a decade ago by Her Majesty's Inspectors (DES 1978), following a survey of a representative sample of primary schools. This report drew attention to the fact that a quarter of the sampled schools did no history or geography, either separately or thematically in topics or projects; there was no observational or experimental science in 80 per cent of the observed classrooms.

The overall framework for assessment has been provided by the Task Group on Assessment and Testing (TGAT) which reported in early 1988(c). TGAT gave priority to four main criteria in its proposals: that the national system should be criterion-referenced; that the results should be formative ('feeding forward' as well as 'feeding back'); that the assessments should be moderated; that they should relate to a clear structure of progression. The group proposed a ten-level matrix to map out this progression, with the integral plan that the attainments of seven-year-olds (to be monitored at 'key stage one') should be clustered around level two and that attainments of 11-year-olds (monitored at 'key stage two') should be clustered around level four (DES 1988c).

In response to the proposals of the report of the working party on English (DES 1988b), the National Curriculum Council recommended five attainment targets; one for reading, one for speaking and listening (the working party had proposed two targets for reading) and three targets for writing (conveying meaning, spelling and handwriting). At the time of writing only the targets for key stage one have been legally formalised (DES 1989), but it is not difficult to find in these targets signs of the concessions and demands noted above.

In the attainment targets for conveying meaning in writing at level one, for instance, there is a concession to children 'using pictures, symbols or isolated letters, words or phrases to communicate meaning'; by level two the target is more orthodox – to 'produce, independently, pieces of writing using complete sentences, some of them demarcated with capital letters and full stops or question marks.' (There are also three other targets related to chronological and non-chronological writing and rudimentary story structure.)

The emphasis on 'complete sentences' is particularly interesting in the light of the work of Kress (1982), who argues that children's concepts of a sentence are relatively slow to develop, because the syntactical structure of speech is grouped more in chains of clauses than sentences. He suggests that children may at first produce textual rather than syntactical units, where perhaps two or three sentences are run together and punctuated as if they were one. He goes on to argue that it is only when children can structure writing in paragraphs that the concept of a sentence becomes properly clear, as the 'minimum unit of argument'. (p.96). There is, therefore, a clear implication that children can benefit considerably from having their attention drawn to the structure of written language when being read to, so that they can begin to internalise its distinctive features. These equitable concessions to 'emergence' and 'initiation' are evident throughout the National Curriculum proposals.

In the targets for spelling, level one allows for 'showing an understanding of the difference between drawing and writing and between numbers and letters'; 'writing some letter shapes in response to speech sounds and letter names' and using 'at least single letters or groups of letters to represent whole words or parts of words.' Level two, however, is more insistent on 'the production of recognisable . . . spelling of a range of common words' in the course of children's writing, 'correct spelling of simple monosyllabic words which observe common patterns' and the growing recognition and application of spelling patterns in a wider range of words.

In handwriting the shift in emphasis is similar: from 'beginning to form letters with some control over the size, shape and orientation of letters or lines of writing' in level one to the production of 'legible upper and lower case letters consistently in one style' with 'recognisable form' and 'proper orientation' in level two.

The attainment target for reading also accommodates the range of perspectives which have informed work in this area in recent years. While level one allows for 'recognising that print is used to carry meaning' and beginning to 'recognise individual words or letters in context', level two specifies the accurate reading and understanding of 'straightforward signs, labels and notices', 'the use of picture and context cues, words recognised on sight and phonic cues in reading.' It also allows for the demonstration of a 'knowledge of the alphabet in using word books and simple dictionaries' and a number of other aspects of responsive reading and increasing fluency.

Perspectives on learning to read

The target statements make distinctive use of insights into the reading process which have developed in the past two decades or so, in which attention has shifted beyond word recognition and word analysis skills to the use of contextual cues and the sense of readership and authorship. The study of the contextual cues has highlighted how young readers can be helped to predict and anticipate syntactic sequences and the evolving pattern of meaning in texts. It is not easy to detect how this awareness develops in children, but it is obviously closely linked to the experiences of being read to and the consequent sensitivity to the possible syntactic variations in certain kinds of text. The organisation of stories and poems is likely to be more familiar than that of information and other non-chronological types of text and therefore children may well gain relatively more from having these sorts of text effectively read aloud to them and from having their distinctive features pointed out to them.

The comfortable use of prediction and sampling of texts in the fluent reading process has led Frank Smith (1978) to launch his well-known slogan that children 'learn to read by reading' and these words do have value in alerting us to the importance of the quality of the text in generating effective reading development. Traditional reading schemes have been justifiably criticised in this light and it has been found possible to read such texts aloud but *backwards* (in sentence or phrase order) to groups of adults without their noticing what was being done, so weak was the style and cohesion of the artificially contrived text (Beard 1990).

At the same time, there has been a growing feeling that Smith's slogan can be taken too far. As was suggested above, it can imply that learning to read is a less demanding process than many children seem to find it to be. Smith is also not clear on how children should be taught, perhaps because he has never been a schoolteacher. These inadequacies have brought criticisms from psychologists who have worked extensively with children. A recent critique has come from Oakhill and Garnham (1988) who suggest that Smith overgeneralises from studies of skilled adult reading to children learning to read. They warn that, in general, contextual information is available too late to aid word identification and that readers have usually identified a word from its appearance before they have had time to decide what words are likely to appear in the current context. They go on to say that '. . . decoding must be *taught*. It cannot be expected to materialise as a by-product of intelligent guesswork.' (pp.96–7).

Thus, as with currently influential theories of early writing development, there is some unease that there could be a danger of neglecting the nature and structure of the written language itself. Oakhill and Garnham provide a very detailed discussion of how children learn to read words, while recognising the motivating influence of engaging and informative texts. Effective word recognition seems to rely upon a number of skills and insights. Oakhill and Garnham stress three abilities in particular. First, children need to realise that the squiggles on the page are systematically related to what is read from the page by parents and teachers. Second, they have to acquire the concept of 'a word'. Third, they are greatly assisted by the ability to subdivide written and spoken language into the recurring units of letters and sounds (phonemes), an essential ability for recognising new words. Children will also be helped by being able to talk about written language and to pay attention to features of language that they have previously ignored, taking up the findings of Wells that were referred to earlier.

237

Contemporary teaching approaches have tended to take account of this kind of perspective. The rationale behind published schemes for the teaching of reading and more individualised collections of 'real books' (Bennett 1985) have tended to promote the building up of children's sight vocabulary within a certain narrative context and, particularly in the individualised approaches, a concern to encourage a 'whole book experience' of enjoyment, reflection and establishing a tacit rapport with the book's author (Meek 1988). Surprisingly, however, very few of these schemes and approaches have exploited the context of environmental print – the signs, labels, notices and instructions which forge for children a continual link between print and action. One notable exception is the *Link-Up* scheme.

Often running alongside such teaching approaches a language experience approach has been used, in which children's own spoken language is used in the composing of texts for them to read and write, exemplified in *Breakthrough to Literacy*. Teaching emphases have evolved to include greater shared reading of the text by the teacher or parent. These approaches vary from the more open-ended 'apprenticeship approach' (Waterland 1985) to the more structured and systematic 'paired reading' in which the adult (or peer) reads simultaneously with the child unless the child signals that he/she can continue independently.

Simultaneous reading is resumed when the child is unable to continue unaided (Morgan 1986). Nevertheless, shared reading approaches in general lack a framework for responding to children's 'miscues' in reading, especially those which indicate a weakness in the kinds of word analysis specified by Oakhill and Garnham. One researcher who has argued for many years that trends in teaching have been in danger of underemphasising letter-sound relationships is Joyce Morris. In an influential paper (1984), she argues that the spelling system of English is more patterned than is often realised and that the teaching of reading can be better informed by considering the more common letter groups which are associated with the 44 phonemes of RP (received pronunciation), the most pervasive English accent. This analysis has led to the listing of 24 'consonant sounds' and 20 'vowel sounds' and a grouping of the more commonly associated letter groups. For the 'vowel sound' /ei/ (as shown in the international phonetic alphabet), the letter groups are *a*pe, r*ai*n, and pl*ay*; for the 'vowel sound' /ai/, the letter groups are *i*ce, p*ie* and h*i*gh. The full analysis covers 396 such correspondences but the main framework of the system is displayed in an adapted form in Beard (1990).

Further cautions about the dangers of neglecting the more specific phonological aspects of learning to read have come from the results of the longitudinal research involving over 400 children carried out by Bryant and Bradley (1985) which draw attention to the ability to detect rhyme and alliteration in the early stages of learning to read. Weaknesses in this ability at the age of four were found to be more associated with under-achievement in reading four years later than other, perhaps more plausible, factors. It is always necessary to be cautious in generalising from research to practice, but the implications of the work of Morris and Bryant and Bradley are that many children are likely to benefit in a variety of ways from the early experience of traditional rhymes and 'I spy' games, as well as the imaginative word-play of our legacy of rhyming verse, which can be savoured by ear as well as by eye.

The influence of home and school

For some years now, other researchers have also tried to establish, like Bryant and Bradley, the more significant factors which are associated with early success in reading, especially in early reading. Marie Clay's work in New Zealand (1979) has been largely concerned with the prevention of reading difficulties and has led her to conclude that the following areas of pre-school development are critical for progress in reading:

- children's ability to control their own behaviour
- their language development
- their auditory discrimination abilities
- their visual perception of word forms
- their sense of security and self-confidence

This kind of constellation of factors has been found in studies of young fluent readers (for example Clark 1976) and has been confirmed in scholarly research reviews of the factors associated with 'reading readiness' (Downing and Thackray 1975). In recent years, however, British research has turned towards the potential of greater collaboration between school and home in trying to maximise the influence of the web of experiences and relationships surrounding children in promoting their literacy development. The most significant findings have come from children reading aloud to their parents on a regular basis, even though their parents may be illiterate or not speakers of English as a first language (Tizard *et al.* 1982). Some relative success has also come from 'paired reading' approaches (Topping and Wolfendale 1985), which were described above.

Literacy development in the later primary years

There was a good deal of research into these later years in the 1970s and early 1980s, funded by the Schools Council and this work has provided a promising legacy of possibilities for classroom practice. In reading, it is possible to differentiate between two strands of this development: extensive voluntary reading of literature and the further development of reading to learn abilities, concerned with improving the quality of reading comprehension and information-retrieval strategies. In writing, development is likely to involve a growing capacity to write with increased sophistication and with greater conscious control, for a wider range of purposes and audiences.

There is also the more controversial area of the fostering of 'language awareness' and grammatical reference, to which the Kingman Report addresses itself (DES 1988a).

In the reading of literature, there has been a general unease for some years about the gulf between the apparent quality and range of texts available and the actual patterns of children's reading, which are at risk in a marked decrease in the 10 to 14 age range (Whitehead 1977) and from the disproportionate influence of popular cult authors such as Enid Blyton, Roald Dahl and Judy Blume, about whom teachers, parents and critics may have misgivings, though for varying reasons. It is easy to underestimate the appeal of such authors; by the early 1970s Blyton had been translated into over 140 languages. The National Curriculum has tried to restore a sense of proportion to the debates in this area by publishing a (controversial) list of recommended authors in its first discussion document (DES 1988b) and by stressing the civilising and psychological values of personal engagement with literature through the primary and adolescent years.

The Effective Use of Reading was the self-explanatory title of a major research report on the development of 'reading to learn' across the curriculum in the 1970s (Lunzer and Gardner 1979 and 1984). The research showed how children can be helped to read more effectively if they are helped to set a specific purpose for study reading and helped to interrogate a text by 'directed activities'. These include labelling or underlining its more significant content or by completing 'modified text' activities in which versions of the text are presented to groups of children to reorder, to fill in deleted words or to predict the content of the next instalment. Other 'critical reading' activities can be built into this, including the detection of bias or the consideration of specific text demands such as technical vocabulary or unusual syntax, as well as the information retrieval skills needed to access additional sources of information.

There are a number of ambitious frameworks for looking at the growth of writing competence in this age range, concentrating on the growth of vocabulary and syntax (Harpin 1976); levels of abstraction (Moffett 1968); the personal growth of the 'communicative individual (moral, stylistic, cognitive and affective) (Wilkinson 1980); and cognitive stages (Bereiter 1980). These models are discussed in Beard (1984). The National Curriculum, however, is likely to embrace the framework adopted in its earlier publication, related to the distinction between chronological and non-chronological writing. This distinction can be found in Moffett's work and has been taken up by one of the members of the English working party, Katharine Perera (1984). It draws upon the theory discussed earlier that children can relate easily to narrating and reporting on the basis of their perception of a time line. Non-chronological writing, like descriptions or arguments, are more demanding because they lack an underlying personal structure of this kind and they may need different types of cohesive link.

One way of looking at how these different kinds of writing are manifested can be found in the work of the American writer, James Kinneavy (1971 and 1976). He uses the ancient notion of the communication triangle, involving writer, audience, text and context, to show how different writing aims can lead to different outcomes. 'Writer-centred' or 'expressive' writing may be to share news or even to reflect upon oneself, as in prayers, diaries and journals. 'Context-centred' or 'referential' writing may inform others about the reality of the world as in reports and essays. 'Text-centred' or 'literary' writing concentrates on getting 'the best words in the best order' in stories, poems and jokes, where artistic merit is particularly important. Finally 'audience-centred' or 'persuasive' writing is concerned to change behaviour, attitude or belief. Therefore growth in writing in the later primary years can be judged by the increasing competence to use a journal for introspection; to write accurate reports of experiments and observations; to construct extended stories, poetic forms like haiku, acrostics and some rhyming verse; and to begin to use writing to discuss, argue and debate. These aims can be pursued by using the different modes of writing, such as description, classification, narrative and evaluation, as well as increasingly diverse styles and registers. There will be greater use of different planning, composing and drafting strategies and greater mastery of the syntax and vocabulary of standard English. The ability to talk 'technically' about the forms and possibilities of written language is likely to be growing too, although the effect of directly teaching this remains inconclusive. The Kingman Report, however, argues convincingly that there is likely to be no advantage in ignorance of specific ways of referring to language and that we can all benefit from reflecting on language 'disinterestedly and illuminatingly' (DES 1988a).

Towards a second language

The learning of a second language has much to draw upon, then, from the literacy of the language learner. Learning to read and write successfully can provide unique insights into the structure and fabric of language, into the relative formality of written syntax and the subtle interplay between word choice and the nuances of meaning within a particular context. It offers a permanent link with the cultural legacy of a society and an omnipresent opportunity to contribute to its 'mind-pool'. Most of all, perhaps, it trains individuals to think beyond an immediate context and to consider language as a tool for crafted communication, in settings other than their own and into which the possibilities of a second language can be realised.

Bibliography

Ahlberg, A. and J. 1978. *Each Peach Pear Plum*. London: Penguin.

Alexander, R.J. 1988. 'Garden or jungle? Teacher development and informal primary education.' in Blyth, W.A.L. (ed). *Informal Primary Education Today: Essays and Studies*. London: Falmer Press.

Applebee, A.N. 1978. *The Child's Concept of Story*. Chicago: University of Chicago Press.

Beard, R. 1984. *Children's Writing in the Primary School*. Sevenoaks: Hodder & Stoughton Educational.

Beard, R. 1990. *Developing Reading 3–13*. Sevenoaks: Hodder & Stoughton Educational.

Bennett, J. 1985. *Learning to Read with Picture Books*. Stroud: Thimble Press.

Bennett, N. 1976. *Teaching Styles and Pupil Progress*. London: Open Books.

Bereiter, C. 1980. 'Development in writing.' in Gregg, L.W. and E.R. Steinberg (eds). *Cognitive Processes in Writing*. Hillsdale, New Jersey: Lawrence Erlbaum.

Bereiter, C. and M. Scardamalia. 1987. *The Psychology of Written Composition*. Hillsdale, New Jersey: Lawrence Erlbaum.

Blake, Q. 1980. *Mr Magnolia*. London: Penguin.

Bloome, D. (ed). 1987. *Literacy and Schooling*. Norwood, New Jersey: Ablex Publishing.

Bryant, P. and L. Bradley. 1985. *Children's Reading Problems*. Oxford: Basil Blackwell.

Butler, D. and D. Kavanagh. 1980. *The British General Election of 1979*. Basingstoke: Macmillan.

Central Advisory Committee for Education (CACE). 1967. *Children and their Primary Schools (the Plowden Report)*. London: HMSO.

Clark, M. 1976. *Young Fluent Readers*. London: Heinemann.

Clay, M.M. 1979. *Reading: the Patterning of Complex Behaviour*. London: Heinemann.

Department of Education and Science (DES). 1975. *A Language for Life (the Bullock Report)*. London: HMSO.

DES 1978. *Primary Education in England*. London: HMSO.

DES 1988a. *Report of the Committee of Inquiry into the Teaching of English Language (the Kingman Report)*. London: HMSO.

DES 1988b. *English for Ages 5 to 11 (the Cox Report)*. London: HMSO.

DES 1988c. *National Curriculum: Task Group on Assessment and Testing – a Report*. London: HMSO.

DES 1989. *English in the National Curriculum*. London: HMSO.

Donaldson, M. 1989. *Sense and Sensibility: Some Thoughts on the Teaching of Literacy*. Reading: University of Reading, Reading and Language Information Centre.

Downing, J. and D. Thackray. 1975. *Reading Readiness*. Sevenoaks: Hodder & Stoughton Educational.

Ferreiro, E. and A. Teberosky. 1983. *Literacy Before Schooling*. Exeter, New Hampshire: Heinemann.

Galton, M. *et al*. 1980. *Inside the Primary Classroom*. London: Routledge & Kegan Paul.

Goodman, K. (1986). *What's Whole in Whole Language?* Portsmouth, New Jersey: Heinemann Educational.

Griffiths, M. and G. Wells. 1983. 'Who writes what, and why.' in Kroll, B.M. and G. Wells. *Explorations in the Development of Writing*. Chichester: John Wiley.

Hall, N. 1987. *The Emergence of Literacy*. Sevenoaks: Hodder & Stoughton Educational.

Harpin, W. 1976. *The Second R*. London: Allen & Unwin.

Heath, S.B. 1983. *Ways with Words: Language, Life, and Work in Communities and Classrooms*. Cambridge: Cambridge University Press.

Hutchins, P. 1970. *Rosie's Walk*. London: Penguin.

Kinneavy, J.L. 1971. *A Theory of Discourse*. Englewood Cliffs, New Jersey: Prentice Hall.

Kinneavy, J.L. *et al*. 1976. *Writing: Basic Modes of Organisation*. Dubuque, Iowa: Kendall Hunt.

Kress, G. 1982. *Learning to Write*. London: Routledge & Kegan Paul.

Lunzer, E. and K. Gardner. (eds). 1979. *The Effective Use of Reading*. London: Heinemann Educational for the Schools Council.

Lunzer, E. and K. Gardner. 1984. *Learning from the Written Word*. Edinburgh: Oliver & Boyd.

Meek, M. 1988. *How Texts Teach what Readers Learn*. Stroud: Thimble Press.

Moffett, J. 1968. *Teaching the Universe of Discourse*. Boston: Houghton Mifflin.

Morgan, R. 1986. *Helping Children Read*. London: Methuen.

Morris, J.M. 1984. 'Phonics 44 for initial literacy in English.' *Reading* 18,1, 13–23.

Mortimore, P. *et al*. 1988. *School Matters: the Junior Years*. London: Open Books.

Oakhill, J. and **A. Garnham.** 1988. *Becoming a Skilled Reader.* Oxford: Basil Blackwell.

Perera, K. 1984. *Children's Writing and Reading.* Oxford: Basil Blackwell.

Peters, M. 1985. *Spelling: Caught or Taught? A New Look.* London: Routledge & Kegan Paul.

Peters, R.S. *et al.* (eds). 1967. *Perspectives on Plowden.* London: Routledge & Kegan Paul.

Sassoon, R. 1989. 'You've got to hand it to them.' *Times Educational Supplement,* 17 February.

Smith, F. 1978. *Reading.* Cambridge: Cambridge University Press.

Tizard, B. *et al.* 1988. *Young Children at School in the Inner City.* Hove: Lawrence Erlbaum.

Tizard, J. *et al.* 1982. 'Collaboration between teachers and parents in assisting children's reading.' *British Journal of Educational Psychology* 52, 1–15.

Topping, K. and **S. Wolfendale.** (eds). 1985. *Parental Involvement in Children's Reading.* London: Croom Helm.

Wade, B. 1984. *Story at Home and School.* University of Birmingham: Educational Publications No. 10.

Waterland, L. 1985. *Read with Me: an Apprenticeship Approach to Reading.* Stroud: Thimble Press.

Wells, G. 1985. *Language, Learning and Education.* Slough: Nelson/NFER.

Wilkinson, A. *et al.* 1980. *Assessing Language Development.* Oxford: Oxford University Press.

Whitehead, F. *et al.* 1977. *Children and their Books.* Basingstoke: Macmillan Education for the Schools Council.

Nigel Hall, Manchester Polytechnic, England

18 Literacy as social experience

This paper takes up the theme of Roger Beard's paper, but addresses literacy specifically as a form of social experience. We do not merely acquire literacy, we also operate in a literate society, and coming to terms with that is a very important part of growing up. The school's role in that process is crucial.

At age four, Shaun changed his name to Ponch, asked for a black wig and began playing CHIPS (Californian Highway Patrol). This involved zooming around on his two wheeler with a pencil and pad tucked in his back pocket. Like his macho, motorcycle riding TV hero, my son, Ponch, issued hundreds of tickets to the law abiding citizens of Wagga over the next few years. *(Kammler 1984, p.61).*

FOR MOST of this century the teaching of literacy has been based upon ideas drawn from psychology. In particular those ideas have reflected a belief that becoming literate is an individual learning process involving the mastery of a set of discrete skills. Such ideas have manifested themselves in practices which make children work on their own in silence, reduce the teacher's role to one of 'telling' and break up the things to be learnt into the smallest possible decontextualised pieces.

Clearly all learning is ultimately individual in the sense that the changes which we call 'learning' actually occur in people's minds, but it is a serious mistake to see learning as a purely individual phenomenon.

In particular this is true of learning about literacy. As Scribner (1984) says, 'the most single compelling fact about literacy is it is a social achievement.' (p.7)

Literacy is a state created by people. Literacy did not exist somewhere in the world waiting to be discovered. It is something that was developed by people as a response to their needs. It is people who use literacy, it is people who learn literacy and it is people who are influenced by literacy. It is people who use literacy to mediate all aspects of their interaction with other people in the world. Becoming literate has to be seen as a social process and literacy has to be seen as a social phenomenon.

We have only to examine our daily lives to understand that literacy is a social process. We are all the time using literacy in ways that derive from or entail interaction with other people. Our everyday lives as workers, students, shoppers, travellers, players, lovers, parents are mediated by print. These everyday concrete experiences with print can, however, blind us to the more fundamental ways in which literacy is a social phenomenon.

Literacy is social in a number of ways:

- It is social in an historical sense in that societies are irrevocably changed once literacy is embedded in the lifestyles of communities. Thus any member of a literate society grows up surrounded by the consequences of such changes.

- It is social in a cultural sense in that many of the values, attitudes and beliefs of society are often embedded within literacy and are transmitted directly and indirectly through literacy-related practices.

- It is social in a functional sense in that literacy influences in both positive and negative ways the daily lives of people living in literate societies. It is this functional aspect of literacy that is most accessible to the consciousness of young children.

- It is social in an educational sense in that the place of teaching literacy is most frequently the classroom, where interaction between individuals and groups is a constant feature of engagement in literacy practices.

The learning of literacy is most frequently associated with the last of the four categories. However, it is clear that a child learning to read and write is not simply influenced by what goes on in the classroom. He/She grows up in a culture which uses literacy for everyday purposes, which enshrines and transmits values through print and which carries with it the technological and bureaucratic consequences of adopting literacy. Of course as different areas of the world, or indeed different areas within a culture or community, vary in the ways they use or are influenced by literacy, so children growing up will experience literacy in very different circumstances.

The four areas outlined above are not mutually exclusive. On the contrary they are all operating in every way at all times. Their division into areas is not simply a device to allow scrutiny in this paper. They represent a move from generality to particularity. As teachers of children we are mostly engaged in the greatest level of particularity; that is, we work in classrooms with children and concentrate in special ways on helping them acquire the ability to use literacy purposefully. However, our classrooms, our schools and our educational systems are influenced by or indeed are a product of the other three senses – historical, cultural and functional.

If we examine the behaviour of Ponch cited at the beginning of this paper, the mutuality between these areas can be seen clearly. Ponch survives happily in and makes sense of a society which reflects changes caused by literacy; in this instance its legal and law maintenance systems. He is growing up in a world which transmits many of its cultural values through literacy and uses literacy to maintain its social structure; in this instance the particular type of social control exercised is traffic control.

His activity of 'issuing' tickets uses literacy to mediate between his behaviour as an intended legal officer and that of members of the public. His knowledge, represented by his issuing of tickets, is part of the range of skills which will enable him to see sense in the activity of being taught to read and write in conventional ways when he goes to school. The whole activity is a literate one and one which reflects the social nature of literacy processes.

This paper examines the four areas outlined above in more detail. Space will not allow more than an introduction to each area. The functional and educational senses are, perhaps, the most central of the four to our primary concerns as educators of young children and are examined in a little more detail.

Literacy as social in an historical sense

The Scollons were able to say of their two-year-old daughter, Rachel, that she was, 'In most ways literate before she learned to read, and that for her learning to read was little more than learning spelling conventions because of the systematic preparation in the literate orientation that we had given her' (Scollon and Scollon 1981). By systematic they do not mean administering exercises, but surrounding Rachel with ways of looking at the world that derive from a literate perspective. The Scollons were able to say this of two-year-old Rachel because although she was unable in any technical sense to read and write, she was able to do things with language that owed more to a tradition of literacy than to a tradition of oracy. Rachel was growing up within a set of cultural norms that the Scollons labelled 'essayist' literacy, and she had taken these norms on board in the ways in which she talked and in the structures which she used when she talked.

In a society which develops within the 'essayist' tradition, language, and especially written text, is able to function in a decontextualised way. Such text is able to stand on its own. It can be carried anywhere, examined anywhere and used anywhere. Such text lends itself to rational, scientific or logical examination.

A society which has developed within an essayist tradition is a society which has developed ways of ordering knowledge and systematic ways of handling that knowledge. Indeed many commentators have subscribed, either in general or specific terms, to the view that such technological and bureaucratic development is a consequence both of literacy and the spreading of literacy through printing. (Goody 1977, Foucault 1973, Ong 1982, Olsen 1975). This is not to say that literacy caused those changes, but that literacy may have contributed to the circumstances being appropriate for such change. Writing may not in itself have caused intellectual change to occur, but written language was open to inspection and analysis in a way which speech (until the invention of the tape recorder) was not. Once the text could be analysed it could be reorganised, reclassified and systematised. Thus 'knowledge' could be established more securely, interrogated more thoroughly and developed more quickly.

One consequence of this perspective is that children growing up and living within an 'essayist' culture who are illiterate in a technical sense are, nevertheless, likely to possess a literate stance towards life. They are, as Olsen, Torrance and Hildyard (1985) point out, 'speaking a written language'. They are using language that has been influenced in its development by literacy. They are also taking for granted that such language is an inevitable part of life.

For Ponch, the child cited at the beginning of this paper, the world is a place where it is quite reasonable to hand out parking tickets. He may not appreciate that this activity is embedded within several larger frameworks which place the activity within processes and institutions that are a product of the growth of a literate society. However, Ponch, albeit unknowingly, is behaving in a way which owes much to the historical relationship between literacy and society.

For some societies the acquaintance with literacy has been a long one. For others it has been brief. Indeed there are many languages for which there is no written form. Children growing up in societies which derive from an oral tradition will have a quite different experience of language and literacy from those children growing up in a society with a literate tradition. A seminal study in this area is that by Scollon and Scollon (1981).

The Scollons examined the differences between their own daughter and children brought up in an Athabaskan village in Canada, in the ability to use certain types of narrative. When telling a story their two-year-old daughter, Rachel, was able to orchestrate her narrative using a whole set of devices that derived from her upbringing in an essayist tradition. Rachel knew something about literacy. She had been exposed to books, story readings and story tellings in a literate mode; 'She asked much more often to be read stories than to be given special foods.' Rachel knew that literacy involved writing and knew that story telling in an essayist tradition had a definite prosodic structure that was different from the prosodic structure of conversation. Rachel knew it was appropriate for her to display her literate abilities in front of adults. By age two her parents were able to say she had, where literacy was concerned, 'achieved a typification of a set of activities and behaviours that corresponded to ours.' (p.64)

For the Athabaskan children (even at age ten or eleven) reading was a school-based and religious experience, and one which was reserved for people who were much older than Rachel. The children did not see it as appropriate to display their literacy behaviours in front of adults. The children had a typification for literacy but it was one that was 'unidirectional; one read but did not write. Literacy was socially located not in the home but in the church and subsidiarily in the school.'

When telling a story in a display mode, Rachel used no hesitation phenomena; there were no 'ums' and 'ers'. She placed herself as the narrator not the actor even when the story concerned herself. She was able to fictionalise herself, that is separate herself from the content of what she was telling. Such an ability is fundamental to the essayist tradition of literacy. Rachel is beginning to use language in a disembedded, decontextualised way. She can distance authorship from the text. The Athabaskan children told their stories differently. They used a face-to-face conversational stance, units which invited audience response, the grammatical structure of speech rather than writing, and they did not fictionalise themselves.

The Scollons are not making value judgements about the relative worth of the two perspectives. Each is a consequence of a particular historical/cultural tradition and each is appropriate to the particular lifestyles of the respective communities. However, the consequences for formal education are important. Much of the world's schooling involves a growing ability to take information from written text. Much of the world's schooling expects children to display their knowledge to teachers and other adults. Much of the world's schooling expects children to develop an ability to engage in 'disembedded' thinking (Donaldson 1976), that is the ability to use language to reflect upon thinking itself. In those three important areas Rachel, at the age of two, was already demonstrating competence, whereas the much older Athabaskan children were not. The influence of western education systems upon the world, their languages, their sciences, their bureaucracies, mean more and more that achieving success in education demands developing an ability to work within the historical/cultural perspective of the essayist tradition. In many respects it is the ultimate western colonial imposition.

Literacy and the transmission of culture

One consequence of societies becoming literate was the ability to record life in more specific ways than had previously been possible. The invention of printing speeded up this process. The existence of semi-permanent records provides a society with an identity which can be preserved. Its customs, beliefs, laws and values are not only enshrined in print but can now be transmitted from generation to generation in a standard form. This does not only happen in a direct way. Both the content of the transmission and the means of transmission have messages for future generations.

Of course the transmission of culture from one generation to the next is surrounded by many complex issues. Who is to decide what is to be transmitted and who is to determine how it is to be transmitted? Through the political control of education and the media, governments of all persuasions seek to ensure that future generations adopt their views and values. Literacy is often seen as a means to power, both in a personal and in a political sense. Illiteracy is seen as inhibiting opportunities and development, and is often associated with poverty and powerlessness. Being literate is seen as a 'state of grace' (Scribner 1984); that is, a person who is literate is viewed as being endowed with special virtues, is seen as educated and is perceived as empowered.

A person who is literate has access to the written heritage, and it is a conspicuous feature of history that the heritage studied is usually that of literate people. It was they, after all, who were able to leave written records of trade, of achievements, of battles, of inventions and of social taste. Thus people's notions of what counts as their heritage are filtered through and mediated by literacy.

Literacy, however, can also be a means of changing society. It offers access not only to the preferred record but also to alternative views of the world.

Societies operate in different ways to control their citizens' access to alternative writings. The soft form of control could be called 'selection'. The harder form of control must be called 'censorship'. As teachers we are all involved in selection. We guide children in their choices of what to read and how to think about what they read. This is inevitable; children cannot read everything. However, in our selection we choose to mark out certain experiences as valuable, noble, worthy, interesting and so on. By doing so we are inevitably using literacy to transmit values and beliefs.

Perhaps some of the clearest examples of this are in the field of literature. Until recently when children in England studied English literature they tended to study the works of dead authors whose reputation has stood the test of time: Chaucer, Shakespeare, Milton, Donne, Pope, Wordsworth, Dickens and so on. Indeed many of the readers of this book who studied English may also have found themselves studying these authors, and may, if they are also teaching advanced level, be examining these authors' texts with their students.

When teachers teach these or equivalent texts, they are not just teaching the content, that is, what the author wrote. They are passing on messages about what kinds of authorship are valued by society and about how those texts should be interpreted given current social norms, and they are inducting children into a perspective on the world. Literacy is being used to transmit a whole range of cultural messages. Through autobiography, biography, memoirs, diaries, journals, newspapers, manifestos, novels, poems, advertisements and so on, we declare not just our facts but our values, beliefs and attitudes.

Understanding a language clearly means more than understanding its grammar or its vocabulary. When children are learning to read and write a foreign language they are having to learn not just a language but a culture as well. Through literacy they have to engage with that culture and all that is transmitted through the literature of that culture. What marks out a fluent user of English as a foreign language is not just that user's command of the technical features of the language (although that helps) but his/her ability to contextualise the language within the cultural norms and expectations of native English users (although of course all native English users do not share the same expectations). It is these cultural factors which allow phenomena like irony or innuendo to operate effectively.

There is a story about a translator of one of Harold Pinter's plays who came across a line during an interrogation scene which read, 'Who watered the wicket at Melbourne?' The translator looked up this strange word 'wicket' in the dictionary and found that one meaning was 'a church gate'. Unable to make sense of any other meaning the line was translated as, 'Who watered the church gate at Melbourne?' Unfortunately the translator's lack of familiarity with one of England's national games, cricket (although the translator is not the only person baffled by the mysteries and rituals of this game), meant that the line lost all its effect and appropriateness. Melbourne is the site of a famous cricket ground. Very sensitive cricket matches are played on that ground. The wicket is the central grass strip on which the most important action takes place. It would be unfair, and illicit practice, to interfere in any way with the wicket, especially by watering it. Thus the line as written by Pinter has embedded within it reference to the so-called British sense of 'fair play' in sport and the general notion of an Englishman's belief in his readiness to be fair. While Pinter is making use of a cultural event by using it in literature, he is also examining and perhaps questioning its significance for English readers and listeners. Thus cultural beliefs (and in this case stereotypes) are transmitted or examined through literacy.

While young children are unlikely to be wrestling with the intricacies and subtleties of Pinter, they are nevertheless in the interesting and complex position of reading and writing a foreign language, while bringing to it cultural values of their own. The possibilities for cultural interaction through literacy are immense.

Literacy as social in a functional sense

If literacy was removed from the world overnight, life would be very different. It would not just be a case of all the signs, labels, adverts and so on disappearing from view. All the social functions that depended on literacy would grind to a halt. Trade would stop, science would stop, industry would stop, bureaucracy would stop, communication systems would stop. Communication with other people would become quite difficult and in most cases impossible. The effects would be both obvious and subtle but the consequences would be devastating. The process of discovering how to live without literacy would be exceptionally threatening.

So much of our everyday life involves literacy, both consciously and unconsciously. While it would be an interesting exercise to keep a diary of all our engagements with literacy for a week, such a task would be virtually impossible. Where does an engagement with literacy stop and start? What about all the environmental print that surrounds so many of us all the time? Are we engaging with it when we pass it or glance at it? Literacy is addictive. Once one is literate it is almost impossible to stop looking at words. For children growing up in a world which is full of print, and full of adults using that print, it is almost impossible to avoid coming to some conclusion about what it all represents.

For children in western societies literacy is a fact of everyday existence. They cannot opt out of the print world. Even families where books are seldom read will probably still write and receive some letters, get junk mail, buy food in packets and tins, look at TV guides, glance at comics or newspapers, have print in and on their clothes. They may have to fill in forms, buy tickets, receive wage slips and so on. The all-pervasive nature of print tends to make us take it for granted. This is so even for researchers. The author of one large project on family literacy (Leichter 1984) found that although the researchers were cued up to look for print in homes, they overlooked for a long time all the print that appeared on television in the homes that they were studying. She wrote, 'Locating literacy events in the stream of everyday family activities is a substantial task, especially if one wishes to avoid defining literacy in terms of previously held conceptions.'

Children who grow up in print-orientated societies cannot and do not ignore the existence of print and its effects. How could they? All around them are these 'marks'. All around them are people doing things with these marks. Societies have usually operated upon the principle that children go to school to learn to read and write, and that prior to formal schooling children know nothing of any significance about print (Hall 1987). However as Ferreiro and Teberosky (1983) point out:

> We have searched unsuccessfully in this literature for reference to children themselves, thinking children who seek knowledge, children we have discovered through Piagetian theory. The children we know are learners who actively try to understand the world around them, to answer questions the world poses . . . it is absurd to imagine that four-to five-year-old children growing up in an urban environment that displays print everywhere (on toys, on billboards and road signs, or their clothes, on TV) do not develop any ideas about this cultural object until they find themselves sitting in front of a teacher. (p.12)

In their research with young children in Argentina, Ferreiro and Teberosky found that far from ignoring print children were trying in many reasonable ways to make sense of it. Of course with limited experience the 'sense' that they came to was often quite different from the 'sense' made of print by adults. However, as Ferreiro and Teberosky showed in a detailed set of investigations, the conclusions children came to about print (a) were extremely reasonable when judged against their limited experience, (b) progressed with accumulating experience to better and better approxima-tion of conventional notions about literacy, and (c) were better grounded in the reality of print and its uses than were the educational assumptions about print which would be imposed upon them once they started formal schooling.

The young children they studied saw literacy as something that made sense. It could be used to do things that related to real-world experience; literacy was tied to social practice. Once they began formal schooling 'instead of learning to do things that entailed reading and writing, one learned to "read" and "write" in courses designed to teach nothing but reading and writing' (Nespor 1987, p.42). This early ability to make sense of literacy in non-school ways is seen again in the work of Heath (1983). Heath, over a ten-year period, documented the way children in a number of different communities were inducted into language and literacy. In one working class black community the children received no pre-school instruction in literacy, had few if any books, had few if any conventional stories, but did have to use literacy in order to survive life in their community. She writes,

> Trackton children are sent to the store almost as soon as they can walk, and since they are told to 'watch out for Mr Dogan's prices', they must learn to read price changes there from week to week for commonly purchased items and remember them for comparison with prices in the supermarket. As early as ages four, Teegie, Lem, Gary and Gary B. could scan the price tag, which might contain several pieces of information, on familiar items and pick out the price. (p.192)

These children used literacy in a highly appropriate way, out of functional necessity. They knew nothing of the conventional, formal processes of learning to read and write. However, 'Jointly or in group affairs, the children of Trackton read to learn before they go to school to learn to read.' Heath makes it explicit that print held considerable meaning for those children but it was a meaning which resided in the purpose of literacy, rather than its formal grapho-phonemic structures.

> Trackton children had learned before school that they could read to learn, and they had developed expectancies of print. The graphic and everyday life contexts of writing were often critical to their interpretations of the meaning of print, for print to them was not isolated bits and pieces of lines and circles, but messages with varying internal structures, purposes and uses. (p.195)

Schooling for these children was a disaster. Literacy in school ceased to have any relevance to the world outside school. All the meaningfulness disappeared in decontextualised exercises and rituals. Freire (1972) says of adult literacy learning, 'Only someone with a mechanistic mentality . . . could reduce adult literacy learning to a purely technical action.' The same must be said of some teachers of children. The social, authentic nature of literacy-related behaviours can be lost beneath a mass of technical prescriptions.

Children's experience of literacy during their early years is, for the most part, experience of literacy as part of a complete and social event. The focus is on the complete event or on the aim of the event. Of course situations do occur where the focus is directly on the nature of the literacy, just as in oral language the focus can be on the language. Parents do buy alphabet books or other instructional books, particularly as children approach formal schooling. Children themselves often initiate print focused events, for instance when asking, 'What does that say?' or when they begin to recognise features of their own names. However, the overriding impression is of literacy as part of a larger meaningful event and this is reflected in their play. Ponch wrote tickets for parking violations (Kammler 1984), the children in the study by Hall *et al.* (1987) wrote to record orders in their restaurants, Paul Bissex (1980) wrote to gain his mother's attention, and the children of Trackton read in order to buy groceries (Heath 1983). A particularly clear example of the way in which literacy is embedded in social activity was recorded by Tizard and Hughes (1984). They reproduce a transcription of a conversation between a mother and her 14 year old child. The mother had been making a shopping list and was discussing it with the child:

MOTHER: We've only got that little bit of shopping to get now (shows Pauline the list).

CHILD: Mummy? Can I have one of them drinks? Can I?

MOTHER: Get some more drink?

CHILD: Yeah. Can write it down on there (points to where she wants it written on the list). Up here.

MOTHER: I'll get you some when I go tomorrow.

CHILD: Aw! (disappointed)

MOTHER: All right? Cause I'm not getting it today.

CHILD: No . . . In the 'Vivo's'?

MOTHER: Haven't got Daddy's money yet.

CHILD: I've got no money.

MOTHER: No, I haven't got enough to get my shopping. All of it.

CHILD: Not all of it?

MOTHER: Irene's just taken five pounds. She'll bring some change back. If she's got some, she'll bring some change back. It's not enough to get all that. Is it? (points to the shopping list)

CHILD: No.

MOTHER: See? So when Daddy gets paid I'll get some more money and then I'll go and get the rest.

CHILD: Yeah. That's nice, isn't it, Mum?

MOTHER: Mn . . . I got one, two, three, four, five, six, seven, eight, nine, ten, eleven, twelve. (counts items on list)

CHILD: (joins in counting) Nine, ten, eleven.

MOTHER: Fourteen, fifteen, sixteen, seventeen, eighteen bits.

CHILD: Mum, let's have a look! (Mother shows the child the list) Do it again.

MOTHER: We gotta get rice, tea, braising steak, cheese, pickle, carrots, fish, chicken, bread, eggs, bacon, beefburgers, beans . . . Oh, Irene's gone to get them (crosses off beans) . . . peas, ham, corned beef.

CHILD: And what's that (points to word on the list)?

MOTHER: That's lemon drink. (crosses off 'lemon drink') She's just gone down to get that one. See? (pp.74–5)

This is a very complex episode. A whole range of factors are embedded in the achievement of creating a shopping list. However, clearly a number of literacy-related events occur. The child witnesses that a written list is a useful way to organise and plan events; that one can redraft written language; that written language is composed of elements; that one can refer back to a written list for information; that there is a relationship between written language and oral language. This family was classed by the researchers as working class and they comment,

> It is often suggested that working class children do not have much experience of their parents engaging in 'literate' activities: yet a shopping list provides an extremely vivid demonstration of the way in which written language may be used within a meaningful human activity.

The power of the written word lies in its ability to link up different contexts in space or time, and here it is doing precisely that – forming a link between the home, where the decisions and choices are made, and the shop, where they are carried out. The demonstrations available to the child about literacy are totally embedded within a holistic social experience. It is, in essence, literacy embedded within economic activity. That children do take notice of such demonstrations can be seen in a transcript of children engaging in shopping play, in which the conversation of Puerto-Rican children is almost identical to that of Pauline and her mother in England (Jacobs 1984).

It is inevitably the case that such learning about print and its uses can only occur in situations where print exists in the environment in significant amounts, where adults frequently use this print and where children are encouraged to participate in print-related activities such as listening to stories and making shopping lists. Even in western print-orientated societies, as the work of Heath (1983), Taylor (1983) and Taylor and Dorsey-Gaines (1988) illustrates so vividly, different communities within a culture will assign different values and meanings to reading and writing. It is clearly the case that even within a country which has taken on the essayist tradition, different social groups will vary in their commitment to it, their knowledge of it and their ability to make use of it.

Children in print-orientated societies do not all grow up having the same understandings about print. Thus the expectations that they bring to formal schooling will vary from one child to another, and this might make a considerable difference to their ability to make sense not only of literacy but of schooling.

Literacy as social experience in schooling

Schooling is the process which many societies select as their formal mode for the transmission of culture. As such the process is bound up with a culture's history and, as might be expected, a variety of cultures gives rise to a variety of ways of schooling. In western societies schooling shares many character-istics, the main one of which for our purposes is that schooling is a book-based activity. It is very much concerned with helping children learn to 'take' from books. As knowledge has become increasingly enshrined in books and less easily the property of individual teachers, so the 'taking' from books becomes the only efficient way of gaining access to the width of knowledge available. The avowed aim of much western education is to encourage an analytic response to what is read. Rather than recitation or copying, it is the analysis of texts which is seen as fundamental to the goal of being an educated person. In other words, schooling has invested heavily in literacy.

Along with the books, schooling has taken the ways of using language that derive from the essayist tradition. Children are encouraged to use language in an increasingly depersonalised way. Such language is of course the language of science, of analysis and of objectivity. Thus when attending school, children do not simply learn to read and write, they learn the process of schooling and all that implies about being a learner and being a pupil. Becoming and being literate is intimately bound up with the social process of schooling. The interactions which play a major role in this defining of schooling mostly take place in classrooms.

Classrooms are places where people meet to engage in a formal or semi-formal relationship with the intention of engaging in teaching or learning or both. Such engagements are inevitably social. Learning literacy in classrooms is no different. As Bloome (1985) suggests for reading:

> Reading involves social relationships among people: among teachers
> and students, among students, among parents and children and among
> authors and readers. The social relationships involved in reading include
> establishing social groups and ways of interacting with others, gaining
> and maintaining status and social position; and acquiring culturally
> appropriate ways of thinking, problem-solving, valuing, and feeling.
> (p.134)

For literacy in general it involves relations between a student and his/her culture, as instanced by the material read or written. It involved relationships between students and other students, between students and teachers, between students and parents. It involves relationships between the students (as readers) and the authors of the texts they read. However, the teaching of literacy involves more than the teacher possessing the content of what is to be taught. There also has to be a means by which it is taught. Students when learning literacy are learning rather more than just literacy. As Wolf and Perry (1988) point out,

> But in the process of becoming literate, children learn more than just the
> rules for encoding or decoding print. Just as schooling provides children
> with implicit definitions of work and play or the differences between
> parents and teachers, children also construct an implicit definition of
> what is – and what isn't – involved in 'being literate' (p.44)

And in order to gain access to these explicit and implicit understandings of literacy, 'In the process, he must acquire certain social knowledge and communicative abilities in order to participate fully and successfully as a student across its many learning contexts' (Kantor 1988 p.25).

A student has to learn both the social text and the academic text (Green, Weade and Graham 1988). The social text

> refers to information about expectations for participation (for example
> who can talk, when, where, in what ways, with whom, for what
> purposes), which in turn sets the procedures for lesson participation (for
> example answer in turn, wait to be called on). The academic text refers
> to the content of the lessons and the structure of this content. (p.13)

As Green, Weade and Graham point out, those two texts co-occur and are interrelated. As teachers present academic content they are simultaneously signalling how the lesson is to be accomplished. Thus any academic content is both taught and learned through a social text. Children are on the whole pretty good at picking up the 'social texts' of schooling. Even in nursery and kindergarten children learn what counts as appropriate knowledge and how it is appropriately displayed (Kantor 1988, Fernie 1988). Literacy is no exception as studies show in kindergarten (Cochran-Smith 1984), in first grade (Rasinski and DeFord 1988), in elementary school (Green, Weade and Graham 1988) and in secondary level (Barnes 1976, Bloome 1987).

For children the process of becoming literate and maintaining literacy is embedded in a mass of interactions which dictate that literacy in schools is a social process. As Bloome (1985) points out, becoming literate in classrooms is social even when the classroom situation looks non-interactive. He describes a classroom:

> In Mr Smith's second-grade classroom, students sit at individual desks. During the daily silent reading, students are not allowed to talk with each other, pass notes, make eye contact, sleep, ask questions of the teacher or look at the clock. Students are required to be looking at their books. Deviations from the rules may result in reprimand or punishment.

It might appear as if the social context of literacy has been stripped away in this classroom. However, the situation remains a social context. Students have to display a certain type of social behaviour in order to be counted as participating appropriately. They have to signal continuously that they are part of the class and are accepting the group norms. As Bloome says, 'Simply put, the social context is one of forced isolation and individualism.' Quite clearly the children are not just learning from what they are reading. They are acquiring a perspective on how reading should be taught and how they should behave as learners. They may also be acquiring a definition of what it means to be literate and to be a reader. Johns (1976) refers to a child who when asked what reading was replied, 'Reading is stand-up, sit-down.' When the child was asked to explain what he meant, he said that the teacher told him to stand up when he read. He would continue reading until he made a mistake and was then asked to sit down. Hence reading was perceived as a 'stand-up, sit-down' process. In such situations children can learn to fear literacy, to despise it, to avoid it and to believe it is a process of procedural display rather than a meaningful and personally significant experience.

One teacher (reported in Hall 1987) was trying to help her class of five-year-olds develop an understanding of why people learned to read and write. Finding it rather heavy going, she suddenly told them that she had a book by the side of her bed at home and asked them why it was there. There was a long pause and then one child said, 'So you can practise.' When she told them she did not have to practise and could read anything, there was general disbelief among the children. Eventually one child produced a book with some very tiny print and said, 'Go on, read that, then.' When she did the children were amazed. The interesting question is, did the children, as a result of their own classroom experiences of practising reading, believe that a lifetime of practising reading lay ahead of them? Had their experiences defined for them that reading was practising, just as the child cited by Johns believed that reading was a stand-up, sit-down process.

Teachers, through the way they select the content of their lessons, the way they organise their lessons, the way they select their resources, the way they behave towards the materials and content and the way they respond to children, are always consciously or unconsciously offering demonstrations relating to their attitudes, values and beliefs about literacy. Children are very sensitive towards these teacher demonstrations. Different teachers and different schools demonstrate a different ethos with regard to literacy. The social context of literacy in school may or may not match the social context of literacy the children experience at home. As Heath (1982) has shown so vividly, the consequences of this match or mismatch can be dramatic indeed. For children who experience a match, the move into the literacy of schooling is one of continuous experience. Such is likely to be the case for Rachel, the daughter of the Scollons. For the children in the Trackton community, the mismatch was one which few of them ever resolved. The consequences of the cultural clash where literacy (and other aspects of life) was concerned, meant that they seldom achieved anything further than a very basic functional literacy, the seeds of which were anyway sown not by school but by their pre-school experiences. Those children who in the pre-school days had been 'reading to learn', found themselves unable to learn to read. The social context of literacy within the school defeated them.

Some children hang on to the reality of literacy in their own cultural terms. Heath (1983) reports the following children's conversation overheard while they were on their way home from school.

SALLY: That story, you just told, you know that ain't so.
WENDY: I'm not tellin' no story, uh-er-ah, no I'm telling the kind Miss Wash (her teacher) talks about.
SALLY: Mamma won't let you get away with that kinda excuse. You know better.
WENDY: What are you so, uh, excited about. We got one kinda story mamma knows about, and a whole 'nother one we do at school. They're different and you know it.

At home these children, from what Heath calls the Roadville community, knew that their parents and their parents' community, a very religious one, saw fictional stories as lies. The children were forced into a different literacy reality at school with its emphasis on fictional narrative. Fortunately in this instance the children were able to hold both models distinct.

Conclusion

The overriding message of this chapter is that teachers of literacy cannot judge their work as being culturally neutral. No matter how hard some teachers may concentrate on narrow individual skills, every move in literacy

257

education drags along with it a whole range of inbuilt historical and cultural assumptions and associations. This is as true for the teachers of English as a foreign language as it is true for teachers of English to native speakers. In the teaching of literacy in England, the United States and Australia, there have been sustained attempts during the last 15 years to develop ways of teaching which acknowledge this essential social nature of literacy. The work of Goodman (1986), Butler and Turbill (1984), Meek (1981), Harste, Woodward and Burke (1984), Hall (1989), Graves (1983) and Wells (1987) is all directed to providing experiences for children which recognise the social dimension of becoming literate.

This chapter began with Ponch playing in the streets of Wagga. Ponch, without being too aware of it, knows that literacy is social experience. It is something which involves him with other people and it is something that allows him to influence other people. The event of 'issuing tickets' is for him just a game. However, it is in reality so much more than that. It is the expression of literacy as a social phenomenon. Ponch and literacy are tied together by historical, cultural, functional and educational ties. No matter how much Ponch will in the future be engaged in skills-based individual work in literacy, he cannot escape the constraints and freedoms offered by the social nature of literacy experience. For Ponch literacy will always, and inevitably, be 'something that exists between people and something that connects individuals to a range of experiences and to different points in time' (Schieffelin and Cochran-Smith 1984).

Bibliography

Barnes, D. 1976. *From Communication to Curriculum.* London: Penguin.

Bissex, G. 1980. *Gnys at Wrk.* Cambridge, Massachusetts: Harvard University Press.

Bloome, D. 1985. 'Reading as a social process.' *Language Arts* 62/2.

Bloome, D. 1987. 'Reading as a social process in a middle school classroom.' in **Bloome, D.** (ed). *Literacy and Schooling.* Norwood, New Jersey: Ablex.

Butler, A. and J. Turbill. 1984. *Towards a Reading-Writing Classroom.* Rozelle, New South Wales: Primary English Teaching Association.

Cochran-Smith, M. 1984. *The Making of a Reader.* Norwood, New Jersey: Ablex.

Donaldson, M. 1978. *Children's Minds.* London: Fontana.

Fernie, D. 1988. 'Becoming a student: messages from first settings.' *Theory into Practice* 37/1:3–10.

Ferreiro, E. and A. Teberosky. 1983. *Literacy before Schooling.* New Hampshire: Heinemann Educational Books.

Foucault, M. 1973. *The Order of Things.* New York: Random House.

Freire, P. 1972. *Cultural Action for Freedom.* London: Penguin.

Goodman, K. 1986. *What's Whole about Whole Language?* New Hampshire: Heinemann Educational Books.

Goody, J. 1977. *The Domestication of the Savage Mind.* Cambridge: Cambridge University Press.

Graves, D. 1984. *Writing: Teachers and Children at Work.* New Hampshire: Heinemann Educational Books.

Green, J., R. Weade and K. Graham. 1988. 'Lesson construction and student participation: a socio-linguistic analysis.' in **Green, J.** and **J. Harker** (eds). *Multiple Perspective Analysis of Classroom Discourse.* Norwood, New Jersey: Ablex.

Hall, N. 1987. *The Emergence of Literacy.* Sevenoaks: Hodder & Stoughton.

Hall, N. 1989. *Writing with Reason: the Emergence of Authorship in Young Children.* Sevenoaks: Hodder & Stoughton.

Hall, N. *et al.* 1987. 'The literate home corner.' in **Smith, P.** (ed). *Parents and Teachers Together.* London: Macmillan.

Harste, J., V. Woodward and **C. Burke.** 1984. *Language Stories and Literacy Lessons.* New Hampshire: Heinemann Educational Books.

Heath, S.B. 1983. *Ways with Words.* Cambridge: Cambridge University Press.

Jacobs, E. 1984. 'Learning literacy through play: Puerto-Rican kindergarten children.' in **Goelman, H., A. Oberg** and **F. Smith.** (eds). *Awakening to Literacy.* New Hampshire: Heinemann Educational Books.

Johns, J. 1976. 'Reading is stand-up, sit down.' *Journal of the New England Reading Association* 12/1:10–14.

Kammler, B. 1984. 'Ponch writes again: a child at play.' *Australian Journal of Reading* 7/2:61–70.

Kantor, R. 1988. 'Creating school meaning in pre-school curriculum.' *Theory into Practice* 37/1:25–35.

Leichter, H. 1984. 'Families as environments for literacy.' in **Goelman, H., A. Oberg** and **F. Smith.** (eds). *Awakening to Literacy.* New Hampshire: Heinemann Educational Books.

Meek, M. 1981. *Learning to Read.* London: Bodley Head.

Nespor, J. 1987. 'The construction of school knowledge: a case study.' *Journal of Education* 169/2:34–54.

Olsen, D. 1975. 'Review of "Towards a literate society".' *Proceedings of National Academy of Education* 2:109–178.

Olsen, D., N. Torrance and **A. Hildyard.** 1985. *Literacy, Language and Learning.* Cambridge: Cambridge University Press.

Ong, W. 1982. *Literacy and Orality.* London: Methuen.

Rasinski, T. and **D. DeFord.** 1988. 'First-grader's conceptions of literacy: a matter of schooling.' *Theory into Practice* 37/–1:53–61.

Schieffelin, B. and **M. Cochran-Smith.** 1984. 'Learning to read culturally' in **Goelman, H., A. Oberg** and **F. Smith.** (eds). *Awakening to Literacy.* New Hampshire: Heinemann Educational Books.

Scribner, S. 1984. 'Literacy in three metaphors.' *American Journal of Education.* 93/1:6–21.

Scollon, R. and **S. Scollon.** 1981. *Narrative, Literacy and Face in Interethnic Communication.* Norwood, New Jersey: Ablex.

Taylor, D. 1983. *Family Literacy.* New Hampshire: Heinemann Educational Books.

Taylor, D. and **C. Dorsey-Gaines.** 1988. *Growing up Literate.* New Hampshire: Heinemann Educational Books.

Tizard, B. and **M. Hughes.** 1984. *Young Children Learning.* London: Fontana.

Wells, G. 1987. *The Meaning Makers.* New Hampshire: Heinemann Educational Books.

Wolf, D. and **M. Perry.** 1988. 'Becoming literate: beyond scribes and clerks.' *Theory into Practice* 37/1:44–52.

Diane Shorrocks, University of Leeds, England

19 The development of children's thinking and understanding

Diane Shorrocks takes us through the processes of development and maturation outside language, but interacting all the time with language development. Underlying all the practice described in Section One of this book are the theories which attempt to explain the development of thinking and understanding, as examined in this paper.

CHILDREN GROW AND CHANGE in many ways. They grow physically, they gain greater social independence and emotional maturity, they learn to communicate more effectively and they come to understand progressively more about the world. Although these aspects are often considered separately, we must remember that the whole child is our basic focus. What I have to say in this paper is mainly concerned with communication and understanding, but the wider canvas is always in the background.

Whenever we consider an aspect of children's development, an important issue immediately arises – is the process best explained in terms of inborn factors or the influence of external forces? Phrases like 'nature versus nurture' or 'heredity versus environment' are used and arguments have been put on both sides over the years. Some, like the American developmental psychologist Gesell, have described development as a simple process of maturation, with certain characteristics almost pre-programmed into the child. Others, following a behaviourist psychology line, stress the role of the environment in creating and shaping any individual. More recently, the spirit of compromise has reared its head. It seems more reasonable to suggest that what any child eventually develops in terms of characteristics and skills is going to be the result of very complex interactions between inborn potentials and environmental responses and experiences. Both the 'child' and his/her 'environment' are in a state of constant change as a result of transactions between them. Children are active participants in their own development. A simple input-output view is grossly misleading.

This chapter is about the development of children's mental capacities – how they represent the world to themselves, how they come to be able to think, plan, solve problems and understand. This may seem rather odd in a book concerned with language teaching. Let us not forget, however, that when we understand, learn and produce language, we are using high-level mental processes, and gaining insight into these is important. Coming to terms with a first or second language in its oral and written forms involves children in some of the most complex mental (cognitive) activity they will ever experience.

Children's thinking and understanding

The terms *thinking* and *understanding* are often used rather loosely so perhaps some definitions are in order. Both imply mental activity and both occur internally in the mind. When we talk about another person's thinking or what they understand, we are inferring indirectly what we presume to be going on inside, on the basis of what they do and say. But that is all our judgements really are – inferences. Thinking seems to involve the manipulation of ideas from memory and can cover many different kinds of mental activity. Often, however, it implies manipulating ideas towards a particular goal, for instance solving a problem. Understanding seems to involve getting at the full meaning of a situation or piece of information, seeing links and relationships.

Let me begin by presenting you with a problem that requires some quite complicated thinking on your part. I give you a length of string and a series of small weights that you can attach to the end of it. I ask you to make a pendulum (see Figure 1) and try to discover which of these factors influences how fast the pendulum swings – how long the string is, how much weight is at the end of it, how high the weight is held when it is pushed and how hard it is pushed. This is clearly a complex problem. How would you tackle it?

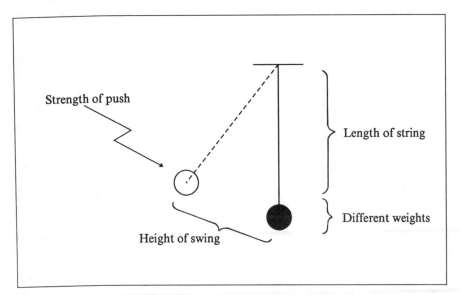

Figure 1 The pendulum problem.

As a mature and logical thinker you would probably say to yourself, 'there are four factors to consider so I'll test out each possibility and thereby try to come up with a rational answer.' In so doing you would be setting up a plan, making systematic tests, recording your results and arriving at a soundly based conclusion. I won't give any solution, since the main issue here is *how* the conclusions are reached. But if I gave the same problem to six- or seven-year-olds, what would their response be? Our experience or intuition would probably tell us that they would behave in a much more random, trial-and-error kind of way and that they would be unlikely to find a valid answer to the problem. Why should this be? Are children less efficient and capable thinkers? Perhaps they are literally unable to think in a logical and abstract way, or is it just a matter of experience, so that with help they could solve the problem. This is one of the main questions I will deal with in this chapter: is children's thinking and view of the world fundamentally different from that of adults? If so, how does it change and what causes it to change? If not, what does the most recent research tell us about helping children to become more efficient thinkers?

In addressing this issue we cannot ignore the work of the eminent researcher, Piaget. His lifetime of work on this topic is central, even though many of his ideas have been questioned.

Piaget's views on the development of children's thinking

Beginning his career as a biologist, Piaget moved on to study the question of how knowledge emerged and developed in the human race, especially the logical, scientific knowledge that we now possess. This was no straightforward task, but he reasoned that studying how thinking, and in particular logical thinking, develops in children might give some insights about its emergence in the human race. His work has this very specialised focus.

He obtained his information about children by observing them very closely and by means of the 'clinical interview'. In this procedure, the child (individually) is presented with a problem to solve or a situation to explain, much as I have just done with you and the pendulum problem. He/she is observed doing this and then asked questions about it. Based on this kind of evidence, Piaget developed his theory.

A central idea is that of adaptation. We are all constantly adapting to the world – this is how he defines intelligence. From birth the world outside begins to impinge on us and as a result of our earliest dealings with this environment we begin to develop sets of ideas or concepts which allow us to begin to relate to, classify and to predict what is happening around us. Throughout childhood into adolescence and maturity, these ideas and concepts become more complex and interlinked and hence more powerful and useful.

According to Piaget, two kinds of process are at work to bring this adaptation about. When we come upon a new object or experience, our existing ideas and concepts will give us some clue about how to recognise and interpret it. For example imagine a young boy who has experience of playing with a large round soft ball but who one day comes across a small round hard object. He can use his previous experience to begin to work out what it might be and therefore to begin to deal with it. Perhaps it could be rolled or thrown? As he rolls it, however, it becomes clear that it is heavier and rolls further than his large round soft one. This nicely illustrates the two processes. Previous experience had provided a framework into which the new object can be integrated – the process of *assimilation*. At the same time, that framework becomes extended a little as a result of engaging with the new object, the concept of 'ball' is now a little broader, a little richer. This enriched concept will in turn allow the child to see and recognise yet more possibilities in the world next time. This is the process of *accommodation*.

Assimilation and accommodation processes work in a complementary way with each other to give organisation to our ever-growing knowledge and understanding. They apply across all age ranges, to adults and children alike. What we already know influences how we are able to recognise and interpret new information and experiences and under appropriate circumstances modifies, changes or extends that knowledge.

However, from time to time in the course of the child's development, these 'modifications' are so wide-ranging and revolutionary that we could say that a different kind of thinking has emerged: these are the famous 'stages' for which Piaget seems to be mostly known. They are the part of his theory that has been most questioned so I will say little about them. In very general terms, the move is from highly limited concepts in early infancy to complex, abstract and logical thinking in adolescence and adulthood. The baby comes to know the world by direct actions upon it – a period of *practical intelligence*. These actions become more and more internalised and so allow the manipulation of ideas in the mind. Because of this, throughout middle childhood, the possibility of more logical and abstract thinking gradually emerges. The supposed endpoint of this is the kind of thinking I asked you to engage in with the pendulum problem.

The questioning of Piaget's theory

Criticisms of Piaget's theory and findings have been many and I have already hinted at a few. The following points summarise some of the main ones:

1 As we have seen, his focus was on a particular aspect of children's development – the capacity to think logically and scientifically – and his practical work with children was devised to probe this. It has been suggested that this is only a small part of the richness of human thinking and culture and that it omits much that is significant about human understanding.

2 Because the tasks he set for children were focused in this way, with fairly strict formats and questions, he may have obtained a rather biased view of children's abilities. Other workers (Margaret Donaldson, for instance)

have modified the tasks, making them more comprehensible to children, more grounded in commonsense situations and have obtained more positive results. In other words Piaget seems to have underestimated the abilities of children, especially young ones. Research by Peter Bryant, Ann Brown, Elizabeth Robinson and others has shown that under more propitious circumstances, even quite young children can think with a degree of logic, remember with some efficiency and can see the world from another person's position. This kind of information could lead us to the equally unfortunate position of overestimating children and expecting too much of them: what we need is a realistic and balanced view.

3 The idea that children's thinking passes through certain definable stages has been one of the most contentious parts of Piaget's work. Indeed it is the part that he himself modified towards the end of his work. It is also unfortunately the part that has permeated teachers' ideas most, often with negative consequences as we shall see in later sections of this chapter. If we use the term *stage* in a strict sense, we imply that the characteristics within that stage are clear-cut and coherent, and measurably different from the characteristics of other stages. We also imply that the mechanisms of change are understood and that when the transitions occur, they do so across the board.

Neither of these implications can be applied to Piaget's findings on children's thinking – his terms of reference are much fuzzier. Characteristics of thinking within several of the stages are rather variable and transitions across stages are not uniform. Since this is the case, it is not easy to see the merit in using the idea at all.

4 A view widely held among researchers (as we shall see later) is that language plays an important part in the development of children's thinking and understanding. Piaget does not seem to agree with this view: for him language does play a role but it is not the driving force. Perhaps because of this he does not seem to consider the significance of the language used in his practical work with children. Presenting children with a task and then discussing it on a one-to-one basis with an adult, where the adult uses probing questions, may indeed give us insights into children's thinking and view of the world. But we must also be aware of the limitations of the approach. In this situation we have two sources of evidence from the children – what they do and what they say. Information from both these sources is problematic, since all behaviour needs interpreting and verbal responses may be ambiguous and partial. Problems of interpretation in the communication process have been underplayed in Piaget's work.

Even more surprising is how strange and complex some of the questions asked of the children are. Imagine your own response if you were faced with a tray of beads, some wooden and some painted white, and were asked, 'Are there more white beads than beads?' As rational adults we would have to think twice about the 'sets' and 'sub-sets' involved, but these were children under five!

Imagine also the possibility that the child interprets the whole interview situation in a way not anticipated by the adult. It would be a rare child who was not a little apprehensive and puzzled as to why this grown-up should be asking all these peculiar questions about something that was not particularly interesting in the first place. To cap it all, in some of the tasks the same question is asked twice, once at the beginning and again after the materials have been moved. Many children would assume that they had got it wrong the first time, since this is usually what asking a question a second time means at school. In this context, however, sticking by your judgement is what is required.

Piaget does not seem to regard language and communication as problem spaces *per se*. For him language seems to be 'transparent' – a straightforward vehicle and means of access, not an 'opaque' area of experience which needs considering and working out in its own right.

5 Unlike many others, as we shall see, Piaget does not give much of a role to adults in this process of development. Social relationships and the social context are broadly acknowledged as factors, but they are not seriously investigated in his work. Children seem to have to do all the work for themselves, with parent or teacher intervention having only minimal effect. We will consider the implications of this later.

These points convey a flavour of the major problems in Piaget's work. They do not imply, however, that he can be dismissed out of hand. He has made a massive contribution towards the current view of children. An enormous volume of information based on systematic study has arisen as a result of others trying to verify or refute aspects of his theory. And for many years, his view of development was the most coherent alternative to that of behaviourist psychology; a view which suggests that children are passive receivers, responders to stimuli from the environment, being progressively shaped by processes of reward and reinforcement.

In recent years, however, another framework has emerged and it is to this we now turn.

The information processing framework

The growth of computer technology over the past two decades or so has provided some suggestive ideas about how the human mind works. The computer takes in information, represents it internally, then processes it and manipulates it in various ways. Perhaps there are some parallels here with human functioning: we too take in information, store, retrieve, utilise and transform it.

To develop this a little further, consider your own situation as you read this. You may be alone, with other people, indoors or outside, in a variety of contexts. There are undoubtedly many things going on around you, all your senses are potentially being bombarded by sounds, sights, smells and so on. You are ignoring most of them, screening them out, in favour of attending to the activity that is your central focus at the moment. This very first stage of taking in information is clearly a highly selective process. Our attention is a limited resource which we have to deploy selectively.

What is also clear is that there is no such thing as just seeing or just hearing. There is now a great deal of experimental evidence to show that we constantly try to give meaning to what we see and hear. If we are presented with an ambiguous piece of text or an ambiguous picture or sketch, we attempt to impose meaning on it, to interpret it in some way. This is why the term *perception* is used rather than *seeing* or *hearing*.

Once information has been attended to and perceived, it can be worked on; we can make more sense of it, make links with other knowledge, see relationships, maybe think of ways to try to remember it. The more these processes happen, the more likely we are to incorporate the new information or experience into our framework of existing knowledge and understanding. Two important processes of this kind are (a) rehearsal strategies, where various ways of remembering are put into practice, and (b) 'chunking', where the information is grouped or categorised in order to create fewer but larger units of information. An example of this would be grouping the digits of a telephone number into two or three 'chunks' in order to store and recall it more efficiently.

The knowledge we have already accumulated and stored is a major influence on what we choose to attend to and how we deal with it. This long term store must contain all a person knows about the world, all previous experiences, all previous events, all information built so far. In principle, it seems to be unlimited in capacity: it is thought that little is ever erased from long term memory, but access to it may become difficult. It must contain knowledge of many kinds, straightforward information (how high Mount Everest is) and procedural knowledge (how to open a tin). We all know many things: how to write or type; the names of our grandparents; what a bus looks like; how to remember a list of items; the colour red; the sensation of pain; a memory of where we used to live or particular events in our childhood. We also know something about what is in and what is not in our memory (I know that I don't know about calculus, for instance) and that some things are more difficult to learn and understand than others. In other words, we know something about knowing and learning – a topic we shall return to later.

Without this complex knowledge/memory system we could not function in the world, we would have no way of linking the past to the present or the future. When we talk to others, read or carry out a simple task such as recognising an object, we use these memory systems and thought processes. Therefore the more organised this information is, the more likely we are to be able to access it quickly, retrieve it and utilise it. Think of a large library of books without a pattern of organisation, without an index system – whether or not we could find a piece of information would be determined by trial and error, a very random process.

How does this system develop?

We can use this alternative approach to throw light on children's developing skills and thinking, in relation to those of adults. Take the idea of *novice* and *expert* as the starting point. When we are just beginning to try to learn a new skill, face a new task or solve a new problem, we are novices. Somehow our approach is fragmented and partial, we don't seem to have a feel for the whole task or see how the whole thing fits together. Imagine learning to drive a car or ride a bicycle. At first there seems to be too much to concentrate on at once and if we focus on one part, we lose control of another. But once we have mastered it, everything seems to fit together smoothly, we can perform efficiently and flexibly. The skills become more and more automatic and as this happens, progressively more of our attention becomes freed so we can begin to focus on new information, for example other aspects of the task.

Children are in many ways novices, becoming and being helped to become more expert in a variety of information processing skills and understandings – walking, talking, riding a bike, reading, solving problems, remembering and many more. There is now accumulating evidence that children's abilities do change in this way. There are many aspects but I will focus on just three to convey the general idea:

1 Remembering sequences of numbers

Having to memorise a string of numbers is a popular task in psychology experiments. Children of, say, three can't cope very well when there are more than three or four numbers; five-year-olds do better, recalling perhaps five or six numbers; by the age of about eight, most children can remember as many as an adult, say seven or more. This may partly be a change in capacity, but it is also to do with strategies for remembering – grouping numbers into 'chunks', as we saw earlier.

2 Applying more general memory strategies

Even very young children seem to understand what it means to remember, although they may not be very good at it. In one experiment, two-year-olds were shown a sweet being hidden under one of three cups, and were then asked to remember which cup it was under while the adult left the room for a while. Hidden cameras showed their behaviour when alone, trying to remember the location of the sweet. Some stared very hard at it and some kept touching the appropriate cup. They knew what they were supposed to do and had some very basic strategies for doing it. If five-year-olds and 11-year-olds are given a set of various objects and asked to group and classify them, they perform differently. The younger ones can order and classify, but often in a random and changing way, whereas the older

267

children can group consistently, using appropriate strategies much as an adult would. However, when the younger ones are guided and helped to apply such strategies, they can do it too; they just don't appear to do so spontaneously. Progressively they can come to use more powerful rules and procedures.

3 Scanning pictures

When it comes to taking information from pictures, being asked to look for similarities and differences across two pictures, for instance, there are again differences between five-year-olds and older children in the way they tackle the problem. Using equipment that monitors eye-movements, it can be seen that the scanning patterns of the younger ones have a rather fragmented and impulsive character, while by age seven or eight the scanning is much more systematic and analytic.

Evidence such as this nicely demonstrates the kinds of change that are happening during this middle childhood period. Random and unskilled approaches gradually become more automatic, fluent and strategic, and what is more we can help in the process. Even quite high level thinking and cognitive skills can be taught giving us a rather different way of looking at children and their abilities. Their thinking and understanding may not be as radically and unchangeably different from that of adults, as Piaget suggests; instead it might just be less far along a very similar road. In fact under some circumstances, it might even be more efficient than that of adults.

As an example, take the game of chess – a highly complex activity which has proved fertile ground for experimental work to test these ideas. The pieces on a chessboard can only move in certain ways, and particular patterns emerge as any game progresses. Chase and Simon (1973) asked chess players with varying degrees of experience and skill to look at and then remember and reconstruct from memory particular patterns of pieces on a board. The more skilled players could do so with much greater success than beginners. But where the pieces had been arranged randomly rather than in predictable chess configurations, all players performed equally. The experts did not generally have superior memories, therefore, but what they did have was particular expertise, a large 'vocabulary' of possible patterns stored in memory which enabled them to see groups of pieces as meaningful 'chunks', and the ability to remember them more efficiently.

Further experiments by Chi (1978) add an interesting dimension to this, however. She set a similar chess piece problem to two groups of expert and novice players. Once again, the experts out-performed the novices, but in this case the novices were adults and the experts were ten-year-old children.

This confirms the idea that children may not have radically different capacities from those of adults and in some ways, when they have appropriate experience, their performance can be superior. When we look at accumulating knowledge in this more individualised skills-based way, the whole issue becomes more open-ended; apparent in-built constraints on what children can learn seem much fewer. Perhaps, as Bruner has suggested, we can teach anything to any child at more or less any point, provided our method and interventions are appropriate and geared to the needs of the individual. We can potentially teach children how to think and learn, which is very different from the Piagetian view.

Knowing about knowing and learning how to learn

As adults, part of the stored knowledge we possess will include something about what we know, what kind of procedures to apply in particular situations and recognising when we do not understand. The term given to these aspects of our knowing is *metacognition* and it is of great significance since it enables us to monitor our own functioning and therefore to learn and think more efficiently.

As we saw earlier, even young children seem to have some rudimentary insights into their own thinking. They seem to be aware that they forget things, that trying to remember many things is harder than remembering a few and that certain tasks are harder than others. Planning and knowing what kind of approach or strategy to adopt are important self-monitoring skills and young children and those experiencing learning difficulties often lack them. Ann Brown (1982) puts this well when she explains the importance of these processes in becoming a more efficient learner:

> To be an effective learner, she will need to know something about her own characteristics, her available learning activities, the demand characteristics of the various learning tasks and the inherent structure of the materials. She must tailor her activities finely to the demands of all these forces to be a flexible and effective learner. In other words, she must learn how to learn. (p.106)

Karmiloff-Smith (1984) has studied the processes by which children grapple with new problems, processes as diverse as making circuits, reading maps and learning new grammatical structures. On the basis of her experiments and findings, she puts forward a three-phase sequence in children's problem-solving. In the first phase, when presented with a new problem or materials, children seem driven and dominated by them, with little apparent organisation to their behaviour. Using positive and negative feedback from direct dealings with the problem they may solve it, but not very effectively. Then a second phase emerges, when they seem to rethink their earlier procedures and create an internal representation or plan, which may be over-simplified in an attempt to deal with the whole situation. This is a reflective, almost metaprocedural stage which they then try to impose on the materials or problem. The result is often a decline in the quality of actual performance, solving the problem less efficiently. In the final phase, however, the internal representation and the external experiences/behaviour are brought into line with each other, and the result is an organised and fluent solving of the problem.

This sequence draws attention to the importance of internal representation and reflection – the metacognitive aspects – and has special significance when we apply it to language learning. When children learn a new grammatical structure or item of complex vocabulary, they frequently go through a regressive phase when they fail to use it properly after having apparently mastered it. We can use these ideas to throw light on why this should be. It may be a case of overloading the information processing system with so much that is new and requiring attention, but it could also be this reflective phase of learning, where internal sorting-out processes are going on.

Differences between individuals

All individuals are unique in terms of their physical characteristics, personality and facility in performing certain activities. Yet all the approaches we have considered so far speak in general terms about processes that broadly apply to everyone. For some purposes this has to be the case, but in educational contexts it is important to recognise that within these general patterns, each child's experience, interests and knowledge will be unique. Since each of us constructs our own understanding of the world, the ways in which we view situations, interpret events and approach tasks will reflect this. As educators it is vital to take this on board if we are to achieve any kind of match between activity on the one hand and the child on the other.

The idea of individual differences is well entrenched in psychology and much time, energy and paper have been spent trying to measure them. This is especially true of the complex and elusive idea of *intelligence*. For the best part of this century debate has raged as to what it is and whether it can be measured. There have been almost as many definitions as definers – 'the ability to learn or to profit by experience', 'the ability to carry out abstract thinking', 'the capacity for knowledge'. Definitions are culturally influenced too, with North American surveys throwing up traits such as 'clever', 'efficient' or 'energetic', while studies among rural African groups mention 'mental order', 'inventiveness', 'unselfishness' and contradictorily 'mental turmoil' (Sternberg 1985).

In education contexts, given the controversy and debate that still surround the idea of general 'intelligence', we should perhaps question its usefulness. It is not necessarily helpful to label children 'intelligent' or 'lacking in intelligence' as though it were a fixed and unchangeable quality which they either have or have not. If we take seriously the kinds of views that I have been outlining here, then it seems more appropriate to view the issue as helping all children to think and learn more effectively and to adapt in flexible ways to new situations.

Learning, thinking and teaching

One of the criticisms of Piaget's work is that it underplays the importance of the social context and the possibility of adult intervention. Two theorists who have taken these ideas further are Bruner and Vygotsky. Although from different time periods and cultures (America and Russia), their ideas are closely related. Looking back on his work in his autobiography (1983), Bruner says that he has

> tried to unravel how the primitive operations of the baby's mind got converted to the subtle arts and sciences and intuitions of an adult. In the end, I concluded that man could not have made that voyage without the ready-made tools of a culture and its language, that mental growth comes as much from the outside in as from the inside out. (p.278)

What other people around the child do, within a culture and often through language, is to help the child to go beyond, to 'reach the higher ground' of understanding in ever more complex and abstract forms. Adults provide the 'scaffolding' that enables the child to do this.

For Vygotsky (1978) too, 'human learning presupposes a specific social nature and a process by which children grow into the intellectual life of those around them'. (p.88)

If we start with the assumption of a kind of 'a-social' child, then we are lead down the path that Piaget takes. But if we assume that babies are highly tuned-in and responsive to those around them from the beginning, and there is good evidence that they are, then we can suggest that they learn in part from others. Social transaction is one of the basic means of development and education, not isolated endeavour.

This leads us to Vygotsky's 'zone of proximal development', which has to do with the ways in which we can intervene and arrange activities to help push the child along. He defines this zone as 'the distance between the actual developmental level as determined by independent problem-solving and the level of potential development as determined through problem-solving under adult guidance or in collaboration with more capable peers.' (p.86)

The adult or more capable peer structures the activity, acting almost as the 'consciousness' of the child in a metacognitive way until such time as the child can reflect on and internalise the strategies and then take control. The move is from solutions created between two minds, towards internalised solutions within the individual child – from the *intermental* to the *intramental*, to use Vygotsky's terminology.

The proof of the pudding with the developmental theories we have discussed lies not only in their logic but in their practical effectiveness. Piagetian approaches allow little room for action by adults and, worse, they may have lead to a degree of inertia on the part of teachers, feeling powerless in the face of the apparently inexorable 'internal' developmental process. Intervention could lead, according to Piaget, to superficial rote learning and not to genuine understanding and progress. In some ways this is an important point to make, since we clearly don't want children to experience 'empty' learning, but neither do we want artificially to constrain and inhibit them because they have not reached a particular 'stage'. Teaching is defined as facilitating learning. To do this effectively we need to discover as precisely as possible what the child knows and can do, and then

271

build on this, giving support along the way. This is what the most 'enabling' parents do intuitively and they are the first and perhaps most significant teachers of their children. We can learn from the strategies of the most effective parents.

While the earliest developments happen in the home, there is increasing evidence that schooling has its own kind of impact on thinking, in particular ways and for particular reasons. First, placing children alongside many others brings them face-to-face with alternative viewpoints, all set within a specialised institution with its own culture and rules. The potential for learning from others, peers as well as teachers, is enormous.

Second, schools have impact on thinking via the introduction of literacy. Most children first come up against reading and writing in the school context and are thus introduced to the 'literate' language of text. This differs from oral language in significant ways – it is grammatically more complex and uses more unusual vocabulary. If we accept that the language we use is all tied up with our thinking, then learning literate forms creates the potential for more organised and complex thought. The work of Perera (1984) is interesting to read in this context.

Some conclusions and implications for language learning

This summary brings together the points I have tried to make throughout this chapter on how children's thinking and understanding develops:

1 The work of Piaget cannot be ignored – even though some parts have been heavily criticised, many of his insights remain useful. The notion that knowledge creating is a constructive process is central.
2 Other frameworks, in particular information processing, also offer important insights.
3 There is no such thing as just *seeing* or just *hearing*; both of these processes are highly selective and full of interpretation on our part. We never just 'take in' material.
4 What we already know will have a major influence on what we choose to attend to and what and how we learn. There will be much individual variation in this.
5 The idea of *skill* is an important one. This term does not mean rigid procedures which are drummed in. In this context it implies efficient but flexible creation of patterns and strategies. Thinking, along with many other sorts of activity, is a cognitive skill which can be developed in children.
6 As we become more experienced and skilled, we can deploy less attention to a particular activity and therefore free more of our limited resources to apply to other things. We move from being a novice to becoming a more expert performer or understander. Information becomes transformed into knowledge.

7 Becoming aware of how we think and learn seems to be important. Helping children to understand more about their own strategies and procedures of learning and thinking may be significant in the development process.

8 Views about the nature of children's development have massive implications for the role of the teacher. Within the framework outlined here, effective teaching means sensitive and well-informed intervention in the development process.

Learning a first or second language can be viewed in these terms. Children actively work at language learning, they are not just passive receivers. And what seems obvious to the teacher is not always obvious to the child: they may not hear what we hear or see what we see. Imagine what it feels like when you listen to a conversation in another language, one with which you are totally unfamiliar. It sounds like a stream of sound which you cannot even begin to 'hear'. Word and sentence boundaries only become distinguishable when you know what to listen for. As teachers of language we have to do our best to ensure that what we say will be within reach of the child's ear and mind, as David Wood (1988) says.

Research on children learning their first language increasingly stresses that there is much individual variation in the rate at which children progress and the strategies they use (see Shorrocks 1989 and Wells 1987). Not all children start off at the same age or progress in the same neat single-word-two-word-combinations-phrases sequence. If this is the case with the first language, it is equally applicable when learning a second. Some children will just need to listen for some time before they venture to 'produce', while others will rush in and have a go from the beginning. Some will start by using whole phrases and gradually work out the units that go to make them, but others will use a limited number of words singly and gradually work out how they all fit together.

As they become more expert in vocabulary, structures and communication strategies they can gradually begin to hear more and understand more with the spare attention resources. Communicative strategies and procedures become more fluent, flexible and automatic, and as this repertoire becomes more extensive and varied, so they will be able to elicit more complex information and responses from those with whom they communicate. The more varied the range of communication contexts they are exposed to, the greater are the possibilities for this, remembering, however, that individuals will vary in their willingness and approaches. As I indicated at the beginning, learning and using language is a high-level, cognitive, problem-solving activity. Greater understanding of these processes should enable us to become more effective teachers.

Bibliography

References

Brown, A.L. 1975. 'The development of memory: knowing, knowing about knowing and knowing how to know.' in Reese, H.W. (ed). *Advances in Child Development and Behaviour*, Vol 10. New York: Academic Press.

Brown, A.L. *et al.* 1983. 'Learning, remembering and understanding.' in Flavell, J.H. and E. Markman (eds). *Handbook of Child Psychology*, Vol 3. New York: Wiley.

Brown, A.L. and J.S. Deloach. 1987. 'The early emergence of planning skills in children.' in Bruner, J. and H. Haste (eds). *Making Sense: the Child's Construction of the World*. London: Methuen.

Bruner, J.S. 1983. *In Search of Mind*. New York: Harper & Row.

Bryant, P.E. 1974. *Perception and Understanding in Young Children*. London: Methuen.

Chase, W.G. and H.A. Simon. 1973. 'Perception in chess.' *Cognitive Psychology*, Vol 4, pp.55–81.

Chi, M.T.H. 1978. 'Knowledge structures and memory development.' in Siegler, R.S. (ed). *Children's Thinking: What Develops*. Hillsdale: Lawrence Erlbaum.

Donaldson, M. 1978. *Children's Minds*. London: Fontana.

Gesell, A. 1977. *The Child from Five to Ten*. New York: Harper & Row.

Karmiloff-Smith, A. 1984. 'Children's problem-solving.' in Lamb, M.E., A.L. Brown and B. Rogoff (eds). *Advances in Developmental Psychology*. New Jersey: Lawrence Erlbaum.

Perera, K. 1984. *Children's Writing and Reading*. Oxford: Basil Blackwell.

Robinson, E. 1983. 'Metacognitive development.' in Meadows, S. (ed). *Developing Thinking: Approaches to Children's Cognitive Development*. London: Methuen.

Shorrocks, D. 1989. 'The development of language and communication.' in Sugden, D. (ed). *Cognitive Approaches in Special Education*. London: Falmer.

Sternberg, R.J. 1985. *Human Abilities: an Information Processing Approach*. New York: Freeman.

Vygotsky, L.S. 1978. *Mind in Society*. Cambridge, Massachusetts: Harvard University Press.

Wells, G. 1986. *The Meaning Makers*. London: Hodder & Stoughton.

Wood, D. 1988. *How Children Think and Learn*. Oxford: Basil Blackwell.

Further reading

Some useful follow-up reading which is not too technical is listed here. Some titles have already been mentioned in the list of references.

Bruner, J.S. 1966. *Towards a Theory of Instruction*. Cambridge, Massachusetts: Harvard University Press.

Bruner, J.S. 1983. *Child's Talk: Learning to Use Language*. Oxford: Oxford University Press.

Howe, M.J.A. 1984. *A Teacher's Guide to the Psychology of Learning*. Oxford: Basil Blackwell.

Kail, R. 1979. *The Development of Memory in Children*. San Francisco: Freeman.

Meadows, S. 1986. *Understanding Child Development*. London: Hutchinson.

Wells, G. 1985. *Language, Learning and Education*. Slough: NFER/Nelson.

Wood, D. 1986. *How Children Think and Learn*. Oxford: Basil Blackwell.

Philip Riley, CRAPEL, University of Nancy II, France

20 What's your background?

The culture and identity of the bilingual child

Second language learners are different from other primary learners in one crucial way – they are moving into bilingualism. Philip Riley looks at significant issues of culture and identity for bilingual children and raises important questions for teachers and for parents.

THE OVERALL AIM of this paper is to investigate certain aspects of what it means to be a bilingual child, not just in linguistic terms, but socially and psychologically. We will be looking at the child's *sense of reality*, at how he/she thinks the world works and, in particular, at *social reality* – how society is organised and how people function within it.

Social reality consists of common sense, of what (we think) we know. The nature of this *knowledge*, that is, the different things we know and know how to do, determines our *culture*. Our culture also includes the ways in which knowledge is acquired and communicated, formulated and stocked. Culture largely defines our *social identity*, which is conferred by virtue of our membership of the various social groups and sub-groups which exist within society.

The main way in which a particular kind of knowledge is acquired is through interaction and *negotiation* with members of the group in question. The principal mechanism of this process of *social* learning is language, which also serves, therefore, as one of the most powerful symbols of group membership.

In varying degrees, bilingual children may acquire and assimilate two cultures and two social identities or construct a culture and an identity which contains elements of both. However, both as individuals and in terms of the situations in which they live, bilingual children vary enormously. So it would be unrealistic to imagine that a single, straightforward account of *the* bilingual child could ever be given. Instead, an attempt will be made to provide readers with a set of notions (the terms italicised above) which they can use to describe and, it is hoped, better understand the particular children and situations they are concerned with.

Getting yourself organised

Culture as knowledge

Let us start with two notions which are closely related to the bilingual child's personality and life – *culture* and *identity*. The word 'culture' has a number of different meanings including:

a) One very common meaning is 'works of art': Michelangelo's *David*, the Goldberg Variations, *Swan Lake*, Salisbury Cathedral, *Les Misérables*.

b) A somewhat similar, but much broader, meaning refers to all the objects produced by a given group, not just those which are highly prized aesthetically: pots and pans, fabrics and items of clothing, weapons, toys, tools – everything in the environment which is artificial, made by humankind, as opposed to being part of nature.

These meanings of 'culture' are useful in everyday conversations, but when we need to define the word more exactly, for example if we want to say what an individual's culture *is*, we find them lacking for a number of reasons. Some of these are matters of demarcation. If we decide to limit culture to works of art, who is to decide which works are and which are not 'art'? Again, if we extend culture to everything that is manmade, what do we do about a stone that is used as a tool and when is a flower 'arranged'? Indeed, is it possible to make neat distinctions between the 'natural' and the 'artificial' in the face of evidence that perception itself, our way of processing and interpreting the environment, varies from one ethnic group to another?

While these questions are interesting and important, a more crucial problem in the present context concerns the relationship between culture and language. It is this: humankind does not only make concrete objects, whether works of art or pots and pans, we also make social objects, 'things' like an invitation, the rank of sergeant, school, a lie, shopping, a birthday, duty, marriage, shaggy dog stories, fun and promises.

Now whereas natural objects – stones, trees, animals – exist and continue to exist whether or not we notice or name them, social objects only exist because we act as if they were there and because we have names for them. To the people concerned, marriages, promotion to the rank of sergeant, promises and birthdays are just as real as any object and they act accordingly. 'Whatever is perceived as real, is real in its effects,' as Thomas's Law puts it.

This means that any approach to culture which goes beyond simply listing or describing concrete objects – which aims, for instance, to describe culture as something an individual *has* – necessarily has to take social objects into consideration. However, we cannot stop there. As we have just seen, social objects do not exist in the way concrete objects do. They exist in people's heads and in their behaviour. Each of us carries around a mental image of our society and how it functions. This image is shared to a greater or lesser extent by our fellows. It is made up of shared ideas on every possible aspect of social structure and activity: when, who and how you marry; what your relationship with your spouse will be like; how a sergeant or schoolchild or priest is supposed to behave and how others are expected to behave towards them; what you do or say on somebody's birthday; what schools, banks, churches and football fields are and what you do there; who does the shopping, when, where and how; what and when you eat . . . . These considerations lead us to adopt a third approach to culture:

c) Culture is knowledge. Not in the scientific sense of objectively verifiable facts, but in the ideological sense. It is a set of ideas, information, beliefs, values, rules and capacities – everything which makes that particular society tick and which its members need to know if they are to participate competently in its activities.

This 'socio-cultural knowledge' includes every domain of social activity: religion, politics, sports, occupations, the arts, leisure, defence, medicine, education, science and language.

There are two important implications here. The first is that culture is something which is *learnt,* since it is neither part of our biological inheritance nor of the natural environment. Culture, that is, is transmitted socially, enabling the group and its members to survive as a group. The forms that transmission takes – the ways in which we bring up children, our rearing and educational practices – are themselves part of culture. In all human societies, language plays a major role in this process, since it is both the repository of culture (the notions and distinctions expressed in its vocabulary and grammar) and the medium by which meaning is created and shared in interaction.

The second point is that culture is *variable.* We do not all know the same things. This sounds obvious, yet every time we speak of 'French culture' or 'Indian culture' or the 'British Way of Life' we are in danger of forgetting it. Cultural knowledge is not uniform or indivisible, something which you do or do not have as a whole. Each of us acquires a specific selection of socio-cultural knowledge according to the nature, range and quality of our participation in society – this is, according to the lives we lead.

It is to this relationship between knowledge and social identity which we now turn.

Knowledge and identity

Because we do not all have the same experiences, live in the same place, know the same people, play the same roles or do the same things, different people learn different things – they have different cultures. What we know, then, is very closely related to who we are, to our social position. Moreover, no individual can be a member of all the social groups which make up a given society, since many of them are in a mutually exclusive, either-or relationship:

Examples	Aspects
Male, female	Sex
Teenager, middle-aged, pensioner, child	Age group
Londoner, Liverpudlian	Residence
Deaf, hearing	Audition
Rich, poor	Wealth
Lawyer, welder, supermarket cashier, optician	Profession
Catholic, Atheist, Muslim, Plymouth Brethren	Religion
Green, Socialist, Conservative	Politics
Chess player, synchronised swimmer	Pastimes
Married, single, divorced	Marital status
An only child, one of eight	Order of birth
Jamaican, Irish, Pakistani	Ethnicity
Speaker of English, Urdu, French	Language(s)

Figure 1 Aspects of social identity.

Such a list as in Figure 1 could be extended indefinitely but if one is at first reminded of those books for children where the pages are cut into three parts, enabling the reader to make vast numbers of different and unlikely combinations (a chinaman wearing a kilt and clogs), a little reflection shows that the real-life facts of the matter are far more complex than any fiction. Not only does every society have a considerable repertoire of such categories but they are continually shifting or being redefined. Today's shadow cabinet is tomorrow's government and the same is true for the individual who attains the age of majority, marries or divorces, qualifies as an accountant; he/she is constantly changing or entering groups. The social identity of the individual, then, is a particular combination of the social classifications available; some of them we are born to, some are achieved and some are thrust upon us.

Two further points can be made in this respect. First, the idea that there is a close relationship between knowledge and group membership is not just sociological theorising: almost every group, from teenage gang to professional association has some kind of knowledge-based entry qualification and one which is very often linguistic in form whether it is a secret oath or a written examination paper. Second, we expect people who are members of particular groups to know certain things: a car mechanic should know how to change an exhaust pipe, a Catholic should know the Catechism, a bird-watcher should recognise a white-rumped sandpiper. And it is on the basis of such attributions of knowledge that we perceive and interact with others.

In order to summarise and illustrate the approach to culture and social identity which has been adopted here and to underline the role of language as the principal channel of socio-cultural knowledge, let us consider the list of words and phrases in Figure 2.

a boozer-cruiser	molysmology	Wai	azimuth
fascine	kukka	an accumulator	1066
conkers	the Roberval Enigma	bur-chervil	meals-on-wheels
Twickenham	scrimshaw	the Old Man's Gardens	pay and display
a flash butt weld	adabiatisme	endogamy	muñeca
gvias-eydes	mandamus	Free House	monetarism
SWALK	Borstal	mistletoe	DIY
recaption	fondue	tnoyim	national curriculum
ystävä	lines	squash	sisu
Citizens	källarvåning	a chip butty	the Provos
a double top	a diaper pattern	nano	MoS_2

Figure 2

Now it is highly unlikely that any single person knows all these words. It is also unlikely (given that you are reading this book) that you do not know any of them. But what is it that determines not just how many and in what detail but which particular combinations of these items you know? To a large extent, it is your social identity. You are much more likely to know *caption* and *mandamus* if you know something about English law, *a double top* if you are a darts player, *the Old Man's Gardens* if you spent your childhood near the Royal Hospital, Chelsea, *bur-chervil* and *fascine* if you are interested in botany and historical architecture respectively, *a boozer-cruiser* if you are in the habit of pub-crawling in areas where brewing companies provide transport . . .

The quality of our knowledge of any item also varies: *a flash butt weld* will be just a sort of weld to non-welders and *meals-on-wheels* will be much more than a social service for an old age pensioner who relies on them coming at 12.30 pm, Monday to Saturday (and on Fridays they always give you a choice of meat or fish.)

The possible combinations seem infinite (a retired welder who has his lunch brought round every day? a child who speaks English, Urdu and French?) yet in fact this is an extremely simplified example. For instance, we have not yet taken into account the fact that items on this list will probably trigger off different domains of knowledge for different people. When you saw *accumulator* did you think of a sort of bet or a sort of battery? Does *squash* go with 'orange' or 'court'? Are *lines* more closely related to school geometry or school punishment? Our knowledge and our interpretation of these items will depend largely on our social identity.

So far, we have limited our attention to words and expressions that can be regarded as being in some sense 'English', although the fact that many people would contest the status of, say, *mandamus* or *boozer-cruiser* shows us that it is no easier to delimit a language than it is to delimit a culture. If we turn to other items such as *muñeca*, *ystävä*, *källarvåning* and *gvias-eydes*, we would probably say that you 'need to know' Spanish, Finnish, Swedish and Yiddish to understand them. In other words, knowledge of Spanish or Finnish is related to identity in much the same way as knowledge of welding or darts. Combinations of languages – forms of bilingualism – are in this respect similar to combinations of other areas of knowledge.

There is, however, an important difference between bilinguals and monolinguals and the way their knowledge is distributed. Whereas by definition everything a monolingual knows he/she knows in one and the same language, for the bilingual the situation is obviously more complex. Some things he/she will know in both languages, some things only in one or the other.

This sounds strange if you are used to thinking of bilinguals as people who are absolutely competent in two languages. But if we stop and think for a minute, we see that this is an impossible demand. Even when we restricted our attention to the English items on the list, we saw that it was quite possible for an English-only speaker to have 'gaps' in the way his/her knowledge is distributed or to know some things much better than others and that this state of affairs is directly related to the individual's social identity. This is equally true for the bilingual but in addition the knowledge may be distributed between two languages.

Consider the case of Magnus, a Swedish-French bilingual teenager who is learning to drive in France and in French. You cannot attend school or learn to drive in two countries at the same time, and so these two areas of knowledge and experience will be French. However, at home and on holidays Magnus speaks (and cooks and sails) in Swedish. He will probably have a certain amount of difficulty talking about driving or the Treaty of Westphalia in Swedish or talking about sailing or meatballs in French. Certain aspects of his social identity (schoolboy, sailor) will be more closely identified with one or other of his languages, according to the circumstances in which the relevant knowledge and experience was acquired.

Who do you think you are?

Where does our sense of social identity come from? How do we know who we are and what our place in society is? Such questions are obviously extremely complex, but it is possible to identify two main answers without undue oversimplification.

First, we know such things because other people tell us all the time and they tell us in no uncertain way. Society is continually bombarding its members with instructions, information and feedback – 'This is how little boys/people on Social Security/customers/barmen/Muslims should behave.' *Social* identity is necessarily conferred and validated by others. Society holds up a mirror in which individual members see themselves. There is usually a fair degree of congruence between what the individual believes or expects to see and the image which is reflected back, between 'I' and 'me'. That is, our behaviour produces the results we expect. When this is not the case, a reappraisal becomes necessary, a realisation which can also be brought home forcefully by others – 'Who do you think you are?', 'Sorry, members only', 'Don't call us, we'll call you.' 'You're wrong/mad/wicked/a failure . . . .'

Second, such behaviour is to a large extent only possible because, as we saw earlier, our language has provided us with the tools and categories necessary to classify people in general. Terms such as Catholic, foreigner and neighbour provide the scaffolding for our social reality: without them, the world around us would not make sense. The bilingual child, then, has to operate two such systems, which means deciding which system to apply to which people, including him/herself, and in what situations. This may involve relatively simple choices – 'What language do I use to address this new acquaintance?' – but even this will be an explicit statement of the child's system of social categorisation, 'I think you are a member of such-and-such a group.'

The acquisition of these social categories is a highly complex process, so it is rather surprising to find that it occurs within a limited and precise time 'window' in the child's development: between three-and-a-half and five years old. All children compile their personal 'Who's Who' during this period, but the bilingual child has to add an additional '. . . and who speaks what?' This is further complicated by the fact that the notion of 'a language' and of particular categories of language (German, Cantonese and so on) is amongst the social classifications being learnt. So it is by no means unusual for such children to ask questions such as 'What language am I speaking to you in?' or to use regularly paraphrases such as 'the language I speak to Daddy' rather than 'English'. Such questions should not be seen as signs of confusion. On the contrary, they are clear evidence that the child is becoming aware of his/her bilingualism and of its role in constructing social reality.

It is here that the relative status of the child's language or languages plays a crucial role in the definition of self-image and social identity. In very general terms, if both a child's languages are valued by both of the speech communities concerned then bilingualism will be experienced as something positive and enriching. On the other hand, if for some reason (political or racial tension, the weight of a colonial past, 'modern' versus 'old-fashioned' or even 'primitive' values) there is a disparity between the perceived values of the two languages, bilingualism may well be experienced as something conflictual, though still necessary. These two kinds of bilingualism, often called *additive* and *subtractive*, are really poles on a scale, rather than watertight categories. They stand in a more-or-less relationship rather than an either-or one and this relationship is in turn the product of a wide variety of social and psychological factors. This means that, although there clearly is a correlation between forms of bilingualism and social identity, it is not a simple one of cause and effect.

Schematically, we can identify three main possible combinations between language and cultural identity:

1 First, there is the bilingual who is also bicultural, equally at home in two different cultures or countries.

2 Second, there is the bilingual whose culture is clearly aligned with one of the two language groups concerned. Such a person is bilingual but monocultural. Where cultural or self-identification is with what can be regarded as a second language (in that it was acquired later or is not the family language for example) it is usually the result of a shift of cultural allegiance of some kind, either between generations or because the social conditions of the individual concerned have changed radically. This would be the case for many immigrants, but can also result from social or educational mobility.

3 An adult or child engaged in the process of *acculturation*, that is shifting from one cultural allegiance to another, may go through a period of uncertainty as to his/her cultural identity. In some cases, this period may be extended and may involve a sense of belonging to no group. This *anomie*, for reasons which have been touched on earlier, is characterised by a feeling of general meaninglessness. Anomie used to be presented as the great 'danger' of bilingualism and it is certainly distressing by all accounts. Nonetheless, recent work has led many researchers to play down its importance. Partly this is because of the general point made earlier that it is simplistic to relate bilingualism and cultural identity directly without taking into account a host of other social and psychological factors. Partly, though, it is quite clear that it may be just a passing phase (and one of the kind that many people, in particular adolescents, go through whether they are bilinguals or not). More important is the growing realisation that every individual's culture is a patchwork and that many bilinguals are perfectly content to share parts of what monolinguals see as different cultures. What is more, rather than considering themselves as excluded by two monolingual groups, bilinguals often identify very strongly with other bilinguals; their sense of group membership, the basis of social identity, uses bilingualism as a defining characteristic. Not surprisingly, this has striking linguistic repercussions: when bilinguals interact with fellow bilinguals they often use *both* languages and cultures in an especially rich and sensitive mode of communication. We will return to this phenomenon – *code switching* – in the next section.

Getting your acts together

You know what I mean?

A few years ago, my family and I rented a house for a short holiday. On the evening of our arrival we went into the kitchen to prepare a meal and set the table. To the extent that the kitchen (as well as ways of cooking, setting the table and so on) was like the kitchen we were used to, we had no difficulty in finding and using what we needed, even though we had never been in that particular kitchen before. The rubbish bin was under the sink, the knives and forks were in the table drawer and everything was going smoothly – until we tried to find the salt. We hunted high and low but to no avail and in the end had to telephone the owners. 'Oh, sorry,' they said. 'We thought you knew – it's in the fridge.'

In conversation generally, if things are not as we expect them to be or if we assume that our interlocutors know things which in fact they do not, the inevitable result is communicative failure or misunderstanding of some kind.

In this section we will be looking first at some of the ways in which background knowledge, such as where the salt is kept, penetrates discourse. We will be discussing how we use it to create meanings which are shared with our interlocutors and what we can do when we run into problems. We will then go on to investigate aspects of these matters which are characteristic of bilingual discourse.

Background knowledge in conversation

Here, in translation, are three snippets of conversation involving French schoolchildren:

1 A: No school today?
  B: It's Wednesday.

2 A: Why are you crying?
  B: I've forgotten my canteen ticket.
  A: You can have one of mine.
  B: I'm from Lay St Christophe.

3 A: What's for lunch?
  B: Pizza.
  A: Why isn't Bénédicte coming home?
  B: It's Friday.

To understand each of these exchanges, we need to know certain things.

In the first snippet, A, an adult, meets B, a small child, in the street, asks why the child is not at school and receives as a reply the day of the week. To make sense of this exchange, you need to be able to supply the missing link: by and large, French schools are closed on Wednesdays. This is ostensibly to allow children to attend Catechism classes whilst continuing to respect the separation of church and state, but the extent to which A and B are aware of these historical and political ramifications may also vary considerably.

Extract 2 is part of a conversation between two children. In their first exchange, the fact that you have forgotten your canteen ticket is given as an adequate reason for crying, presumably because it might mean getting into trouble, going without lunch and so on. The symbolic value of a ticket is itself a sophisticated piece of background knowledge: when Child A then offers one of her tickets, she demonstrates that she has mastered this knowledge. However, she receives as a reply the name of the village where B lives. To make sense of this, you have to know (at least) the following points:

a) Lay St Christophe is some ten kilometres away from the centre of the town where the school is situated.

b) Children whose home is not in town but who attend a town school do not benefit from town-subsidised meal prices: they have to pay the full rate.

c) Subsidised meal tickets are different from full-price meal tickets.

Our third quotation comes from a mother-child conversation. A is a small boy. When told that there will be pizza for lunch, he draws the conclusion that his sister, Bénédicte, will not be eating at home. What has enabled him to reach this conclusion? Simply that his sister hates pizza and so his mother provides it for lunch when she is not there. As to why she isn't there, the reply is the day of the week. In fact on Fridays Bénédicte goes straight on to her music lesson.

Superficially 1 and 3 are very similar, in that both depend on knowing what happens on a certain day of the week. There is, however, an extremely important difference between the two cases. In 1 the knowledge in question (no school on Wednesdays) is something everybody knows; anyone who has ever had anything to do with the French educational system can be expected to know this. In other words it is true of the vast majority of the French population. In 3 the key to understanding the exchange is the information that on Fridays Bénédicte has her piano leson. In this case, the class of people who possess the information in question is a very limited one indeed (Bénédicte's parents, her brother and her piano teacher, probably – a maximum of five).

As we saw earlier, knowledge is not distributed evenly, with everyone knowing the same things. If it were, it would be tantamount to saying that everyone knew everything and that would make communication complete-ly superfluous. The particular selection of knowledge which we acquire varies according to the nature and quality of our participation in social life: In what circles do we move? What kinds of situation are we involved in and in what roles? Who do we meet, what do they know and what is our social relationship with them? Some knowledge we will have in common with the other members of the smallest social groups we belong to – a couple, a family. Other knowledge may be slightly wider spread — the members of a volleyball team or the people who drink in a particular pub. The bounds of the social groups may be set wider still and wider — everyone living in a particular region or who has received a certain form of schooling, say.

This is why, if we wish to communicate effectively with someone, we need to know what they know, so that we can judge what they do and do not 'need to be told'. This is where 'membershipping' — the process of social categorisation — comes in. Let us look at this from the point of view of its linguistic and communicative effects. Take the following simplified case. A is a Londoner. He meets someone whose accent identifies him as a Londoner too, and who asks, 'Where are you from?', to which he replies, 'Fulham'. Next he meets someone who, although recognisably British, is clearly not a Londoner. Again, he is asked, 'Where are you from?' and he replies, 'London'. Later, on holiday in France, he is asked the same question by the hotel receptionist. This time he replies, 'England'. Presumably, if he landed on Mars, he would inform the inhabitants that he was from 'Earth', but we do not need to push the argument so far to show that we select and formulate our conversational messages on the basis of what we think other people might know: it is improbable that someone who does not even know England is likely to know where Fulham is.

This can be seen in how we change when we receive information about our interlocutors which makes us modify our perception of them and in particular the knowledge we attribute to them. For example, if the conversation with the French hotel receptionist mentioned above proceeds as follows, A would certainly have to shift ground:

R: Where are you from?
A: England.
R: Oh yes, what part?
A: London.
R: Oh, I love London. I worked in a travel agency right next to South Kensington Station for five years.
A: Really! Well, if you go up Sydney Place and turn right on the Fulham Road and walk about 200 yards . . .

The negotiation of meaning

As we have seen, speakers need to know what their addressees know in order to decide what they need to be told and how. If we attribute knowledge to people which they do not in fact possess, they will not be able to understand what we say: if we keep telling them what they already know they will find us at best boring and at worst feel rejected, since this is a clear signal that we do not consider them to be members of our group. We make use of a very wide range of clues when assessing people's knowledge: uniform and grey hair, for example, but above all language, including accent and speaking style, in the widest sense.

Language also provides us with the mechanisms and tools necessary to evaluate the knowledge of our addressees, to check on our evaluation in cases of uncertainty, and above all to identify, give or acquire missing knowledge when there is a communicative problem of some kind. This process is known as the negotiation of meaning. Consider the following passage from a conversation between a father and his daughter. The child is recounting an afternoon's visit to the park in the middle of town with friends.

CHILD: . . . and the goats didn't like the bread but they ate the carrots.

ADULT: Yeah, yeah, I suppose they get too much bread all the time. What about you? Did you have anything?

CHILD: Caroline had an ice and I had one of those . . . you know . . .

ADULT: An ice-lolly?

CHILD: No, it's not cold. It's like bread . . .

ADULT: Hamburger?

CHILD: . . . only, no, only sweet and . . .

ADULT: Oh I – a a waffle. You know, you put sugar and cream on . . .

CHILD: Yeah, a waffle.

In the course of this conversation, the child ran up against a communicative problem: she did not know the right word for a particular aspect of her world. In the negotiation which followed, she tried to elicit this knowledge from her father by providing him with a description ('sweet') an analogy ('like bread') and differences ('not cold'). Her father collaborated by putting forward a series of hypotheses: two of them were wrong, but nonetheless helped the child by providing points of comparison ('ice lolly', 'hamburger'). When he believed he had correctly identified the object, he checked his hypothesis by providing supplementary information ('you put sugar and cream on') which the child was able to confirm ('Yeah, a waffle').

Three points can be made regarding this exchange. The first is that the participants collaborated to establish common ground, to identify what it was they were talking about. Second, this negotiation of meaning is obviously very closely related to *learning*. At the beginning of the conversation the child did not know the word 'waffle', at the end she did. By sharing this knowledge with his child, the father had made a tiny but real contribution to her culture. Learning is a social process and language is both instrument and content, both how learning is achieved and what is learnt.

Third, this passage clearly shows that speakers have a range of different techniques available to enable them to negotiate. When the child said 'one of those . . . you know', for example, she was clearly asking for the adult to intervene, which he promptly did. The various kinds of description, paraphrase and analogy which have already been noted are also examples of such *strategies* which have been the subject of intense research over the past 15 years or so and it is now generally agreed that they play a crucial role not just in communication but in the acquisition of language and knowledge, including social categories of every kind.

For all children, whether monolingual or bilingual, the ability to apply such strategies is of the utmost importance, since they canalise and filter social knowledge, both quantitatively and qualitatively. However, there are differences between the two groups: the most important of these is that bilinguals can use strategies based on both languages, such as translation or borrowing. Such strategies are used when the speaker is unable or unwilling to use the other language equivalent – unable because of a lack of vocabulary, for example, unwilling because it simply does not seem appropriate to do so. A *'tarte aux grenouilles'* is just not 'frog pie' any more than a *'château'* is a 'castle'. Here is a French/English bilingual child talking about her schoolday:

CHILD: We went out in the *cours* and I dropped my my, how do you say *'cahier de contrôle'*?

ADULT: Er.

CHILD: Anyway, I dropped it into a puddle and Monsieur Dap said . . .

By borrowing the word *'cours'* and by asking for a translation of *'cahier de contrôle'* (but not waiting for it) this child shows that she perceives the situation as bilingual, one where she can call on both systems, because she knows her father speaks French and because this is a conversation where her French world (school) and her English world (home) overlap. Communicatively speaking, this code-switching makes good sense – it is more accurate and more efficient. Indeed, in certain cases of this kind, children may opt for a complete switch of language, using only the school language to talk about school or consistently replying to their parents only in the school language. Such behaviour is often misconstrued by outside observers (especially if they themselves only speak one of the languages concerned) since they see it either as 'mixing' or as 'failed bilingualism'. In fact, it is a systematic reflection of the child's sense of social reality and his/her social identity. Numerous studies have shown that the same child in a monolingual situation will use only the strategies appropriate to that language and this includes children who 'refuse' to speak their parents' language at home.

Conclusion

In recent years, the ways in which children acquire language has been subject to intense scrutiny by linguists and psychologists. While many aspects of this process are still hotly debated, there is a growing consensus amongst specialists about one characteristic feature that comes as a surprise to laypeople. It is this. Between the ages of approximately nine to 16 months, children everywhere develop the same language – the *protolanguage* – which does not appear to be influenced by the particular language which is spoken around them. Only after this period does the child start to learn a particular language or languages, French, Finnish, Chinese or whatever.

This means that, despite their many differences, all languages share a number of common characteristics, particularly as regards the fundamental notions and functions they express, such as time and space and understanding or interacting with the environment. The specific way in which a given language handles or maps out these universals – the mother tongue – is learnt by children from some time in the latter half of their second year onwards. Progressively finer distinctions, oppositions and classifications are acquired which enable the child to make sense of his/her world: these distinctions make up the lexical and grammatical systems of the language in question. In M.A.K. Halliday's words (1988): 'Language is not *how we know* something else, it is *what we know*; knowledge is not something that is encoded in language – knowledge is made of language.'

Even when presented in such a schematic fashion, these ideas clearly have important implications for bilingualism. Indeed, it could be argued that if there were no protolanguage/universals, bilingualism would either be impossible or would result in totally schizoid individuals. Instead, we have children acquiring two (or even six or seven!) different sets of coordinates for mapping out common areas of experience. Again, the protolanguage theory also goes a long way to explain why bilingual children go through a 'mixing' phase at plus or minus two years old.

A third implication, and the most important one in this context, is that while the protolanguage can be regarded as innate, since it develops independently of the social and linguistic environment, its characteristics being determined by the 'systems constraints' of the human brain, the mother tongue(s) must be acquired socially, through interaction with others. The acquisition of the language system(s), of finer and finer shades of meaning will continue for the rest of the child's life. It is no coincidence, therefore, that the onset of this stage in the child's linguistic development is paralleled with an increasing ability to see and say things from the addressee's point of view.

Bibliography

Baetens-Beardsmore, H. 1982. *Bilingualism: Basic Principles.* Clevedon: Tieto Press.

Harding, E. and P. Riley. 1986. *The Bilingual Family: a Handbook for Parents.* Cambridge: Cambridge University Press.

Saunders, G. 1983. *Bilingual Children: Guidance for the Family.* Avon: Multilingual Matters.

A.P.R. Howatt, University of Edinburgh, Scotland

21 Teaching languages to young learners: patterns of history

Anyone who has progressed this far in a book on teaching young children will be wondering how we came to be where we are. This paper offers a historical account of teaching language to young learners, to remind us that few arguments are new and few ideas are unique to a particular time. The principles and practices outlined throughout the rest of this book grew out of the events and arguments recorded here.

U NTIL VERY RECENT TIMES, learning foreign languages was 'generally a mark of privileged or advanced schooling'[1]. This comment by H.H. Stern and Alice Weinrib provides a useful point of departure for an historical perspective on the teaching of foreign languages to young learners. Privilege was the hallmark of schooling throughout Europe for centuries and when basic elementary education for all finally arrived in the late nineteenth century, it did not include foreign languages which were restricted to the (selective) secondary schools. Recently there have been determined attempts to extend opportunities for foreign language learning to groups who had been excluded in the past, 'less academic' pupils, for instance, and younger learners. While such aims are well-intentioned, they do not always meet with the enthusiasm that might be expected. Teaching foreign languages to young learners is not as simple as it may appear at first sight; it implies an arrangement of priorities which is not easy for everyone to accept, particularly if it is perceived as a threat to the teaching of the mother tongue. These tensions have a long history.

Until the eighteenth century, formal education in Europe consisted almost exclusively of the teaching of foreign languages, Latin mostly but also some Greek and Hebrew, to young boys between the ages of eight and 14. While in the Middle Ages there had been clear practical uses for Latin skills, most obviously in the church but also in secular activities such as administration and the law, gradually the vernacular languages began to take over functions and uses hitherto reserved for Latin. This trend was accelerated in the fifteenth century by a growing awareness of national identity facilitated by developments such as the invention and spread of printing. By 1500 the stage was set for what might have been a major educational shift away from Latin and towards the vernacular languages, but the opposite happened. There was a revival of interest in the history and culture of the ancient world led by scholars like Erasmus, Vives and other Renaissance humanists which revitalised the study of the classical languages and encouraged a deeper knowledge of the literature of antiquity.

Inspired by the humanists and the cultural achievements of the Renaissance, a new energy was apparent in European education. In England, for instance, the grammar schools were charged with the public duty of providing free tuition in the classics to all who could benefit from it. Under the leadership of Henry VIII a standard grammar, written by a number of hands but traditionally attributed to William Lily[2], was compiled and made compulsory for all schools. Pupils were not admitted until they could prove they were reasonably literate and from their first day at school at the age of seven or eight they were given Lily's grammar, which was written in Latin, and were required to learn it by heart. From time to time their work was 'heard' by the teacher in question-and-answer sessions which were also conducted in Latin. In some schools learning Latin grammar by rote was the sole activity six long days a week for six long years. In the better schools, however, the youngsters went on to literature and translation, beginning with legends and fables and then more demanding texts. The aim was twofold: first to discipline the mind through rigorous grammatical training and second to inculcate the moral virtues and values of the ancient world through contact with its literature and culture.

The prestige of the Renaissance grammar schools remained unchallenged for nearly two centuries but it is worth noting that this was also the period of the most spectacular development of English and most of the other mother tongues of Europe. A set of increasingly versatile vernacular languages grew up capable of meeting the communicative demands of an ever-widening range of contexts of discourse, but none of this was taught at school. 'English' did not appear on any school curriculum until the late seventeenth century and the grammar schools continued to reject it until reform was forced upon them in the mid-nineteenth century. It would be easy to dismiss such neglect as merely inertia and conservatism but this would not be wholly justified. The classics continued to find support long after they ceased to teach practical skills because they dealt in knowledge which defined the concept of learning itself. Latin and Greek were popularly referred to as 'the learned languages' and knowing them opened the way to membership of a stable and lasting culture which not only embraced the European continent but had begun to spread beyond.

The classicists did not, however, have everything their own way. Modern foreign languages, particularly French, were increasingly found in schools, but the issue which aroused the greatest interest throughout the whole period was that of the mother tongue and its role in a well-designed system of education for young children. From the mid sixteenth century onwards one educational reformer after another across Europe preached the same message: education should grow out of the child's experience of the mother tongue and foreign languages (particularly Latin) should be relegated to a subsidiary role.

One of the earliest champions of the vernacular in England was a teacher in Elizabethan London called Richard Mulcaster who spoke up eloquently for the use of English in his *First Part of the Elementarie* in 1582. Reminding his audience that English was the language of 'our liberty and freedom' whereas Latin 'remembered us of our thraldom and bondage,' he concluded: 'I love Rome but London better; I favour Italy, but England more; I honour the Latin but I worship the English.'[3] His book sets out a programme for the codification of the English language as a necessary prerequisite for any serious system of vernacular schooling and he offered a set of rules and principles which made a significant contribution to the standardisation of the English spelling system in the early seventeenth century.

Further afield in Europe Wolfgang Ratke opened the first German mother tongue school at Koethen in Saxony in the 1620s but in spite of arousing considerable public interest the venture eventually failed through lack of sensible practical planning. Ratke's basic principle, expressed in his *Methodus*[4] of 1626, has been restated in different guises by educational innovators up to the present day: 'In everything we should follow the order of Nature. There is a certain natural sequence along which the human intelligence moves in acquiring knowledge. This sequence must be studied and instruction must be based on the knowledge of it.'[5] This precept was developed into a set of pedagogical rules but the key innovation was the mother tongue principle: 'First let the mother tongue be studied, and teach everything through the mother tongue, so that the learner's attention may not be diverted to the language.'[6] Ratke's last remark draws attention to the fact that serious educational damage can be caused by too heavy an emphasis on linguistic form at the expense of meaning. Ratke's follower, the great Comenius, underlined the central role of the mother tongue in the child's exploration of meaning in his *Great Didactic* originally published in Czech around 1630: 'First of all the mother tongue must be learned,' a process which will take several years 'since it is intimately connected with the gradual unfolding of the objective world to the senses.'[7] Foreign languages should not be taught until the child was ten years old (late by the standards of the time) and should not take up too much time. Latin, for instance, should require no more than two years and other less important languages half that time. Elsewhere in Europe there were a few short-lived experiments to establish vernacular-based schools. In mid seventeenth century France, for instance, the famous 'Little Schools' (*'petites écoles'*, a term similar to the English 'petty schools') of Port-Royal were heavily committed to the mother tongue principle and gave considerable prominence to reading and the development of a feeling for literature in French[8].

Towards the end of the century in Britain John Locke elaborated these points further in *Some Thoughts Concerning Education* (1693), an essay containing supremely sensible advice on a modern system of education to replace the horrors of the grammar schools: 'To speak or write better Latin than English, may make a man be talked of, but he would find it more to his purpose to express himself well in his own tongue.'[9] Locke was also a strong supporter of early modern foreign language teaching since living languages were typically taught by resident native-speaking tutors following 'natural' conversation methods that could usefully be copied by the classics:

> As soon as he can speak English, 'tis time for him to learn some other Language. This nobody doubts of, when French is proposed. And the reason is, because people are accustomed to the right way of teaching that language, which is by talking it into children in constant conversation and not by grammatical rules. The Latin tongue would easily be taught the same way if his tutor, being constantly with him, would talk nothing else to him and make him answer still in the same language. But because French is a living language, and to be used more in speaking, that should be first learn'd, that the yet pliant organs of speech might be accustomed to a due formation of those sounds, and he get the habit of pronouncing French well, which is the harder to be done the longer it is delay'd.[10]

This last point about pliant speech organs was to surface again two or more centuries later. The vernacular movement gradually gathered support throughout the eighteenth century[11] but progress was slow and it was always seen as 'second best' to the traditional if increasingly moribund Latin grammar school tradition.

One specific issue separated the two systems more than any other, namely the teaching of grammar. Time and again it was pointed out that young children would learn Latin grammar better and more quickly if they learnt English grammar first. 'My drift and scope therefore is, to have a child so well versed in his mother's tongue before he meddle with Latin,' said an early enthusiast Joshua Poole in 1646, 'that when he comes to the construing of a Latin author, he shall from the signification of his words in construing, be in some good measure able to tell distinctly what part of speech every word is.'[12] Fifty years later, Joseph Aickin again stressed the importance of the mother tongue as the medium of instruction throughout the education system: 'It were to be desired that all learning were to be taught in our mother tongue, then youth might not only imbibe the inferior sciences, but even philosophy, divinity and law in their tender years, and might be serviceable in church and state sooner than they can now attain to the knowledge of the tongues'[13] and Daniel Duncan's plea in 1731 expressed in public what many must have felt in private: 'The learning of dead languages is a yoke that neither we nor our fore-fathers could ever bear when we were children. And I fancy the loathsomeness of that dry study comes for want of reasoning previously with them enough about the nature of words and their dependency on one another in their own mother tongue.'[14] Finally, two heavyweight views from later in the century – first, Joseph Priestley's succinct conclusion in 1761: 'The propriety of introducing the English grammar into English schools cannot be disputed'[15] and lastly, the much-maligned Robert Lowth asserted with admirable common sense, 'To enter at once upon the science of grammar and the study of a foreign language is to encounter two difficulties together, each of which would be much lessened by being taken separately in its proper order.'[16]

Lowth's *Short Introduction to English Grammar*, the influential prescriptive grammar that the twentieth century loves to hate, was published in 1762 and so, by an entertaining coincidence, was Rousseau's *Emile*, or *Education*, the equally influential quasi-novel about teaching, learning and childhood that has been the bible of liberal educationalists ever since. So much for generalisations about 'the eighteenth century'.

Emile is designed as a 'story' which describes the education of a boy of the same name and it is a rich source of ideas and principles which have since become the stock-in-trade of progressive education. There is, for instance, Rousseau's insistence on the central importance of experience where the teacher provides a series of opportunities for learning and avoids imposing a fixed curriculum. There is also a heavy emphasis on the internal development of the individual child (Emile has no classmates) through a continuous process of discovery carried out at his own pace in his own way. Above all, there is the constant appeal to 'Nature' and the rejection of everything that hints at artifice. Nature for Rousseau, as for his fellow romantic Wordsworth, 'ran through all things' and, also like Wordsworth, his guiding metaphor was biological: 'plants are fashioned by cultivation, man by education.'[17] The task of the educator is to discover the internal forces of Nature and construct a learning scheme consistent with them. It has to be remembered that Emile is not a miniature adult with ill-formed ('childish') versions of adult qualities, but a child with qualities of his own which are unknown to the adult. This perception is crucial to Rousseau's philosophy. Trying to reason with a child as Locke, for instance, suggested is pointless: 'Those children who have been constantly reasoned with strike me as exceedingly silly . . .' Rousseau claimed, 'If children understood reason, they would not need education.'[18]

Of the greatest importance to the child's development is constant contact with meaningful experience, beginning with the world of the senses, and the exploration of this experience through talk. The teacher's role is not to initiate but to respond to the child's discovery of meaning through discussion. In particular, the teacher must never pre-empt this crucial process of discovery by replacing the genuine experience of the real world with the artificial experience of language: 'Words! Words! Words! . . . You will be surprised to find that I reckon the study of languages among the useless lumber of education.'[19]

Rousseau's passionate rejection of foreign languages and even of literacy in the mother tongue ('reading is the curse of childhood'[20]) seems excessive but it was designed to emphasise a central point concerning the relationship between form and meaning. Premature concentration on language at the expense of experience meant that linguistic forms became divorced from the meanings they were intended to convey. Teaching such empty forms was worse than useless, it was a betrayal of the purpose of education itself ('the symbols are of no value without the idea of the things symbolised'[21]). In

Rousseau's view this form-meaning divorce was inevitable in the case of foreign language teaching ('I do not believe any child under twelve or fifteen ever really acquired two languages . . . you may give children as many synonyms as you like [i.e. foreign language vocabulary]; it is not their language but their words that you change; they will never have but one language'[22]).

What Rousseau is saying is that the acquisition of the mother tongue is a special event – in accord with 'Nature' – but that languages learnt later are little more than artificial displays of verbal expertise. This distrust of verbalism was a theme which ran through the work of Rousseau's disciples and successors – Pestalozzi for instance and his follower, Froebel, both educational innovators whose principal interest concerned the welfare of very young learners. Moreover there is no doubt that the mother tongue tradition as elaborated by Rousseau has left a lasting legacy which plays a powerful role in conditioning the views of teachers, parents and others towards the teaching of foreign languages to children of primary school age at the present time. There may be strong practical reasons for teaching languages in schools, but practical relevance to the adult world is seen as essentially an argument for the secondary school. The primary school is concerned with more basic processes, and there are many who remain unconvinced that teaching or using languages other than the mother tongue can ever be fully justified. At best foreign languages are distracting, at worst actively damaging to the young child's perceptions of meaning in the outside world.

Rousseau's provocative but rather vague philosophising was made more practical and concrete by the work of his successors. Pestalozzi, for instance, developed the technique of the so-called 'object lesson', a procedure which took as its starting point a simple artefact such as a cup or a coat that the children were encouraged to explore by describing its qualities, functions and so on. In this way language was stimulated and developed through direct experience of the world of the senses, a concept developed further by Pestalozzi's disciple Froebel in his system of education for very young children called the 'Kindergarten' (not, as is sometimes thought, a garden where children can play, but a garden where children are, as it were, 'grown', like Rousseau's plants). The 'object lesson' had a significant influence on the history of language teaching methodology in the mid 1860s when a follower of Pestalozzi from Germany called Gottlieb Heness was inspired by the theory to conduct a small-scale experiment in which he taught German as a foreign language to the children of the staff at Yale University using objects of various kinds and a 'conversational' method that totally avoided the use of the native language[23]. The experiment was a success and Heness was sufficiently encouraged to open a school of languages in Boston with a like-minded Frenchman called Lambert Sauveur. Together they founded what became known, in true Rousseau style, as the 'Natural Method' of language teaching. This was the fore-runner of the better-known 'Direct Method' associated initially with the schools of Berlitz, the first of which was opened in nearby Rhode Island in 1878[24].

On the face of it the emergence of direct methods of language teaching in the tradition of Rousseau and Pestalozzi might seem to promise a more positive attitude towards languages among teachers of young children. Here apparently was a methodology which would fold foreign languages into the activities of the classroom in an entirely natural way. In fact, however, direct methods attracted two serious criticisms. The first was the practical problem that they were monolingual methods which required a native-like level of proficiency which was unrealistic in the circumstances. The second was the more fundamental objection that natural or direct methods tended to trivialise the learning process[25]. Whereas the original Pestalozzian object lessons had been genuine explorations of the relationship between meanings and words, the direct method adaptations were little more than labelling exercises ('This is a book. This book is green.' and so on) in which new foreign language words were attached to long-familiar concepts, precisely the empty verbalism that Rousseau had rejected in 1762.

Leaving aside new ideas in methodology, which were not entirely convincing anyway, the broader trends of educational change in the nineteenth century served to reinforce the view that foreign languages (particularly the classics) were unsuited to the needs of mass elementary education and should be confined to the secondary level of schooling where they would do the least damage. The aim was not 'how can the masses participate in foreign language education?' but 'how can the new reforms be protected from interference by the powerful classicist lobby?' In England, the situation was particularly unfortunate since the transformation of much of the old 'Latin' grammar school system into an expensive private sector of exclusive ('public') secondary schools encouraged the growth of a 'feeder' system of 'preparatory schools' for young children aged eight to 13. These 'prep schools' taught Latin and French because the 'public schools' made it worth their while to do so, but the state elementary schools (which grew substantially in numbers after 1870) did not follow suit. The inevitable result was that there were two sharply divided systems of education in which foreign languages played a crucial role and transfer between them was virtually impossible.

The outcome of all this was a situation in which the traditionalists from the private schools wanted to continue the 'early-start' practice of teaching foreign languages to eight-year-olds but the reformers from the public sector argued for a 'late-start' policy reserving languages for the secondary schools only. Eventually the two sides met on a government committee chaired by Stanley Leathes which was set up in 1916 by the Board of Education (the forerunner of the present Ministry) to look into the whole question of 'modern studies' including the future of foreign languages. The starting age for foreign language teaching was a major controversy and the discord led to the publication of a set of detailed 'Reservations' by a minority[26]. The majority ('reformers') view was expressed in Conclusion 15: 'Under present circumstances it is not desirable to introduce modern languages into the great majority of Elementary Schools'[27] and Conclusion 24: 'It appears to the majority of us far from certain that the early beginning of foreign languages at schools is advantageous to their study or to education in general.'[28]

In their 'Reservations' the 'traditionalists' argued that the late-start policy represented a 'very drastic change'[29] which would in practice mean a serious threat to the teaching of Latin in particular. If the first foreign language (typically French) were to be delayed until the age of 12, Latin could not begin much before 14. Among other things, this would have placed a great strain on the cosy relationship between the 'public schools' and the universities, and lessened their commercial attractiveness. Most of this was of course relegated to the sub-text of the report. On the surface there was a lot of concerned talk about attainment requiring 'time and constant practice in the earlier stages'[30] and, picking up the point Locke had made back in 1693, young children were better at pronouncing foreign languages: 'it is probably agreed by all that young pupils have more readiness in catching and imitating the sounds of a foreign language than those who are older; we believe that it is a very great advantage that this difficult and tedious process should be got through at an early age, when time can best be spared for it.'[31]

Like most government reports Leathes' gave expression to a climate of opinion at the time, but it did not seriously challenge the system. From now on foreign languages in the private sector were privileged but not necessarily advanced whereas in the public sector they were both. Very little changed until the early 1960s when the absence of foreign languages from most of the state education sector was seriously questioned. Part of the response was a large-scale project to introduce the teaching of French to primary school children. The real solution, however, was to introduce foreign languages to all children in the secondary schools but that had to wait for another decade.

For much of its lifespan the twentieth century has shown remarkable faith in the solubility of problems. All that was required was a convincing theory and a methodology for applying it to a practical situation. The new social and human sciences ought to be able to supply the former and practical research would take care of the latter. The obvious theory in the present context was the one already alluded to by John Locke back in 1693, by the 'direct method' enthusiasts and by many others: the notion of a 'natural method' of foreign language teaching mimetic of the universally effective processes of first language acquisition. There ought to be a way of teaching languages which would 'plug in' to the seemingly inexhaustible capacities of young children to learn languages without any of the frustration and general slog experienced by older learners.

In 1953 a psychologist called William Penfield[32] appeared to answer the call in a paper which supported the view that pre-adolescent children were particularly well-suited to the acquisition of foreign languages since their responses were still flexible enough to cope with the demands of new speech habits. Since this flexibility was lost at puberty, it made sense to begin the teaching of foreign languages at a much younger age than hitherto. This research helped to launch a series of initiatives in American elementary schools known generically as FLES (Foreign Languages in the Elementary School) programmes and the scheme was helped along its way by a National Conference called by the US Commissioner of Education.

The FLES programme[33] continued until the mid 60s with some success[34], but the breakthrough suggested by the new ideas failed to materialise. Young children learnt reasonably well, but they learnt slowly and very little was gained by the early start. The late-start children simply caught up.

In Britain before the 1970s foreign languages were reserved for bright adolescents, the top 20 per cent or so who had passed the entrance test to the grammar schools. A British FLES-type programme was, therefore, doubly attractive. First, if successful, it would undermine the argument that only clever children with special gifts could learn foreign languages and at the same time it would give all children a chance of learning a foreign language before facing the hurdle of the secondary school selection test.

In 1961–2 a small but highly publicised experiment to teach French to primary school children was carried out by a native-speaking teacher in Leeds. The fame of this initiative provided the nudge and the avalanche duly slid down the hillside in the shape of a government-funded pilot scheme for teaching French in a substantial number of primary schools in England and Wales[35]. A complex and expensive support system was created with the help of the Nuffield Foundation and later the Schools Council for the production of materials[36], the National Foundation for Educational Research (NFER) was enlisted to evaluate and assess the project, and local education authorities, colleges of education and so on were involved in various capacities. By the mid 60s the scheme had blossomed into a multi-million pound project involving the production of audio-visual courses not only for primary and secondary French but also secondary German, Spanish and Russian which, it was believed (wrongly as it turned out), would benefit from the new policy.

Ten years and three NFER reports later[37], the project came to an end. The basic outcome was that the amount of time and effort that had to be invested in the teaching of French to eight-year-olds was out of proportion to the amount of learning that was actually achieved. As in FLES, the late-starters in the secondary schools caught up. As Burstall, the chief researcher for NFER put it: 'The achievement of skill in a foreign language is primarily a function of the amount of time spent studying that language, but is also affected by the age of the learner, older learners tending to be more efficient than younger ones' and in a parting shot at the work which had set everything going 20 years earlier: 'Penfield's contention that the first ten years of life constitute a 'critical period' for foreign language acquisition remains unsupported by direct experimental evidence.'[38]

French did not become part of the normal pattern of work in the primary schools as the project founders had hoped. This was a disappointment for everyone involved, but it could hardly have come as much of a surprise. Apart from the negative results of the NFER reports, the expansionist atmosphere of the early 60s had evaporated long since and the basic motivation for primary French – introducing foreign languages to all children – had come about anyway through the reorganisation of the secondary schools and the abolition of selection. If FLES, primary French and similar movements in other countries[39] proved anything, it was that if young children possessed a special talent for language acquisition, it did not show itself in the context of the typical school classroom.

Our discussion so far has been based on the unexamined assumption that all educational options are open and societies are free to choose whether to teach foreign languages, to whom, when, at what stage and so on. Such freedom is possible only if there is no serious difficulty in deciding what language is the normal medium of instruction in the schools and therefore which languages are 'foreign'. Until recently this pattern has been the norm in countries which are, or see themselves as being, largely monolingual, most of Europe and the Americas, for instance, the Middle East and East Asia. In other parts of the world, however, India for example and most of sub-Saharan Africa, extensive multilingualism means that language planning decisions such as the choice of the medium of instruction are very much more complex.[40]

In recent times there have been far-reaching changes in the patterns of language use throughout the world and in people's perceptions of their significance. Large-scale shifts of population since 1950 have resulted in substantial linguistic minorities in countries where they did not exist before. Moreover, attitudes towards minority languages have changed and there is a more positive concern for conservation and maintenance. One practical outcome has been the expansion of bilingual education programmes in areas of the world like Britain, for instance, or North America where one language is dominant and on the whole they have proved successful in promoting practical second language skills among very young children. The essential feature of such schemes has been the use of each of the two languages as the medium of instruction at different stages of the programme. One of the best-known and most successful examples of bilingual education was the Canadian scheme which pioneered the notion of 'immersion'[41] where the children used the second language for all school purposes for a specific part of each day or for a specific length of time. The Canadian programme was remarkable for the strength of commitment it revealed among majority-language speakers to encourage the learning of the minority language and for the maintenance of that commitment over a long period of time.

The Canadian experience is a reminder of the fact that the most consistently successful contexts for second language learning have been those where the second language is used for normal communication purposes and acquisition is incidental to the pursuit of some other activity. Using the second language as the medium of communication (including instruction) at school is an obvious context. The fact that young children benefit from such natural language acquisition situations is well-known but why they do is more mysterious. Perhaps, as Locke and others believed, it has something to do with the supposed 'flexibility' and 'adaptability' of young children, perhaps it depends on the way that adults talk to children to help them understand. There could be many reasons. But, rightly or wrongly, education in a second language is regarded by most people as inferior to education in the mother tongue. Perhaps there is some 'middle way' in which, for instance, teaching can be deliberately designed to encourage the incidental acquisition of the second language in the course of doing a set of activities and tasks of various kinds. There are signs that the late twentieth century has begun to explore the issue[42].

What this paper has tried to show is that the role of language in the education of young children has always provoked a variety of views, particularly on the crucial question of the mother tongue. For some people the mother tongue can happily co-exist with other languages or even be set on one side completely and an educationally more significant language – Latin in the past, English in some contexts today – can be substituted for it. Others, however, accord a privileged status to the mother tongue as the language through which some of the child's deepest and most permanent perceptions have been formed and developed. Since this early experience is held to be the foundation on which all later learning and understanding is based, the mother tongue must be placed at the core of the education system. Foreign languages are essentially peripheral skills which can be acquired as and when they are needed. There are intermediate positions, less uncompromising attitudes and so on, but the various patterns of thought arouse strong allegiances and history can provide support for most of them.

Notes

Spelling has been modernised except in the bibliography.

1 Stern & Weinrib (1978: 152)
2 *Brevissima Institutio* or *A Short Introduction of Grammar* by William Lily (c. 1466–1522).
3 Quick (1895: 534). Richard Mulcaster (c. 1530–1611).
4 *Methodus Institutionis nova . . . Ratichii et Ratichianorum* published in Leipzig in 1626. See Quick (1895: 108). Wolfgang Ratke (1571–1635).
5 Quick (1895: 109).
6 *Ibid.* p.111.
7 Keatinge (ed 1910: 205). Jan Amos Comenius (1592–1670).
8 Quick (1895: Chap. 11). Also, Barnard (1913).
9 Axtell (1968: 300). John Locke (1632–1704).
10 *Ibid.* pp.266–7.
11 Hans (1951).
12 Poole (1646: 'To the Reader').
13 Aickin (1693: A3).
14 Duncan (1731: v).
15 Priestley (1761: viii). Joseph Priestley (1733–1804).
16 Lowth (1762: xii). Robert Lowth (1710–1787).
17 Rousseau (1762/1911: 6). Jean-Jacques Rousseau (1712–1778).
18 *Ibid.* p.53.
19 *Ibid.* pp.72–3.
20 *Ibid.* p.80.
21 *Ibid.* p.73.
22 *Ibid.* p.73.
23 Kroeh (1887: 178).
24 cf. Howatt (1984: Chap. 14).
25 Kroeh (1887: 180–1).
26 Leathes (1918: 110–7 & 230–4).
27 *Ibid.* p.208.
28 *Ibid.* p.210–1.
29 *Ibid.* p.231.
30 *Ibid.* p.233.
31 *Ibid.* pp.232–3.
32 Penfield (1953).

33 Andersson (1953); Andersson (1969).
34 Dunkel and Pillet (1962).
35 Schools Council (1969).
36 Spicer (1969).
37 Burstall (1968); Burstall (1970); Burstall *et al.* (1974).

38 Burstall (1978: 17).
39 Stern (1967: Part 2).
40 cf. Dakin *et al.* (1968).
41 cf. Allen & Swain (eds 1984).
42 e.g. Prabhu (1985).

Bibliography

Aickin, J. 1693. *The English Grammar; or the English tongue Reduced to Grammatical Rules.* London.

Allen, P. and M. Swain (eds). 1984. *Language Issues and Education Policies.* ELT Documents 119. Oxford: The British Council & Pergamon Press.

Andersson, T. 1953. *The Teaching of Foreign Languages in the Elementary School.* Boston: Heath.

Andersson, T. 1969. *Foreign Languages in the Elementary School: a Struggle against Mediocrity.* Austin: University of Texas Press.

Axtell, J.L. (ed). 1968. *The Educational Writings of John Locke, a Critical Edition with Introduction and Notes.* Cambridge: Cambridge University Press.

Bantock, G.H. 1980. *Artifice and Nature, 1350–1765. Studies in the History of Educational Theory,* Vol 1. London: Allen & Unwin.

Barnard, H.C. 1913. *The Little Schools of Port-Royal.* Cambridge: Cambridge University Press.

Burstall, C. 1968. *French from Eight; a National Experiment.* Slough: NFER.

Burstall, C. 1970. *French in the Primary School: Attitudes and Achievement.* Slough: NFER.

Burstall, C., M. Jamieson, S. Cohen and M. Hargreaves. 1974. *Primary French in the Balance.* Slough: NFER.

Burstall, C. 1978. 'Factors affecting foreign-language learning: a consideration of some recent research findings.' In Kinsella, V. (ed). 1978: 1–21.

Dakin, J., B. Tiffen and H.G. Widdowson. 1968. *Language in Education: the Problem in Commonwealth Africa and the Indo-Pakistan Subcontinent.* London: Oxford University Press.

Duncan, D. 1731. *A New English Grammar, wherein the Grounds and Nature of the Eight Parts of Speech and their construction is explain'd.* London.

Dunkel, H.B. and R.A. Pillet. 1962. *French in the Elementary School: Five Years' Experience.* Chicago: University of Chicago Press.

Hans, N. 1951. *New Trends in Education in the Eighteenth Century.* London: Routledge & Kegan Paul.

Howatt, A.P.R. 1984. *A History of English Language Teaching.* London: Oxford University Press.

Keatinge, M.W. (ed). 1910. *The Great Didactic of John Amos Comenius.* London: Adam and Charles Black.

Kinsella, V. (ed). 1978. *Language Teaching and Linguistics: Surveys.* Cambridge: Cambridge University Press.

Kroeh, C.F. 1887. 'Methods of teaching modern languages.' *Transactions and Proceedings of the Modern Language Association of America,* III, 1887, 169–185.

Leathes, S. (Chairman). 1918. *Modern Studies: being the Report of the Committee on the Position of Modern Languages in the Educational System of Great Britain.* London: HMSO.

Locke, J. 1693. *Some Thoughts Concerning Education.* (See Axtell (ed). 1968.)

[Lowth, R.] 1762. *A Short Introduction to English Grammar: with Critical Notes.* London.

Penfield, W.G. 1953. 'A consideration of the neurophysiological mechanisms of speech and some educational consequences.' *Proceedings of the American Academy of Arts and Sciences,* 82, 5, 201–214.

Poole, J. 1646. *The English Accidence: or, a Short, Plaine and Easie way for the more speedy attaining to the Latine tongue by the help of the English. Set out for the use and profit of young Children, & framed so, as they may bee exercised in it as soon as they can but indifferently read English.* London.

Prabhu, N.S. 1985. *Second Language Pedagogy.* Oxford: Oxford University Press.

Priestley, J. 1761. *The Rudiments of English Grammar; adapted to the Use of Schools. With Observations on Style.* London.

Quick, R.H. 1895. *Essays on Educational Reformers.* New edition. London: Longmans, Green.

Rousseau, J-J. 1762/1911. *Emile, or Education.* Orig. publ. 1762. Translated by B. Foxley. Everyman's Library. 1911. London: Dent.

Schools Council, The 1969. 'The primary French pilot scheme: an English experiment.' In **Stern, H.H.** (ed). 1969. 95–111.

Spicer, A. 1969. 'The Nuffield foreign languages teaching materials project.' In **Stern, H.H.** (ed). 1969: 146–61.

Stern, H.H. 1967. *Foreign Languages in Primary Education: the Teaching of Foreign or Second Languages to Younger Children.* London: Oxford University Press.

Stern, H.H. (ed). 1969. *Languages and the Young School Child.* London: Oxford University Press.

Stern, H.H. 1969. 'Languages for young children: an introductory survey of current practices and problems.' In **Stern, H.H.** (ed). 1969: 9–35.

Stern, H.H. and **A. Weinrib.** 1978. 'Foreign languages for younger children: trends and assessment.' In **Kinsella, V.** (ed). 1978: 152–72.

Luisa Pantaleoni, University of San Marino

22 Syllabusing at primary level: the Italian perspective

Finally, Luisa Pantaleoni offers us a small piece of comparative education, with an account of an Italian approach to devising syllabuses for primary learners.

L2 SYLLABUSING has been a major issue in the foreign language teaching field for the past 20 years, notably since the notional functional revolution of the mid 1970s questioned the educational value of subject-centred, content-driven, teacher-centred and transmissive methodology. Special emphasis was subsequently given to needs analysis and goals calling for language exponents which were situation-based, geared to the individual learner's needs, appropriate to context and with a high surrender value at all steps along the path. Functioning in the language or knowing about the language? In doubt, the pendulum has been swinging from the *what* (content) to the *how* (methods and techniques) to the *what for* (goals) back to the *what*, depending on school levels and types, educational constraints and research (ranging from second language acquisition to sociolinguistics, from lexicography to psychology to language education in general).

Defining a syllabus

Both curriculum and syllabus entail what to teach, but while the former has to do with institutional as well as classroom goals and considers syllabus design, methodology, assessment and evaluation in the broadest terms, the latter is a more day-to-day, localised guide for the teacher; it is a statement of approach, an instrument for tackling priorities, selecting and sequencing linguistic data; it provides a focus for what should be taught and learnt, as well as a rationale for how that content should be selected and ordered.

Clearly there is constant interplay between syllabus and curriculum, but it would seem that one has first to decide on which syllabus to plan before determining methods of presentation and implementation, which will then possibly affect curriculum development and change.

Factors affecting syllabus design at primary level

Selecting an L2 syllabus at primary level in Italy entails careful examination of the following factors:

1 The end-goals of the course as pre-determined by school authorities (see Ministerial Programme 1985).

2 The pupils' demographic/biographical conditions, that is their social and linguistic background, which can vary considerably depending on social class and geographical area (north/south, country/town, big city/small town, districts within the same metropolitan area and so on).

3 The pupils' cognitive development at the point at which the foreign language is introduced (whether from the first, second or third year onwards).

4 The number of pupils per class, the frequency and duration of classroom periods, the time of day at which the periods fall.

5 The feasibility of interdisciplinary, cross-curricular work (depending on the school's working atmosphere, the teachers' willingness to co-operate and act as a team).

6 The availability and use of audio-visual materials, aids and facilities.

7 The educational triangle, that is parent/teacher/child relationships and environmental constraints.

8 The foreign language teacher who is to make it all possible, whether a specialist teacher wedged into the school context or an L1 primary teacher sensitised to L2 competence and methodologies through specially designed courses.

From a 'political' point of view, factors 1 and 8 are pivotal in the Italian context. Let us first consider factor 1. The end-goals of the L2 primary programme seem to have been correctly identified by the Italian Ministry of Education: 'the study of a foreign language contributes to the broadening of the pupils' cultural, social and human horizon.' Beautiful words. But if language, to use Wittgenstein's words, is 'not only the vehicle of thought but also the driver', then learning a foreign language should give the learners an extra awareness of language through exposure to and experience of a powerful tool of intellectual growth and an invaluable insight into their first language. If, on the other hand, the introduction of a foreign language in the primary curriculum simply means an instrumental early start to the syllabus, extended to 11 years from the former eight, then we will witness a plethora of textbooks with 'nice' illustrations and language material 'cut to size', so to speak, from older learners' materials, watered down to accommodate the stereotypical pseudo-communicative approach which is supposed to be good for the 'dear little souls' and which is sure to delight parents, school heads and advisors.

Does one really want to be gratified by their chirping of 'What's your name?'s and 'How old are you?'s; by their parroting of adult language? Much as one agrees with the view that language is a set of habits and that there is a ritual, formulaic dimension to it which children love and are eager to pick up and use, one cannot help advocating a more 'enlightened' approach to the much debated early introduction of foreign language study at primary level.

As for factor 8, it contains either the seeds of defeat or the potential for success, of early foreign language teaching at large. When it is on a nationwide scale, innovation has to take into account figures, resources, potentialities and constraints which *de facto* are going to affect outcomes. Primary teachers in Italy are not qualified for teaching a foreign language at the moment. Qualifying them will not be a matter of months or years. It will take decades to change pre-service policies in a country where no pre-service training is provided for teachers at university level, in terms of psychology, classroom management, methodologies and subject-specific teaching techniques. Even if conditions were more favourable, massive change does not take place overnight. There would still be the need for a gradual introduction, adjustments, trial-and-error approaches, monitoring, pruning, stitching and ironing. It is unlikely that Italy will find large numbers of qualified primary school specialists among the ranks of practising teachers, nor will it be possible to train adequate contingents in the near future. Besides, this is not perhaps what is wanted. If specialist competence is required and expected, then the whole issue of instrumental rather than educational objectives needs to be addressed in connection with the question of continuity at subsequent levels of schooling, choice of the foreign language to be studied (Does it *have* to be English? What about French, German or Russian? What about bilingual areas along the borders or minority languages?), standards of achievements, quantifiable results and so on.

Interestingly, this does not seem to be the main preoccupation of school authorities, although it may well cause many a sleepless night in the Rome headquarters of the Ministry of Public Instruction. It is far more important to set oneself realistic goals, to aim at results measurable not so much in terms of product-based target behaviour as in terms of sensitivity to cultural diversity, mental and emotional involvement and language awareness derived from a positive learning experience, a relaxed, positive attitude to foreign language learning, confidence, willingness to try, curiosity, creativity. How can this be achieved?

Options in syllabusing

In a structural syllabus, the primary focus is the grammatical structure of the language. Sequences are often established on the basis of intuition and tradition. The grading criteria followed tend to be simplicity, regularity, frequency and contrastive difficulty. Inexperienced teachers invariably opt for this type of syllabus because it reflects their own learning experience (it was the most widely adopted until about 20 years ago). Moreover, it is teacher-centred, it does not seem to require a communicative command of the language, it is norm referenced and soundly 'traditional', with all the positive implications attached to the word from a teacher's point of view.

In a situational syllabus, the emphasis is on the social roles of the participants, their psychological status, the type of conversations they have, the setting. Sequencing criteria are based on a prediction of what situations the learners will have to deal or cope with. Materials tend to be based on phrase-book language easily memorisable but rather soulless, aseptic, uncreative.

In the notional functional syllabus, the semantic content of language and the use that language is put to are the major concerns. The sequencing is established on the basis of intuitive prediction of which core language functions will be more relevant to which users to survive or interact competently in a foreign culture. Adult-oriented in principle (taking its origin from needs analysis, language for special purposes and threshold levels of competence), it calls for a good command of the target language on the part of the teacher and adequate teaching materials often tailored to the needs of the learners.

All three types of syllabus tend to create language competence in terms of building blocks one on top of the other; in other words, they tend to be product-oriented, the end product being represented by the various steps, or blocks, along the way, with the little flag on top as the final outcome at the end of the course. They also have as a common denominator the idea that the chunks of language taught or learnt are *then* put to use for communicative purposes. There is, in other words, a sort of 'rehearsing' dimension to language (you learn your lines, rehearse and then perform on stage) which perhaps accounts for some of the ineffectiveness of lock step teacher-dominated classroom drill and practice.

If, alternatively, language is not seen as an end in itself, but as a means to perform other types of activity – which is basically what happens in real life with the mother tongue – the three syllabuses, each with its pros and cons, each pursuing specific pedagogic, linguistic and operational goals, can successfully be converted into process-oriented, procedural or task-based sets of activities by shifting the focus from usage and rehearsal to real life use.

In the light of the latest research and insight into language learning processes, it seems lucky that, for want of specialist competence, Italy should be 'forced' to favour methodologies which will enhance collaborative learning, cater for individual differences in learning styles, accommodate cognitive skills and capitalise on other disciplines and on the learning environment in general.

It is therefore not so much a question of sour grapes, or of conscience making cowards of us all, as a realistic and informed language policy whereby language – all languages – are viewed as servicing the development of thought and the growth of intelligence. One has only to read the *Italian programme for the listening skill* to see what is meant by language education, *educazione linguistica*. The following activities, intended to develop children's sensitivity to sounds, are self-explanatory enough: 'voice games, lip reading, contrasting a singing and a speaking voice, rhythmical singing accompanied by body movements, whispering, shouting, acting out moods and attitudes, projecting, exploring drama, television, the cinema and the radio in their vocal qualities.' What a wonderful opportunity for interdisciplinary work! How rich and appealing in its diversity and conspicuousness the foreign language will be to the sensitive ears of children! Rhymes, songs, ritual games, jingles and riddles will become the raw material for analysis, comparison and contrast, a first step towards the language awareness that we want to promote and encourage in children from as early as possible. A great deal of peripheral learning will take place all the way through. Observation skills and thinking skills will be fostered by listening activities as well as by cognitive, logical activities, the ones with the highest surrender value in the educational continuum.

Some of the attainment targets listed for mathematics and science, such as locating, classifying, grouping, discriminating, ranking, estimating, sorting, sequencing, measuring, comparing, observing, describing or spotting differences, could be applicable to foreign language activities too. While the amount of language required for such activities would not be daunting either for teachers or pupils, the reinforcement of notions crucial to the child's development of stock concepts and of the related vocabulary would be immensely beneficial. Rather than the irrelevant adult-like dialogues of current FL textbooks, we would teach children the language they need to find out about things (see Halliday's heuristic function) to explain and describe spatial, temporal and causal relations connected with the notions of size, quantity, time, space, cause and effect. A *notional* syllabus: that is what we really want!

A fascinating perspective opens up when we consider, on the one hand, a traditional syllabus where the foreign language is viewed just as a discipline, to be taught in tight-compartment isolation (no matter how 'splendid': efficient specialised mother tongue or bilingual instructors are reported to have failed where less efficient teachers with a special feeling for moods, atmospheres and potentialities have been wildly successful) and, on the other, a notion-based syllabus where the foreign language simply reinforces and services primary school activities done to 'discover the world'. The eight factors illustrated above, worrying as they may appear, cease to be insurmountable obstacles looming in the primary teacher's horizon and become variables to be taken into due account, but no more than that.

One might argue that, after all, it is only a question of emphasis, of terminology, of labelling. In fact, there is a crucial difference between the product-oriented grammatical, situational or functional syllabuses, and the process-oriented notional one we have just illustrated.

If one favours process, one does not bother to cover a given amount of language, say, Units 1 to 12 of the coursebook. Moreover, the children's attention is focused on the activity rather than on the language; tasks and projects become all important. The size of the class, the time factor or the teacher's linguistic competence cease to matter if teachers are good classroom managers and practitioners, with a sense of their audience, a sensitivity for the 'settling' or 'unsettling' quality of the activities they plan, a good rapport with their colleagues, an intelligent and informed attitude to language *per se*. As for classroom language, apart from a realistic use of the mother tongue whenever necessary and advisable, even not particularly proficient users of the foreign language should be able to cope, if intelligently trained and self-trained.

In this respect, there is an urgent need to identify key areas for language improvement, with special emphasis on phonology, classroom language, the language and 'lore' of children, and subject specific vocabulary. It would indeed be advisable to identify a sort of threshold level for children, with inventories of language functions related to games, social interaction among peers and with grown-ups and so on, so that rather than embark on a desperate attempt to cover all-purpose English or French, teachers can concentrate on more restricted codes. As for other competencies, training courses will cater for different needs depending on the teachers' experience of foreign language teaching, primary school teaching and so on. Quite an exciting perspective ahead for Italian school bodies at all levels! To cheer ourselves up, let us read the reports that an Italian teacher asked her pupils to write about a year's work in English (translated from Italian):

> What I learned in English: the colours, numbers from 1 to 30, reading stories, the names of objects and of rooms. English is a beautiful subject because you study words, you draw, you colour. I have some problems when we have to read and when we have tests, because I don't study my English book when I am at home. (Boy aged 9).

> What I like best when we do English is the robot game, when we have to guess who is the pupil who asks questions, and you are blindfolded. Then I like it when we have tests, and many other games that I don't remember. To tell the truth, there is nothing that I don't like because I have a nice teacher, and when she comes for the lesson I am filled with happiness. (Girl aged 8).

In these short texts one can easily detect the teacher's approach and style as well as the pupils' (induced?) attitude to the learning experience. It is against these two major poles that one has to measure policies, resources, results.

In the light of the constraints illustrated above, L2 syllabusing will have to be a meditated and balanced intervention in Italian curricular itineraries – the foreign language, as it were, tiptoeing into existing territories with a view to opening up new educational perspectives. Rather than pursuing operational goals which in the present conditions would not be feasible or, ultimately, necessary or desirable, we have to invest in teacher education at large, striving to develop more professional attitudes to language in a category that *in* language finds the justification of its existence. But *language in general*, mother tongue in particular: language servicing subjects and disciplines. And only as an extra insight into it, a *foreign* language. Otherwise, we will risk considerable disappointment and even damage to later language learning.

The training programmes about to start on a nationwide scale, initially addressed to practising primary teachers with 'some' knowledge of a foreign language (the amount of that knowledge to be measured by placement tests), in addition to sensitising them to all of these issues, will have to put a premium on good will, flexibility, common sense, expertise and knowledge of children, and capacity for action research in the classroom. Teachers will have to become, more than ever before, researchers. The foreign language input will be directed to areas of notions, functions, lexis and structures to be predicted, discussed, planned, taught, experimented with, monitored, assessed, evaluated. Theme-based teaching kits, constructed round notions such as, say, time, space or quantity, with the relevant situation-based vocabulary, will be tried out and reported back on. Ready-made language materials will be assessed with critical, non-slavish attitudes, and adopted in so far as they can offer flexibility, modularity and a potential for creativity and expansion. Special attention will be given to contrastive analysis of linguistic and cultural systems, including, where possible, local dialects. If, to quote from Goethe, 'the more languages we know the better we get to know our mother tongue,' Italy will perhaps be able to boast in 12 or 15 years from now that at least this major goal has been achieved. Early foreign language teaching will at least have produced these results: a sound foundation and a tuning in for the work which is to follow, a better class of primary teacher – for that matter, quite good already! – and, above all, a better insight into, and command of, the mother tongue.

Bibliography

Clark, J.L. 1986. *Curriculum Renewal in School Foreign Language Learning.* Oxford: Oxford University Press.

Halliday, M.A.K. 1973. *Explorations in the Functions of Language.* London: Edward Arnold.

'I Nuovi Programmi della Scuola Elementare.' 1985. *Gazzetto Ufficiale,* 76. Istituto Poligrafico dello Stato.

Vygotsky, L.S. *Mind in Society.* Cambridge, Massachusetts: Harvard University Press.

Titone, R. 1985. *Educare al linguaggio mediante la lingua.* Armando.

Christopher Brumfit

Conclusion

THIS BOOK has attempted to provide an account of the kinds of practices, and the kinds of justifications for them, that good teachers and methodologists are currently producing for young learners coming to English. It will be clear from what is written here that there is an enormous range of possible approaches to teaching young learners. While we have tended to concentrate on integrated and activity-based approaches, there are still references to discrete activities involving relatively passive learning. Different countries have different needs, and so too have different learners. Ultimately, each teacher has independent and personal decisions to make, for the final judgement about what is best will in the end depend on decisions made by individual teachers in individual classrooms. We would like these decisions to be as principled as possible, and the appropriate principles will derive from our understanding of children and their development, of language and its role in society and in human understanding, and of classrooms as social groups. But teachers have to translate the kinds of discussion offered in this book into real ideas, real preparation, real classroom activity. However many ideas we offer here, they can only be examples of types of activity. However many explanations and accounts of research findings we offer, they only have value when tested against the personal experience of teachers who spend every day in the classroom. This is a book to be trusted for what it is – an account of current ideas and current practices. It has tried to be as full, serious and wide-ranging as possible. We hope it provides a strong base for working with young learners.

But it is only a base so that it can be challenged. If you have read this far, you are obviously very committed and serious. You now have the responsibility of testing what we have said, improving upon it, developing it, rejecting and accepting various parts. A similar book, written in 30 years' time, should be different from this one in many ways. You, our readers, should be initiating those changes. Good luck!